Bohemian Grove:

Cult of Conspiracy

Bohemian Grove:

Cult of Conspiracy

Mike Hanson

Foreword by Texe Marrs

 RiverCrest Publishing
1708 Patterson Road • Austin, Texas 78733

Bohemian Grove: Cult of Conspiracy

Copyright © 2012 by Mike Hanson. Published by RiverCrest Publishing, 1708 Patterson Road, Austin, Texas 78733.

Except where credited otherwise, photographs are from the author's private collection. All other photos used with permission.

Front cover photo courtesy of Mary Moore, Bohemian Grove Action Network.

Printed in the United States of America

Library of Congress Catalog Card Number 2012933777
    Categories: 1. History
                2. Secret Societies

ISBN 978-1-930004-69-6

Amor patriae

(Love of country)

This book is for all the great patriots who have dedicated their lives to the restoration of our republic.

"Weaving Spiders Come Not Here"

—William Shakespeare, *A Midsummer Night's Dream*

(Motto and Logo (above) of the Bohemian Club)

Contents

Part II   *PERSONAL STORIES*

List of Illustrations

Acknowledgements

Pro patria vivere et mori

(To live and die for our country)

My first thanks should go to my friend Alex Jones, a great patriot and broadcaster. Together we produced an access television show together for over nine years, as well as eight documentary films. It was Alex who was the only man courageous enough to stand by my side when we were deep in the belly of the beast at Bohemian Grove. It was Alex who risked his neck with me, willing to die if we failed and more than willing to take the inevitable public heat if we succeeded in getting the hidden camera tapes out to the public. I also want to thank Alex's wife Violet Jones, who traveled with us and provided invaluable support, both on location and in posting video clips and still photos of the "Cremation of Care" ceremony to the web within hours of our return.

I must thank the British television network Channel Four, who sponsored our foray into Bohemian Grove. Reporter Jon Ronson and his camera crew helped us get oriented with maps, information, equipment and even the proper "preppy" clothes to wear. Chris Athanas of *Reality Expander* supplied us with the super-small spy cams that we used to document the "Cremation of Care" ceremony. Dr. Peter Phillips, Professor of Sociology at Sonoma State University, was helpful to provide an interview and permission to quote extensively from his 1994 dissertation, *A Relative Advantage*. Also thanks to Mary Moore of the Bohemian Grove Action Network, David Icke, former Nebraska state Senator John DeCamp, and countless others who wish to remain anonymous, for providing photographs, interviews and invaluable information about the Grove, both on and off the record.

For assistance with research, thanks to Steve Blahak and Richard Reeves, Hester Pollard and Patsy Spradling for loaning books and guidance to the project. Special thanks to Catherine Matteson, Texe Marrs for allowing me to plow through his many boxes of material pertaining to the Grove, and Michael Campino in San Francisco for visiting many local archives and libraries on my behalf. Mr. and Mrs. R.H. Rodriguez, local residents of Guerneville, California (near the Grove) kindly assisted by sending me much information on the history of Sonoma County and the Grove. I am also grateful to Keri Jones and Greg Jackson for their tireless hours of research, typing, transcribing and editing, proofreading, locating photographs, and helping to prepare the final manuscript.

This book would not have been possible without the spiritual guidance provided by Leah Lewis and Melissa Taylor, and the constant support of Mike and Michelle Helms, Jimmy Gardner, Kevin Smith, JoAnn Thornton, Big Rob, The Henry and Getterman families, Dessie Andrews, SueAnn Campbell and Jean Overdeer. A very special thanks to Chris and Jimmy Ritter, Jeff Contreras, Chris Athanas, Jeff Davis and former Austin City Councilman George Humphrey for their many years of friendship and production assistance on our local television broadcasts and independent films.

From the bottom of my heart, I thank my entire family—especially my wife, Melissa, my son, Justin, and daughter Krystal.

This book was inspired by the memory of my late grandmother who passed away on October 11, 2001, a month after 9/11.

Most of all, I want to thank God—for *everything*.

—Mike Hanson

Introduction

Imprimatur

(Let it be printed)

"The Bohemian Grove is the greatest men's party on earth."

—Herbert Hoover,
President of the United States

It's said that nowhere in the world do more billionaires and power brokers get together than at the Bohemian Grove in the northern California redwoods. And chances are, this is news to you. You're not alone. Most Americans have never heard of the place.

For two and a half weeks every July, two thousand of the top high rollers in business and government attend the Bohemian Club's summer encampment. Although highly selective, the club has a national membership and is among the most prestigious of affiliations in conservative circles. Its membership is known to include Ronald Reagan, George Bush Sr. and Jr., Gerald Ford, Colin Powell, Henry Kissinger, Newt Gingrich, William F. Buckley, Jr., Frank Borman, Justin Dart, William Randolph Hearst, Jr., Caspar Weinberger, Charles Percy, George Schultz, the late Edward Teller, Merv Griffin, and a large proportion of the directors and chief executive officers of the Fortune 1000. Daniel Ludwig, the richest private citizen on earth, is a Bohemian. Conspiracy nuts think the Bohemian Club meets each summer to plot to take over the world. Get real. These guys ALREADY run the world.

Prominent members of the Bohemian Club have run America's private run-for-profit Federal Reserve Bank, from its very inception in 1913. Alan Greenspan was seen leaving the Bohemian Grove only a month before he was appointed chairman of the Federal Reserve. He had to be a "made man" to be a member of the most powerful cabal on the planet. Historical records also clearly tell us that the Manhattan Project was planned, instituted and operated out of the Bohemian Grove.

The purpose of this book is to draw the public's attention to the fact that many of the major policy decisions which affect our lives are not emanating from Washington, DC, as you might think. Much of America's future domestic and foreign policy, weapons systems, technology, and even wars are being orchestrated in secrecy at the Bohemian Grove. This has taken place very quietly over the past 130 years, right under our noses—and yet, you'd be surprised how few people on the street could name the Bohemian Grove in the same breath as the White House or Camp David.

Why doesn't the general public know about the Bohemian Grove? Because it is a secret organization. Four times in the past the Grove received unwanted publicity. The first came when Attorney General Edwin Meese was reached at the Bohemian Grove when his son died in an automobile accident. The second occurred when President Reagan canceled his annual trip to the Grove because of an international terrorist crisis. The third instance, and perhaps the most embarrassing, happened in 1981, when the new sheriff of Guerneville, a neighboring town, arrested a group of professional prostitutes along with several of their regular customers—all members of the Bohemian Club! The names of the members were never released, and all charges were quietly dropped. The fourth time was when Alex Jones and I infiltrated the Grove and exposed their occult ritual activities in a documentary film containing footage that we shot ourselves with a hidden camera. This film, *Dark Secrets: Inside Bohemian Grove*, sparked worldwide controversy.

While the Bohemian Club is notoriously secretive and publicity-shy, a surprisingly large number of mainstream news articles have been written about the power elite's summer camp through the years, and a good deal of that news coverage is included in these pages.

Maybe you've already seen some of the famous photographs from the University of Berkley (these images can be viewed on UC Berkeley's website) that show many former and current Presidents and vice-presidents lounging underneath the Grove's redwood trees, casually plotting the fate of nations and choosing future rulers. In fact, during the 2000 Grove summer camp, they announced Dick Cheney as George W. Bush's vice-presidential running mate from Bohemian Grove. CNN reported in July of 2000 that the decision had been partially made and that George Bush Jr. had been consulting with George Herbert Walker Bush, the former President and his father, at Bohemian Grove. That was reported on the national news, but it was innocuous, it was *no big deal*, it's just business as usual in the redwoods.

At that very same time, I infiltrated the Bohemian Grove summer camp on July 15, 2000, along with my longtime friend, fellow patriot and filmmaker

Alex Jones. The two of us managed to sneak into the Grove and captured everything we saw on videotape. We recorded the ancient Babylon mystery religion rites that were being practiced there, a bizarre ceremony the Bohemians call "The Cremation of Care."

This strange ritualized custom of cremating Dull Care has been much talked about through the years, but was never seen by the public until our hidden camera footage was released in a film called *Dark Secrets—Inside Bohemian Grove*. Reaction to our film was tremendous: mainly utter shock and dis-belief at the idea of our world leaders taking part in a Druid fire sacrifice. Some people just couldn't accept it, even after seeing the "Cremation of Care" with their own eyes. And everybody I've spoken to in the preparation of this book has a different theory as to what it all means, what the occult symbolism inherent in the ritual is supposed to represent. The Bohemian Club's historical annals even admitted their obsession with the occult, and what they called "Druid rituals." Amongst the great redwood trees they revived ancient ceremonies that in truth had their roots not in the Druids, but in Babylon itself.

We do know that throughout history, elites and rulers have been obsessed with the occult; from Presidents to Governors to the heads of industry. Examples range from John Dee, the Queen's astrologer in Elizabethan England to Hillary Clinton conducting seances in hopes of conversing with Eleanor Roosevelt. We've all read the stories of Presidents and First Ladies obsessed with their astrologers, making national policy decisions upon their recommendations, psychics and shamen in the White House.

I had been warned of the dangers before even attempting to go into the Bohemian Grove. To protect my family, they were not allowed to know about my visit to the Grove until after my safe return. When Alex and I left for California, my wife thought that I was simply going to meet a British reporter in San Francisco, but she had no idea what the story was about or the risks we would have to take to get that story.

Truth be told, neither did I. Supposedly, the plan was to try entering the Grove just by walking through the front gate. At least, that was the original idea. And of course, I naturally assumed that Alex and I would soon be fingered as intruders and promptly thrown out. Or perhaps arrested. I never in my wildest dreams thought we would actually get in and out of there with our cameras *and* our freedom intact. By the grace of God, we *did* bring out the tape and broadcast it immediately. This book is my personal story of what Alex and I went through to get this information out to the people, in an effort to fully document our experience inside Bohemian Grove.

In addition to what we witnessed during the "Cremation of Care," troubling rumors have emerged in more recent years that more is going on in the Bohemian Grove than just a bunch of rich old men having a wild frat party. There have been tales of murder and mayhem, rape, pedophilia, and other sexual perversions, snuff films being made depicting actual ritual sacrifice at the foot of the Grove's 45-foot stone owl statue that serves as their idol. We will explore these rumors in more detail here, and the testimony you will read is very disturbing indeed. It is at this point I feel the need to warn parents that this material is of an adult nature and can be very graphic and violent at times. *It is not suitable for children to read.*

This book is divided into two separate sections. Part I, *Bohemian Babylon*, gives you all the necessary history of the Bohemian Club and it's members, describes life at the Grove in great detail, tells tales not only of the legendary politicking inside the Grove, but the notorious partying as well. Part II, *Personal Stories,* is a series of first-hand accounts from eyewitnesses who have personally visited the Bohemian Grove or those otherwise intimately connected with the subject as known experts. I decided to reserve the first-hand account of my own experience at the Grove for this section of the book, and I've also included interviews with Alex Jones here as well.

In the interest of fairness, I was careful while conducting interviews to assure the participants that their words would not be changed or misinterpreted. All interviews were tape-recorded or documented in writing, and it is for that reason you will find the key interviews within this book printed verbatim, in a Q&A format, exactly as the subject told their story to me. This was vitally important, as many of the subjects had valid concerns regarding accuracy; they had been burned by journalists before. I understand because I've been there, too, and agreed to a transcript format.

This point probably needs no further clarification to the reader, but obviously, this is not going to be a book in support of the Bohemian Grove. If you're looking to read a polite whitewash of their activities, look elsewhere. The Bohemian Club has self-published several books privately that detail the club's history and customs, and the reader is encouraged to read them and hear their side of the story as well.

The people I chose to interview for this project are activists, journalists, college professors, current and former public officials, researchers, even a few exotic dancers and prostitutes who have "worked" the Grove camp. I was fascinated by all of their viewpoints and wanted to ensure that their stories were told. While some may not share my political, religious, or ideological views, we all agree on one thing—we are all strictly opposed to any, repeat ANY of the nation's business being conducted in secret at the Bohemian Grove or anywhere else.

Over the years, books about the Bohemian Grove have been hard to find. The only two books available to the general public, John Van Der Zee's *The Greatest Men's Party On Earth*, and William Domhoff's excellent *The Bohemian Grove and Other Retreats*, both were published over 30 years ago and are long out of print. I believe this book provides a much-needed new resource of information about the Bohemian Grove, and further demonstrates the undeniable occult undercurrents that run through every single part of the Bohemian Grove culture, which other books have failed to explore. This book, being the first published about the Grove since 1974, substantially expands upon the work of previous authors with updated information.

Some people ask me, "so what if our leaders belong to the Bohemian Club? What's wrong with them acting like fraternity brats once a year?" First, I think it engenders a lack of respect. The next time you watch the evening news and spot a world famous personality—be he politician, artist, financier, or corporate executive—ask yourself, "is this one of those guys who mockingly worships an owl, revels around a campfire and puts on women's clothes to perform in a play?"

Second, it endangers national security. To think that more than 1,500 of our national leaders are gathered in one small geographic location at the same time is frightening. They are exposing themselves to possible sabotage or terrorist attack.

Third, "behind closed doors" politics is opposed to everything America stands for.

While the Bohemian Club's membership consists mostly of American leaders, there are plenty of foreign rulers on hand, too—from Queen Elizabeth, who visited the Grove in 1983, to former Chancellor of Germany Helmut Schmidt. In his autobiography, *Men and Powers—A Political Retrospective,* Schmidt said that the Grove was a wonderful place, it was important for his career, its scope is international; and that they did have Druidic rites that he enjoyed very much. So we have the power elite, or at least the higher-level minions of the power elite, who go there to basically be "chosen". If you're a member of the Trilateral Commission or the Council on Foreign Relations, chances are you're a member of the Bohemian Club, too.

In this book, I will attempt to trace the many layers of this complex web and show the reader how Bohemian Grove, outside of the DC beltway, is probably the only other place in America where you can find this many powerful people in one place at one time. This book will give names of the famous and infamous individuals, politicians, corporations, policymakers, public opinion-shapers, and warmongers who attend the Grove. And for your further cross-referencing pleasure, a complete recent club membership list is included in the Appendix section, which lists not only each member's name but also which Grove camp they belong to.

Perhaps my main goal in publishing this book is to illustrate how brilliantly people from all ends of the political spectrum come together on important issues like what goes on inside Bohemian Grove. We may fight like cats and dogs about the 2nd Amendment, legal vs. illegal immigration, religion, the United Nations, or the war in Iraq, but protesting the Bohemians' clearly arrogant and often criminal behavior towards the people they govern is one issue neither the left nor the right disputes. This is not a partisan or even a religious issue. It's bigger than that.

Now, I personally am a Christian, but I am also a reporter. I have always tried to remain objective enough to keep my personal religious beliefs out of the story. But in the case of the Bohemian Grove, I am wholly unable to ignore the obviously and decidedly pagan rituals these powerful men are engaging in. I do find it curious that so-called "conservatives" and some liberals as well, along with religious, academic and cultural leaders meet up for two weeks each year for this "summer fire festival" at the Grove. These are the same people who outwardly claim to be "good Christians" to the public, to their friends and even their families. Do they do this only when they think nobody is watching them? Well, if we weren't watching them before, we are now.

Regardless of your personal religious preference, the very nature of your leaders engaging in this type of ritual in secret should alarm you. Christians, Jews and Muslims can all see how sickening this stuff truly is, and that this runs contrary to the basic principles of their faith. Even if you're an Atheist, it doesn't matter. The point here is—would you let your neighbor even walk your dog or baby-sit your children if they were sacrificing humans in effigy to some 45-foot stone owl god, and chanting, *"Oh, Great Owl of Bohemia"?*

The task of writing a book about my own experience inside the Grove was a daunting one. I really didn't even know how to address a story like this. It's so incredible, so...*bizarre.* This is not the *Blair Witch Project,* or *War of the Worlds.* This is not a hoax—this is real. And it's just massive, the amount of evidence I have to share with you in the pages to follow. Truth is stranger than fiction.

For most of the club's long history, the public could only speculate as to what went on behind those well-guarded gates. Now the truth can finally be told. The entire "Cremation of Care" ritual, which we secretly filmed, will be published in full here for the first time. We will peer behind the deep, green foliage and twisted vines, and the moss-covered brown limbs and trunks of ancient, gnarled trees to discover what *really* goes on at the Bohemian Grove. On this 130-year anniversary of the founding of the Bohemian Club, *Bohemian Grove—Cult of Conspiracy* will uncover the Grove's hidden history and reveal the secrets of the redwoods.

Foreword:
Disturbing Discoveries

Texe Marrs

I first learned about the Bohemian Grove in 1988 from a former Central Intelligence Agency (CIA) officer. Retired from that agency and privy to many of its deepest secrets, he was intent on exposing the sinister plans of elite conspirators. He asked what I knew about a secretive group of powerful men that meets in the redwood groves near Santa Rosa, California, each year in July.

"Absolutely nothing," I responded.

He then went on to tell me strange and incredible things about the Bohemian Grovesters, things that seemed to be both bizarre and almost impossible.

I say "almost" because, just the year before, an insider, a graduate of Yale University, had provided me detailed information about yet another secretive group, the Order of Skull and Bones, headquartered in New Haven, Connecticut. Most "Bonesmen," as they are called, are graduates of the elite, Ivy League Yale University. For a year each actually resided in a building called the "Tomb" where they participated in satanic Masonic rituals, including one in which the newly initiated candidate lay nude in a coffin as a demonic, pagan ritual was conducted in a dark foreboding sanctuary.

The Order of Skull & Bones, I discovered, included some of America's most well-known and most powerful men. Among them—three generations of the Bush Dynasty: Sheldon Prescott Bush, George Herbert Walker Bush, and George W. Bush. There were also Bonesmen who became U.S. Senators, top corporate CEOs, bank presidents, university chancellors and other such famous persons on the Skull & Bones membership rolls.

Having investigated the weird but very real Skull & Bones organization, you might say that I was more ready to believe that similar groups also existed. The CIA operative assured me that the Bohemian Grove was one such occult secret society, and so I energetically sallied forth to find out more about the crazy antics and improbable behavior of the world's most auspicious leaders. Leaders who have been meeting in the mysterious forests some fifty miles from San Francisco since the year 1872.

My Discoveries Were Disturbing

What I dug up during my probing investigation of the Bohemians greatly disturbed me. It still does. In 1991, I recorded a lengthy audiotape summarizing my findings, which I entitled *"The Wicked Men of the Bohemian Grove."* Imagine if you will, hundreds of men—the President of the U.S., perhaps a few guest Prime Ministers, Premiers, or Chancellors from foreign countries, an assortment of oil company titans, Hollywood actors, the heads of corporate giants like IBM, Bechtel, Halliburton, Bank of America, etc.; the Secretaries of State and Defense, the Chairman of the Federal Reserve, and the list goes on—cavorting about, casually and sparsely clothed, urinating on trees and alongside walking and hiking trails, and incredibly behaving in an ungentlemanly, sordid sexual manner.

These men drink tons of alcohol, lounge about, attend special talks, and schmooze with each other for some two weeks. Insiders report that homosexual link-ups are commonplace, and the lust-filled, depraved participants in these encounters exhibit little or no shame in coupling in plain sight.

President Nixon's Personal Observation

Then President Richard M. Nixon is quoted in the White House tapes (available at California's Nixon Presidential Library) as complaining to his White House Chief of Staff, H. R. Haldeman:

> "The Bohemian Grove—which I attend from time to time—is the most faggy goddamned thing you could even imagine, with that San Francisco crowd. I can't shake hands with anybody from San Francisco."

(Note: my apologies for the regrettable profanity but those *were* Nixon's exact words.)

Nevertheless, Nixon also admitted that it was the warm and enthusiastic reception he received after one of his talks at the Bohemian Grove encampment that proved to be the catalyst for his subsequent successful political campaign for the presidency of the United States.

President Ronald Reagan also gave credit to his personal contacts made at the Grove for his election to the White House. Like Nixon, Reagan's talk to the assembled movers and shakers translated later into media support and millions of dollars in the Reagan campaign coffers.

Republicans But Also Some Democrats

Most of the Bohemians are Republican Party types. Republican Presidents Taft, Hoover, Nixon, Ford, Reagan, and both Bushes were (or are) Bohemians. But the membership list also includes some unusual examples of Democrat Party bigwigs.

President Jimmy Carter, for example, attended the Bohemian Grove conclave. Carter, a liberal Democrat, was and is a member of such globalist, pro-New World Order organizations as the Council on Foreign Relations and the Trilateral Commission. No doubt, President Carter's wide-ranging internationalist sympathies held him in esteem among the Bohemian elite, who also are predominantly dogmatic, anti-nationalist New World Order types.

The "Cremation of Care" Ritual

As I explained in *"The Wicked Men of the Bohemian Grove,"* the centerpiece of the two week encampment is the "Cremation of Care" ritual ceremonies. A virtual devilfest, this pagan drama is a massive theatrical production with outstanding actors and actresses (male actors portray the female parts in the drama). Similar to the bacchanalias of ancient Europe in which the various gods and goddesses were worshipped, animalistic idols were venerated, sexual orgies were engaged in, and human beings sacrificed, the Bohemian ritual ranks at the top of the occultic Secret Society dramas.

It appears that the ancient Canaanite and Hebrew deity "Moloch" (also known as Molech, Molekh, Molek, Moloc, and by Tophet, Baal, Chiun, Remphan and other names) is represented at the Bohemian ritual by a 42-foot (some say forty foot) tall owl-like figure. Shrouded in flames, this owl deity is surrounded by Druidic priests and other characters. During the ceremony, chosen "victims" are sacrificed. Their screams and shrieks pierce and shatter the still night air.

Alex Jones and Mike Hanson, who so bravely and clandestinely penetrated the Bohemian Grove activities, say that these sacrificial victims were probably human effigies. But Alex admitted that it can not be ruled out that actual *live* human beings are being murdered.

As you will read later in this book, that possibility is amplified by testimony of pedophilia survivors who report horrifying sexual abuse and torture occurring at the Grove. We know, too, that Britain's late Prime Minister Winston Churchill was covertly a Druid priest as is the current ecclesiastical head of the Church of England, the Archbishop of Canterbury, Rowan Williams.

Certainly, the sordid and disgusting *proven* sexual antics of recent Presidents Clinton and Obama, not to mention those of men like the late Senator Strom Thurmond, Speaker Newt Gingrich, Congressmen Anthony Weiner and Glen Foley, and many others clue us in on the immoral cravings and unseemly sexual conduct of our elected leaders. One can only wonder at the evil and depraved lifestyles of our clergy, our educators and the corporate and other chieftains who attend the Grove

The Importance of This

Thus, their heinously wicked conduct at an isolated, closely guarded encampment amidst towering, historically ancient redwood trees, is not so remarkable, is it? My own investigation of the Bohemian Grove—its history and activities—pales in comparison to what Mike Hanson, author of this excellent book, and his partner, the indomitable Alex Jones, discovered. Mine was investigator, detective, and research work from afar, from a distance. But Hanson and Jones were *there*, at an actual Bohemian Grove conclave. They pretended to be participants, fooled a bevy of security personnel, and miraculously filmed and taped much of the mind-boggling spectacle.

It is thanks to these two men, Hanson and Jones, that you and I are now able to discern the significance of this annual event of the elite. As you will see, the achievement of these two truth-finders in opening the window of discovery is key to the past—and future—history of the world.

The most alarming finding of Hanson and Jones is not the sexual cesspool behavior of the Bohemians, but the fact that these men conduct world and national affairs at their conclaves. Our lives are transformed by legislation conceived and crafted at the Bohemian meetings. Our Presidents and Vice Presidents—even our military generals—are selected by the degenerates who attend the Bohemian encampment. Wars are hatched, economic collapses planned out.

Let no one, then, claim that the annual goings on at the "greatest men's party on earth," as former President Herbert Hoover called it, are inconsequential or unimportant. These are not mere pranks and high-jinx. This is world-class stuff, as sick, depraved, surreal and shabby as are the activities that accompany the monumental decisions that are made at the Grove.

That is why this book by my long-time good friend, Michael Hanson, is so vitally important. Hanson is able to pull back the curtains and expose the mind-set and paradigm of the men who actually rule the world. He helps us to realize that these individuals are not "little gods" or even men of particular high intellect. Many are incredibly base and stupid. Regrettably, their sinister conduct in the redwoods exemplifies their executive decision-making in corporate boardrooms, legislative chambers, courtrooms and elsewhere. Is this why our nation and our world are in the pitiful mess they are in today?

The Bohemians hold the lives of billions of human beings in over 175 nations across the globe in the palm of those hands that former President Richard Nixon said are "faggoty" and unclean. Be wary, dear friends. Your very life and that of your loved ones is at stake here.

—Texe Marrs
Austin, Texas
(May 2012)

Texe Marrs is author of over forty books, including bestsellers *Dark Majesty, Circle of Intrigue, Codex Magica*, and *Conspiracy of the Six-Pointed Star*. A retired U.S. Air Force Officer, he taught at the University of Texas at Austin and for two other universities.

I

BOHEMIAN BABYLON

Chapter I

Praemonitus, praemunitus

(Forewarned, forearmed)

:rets of the Redwoods REVEALED!

`ı . uth can never be reached by just listening to the voice of an authority."

—Sir Francis Bacon

The Bohemian Grove is more properly known as the Midsummer Encampment of the Bohemian Club of San Francisco. It takes place annually each Ides of July in a majestic redwood grove outside Monte Rio, California, and has been going on for well over a century now. Former President Herbert Hoover even called the Grove "the greatest men's party on earth."

That's pretty lofty praise for a President of the United States to heap upon an outdoor summer camp, no matter how exquisite the natural environs may be. So what is the attraction, really? There must be something more than just one *hell* of a great party to make some of the richest and most powerful men in the world clear their busy schedules for two weeks each July, set aside matters of state (we're told), and come running from all corners of the globe.

It's an intensely secretive affair, with a heavy presence of security. No media are allowed in, either as members or guests. Membership lists are guarded like golden eggs, so that few people outside the Grove know who will be attending from one year to the next. (See *Appendix B* for the complete membership list we obtained) Past participants have included every Republican president since Calvin Coolidge, and before him, Theodore Roosevelt and William Howard Taft. Dwight Eisenhower, Richard Nixon, Barry Goldwater, Nelson Rockefeller, Ronald Reagan, George Bush Sr. and Jr., all Bohemians, crafted their future presidential campaigns within the secret and cozy confines of the Bohemian Grove.

Here, heads of state and industry, such as Henry Kissinger, Caspar Weinberger, James Baker, Dick Cheney, Malcolm Forbes, Stephen Bechtel and a host of prominent CEOs, foundation chairs and university presidents mingle with movie stars, musicians, artists, and cultural leaders. About one-fifth of the members are either directors of one or more of the Fortune 1000 companies, corporate CEOs, top governmental officials (current and former) and members of important policy councils or major foundations. The remaining

34

members are mostly regional business/legal elites with a small mix of academics, military officers, artists, or medical doctors. Most of them are Californians, 70 percent or more are political conservatives, and 99 percent of them are white. And all of them are *very, very* rich.

The Bohemian Club's name harkens back to its founding in 1873 by artists and journalists in the Bay Area, just four years after the completion of the transcontinental railroad which finally linked the East with the new golden cities of the West. In those early years, the Bohemian Club boasted among its membership some of the most influential writers and artists of the late 19th and early 20th centuries: Mark Twain, Ambrose Bierce, Bret Harte, Wytter Bynner, Henry M. Stanley, radical reformer Henry George, socialist Jack London. As word spread about the club in the 1910s and 20s, more popular entertainers came into the fold. Stars of stage and screen such as Will Rogers, Bing Crosby, Charlie Chaplin and Douglas Fairbanks, Sr. came to "let their hair down" at the Grove.

The Bohemian Club soon learned the age-old lesson—that art alone couldn't pay the club's annual operating expenses. The membership rolls were then opened to "men of use," as they called the local wealthy businessmen and politicians who joined the club in those years. The money these "men of use" poured into the club's coffers helped subsidize the Grove's "men of talent," while the focus of the club remained fixed upon the arts. But that would soon change as the "men of use" gradually took over the club, changing the artsy bohemian atmosphere of the club into their own private resort. Unofficially, Bohemian Grove became known as a spot where the good-old-boys political network reigned supreme and "art" served as little more than a mere backdrop, a convenient cover for the dealmaking that went on behind closed doors.

THE CITY CLUB

In order to accommodate their rapidly growing membership, the Bohemians moved into a permanent clubhouse at Post and Grant Streets in San Francisco in 1889. The April 18, 1906 San Francisco earthquake and resulting fire destroyed the Bohemian clubhouse, including its library and most of its art. After that, the Club rented various locations for four years, religiously maintaining regular Club activities until the completion of a new clubhouse at the corner of Post and Taylor Streets.

The Club spent $300,000 on the land and the new building. Bohemians purchased long-term bonds as part of the funds and the Pacific Mutual Life Insurance Company loaned the Club $200,000 at 6% interest, according to the August 17, 1908 *San Francisco Chronicle*. The newspaper dutifully reported on all phases of the construction, even affording front-page coverage to the opening of the new clubhouse on November 13, 1910. The *Chronicle* described the Bohemians' new digs breathlessly as a grand architectural achievement:

> *"The new building is four stories in height. On the first floor is the main hall or court in Corinthian style…the lounging room on the south side is in different shades of lake green and antique gold [as well as]…the billiard room, dining room and wine room. The second floor is the library in Elizabethan style and the theater. The third and fourth floors are given over to members' and guest rooms."*

This article on the front page of the *Chronicle* was symbolic of the Club's importance in late Victorian San Francisco. The Club activities were newsworthy events and the early 20th century Bay Area newspapers were filled with accounts of Bohemian Club activities. It was even common for the Bay Area newspapers to report on Bohemian elections and present the platforms of the various candidates for office. Between 1900 and 1915 the *San Francisco Chronicle* ran nearly 400 stories on the Bohemian Club, making it one of the most highly publicized clubs in the San Francisco Bay Area.

These historic newspaper accounts paint a very vivid picture of the club's first fifty years or so, and have been an invaluable tool to me in my research. For example, I was surprised to learn that the first Bohemians actually allowed restricted visits from women, usually curious wives. The hours of 10:00 A.M. to 11:30 A.M. and 2:00 P.M. to 5:00 P.M. every Wednesday were the times members could invite women into the clubhouse. In later years, the rules were changed again to only allow women during special occasions such as art shows and musical recitals. Women were banned from the clubhouse altogether from 1910 to 1933.

By the late 1920's, the Bohemian Club had close to 2,000 members and along with that growth came the need for a larger clubhouse. The members voted in 1930 to increase their dues by $5 a month to create a new building fund. The Lambs Club of New York donated $5,000 to the Bohemians towards the purchase of a new clubhouse. By December 1931, financing for $800,000 had been arranged to initiate building the new City Club. In the summer of 1933 the Bohemians took up temporary residence at the Sir Francis Drake Hotel when the dismantling of the old clubhouse began. In May of 1933, women were finally invited back into the clubhouse (for the first time since 1910) to a reception honoring the old building's demise.

The formal dedication of the new clubhouse occurred October 13, 1934 with the oldest living Bohemian unlocking the doors. The *Chronicle* story on Sunday, October 14th was significantly shorter and more subdued than the *Chronicle* article covering the 1910 opening. Instead of describing the grandeur of the new clubhouse the Chronicle simply stated that "the new structure adds two floors of bedrooms, and also houses an improved Jinks room or theater seating more than 750, a permanent art gallery, a smaller art gallery, an improved library and a roof solarium."

The 1934 story was very brief, ran without a picture and placed discreetly on the inside pages of the paper, whereas in 1910 the new clubhouse story was front-page news. This is probably due to the fact that the country was in the midst of the great depression, and the opening of a new million dollar clubhouse may have been a sensitive issue given the high levels of unemployment and poverty at that time. Also, San Francisco had just been through a massive General Strike where over 100,000 union workers had walked off their jobs. Businessmen in San Francisco, many of them Bohemian Club members, had been extremely active in anti-strike activities during that summer. The midsummer encampment at the Grove kicked off at the exact same time the General Strike was initiated. This may have been one of those years that Dull Care was not easily banished from the Grove.

A 1947 Howeller camp history gives an account of the dark mood at the camp in the summer of 1934:

> *"We will never forget the summer of 1934...Eager Bohemians who wanted to know about the General Strike in San Francisco thronged General David Barrows, Commander of the California National Guard, coming out of the dining area. So many of them wished to hear the General that in a short time at least seventy-five Bohemians came up to the camp...It was a notable gathering, including the head of the Marine Corps, A.P. Giannini (of Bank of America), and The Hale brothers...Ray Lyman Wilbut, and...Charles W. Field."*

Perhaps the Bohos were beginning to fear that the workers might revolt and storm the proverbial Bastille, doing away with their royal rulers. (Ironically enough, Bastille Day is July 14, the opening day of festivities each year at the Grove.) Clearly, the Grovers were at least somewhat worried that the unwashed masses could penetrate their private camp, for they instituted a new policy at the 1934 encampment: official employee identification cards were to be issued to all Grove workers.

But the natives were still restless. The following summer, during and after the Grove gathering, someone set several mysterious fires near and on Bohemian Grove property. The fires were quite severe, burning for several days, and had the wind shifted, could have threatened the entire Grove. Oddly enough, this incident goes unrecorded in the official annals of the Club. But in the personal papers of John Neylan, located at the Bancroft Library, we find a few more clues. A letter from Marshall Dill, president of the Bohemian Club, to John Neylan dated September 17, 1935, gives us some idea of what the club's concerns were, and how they intended to prevent this sort of "terrorist attack" in the future:

> *"The opinion of those who studied the particular fire was unanimous in the belief that it was of incendiary origin. The week before Labor Day four fires developed within our property and the result is that at the present time, not only is the Grove carefully patrolled and watched but both the Government and the State have their representatives there investigating the possibility of all the fires during the week having been of incendiary origin."* (Neylan papers, Bancroft Library).

Was the Bohemian Club being targeted by activists (today known commonly as "terrorists" under the definitions of the *USA Patriot Act*) in the summer of 1935? Was someone making a political point, or could it have just been a practical joke perpetrated by a few errant local teenagers? We may never know for sure, as no one ever claimed responsibility for starting the fires. We do know that some person or group did set fires at the Grove in 1935 and the Club seems to have chosen to ignore the incident in its historical records and stories. Besides upping security around the Grove considerably, the problem was solved largely by creating an in-house fire department, which now stands at the ready year-round.

STEP INTO MY PARLOR
(Said The Spider To The Fly)

Today the city clubhouse in San Francisco is still very much as it was originally built in 1934. Visiting the City Club is a much more formal experience than the Grove. Dr. Peter Phillips, professor of sociology at Sonoma State University, visited the City Club as part of his research on a doctoral dissertation about the Bohemian Club. He describes the atmosphere in *A Relative Advantage*:

> "When you enter as a guest, you are signed-in by your host. If your host is not present, you are asked to wait in the lounge area while he is paged and can escort you into the Club. Upon entry a large general sitting room is the first area you enter. It comprises dozens of dark leather over-stuffed chairs and couches, and heavy dark wood tables. Numerous paintings adorn the walls and all the current newspapers and magazines are available for your perusal.
>
> The adjacent Cartoon Room is the Club's main bar area. Its name comes from the many historic cartoons, lithographs, and pictures of Club events, plays, and memorials that can be seen on the walls. A dozen ten-person round tables encourage group conversation. The same floor also includes the Bohemian Club library, which would be adequate for a small college. The books fill a large two-story room from floor to ceiling with a balcony circling the second floor. Original rare books authored by famous Bohemians such as Jack London are kept under lock and key. Other than that all books are on the honor system, with a member signing out and returning them at his leisure.
>
> The entire Bohemian Club is filled with artwork done by members: bronze statues, memorabilia (they even have Herbert Hoover's fly rod), and numerous pictures of events and personalities. Upstairs, on the third floor is a 700-person dining room with a stage for Jinks dinners and special celebrations. On the same floor is the famous Grove Room, with its four-wall mural of the Grove exactly as if you were standing at the Civic Center in 1934.
>
> The City Club also has a 750-person theater set up for full stage productions, with sound rooms, and all the normal backstage necessities such as make-up rooms, carpenters' shop, set design areas, and rooms holding thousands of costumes collected over the years. Bohemians even own a 2,500-year-old mummy donated to the Club by an Egyptologist, Jeremiah Lynch in 1914. The mummy, known as Lady Isis, rests in a glass case near the entrance to the Bohemian Theater."

The street level floor has two additional separate entrances, one onto Post Street and one onto Taylor. These are used as entrances for the theater and the art gallery. They served as public entrances in the days before World War II when the Club allowed the San Franciscans to view its annual art displays. Today, entrance to the City Club is by invitation only. The annual art show, while still held, is seen only by Club members and specially invited guests. There are numerous rooms upstairs available for small gatherings and meetings. Few members are long-term residents today, but out-of-town members can reserve a room for overnight stay. City Club hotel rooms are named after various camps at the Grove and decorated accordingly. Tradition is an important aspect of Bohemia and the Clubhouse clearly reflects a long-held concern with that principal. Not much has changed here, just as the Grove still looks about the same today as it did a hundred years ago.

THE GROVE

The Grove is the Bohemians "home away from home", nearly 100 miles distant from the main clubhouse in San Francisco. For the first 50 years of the Bohemian Club's existence, the Grove was comparatively accessible to outsiders. But by the 1930s, as the club gained a reputation for being a favorite hideaway for American Presidents, a shroud of secrecy began to surround the club's membership and the strange rituals that went on inside. Today, you won't even find the Grove listed on most public maps.

At this exclusive private retreat, the members commune with nature in a truly original way. They drink heavily from morning through the night, and bask in their freedom to urinate publicly on ancient redwood trees in the Grove. This strange initiation rite is an old club tradition that baffles outsiders. What kind of fraternity obsesses on the penis' rather mundane biological function this much? Even the Grove's camp cartoons, the *Owl Hoots*, displayed near the Camp Fire Circle each day, depict famous Bohemians peeing on trees. One featured a faux design for a commemorative stamp of club member Anthony Frank, the U.S. Postmaster General, relieving himself on the redwoods.

They also perform pagan rituals like the infamous "Cremation of Care", in which the members wear red-hooded black robes and cremate a coffin effigy of "Dull Care" at the base of a 40 foot owl altar. Some 20% of the Bohemians reportedly engage in homosexual activity, but few of them support gay rights or AIDS research in their official capacities as elected representatives.

The men watch (and participate in) plays and comedy shows in which male actors portray women dressed in drag. Although women are not allowed in the Grove, members often leave at night to enjoy the company of the many prostitutes who come from around the world for this annual event. Employees of the Grove have said that no verbal description can accurately portray the bizarre behavior of the Grove's inhabitants.

Every spring for more than a century, Bohemian Club presidents have summoned their fellow Grovers with this hearty pagan salutation:

> *"Brother Bohemians: The sun is Once Again in the Clutches of the Lion, and the encircling season bids us to the forest—there to celebrate…the awful mysteries!"*

> *"Bohemians come! Find home again in the Grove! Burn CARE and hurl his ashes, whirling, from our glade!"*

> *"Come out Bohemians! Come out and play, come with all the buoyant impetuous rush of youth!"*

The presence of so many powerful men meeting in secret to burn "Dull Care" has led some critics of the Bohos (as they are known) to speculate that more is going on here than a simple two-week romp in the woods. Some critics claim that important public-policy decisions are being made here in secret. Others point to the gathering's bizarre opening ceremony, in which a mock human sacrifice occurs, as evidence of occult activity. Still others say that the two-week sojourn merely provides cover for the powerful to engage in even more twisted behavior, including sexual abuse of prostitutes, CIA MK-Ultra mind-controlled slaves, and children. Then, there are the people who allege ritual murder—yes, *real* human sacrifice.

While the charges of these various critics differ wildly, they have one thing in common. They all seem to agree that the men who meet here deep in the woods are involved in a vast conspiracy that has but one ultimate aim: global domination. Major military contractors, oil companies, banks (including the Federal Reserve), utilities, foundations, museums, universities and national media (broadcast and print) organizations have high-ranking officials as club members or guests. Many members are, or have been, on the board of directors of several of these corporations. You should note that most of the above industries depend heavily on a relationship with government for their profitability.

Longtime Bohemian Dr. Glenn Seaborg once described the Grove as the place "where all the important people in the United States decide an agenda for our country the following year." In the photograph below, they are doing it over a gin fizz breakfast with Dr. Seaborg. (Source: Seaborg Lecture—*My Service with Ten Presidents*. UC Berkeley Archive.)

Breakfast at Owls Nest Camp, Bohemian Grove, July 23, 1967. Around the table, left to right: Preston Hotchkis, the late Ronald Reagan (then Governor of California), former president Dwight Eisenhower, future president Richard Nixon, Glenn Seaborg, Harvey Hancock, Jack Sparks and Edwin Pauley. (University of California—Lawrence Berkeley National Laboratory, Seaborg Archives.)

When powerful people work together, they become even more powerful. This close-knit group determines whether prices rise or fall (by their control of the banking system, money supply, and stock markets), and they make money whichever way markets fluctuate. They determine what our rights are and which laws have effect, by appointing judges. They decide who our highest officials shall be by consensus among themselves, and then sell candidates to us through the media that they own. Important issues and facts omitted from news stories are discussed frankly and openly at the Grove.

What's really going on in the Bohemian Grove? Outsiders may never know for certain. While some researchers are quick to debunk the "conspiracy theories" about child abuse and murder, they do agree that this is by definition, a conspiracy. It was at the Bohemian Grove, after all, where scientists first conceived of the Manhattan Project in 1942, Eisenhower was selected as the Republicans' presidential candidate for 1952, and Richard Nixon talked Ronald Reagan out of running for president in 1968. Most recently, Dick Cheney was selected as George W. Bush's vice-presidential running mate at the Grove during the 2000 election campaign. All of these events transpired in the secret confines of this redwood retreat, known only to the participants involved at the time. The public would not find out until well after the fact, long after the decisions had been made—sometimes weeks later, more often decades later.

Is it "The American Way" to have so much power concentrated in so few hands? Is there any real difference between the public and private sectors when cabinet members come from the boardrooms of large corporations? Is the spending of billions on weapons of war really the will of the American people? Or is it the will of the "Military Industrial Complex" that Eisenhower warned us about in his farewell address?

And what about the occult, the strong mutual interest so many of these powerful men share? In fact, an obsession with the occult amongst elites is nothing new; the tradition certainly didn't *start* at the Grove. Throughout history, rulers have employed magic, astrology, numerology and witchcraft to influence world events in their favor. In this book, I will help to unravel the mystery of the men who have been called the Illuminati, the Black Brotherhood, or simply The Order—the same men you will find inside Bohemian Grove's inner circle. I will reveal their strange worship of a mysterious "god" whom they refer to as the "great owl of Bohemia." And I will expose the hidden depths of what they call their Great Work: "The illumination of mankind by a thousand points of light." With no apologies to George Bush Sr., I must say that the agenda these guys are proposing sounds more like the enslavement of mankind rather than our "illumination."

THE SECRET BROTHERHOOD

In the USA, many people believe that a powerful group of Illuminati Freemasons manipulated and won the War of Independence in 1776 and then took control of the new United States of America. They believe that this Secret Brotherhood has never conceded that control to this day. It is interesting to note the design for the Great Seal of the United States, which contains magical symbols dating to ancient Egypt and beyond, including the pyramid and all-seeing eye of Horus. Above and below this symbol are two Latin phrases, *Annuit Coeptis* and *Novus Ordo Seclorum*. These translate as "Announcing the birth, creation, or arrival" of "A Secular [*Non-Religious*] New Order of Ages". In other words, they were announcing the creation of the New World Order.

The founding of the United States was a massive step forward in the plan for centralized global power. Today, this part of the Great Seal can be found on the back of every US dollar bill, which seems appropriate, given that the Secret Brotherhood controls the American economy. The decision to put the Pyramid and *Novus Ordo Seclorum* symbol on the dollar was made by the 33rd degree Freemason, Franklin D. Roosevelt, in 1935, with the full support and encouragement of his vice president, Henry Wallace, another 33rd degree Mason. The American flag was also designed to reflect Brotherhood symbolism, and the Statue of Liberty was given to American Freemasons by the French Grand Orient (Illuminati) Masonic Order.

Today, the Secret Brotherhood's conspiratorial network includes the mysterious Bilderberg Group; Yale University's prestigious Skull & Bones Society, the clandestine Black Lodges of Freemasonry, and the secretive Knights of Malta. Its diabolical influence reaches into the corridors of power at the White House, the CIA, the Federal Reserve, even the Vatican. And that's just the beginning.

The Secret Brotherhood are men of wealth and position, and the Bohemian Grove is their private, exclusive retreat. Here, they can urinate freely on sacred Sequoia trees, cheat on their wives with prostitutes, engage in fire rituals, worship an owl God, and offer mock human sacrifices upon the altar. Drinking Nembutal fizzes until they pass out, these party animals get up the next morning and plot the fate of nations with a monster hangover.

While the image of our country's leaders performing mock sacrificial rituals deep in a California redwood grove might sound more than a little eccentric, other allegations are even more shocking. In Cathy O'Brien and Mark Phillips' book, *Trance-Formation of America*, sources state that brainwashing; kidnapping, forced sex and ritual murder are practiced at the Grove. The local paper, the Santa Rosa *Sun*, has reported on many weird occurrences in the redwoods. The paper also drew comparisons between the Bohemians and the ancient Cult of Canaan, whose human sacrificial rituals were performed for the god Moloch, named 13 times as the most accursed of demons in the Bible. In the late 1980s, local and state police started investigating suspicious disappearances and human remains found in remote areas of the Grove property, but these investigations were quietly squelched.

The gathering of elite, high-level executives, entertainers, and top political figures alone can raise some suspicion of conspiracy. But strange occult rituals and chanting in the woods is something almost unimaginable to most, especially when these rites of fire sacrifice are done by the likes of the President and Vice President of the United States.

Isn't this the very definition of a *cult*? Not if you listen to former U.S. Attorney General Janet Reno, who ordered the fiery sacrifice of 76 Branch Davidian men, women and children she deemed "cultists" at Waco on April 19, 1993. Soon thereafter, Reno was called upon to defend her indefensible actions, and in typical lawyer language, she gave America a shocking new definition of a "cultist":

> *"A cultist is one who has a strong belief in the Bible and the Second Coming of Christ; who frequently attends Bible studies; who has a high level of financial giving to a Christian cause; who home schools for their children; who has accumulated survival foods and has a strong belief in the Second Amendment; and who distrusts big government. Any of these may qualify [a person as a cultist] but certainly more than one [of these] would cause us to look at this person as a threat,*

and his family as being in a risk situation that qualified for government interference."

—Attorney General Janet Reno, TV news broadcasts, June 26, 1994

The above definition sounds like most regular Americans I know. Does the above paragraph sound like your neighbors? If so, will you move out of the neighborhood in fear? Would you turn them in to the authorities? Should the government spy on them, or worse, *murder them* in a fiery inferno? Such a statement coming from the Attorney General of the United States should outrage us all! Meanwhile, Reno's "boss," Bill Clinton has attended the Bohemian Grove and joyfully participates in a bizarre occult ritual that involves sacrificing a mock human being to an owl God. But that's not cultist behavior, right?

The outrage over the political actions of the Bohemians has spawned an organized opposition group called the Bohemian Grove Action Network, who have held annual demonstrations outside the Grove's main entrance for more than 20 years now. Although the group's leader, Mary Moore, is quick to dismiss the claims of murder and mayhem, she has done an incredible amount of research into the political ramifications of the Grove's close-knit confab of global leaders. She is deeply concerned that both the media and the public are not privy to these important meetings, and so am I. We're certainly not alone. Thanks to the efforts of Mary Moore, as well as a few brave authors, journalists and filmmakers, the word is getting out about Bohemian Grove. Public awareness, curiosity, and in some cases, ire, is being raised. It's about time people started asking questions, and this book aims to provide some of those answers.

Whether the Bohemian Grove is just a friendly camping trip for the rich and powerful, or a dark conspiracy fueled by the power of, and adoration for, an ancient dark owl God, that is for you to decide. This book will give you information from all sides of the political and ideological spectrum, including historical data, inside information from sources who've been there, news reports, analysis, and a study of the occult influences that permeate the Bohemian Club and fascinate the power elite throughout human history.

In the final analysis, the claims of academics and activists aren't that much different. Regardless of political party or religious preferences, everyone I've talked to in the process of writing this book seems to be in agreement that a group of rich and powerful men *are* conspiring to control the world. And that's no "conspiracy theory"—it's a conspiracy *fact*.

Chapter II

Conlige suspectos semper habitos

(Round up the usual suspects)

Whoo Goes There?

"Every year Bohemians find each other somewhat older, or very much older; a little changed, or very much changed; and sometimes transformed from dear friends to cherished memories. But the trees stand, soaring in venerability and strength, redolent of the affection we have had for them, and for the men who have been our companions among these vast trunks."

—Writer and Bohemian Herman Wouk, 1987

It would take nearly an entire chapter to list all of the names of the famous (and infamous) members of the Bohemian Club over the past 130 years. While much has changed through the decades, one thing remains constant: the Bohemian Club always was, still is, and probably always will be, clannishly conservative, with a few exceptions. Even being a blood relation of one of the Bohemians is no guarantee of a membership invitation. For example, it stands to reason that while Republican Teddy Roosevelt was a member of the Bohemian Club, Democrat Franklin Delano Roosevelt was not. Former U.S. Attorney General Robert Kennedy attended the Grove; his brother, President John Fitzgerald Kennedy, did not.

A complete 2010 Bohemian Club membership list is included in Appendix B of this book that reflects mostly current membership. Below is a partial list I've compiled of famous people, many long deceased now, who reflect the club's historical past membership and noted guests:

Notable Names of the Bohemian Club

Eddie Albert (actor)
Luis Alvarez (atomic scientist)
Burt Bacharach (songwriter)
Howard Baker (guest)
James Baker
Ambrose Bierce (writer)
Ray Bolger (entertainer)
Nicholas Brady

Edmund G. "Pat" Brown (former California governor)
Joseph Bryan (Naval Intelligence, Hoover Institution)
Christopher Buckley
William F. Buckley, Jr.
George H.W. Bush
George W. Bush
Jimmy Carter (guest)
Charlie Chaplin (guest)
Richard "Dick" Cheney
A. W. Clausen
Bill Clinton (guest)
Charles Coburn (actor)
Joseph Coors (beer baron)
Walter Cronkite (news anchor)
Bing Crosby (entertainer)
Dwight D. Eisenhower
Queen Elizabeth of England (guest)
Douglas Fairbanks, Sr. (guest)
Leonard Firestone (Firestone Tire Co.)
Henry Ford II
Gerald Ford
Tennessee Ernie Ford (entertainer)
Henry George (radical economist, communist)
Marvin Goldberg (Caltech)
Mikhail Gorbachev (former Russian P.M.)
Merv Griffin (entertainer)
Alexander Haig
Bret Harte (writer)
Fred Hartley (Union Oil Chairman)
Phil Harris (entertainer)
Thomas Haywood
William Randolph Hearst (media baron)
Charlton Heston (actor, former president of the National Rifle Association)
Herbert Hoover
Bob Hope (entertainer)
Robert Kennedy
Henry Kissinger
Ray Kroc (McDonald's)

Ernest O. Lawrence
Jack London (writer)
Art Linkletter (entertainer)
Daniel K. Ludwig (once known as "America's Richest Man")
Edwin Meese
Emil Mosbacher
John Muir (naturalist, founder of the Sierra Club)
Richard Nixon
David Packard (Hewlett-Packard)
Prince Philip (guest)
Lelan Prussia (Bank of America)
Dan Quayle
Ronald Reagan
David Rockefeller
Laurence Rockefeller
Nelson Rockefeller
Will Rogers (guest)
Theodore Roosevelt
Donald Rumsfeld
Helmut Schmidt (former Chancellor of Germany)
George Shultz
William French Smith
Potter Stewart (Judge)
Irving Stone (writer)
Arthur Sullivan
William Howard Taft
Robert Taft
Edward Teller ("father of the H-bomb")
Mark Twain (writer)
Cyrus Vance
Earl Warren
Thomas Watson
Thomas Watson, Jr.
William Webster (former FBI director)
Casper Weinberger
Herman Wouk (writer)

JOIN THE CLUB

Today, a prospective member faces an interrogation that, according to one clubman, 'would satisfy the KGB.' Current membership in the Bohemian Club is about 2,300 men. There is a waiting list of 1,500 notables, all quite eager to pay the $8,500 initiation fee and $2,000-a-year dues. It generally takes from 10 to 15 years or more to get off the waiting list and gain full membership. Some of the older applicants have literally died waiting.

Because club members still require entertainment, "men of talent" pay greatly reduced membership fees, or they work out their dues in trade for their services. For example, when Herman Wouk was accepted into the Bohemian Club, he paid his dues by writing an official history of the club. However, just being famous wasn't always enough to ensure that a membership invitation would be extended.

Such as the case of Charlie Chaplin, the greatest film comedian of the early 20th century. Chaplin was denied full membership in the Bohemian Club, although he was an invited guest to the Grove in 1922. Presumably, it was Chaplin's suspected communist ties that caused the Bohemians to withhold membership privileges from him, for in Chaplin's case, it certainly wasn't a matter of the star not having enough ready cash to pay the club dues. At the time, Chaplin was the wealthiest movie star in the world.

Even Will Rogers, America's favorite humorist and then-unofficial Mayor of Beverly Hills, was denied membership in the Bohemian Club because he made a joke about the Bohemian Grove. Rogers visited the Grove as a guest in 1928 and entertained on the main stage. While Will Rogers "never met a man he didn't like", the Bohos apparently didn't feel the same way about him—his application was denied by the membership committee.

Membership levels since the 1930s have gone up by about a thousand members, give or take a few. There was a Depression-inspired drop in membership through World War II, and then a gradual rise of about 1% per every three years since 1950. Membership categories give an interesting perspective on who really runs the Bohemian Club these days, and it's a far cry from the artsy ideals the original founders intended. In recent years, the power structure grows increasingly unbalanced; about 1500 power elites to roughly 400 artists, musicians, actors, writers, and the like.

Categories of membership are as follows: Regular Members, of which there are about 1,000. Non-resident members number 500 or so. The Regular Professionals category includes 100 well-known thespians, authors, composers and artists. 300 Associate members make up the house band, Grove orchestra and chorus, who receive discounted dues and often even residency status, as the Bohemian Band works year-round. Several other categories make up the balance of membership. The Old Guard category consists of those who have reached 40 years of club membership. And of course, there are honorary members and inactives. Add about 15 Military Officers to that, and about 18 of the much-dreaded foreign consultants, and you've got the idea of who pays the bill for this party. The rest is all background music, so to speak.

The current waiting list for Club is approximately fifteen years, and yes, special preference *does* go to younger men. There is a minimum age requirement to join, however; all potential applicants must be at least 21 years old. The Club has divided the waiting list into ten age groups, from under 30 to over 70. Currently, the majority of Bohos are much older men; the Club averages about 58 deaths per year. This allows an incoming class of fresh, young new members on an annual basis, according to the 1987 Annals of the Bohemian Club.

Currently, Bohemians come from about 37 states and 13 foreign countries. Most out-of-state members come from New York and Washington. Both Texas and Illinois have large contingents at the Grove, as do Arizona and Ohio. Of the 500 non-resident members, close to half actually live in California, but more than 100 miles from the Club, which gives them non-resident status. The largest number of these California non-residents live in the Los Angeles area. It is clear that the San Francisco Bohemian Club is predominately a California-based institution with approximately 85% of all members being residents of the state.

Of the twelve countries represented in Bohemia, England and Canada boast four members each. Germany, Ireland, Panama, Switzerland, India, Hong Kong, Japan, the Bahamas, Bermuda, and the Philippines are all represented here. Non-resident members pay the same dues and initiation fees as resident members, but are not as likely to use the clubhouse on a regular basis in San Francisco. As a result, the city Club isn't too overcrowded, and the Grove is actually a rather pleasant, quiet place in the off-season. Most of the non-resident members only come there once a year for the summer encampment in July, leaving the place for the enjoyment of local Bohemians the rest of the time. Of course, all members are welcome to visit the City Club in San Francisco or the Grove anytime they're in the area, year-round.

Membership in the Bohemian Club has always been by invitation only. Since this is a Club so dedicated to old tradition, the rulebooks have been amended infrequently through the years. Comparisons between 100 year-old rulebooks side-by-side with those of the present day show that not too much has changed about the membership process. Two current non-related Bohemian Club members must sponsor an applicant. Prospective members will fill out a detailed questionnaire, which also asks them about their "artistic or literary talents".

Applicants may submit letters of references from other members in support of their candidacy. Then the investigation kicks into high gear: the membership committee will proceed to write the members listed as known by the applicant, and carefully consider their responses to personal questions about the applicants' character, talent, social potential, and other important requirements of good fellowship. After all of this, the applicant must get nine yes votes from the eleven-person membership committee if he is to be selected.

WELL, *ALMOST* ANYBODY...

Although the Club openly welcomes "men of talent" and "men of use," men of *color* are a different story. Although the Bohemian Club has reluctantly loosened its collar about such matters in recent decades, race is still apparently a factor when considering a potential applicant's suitability for membership. Prior to the 1960s Civil Rights movement, the Bohemian Club was exclusively white. Since then, a few non-white men have been admitted, but as late as the 1990s the best estimates put membership among racial minorities in the Club at less than 1 percent.

Dr. Peter Phillips, Sociology Professor at Sonoma State University and founder of Project Censored, wrote his doctoral dissertation, *A Relative Advantage*, about the Bohemian Club. He was allowed to visit the Grove for his research and noted: "During the Spring Jinks 1994 over two thousand men attended. Of these I observed three African-Americans and one Asian. Every large gathering was a sea of white faces. Predominately white members are a sharp contrast to the waitperson staff at both the Grove and the City Club. By visual observation I estimate the male staff to be approximately a third to half minority. I observed no female employees at my visits to the City Club, although I was told that women do work there. Women employees at the Grove, however, are predominately white."

As we all know by now, women are strictly forbidden as members or guests of the Bohemian Club, at least officially. But what goes on unofficially is quite another story. The Bohos claim that the very presence of women would ruin their freewheeling, frat-party atmosphere. In other words, they would have to *behave*.

Bohemian wives have had concerns for decades. They heard rumors of wild orgies, prostitutes being brought into the Grove by the busload, and other strange sexual goings-on. Even a century ago, wives of the Bohemians began to question their husbands as to what they did over summer vacation—was it all just good clean fun?

After years of steady pressure, the wives were finally allowed to visit the Grove and see for themselves—only *not* during the annual summer encampment in July. The rest of the year, Bohemians were free to bring their wives and children out to the Bohemian Grove for family picnics, swimming, and games of dominoes. According to a 1980 statement from the club's president, women could enter the Grove only under "chaperonage."

The all-maleness of the Club reaches back into a patriarchal past that saw women as inferior humans and encouraged the celebration of male superiority in private associational settings. Despite contemporary "new age" male bonding cultural ideas, the Bohemian Club's patriarchal tradition belies any modern attempt to justify male exclusiveness as a separate but equal process. This is an issue the Bohemians in the future are going to have to face.

"GENTLEMANLY" CONDUCT

Over the last three decades, the Bohemian Club has been involved in a succession of court battles because of its' discriminatory policy against women. During the 1981 Senate confirmation hearings, some female activists called upon Reagan Administration officials to resign from the Bohemian Club. The State of California threatened to revoke the club's liquor license and its tax-exempt status, but still the Bohos fought all the way up to the state Supreme Court. After losing that battle, the Grovers were then forced to at least allow female employees—but the "no gurls allowed" policy still stands when it comes to membership.

The reason? Well, if you ask a Bohemian, he will tell you that the Grovers hold sacred their privilege to walk around in "various states of undress" while at camp. Former California governor Pat Brown has said publicly, on many occasions, that the presence of women would prevent Bohemians from enjoying their right to openly pee on the redwood trees and tell bawdy jokes. That's pretty juvenile reasoning for an organization where the members' average age is 55.

This logic also flies right in the face of the Bohemian Club's own by-laws, which read in Article XXII (1931 Club Rule Book), under the heading "Discipline":

> SECTION 1. Any member who may conduct himself in a manner not becoming a gentleman, either in the Club or elsewhere, or who shall do anything calculated to disturb the harmony or impair the good name of the Club, may be reprimanded, fined, suspended, or expelled.

Might we then conclude that urinating publicly on sacred redwood trees, bringing in prostitutes by the busload, dressing up in drag, drinking alcohol from dawn 'til dusk, celebrating public displays of bizarre erotic art, and engaging in a fire ritual before a 45-foot stone owl is considered "gentlemanly conduct" by the Bohemians? Apparently so. To my knowledge, no Club member has ever been expelled for his participation in these activities, so long as he is suitably discreet about it. But how can a man be "discreet" in a dress and high heels? How exactly does one urinate discreetly in front of hundreds of other men? In actual fact, Bohos are encouraged to do these things; they are sacred club traditions, and naturally, one is expected to join in the fun.

According to an article penned by G. William Domhoff for January 1981 issue *of The Progressive* Magazine, the Bohemians made some rather hilarious excuses in defense of their no-women policy. Describing the proceedings before California's Fair Employment and housing commission in October 1980, Domhoff quotes corporate lawyer Del Fuller (who also happened to be

Secretary of the Bohemian Club) as saying that women would "distract" the more "flirtatious" of the men. He further explained that the men like to let their hair down and become "boisterous," and that they would be "inhibited" by the presence of women. Besides, he added, the men who have to dress up as women for parts in Bohemian plays would be too embarrassed to do so if women were present.

All the legal wrangling to help women gain access to Bohemian Grove was to no avail. Now, some female professionals are taking matters into their own hands. According to a February 19, 2001 *Business Week* article *("Move Over, Bohemian Grove"),* there is now a Belizean Grove, for ladies only. "We aren't waiting for an invitation to Bohemian Grove anymore, because we have our own club," said Mary Lehman Mac Lachlan, president of Chicago's Envest-Net Group, a wealth-management network for financial advisers.

Women may not have a long-standing old-boy network to hook into for job leads, government appointments, or venture-capital deals, but they're rapidly making up for lost time. Groups of professionally accomplished women are building powerful networks of their own, with exotic, exclusive retreats to match the Bohemian Grove. It's a relatively new phenomenon—at this point, still in the experimental stages—the Belizean Grove's first annual gathering occurred in 2001 on Ambergris Caye in Belize, Central America. In comparison to the massive Bohemian encampment, this is a small tea party—only 29 women attended this invitation-only meeting of those who rank high in business, government, and academe.

Participants included venture capitalists and entrepreneurs from Atlanta and Boston, fashion and dot-com executives from New York, and former top-level federal appointees from Washington DC. Also on hand: Sonia Sotomayor, now a U.S. Supreme Court Justice. Attendees spoke on panels that covered such topics as "how to obtain money and power and use them to transform yourself and your community." Unlike the Bohemian Grove guys, the Belize Grove girls don't even try to use the artsy cover as a smokescreen. These ladies get right to the point: *it's about the business, stupid. Of course we're here to network.*

Even the most loyal Bohemians, who adamantly insist that their Club is for social purposes only, occasionally concede that business is indeed conducted at the Grove. Respected historian Kevin Starr, himself a longtime member of the

Bohemian Club, admonished his fellow members in 1977 for their market-place dealings:

> "Weaving spiders come not here" is our motto. This club is vulnerable to criticism when its members outrageously violate that motto, when they use the club, not as an escape from the market place, but as a device of the market place. We are vulnerable to criticism when we grossly violate the heritage handed down to us by our nineteenth century founders.

Starr's critique was in itself an acknowledgment of ongoing business activities inside the Bohemian Club. That these activities do occur is not up for debate anymore. The only question that remains is, how frequently does this taboo dealing take place?

Being in the Club gives a member access to business opportunities well beyond any normal business setting. Some men will and do take advantage of this, while other Bohemians would consider such actions an absolute violation of the "Spirit of Bohemia".

While a few Bohos will admit that, yes, there is policy-setting that occurs at the Bohemian Grove, they will qualify that admission by adding that it is not a formal sit down, negotiation type, behind-the-scenes, deal making process. Rather it is reflected in a mutually shared vision of The Way Things Ought To Be. These Bohemian values are imbedded in the "gentlemanly" traditions of elitism, ethnocentrism, and patriarchy.

While all the written regulations in the world cannot force a man to behave like a gentleman, the Bohemian Club has plenty of rules nonetheless. Before arriving at the Grove, guests are mailed a written statement that describes the main rules of Grove life; no tipping, no cameras (except in camp), no cutting or trimming of trees or branches, no radios, phonographs, video cameras, tape recorders, cellular telephones, televisions, pets, or firearms, and no playing of music from 1:00 a.m. to 9:00 a.m. Due to the high-profile nature of many of the Grove's members and guests, the club even felt it necessary to pass a rule in 1952 forbidding solicitation of autographs!

The Club strives to achieve a well-ordered, "gentlemanly" atmosphere both at the Grove and the City Club. And make no mistake about it—Bohemian men share strong feelings about their Club. The Bohos foster the kind of welcoming, clubby, all-male culture that celebrates tradition with ceremony, while ingraining in each of these men some deeply held values and beliefs. The Club's 131-year history has established a pattern wherein these cultural understandings are religiously passed from generation to generation. More than one young Bohemian camps in the same location as his father and grandfather before him, such as in the case of the Bush family.

FRATERNITY, ELITE MEN'S CLUB, OR SECRET SOCIETY?

Do men join the Bohemian Club for personal friendships and bonding opportunities with other men? The answer to this is an unqualified yes. It is very clear that one of the principal attractions at the Bohemian Club is an opportunity to meet like-minded professional men on an intimate personal basis. The entire Club, especially the Grove experience, encourages friendship building in a shared atmosphere of mutual artistic entertainment and fun. This personal interaction spans decades for many Club members, and deeply held feelings of comradeship and sentimentality towards brother Bohemians are evident in the personal writings and histories of numerous Club members.

With a large majority of Bohemians coming from the corporate world, the Club offers one of the few places in their lives where sentimentality between men is accepted and encouraged. For many the Grove is a reminiscent extension of their college fraternity days, where unbounded alcohol consumption and fellowship reigned supreme.

The Grove experience has a mythic component that triggers the expression of the deepest emotions in the men present, and allows for these feelings to intermingle with others' in the physical beauty of the Grove. Described as the "Spirit of Bohemia," these experiences have been a vital component of the Grove from its earliest inception to the present day.

It is important to recognize how the Bohemian Spirit extends beyond Club boundaries. As explained earlier, the Grove camps create close friendship networks that are often maintained in outside business and social circumstances. The Bohemian Grove offers one of the few places in most of the men's lives where personal friendships and positive feelings towards other men can be expressed. These bonding experiences carry over into men's social networks and become the basis for long-term friendships.

Never forgotten among Bohemians is the belief and idea that they are *important men* in the world, and this gives them the feeling of being truly elite. The Lakeside Chats, jokes about their own excessive wealth, and the exclusive environment of the Club and the Grove camps are completely representative of this shared belief amongst this brotherhood.

The question of whether or not membership in the Bohemian Club affords these men special advantages in the political and business worlds, has been explored exhaustively in previous books and scholarly essays. Therefore, I will not delve into this subject too much here, choosing instead to move forward on the assumption that the answer to that question is, obviously, YES.

Membership has its privileges. Bohemians *do* make business contacts at the Grove. *Of course* deals are being discussed between pairs or small groups of men, but unless you are a careful observer, none of these activities will be obvious. The real standard at the Grove regarding "weaving spiders" is about the same as the "no women allowed" policy—as long as you're not too overt about it, nobody really cares what you do with due discretion.

Perhaps more important than the actual dealmaking at the Grove are the networking possibilities. Bonds of friendship are created here that last a lifetime, and it is very clear that these friendships extend into the commercial and political interests of these men outside the Club. A level of trust between gentlemen is obtained at the Grove, which often is not possible in the day to day business world.

If you are a candidate for political office (particularly Republican), attending the Grove is a definite advantage to your career. This has been going on behind the scenes of American government at all levels for over a century. Politicians and potential candidates have long used the Grove as a place for political networking and consensus building.

A person would have to look very hard to find such a dense concentration of powerful men in one place anywhere else in the United States. The Grove affords these leaders lots of off-the-record discussion time with campmates and other Bohemians about the issues of the day. The Lakeside Chats and other informal talks work toward the building of a collective mindset regarding current political and social issues. This environment provides the foundation for subtle mind control, influencing club members' patterns of thought and political outlook. So subtle, in fact, that the members themselves do not realize how they are being controlled—and if the question were posed to any of them, they would defensively and flatly deny it.

A full recognition of this consensus building process is a key to understanding what makes the Bohemian Club tick. This "Spirit of Bohemia" is the element that makes the collective mindset a reality. Many Bohos describe the Grove as "magical", and a place where "comradeliness" prevails.

While the Bohemian Club certainly qualifies as a kind of fraternity, its' definition also falls into the category of the typical elite men's club, a social tradition handed down from America's British ancestors. English gentlemen's clubs emerged during Great Britain's empire building period as an exclusive place free of troublesome women, underclasses, and non-white persons. London's West End men's clubs, the prototype for American clubs, originated as regular gatherings of local gentlemen in taverns or coffee shops. Sir Walter Raleigh is reported to have founded the Friday Street Club which met at the Mermaid Tavern. Club life in London represented the collective alliance of men with similar tastes and perspectives. Scientific and literary clubs were some of the more honorable associations while gambling and drinking organizations abounded in the 17th and 18th centuries. Some of the more famous early English gentlemen's clubs that are still active to this day are Whites (founded in 1696), Brooks (1774), Carlten (1831) and the Reform Club (1834).

Copied in the United States, elite private men's clubs served the same purposes as their English counterparts. As metropolitan areas emerged, upper crust white males created new clubs throughout the Americas. They understood well that in America, mere money in itself could purchase power, but not social honor. Affiliation with a distinguished club, much like belonging to a good fraternity in college, was (and still is) an essential part of defining oneself as a successful gentleman.

Private men's clubs have existed in America for over 250 years. The first recorded club was the State Club in Schuylkill; a Philadelphia based eating and drinking organization, which was founded in 1732. Harvard University students prompted the formation of the Hasty Pudding Institute in 1770, the

Porcelain Club in 1791. While most of these elite men's clubs usually had discreet occult leanings, New York's Zodiac Club made no effort to conceal its darker interests. Banker JP Morgan founded the super-secret and exclusive Zodiac Club in 1872. Only twelve men, one for each sign of the Zodiac, constitute the club's membership. Within a year, the Bohemian Club, the Zodiac's west-coast spiritual counterpart, was also founded.

Since San Francisco is a much newer city, the Bohemian Club cannot claim the great age of many eastern men's clubs, but it is nonetheless a remote descendant of both the State Club in Schuylkill and New York's Century Association, which in turn was another of the splinter groups to emerge from the old Union Club of Philadelphia. Formed in 1847, the Century's first membership consisted of gentlemen who felt that the Union Club was slighting intellectual and artistic endeavors. This blending of the arts and business served as a model for other clubs throughout the U.S. including the Tavern Clubs of Boston and Chicago, the Cosmos in Washington, DC, the Cactus Club of Denver, the Lotus, Players and Lambs in New York, and the Bohemian Club in San Francisco. From the State in Schuylkill, the Bohemian Club borrowed its emphasis on the great outdoors. Like the Century and Lambs Clubs of New York, the Bohemian Club placed a high priority on arts and letters.

So, what exactly is the Bohemian Club—fraternity, elite social club, or secret society? The answer to this question is simple. All of the above, depending upon which club member you ask, as all Bohos likely have a different subjective impression of what the club actually is. In a later chapter, we will delve into a deeper exploration of the occult aspects of certain elite men's clubs and secret societies, termed by many researchers the "Babylonian Brotherhood," because the basis of their beliefs and ritual practices date back to ancient Babylon. For now, I will give you a brief overview of three of the most infamous such societies: the Bavarian Illuminati, Yale's Skull and Bones Order, and the Thule Society. As you will see, all of these dark side roads lead directly to—and converge upon—the Bohemian Grove.

THE ILLUMINATI

Formally known as the 'Ancient Illuminated Seers of Bavaria', and considered to be the prototype of all secret societies, the Illuminati have had a profound influence upon world events over the past two centuries. The Illuminati were hardly the first secret society. Freemasonry was an extremely influential contemporary secret society with members including American founding fathers George Washington, Benjamin Franklin and Thomas Jefferson. In fact, most of the original signers of the Declaration of Independence were Freemasons. The Freemasons and Illuminati borrowed attributes, titles, degrees, and rituals from each other. Like many of these societies, they were founded as part of the Age of Enlightenment, when men searched for truth within instead of from the Church.

Adam Weishaupt, a law professor at Ingolstadt University, recruited five freemasons from prestigious Masonic lodges to form the Order of Perfectibilists, commonly known as the Bavarian Illuminati, on May 1, 1776. The recruitment of Baron Knigge (a.k.a. Adolf Francis), a major player in the European Masonic scene, is considered to be his greatest coup; under Knigge's guidance, the ranks of the Illuminati grew to over 3,000. At this point, however (1785), it was declared an outlaw conspiracy by the Bavarian government, and Weishaupt quickly disappeared. According to John Robison's *Proofs of a Conspiracy*, the Illuminati organization survived in a somewhat altered form and was the driving force behind the French Revolution.

According to Neil Wilgus in *The Illuminoids*, George Washington had read *Proofs* and felt that the allegations contained therein deserved further investigation. Washington's own correspondence with fellow Masons clearly indicates that he was well aware of subversive forces at work within rival branches of masonic lodges in Europe, and expressed concern that the curse has spread to American lodges. Wilgus also writes that Thomas Jefferson was at least somewhat familiar with Weishaupt's works and felt an admiration for him. It appears Jefferson disagreed with Washington's point of view that the Illuminati had infiltrated American Freemasonry; Jefferson believed that such a thing could not possibly happen in America, since our freedom of speech would have made secrecy unnecessary. Obviously, Jefferson was either a member of this secret brotherhood, or else he was just painfully misguided in this belief, for the Illuminati continues to secretly guide American foreign and domestic policy to this very day.

SKULL AND BONES

Skull and Bones was founded at Yale College in New Haven, Connecticut in 1832. It is the oldest and most prestigious of Yale's seven secret societies. Among the others are Scroll & Key, Book & Snake, Wolf's Head, Eliahu, and Berzelius. This secret fraternity is based at Yale University, where many of the leading members of the U.S. government and the American intelligence community received their formal education. Our current president, George W. Bush, along with his father, former president George Herbert Walker Bush, his grandfather before him, Prescott Bush, and even his great grandfather George Herbert Walker, have all been members of Skull and Bones. Their shared concept of the New World Order is actually an old idea, one which has its origins in the philosophy and beliefs of the Skulls and other affiliated secret societies around the globe.

Bush's opponent in the 2004 presidential race, Senator John Kerry of Massachusetts, is also a Yale grad and proud Bonesman. In this election year, both the Republican and Democratic candidates are members of the same Satanic order. What kind of choice does that leave you, the American voter, when you walk into the voting booth in November?

President Bush appeared on *Meet The Press* on February 8, 2004, in which he was asked a certain question by host (and CFR member) Tim Russert which clearly took him by surprise. Russert asked the president if he knew John Kerry when they were both at Yale. Here is an excerpt:

RUSSERT: You were both in Skull and Bones, the secret society.

BUSH: It's so secret we can't talk about it.

RUSSERT: What does that mean for America? The conspiracy theorists are going to go wild.

BUSH: I'm sure they are. I don't know. I haven't seen the web sites yet. (Laughs)

RUSSERT: Number 322?

BUSH: (No response).

Bush grew visibly uncomfortable and quickly changed the subject. Tim Russert got the exact same answer from John Kerry—and a similar level of discomfort. A few months before, on August 31, 2003, Kerry had appeared on Meet The Press, and was asked the same surprising question by Russert:

RUSSERT: You both were members of Skull and Bones, a secret society at Yale. What does that tell us?

KERRY: Uh, not much, 'cause it's a secret. [Laughs.]

RUSSERT: Is there a secret handshake? Is there a secret code?

KERRY: I wish there were something secret I could manifest…

RUSSERT: 322—a secret number?

KERRY: There are all kinds of secrets, Tim. But one thing that's not a secret: I disagree with this President's direction that he's taking the country.

As it turned out, George W. Bush won the 2004 presidential election. But did it really matter which man, Bush or Kerry, won? They were both members of the same elite secret society family, even if they acted like feuding brothers in front of the cameras. Both Kerry and Bush were pushing the same agenda, which is the agenda of the Bonesmen. The first loyalty of all initiates of Skull & Bones is to Skull & Bones. Their "brothers" in the order are their constituents, not the American people.

Two critics of the Order, historian Antony Sutton and investigative journalist Ron Rosenbaum (himself a Yale graduate), both concluded that Skull & Bones has degenerated since its founding and has taken on more of the occult and ritualistic trappings of the majority of European Freemasonic and Illuminati secret societies. Sutton charges that the Order is secretly known among its initiates as the "Brotherhood of Death" and has become an evil instrument in the hands of America's secret power elite. Rosenbaum claims that the society's Germanic origins are inherently wicked and pre-Nazi. In a long 1977 article in Esquire magazine, Rosenbaum charged that the Skull & Bones building on the Yale campus houses remnants from Hitler's private collection of silver. But upon further investigation, it becomes clear that the Nazi/Skulls connection runs much deeper than a simple set of silverware. In fact, the two worked hand-in-hand to bring Adolf Hitler to power.

In 1910, following the death of Averell Harriman (who presided over Skull and Bones), his widow donated 80 acres of estate property to establish the Eugenics Research Association at Cold Spring Harbor, New York, along with the Eugenics Records Office. The following year, social Darwinism subscriber, John Foster Dulles, revealed his desire to help develop a "super race." He explained that by eliminating "the weakest members of the population," a purer Aryan race might be created. According to several reputable authors, the Dulles brothers directed John D. Rockefeller's management group and law firm at Sullivan and Cromwell on Wall Street, and later administered the American affairs of I.G. Farben, Germany's leading industrial organization linked intimately to Hitler and the rising Third Reich. The Dulles law firm also directed U.S. business affairs for Fritz Thyssen, Hitler's primary financial backer. Thyssen later introduced Allen Dulles to the rising Nazi fuehrer, after which brother John negotiated loans for the Nazis.

All of this activity foreshadowed, in 1928, the Rockefeller financing of the Kaiser Wilhelm Institute for Eugenics, Anthropology and Human Heredity in pre-Nazi Germany. Ernst Rudin, Hitler's chief racial hygienist, was given authority over this institute principally funded by the Rockefellers. Their institute was named for Germany's Kaiser Wilhelm II, who was a solid supporter of early eugenics experiments and occult science to further his royal bloodline. According to Wilhelm II, World War I resulted from a conspiracy between his enemies, the blood kin Czar Nicholas II and King George V, and their affiliated secret societies.

Bonesmen Prescott Bush and George Herbert Walker were directors of the London-affiliated New York banking house of Brown Brothers-Harriman and its various fronts, which funded and directed the military-industrial complex behind Hitler and the Nazi revolution. In 1919, George Herbert Walker had organized W.A. Harriman & Co., which merged with the British Brown Brothers in 1931. In 1924, Averell Harriman and Fritz Thyssen, the German industrialist who began funding Hitler in 1923, set up the Union Banking Corp. in New York to handle funds supplied to it through Thyssen's bank for American investment. Prescott Bush, who had been an officer of the W.A. Harriman bank since 1926, was a director of the Union Banking Corp. from

1934 through 1943. According to government documents, "all of the shares of the Union Banking Corp., were held for the benefit of members of the Thyssen family."

In 1942 the U.S. government investigative report that surfaced during 1945 Senate hearings found that the Union Bank, with Prescott Bush on the board, was an interlocking concern with the German Steel Trust that had produced: 50.8% of Nazi Germany's pig iron, 41.4% of the Reich's universal plate, 36% of their heavy plate, 38.5% of the Nazi's galvanized sheet, 45.5% of Germany's pipes and tubes, 22.1% of their wire, and 35% of Nazi explosives.

So, the next time you hear someone criticize President Bush as a Nazi, understand that this charge is not entirely without foundation. The president's grandfather, Prescott Bush, has documented Nazi ties, and even his father, former president George Herbert Walker Bush, was named after his father's business partner who was an unapologetic Nazi sympathizer and investor. Go figure.

THE THULE SOCIETY

According to numerous historic accounts, Hitler was also an avid student of the occult and a member of the largely secret occult Thule Society that contained members of the British royal family and European banking industry. Thule Society members, with connections to other politically influential leaders in the United States, including members of the Skull and Bones Fraternity at Yale University, are believed to have founded the National Socialist Party in Germany, primarily to initiate World War II. The long-term mission was to create the United Nations, and bring all once-sovereign countries of the planet under the rule of a global government. In other words, the "New World Order" that former president George H.W. Bush spoke so glowingly of on several occasions.

Which leads me to make the obvious assertion that the Skull and Bones Order was clearly a front for Nazi activities in the 20th century and a kind of sister organization to Germany's occult Thule Society. According to a 1940 Skull and Bones document, the initiation ceremony involves the following kinds of things: "New man placed in coffin and carried into central part of building; New man chanted over and reborn into society; Removed from coffin and given robes with symbols on it. A bone with his name on it is tossed into the bone heap at the start of every meeting." Within the Skull & Bones Crypt, also known as "the Tomb," there is what is referred to as a "sacred room" with the number 322 (22x3=66). On the arched wall about the vault entrance is inscribed in German: *"Who was the fool, who was the wise man, beggar or king? Whether poor or rich, all's the same in death."*

The Skull and Bones philosophy, according to several of its most astute critics and historians, emphasizes the "double-cross system." The crossbones on the emblem of the Order symbolically represent the "double-cross". According to this philosophy, anyone who is not an initiate is inferior, and can be lied to and manipulated to further the agenda of the established powers. This is of special importance today, with a leading member of the Skull & Bones/Bohemian Club network occupying the White House.

Here's a look at some of the more powerful people who have been members of the Skull and Bones Order (You will also notice that many of the names below also show up in Bohemian Club member lists): The Bush Family: George Herbert Walker, Prescott Bush, George H.W. Bush, and President George W. Bush. Nicholas Brady, William F. Buckley, Henry Luce, head of Time-Life, which is now AOL/Time Warner, Harold Stanley, founder of Morgan Stanley, Henry P. Davison, senior partner Morgan Guaranty Trust, Artemus Gates, President of New York Trust Company, Union Pacific, TIME, Boeing Company, Senator John Chaffe, Russell W. Davenport, editor of Fortune Magazine, Edmund Pillsbury, head of the powerful flour milling family, The Kellogg family, of the breakfast cereal dynasty, and no surprise, The Rockefeller Oil family.

The truth is we do not know what secret oaths these people have taken. What we *do* know is that the powerful all seem to have ties to the same organizations that collectively have created a one world government that influences you, probably without you even knowing about it.

Using conspiracy theorist logic, you are buying, selling, and electing people who have allegedly taken oaths to manipulate you into furthering their occult ideologies. Some claim that these men and women are Satanic. Now, even if you can't find Lucifer himself hiding behind the "Owl of Bohemia" altar at the Grove, or Baphomet lying in the Skull and Bones "Tomb", you cannot argue that this business cabal doesn't sound just a little bit conspiratorial.

It's hard to ignore the evidence when it's right in front of you. When you see how the Bohemian Club and Yale's Skull and Bones Order interconnected with Nazi Germany's Thule Society, it all starts to make sense. Just as the Bavarian Illuminati interconnected with European and American Freemasonry more than a century before. And all of these secret societies have one important connecting thread—the practice of the same sacred rites used by the high priests and black magicians of ancient Egypt, Tyre, and Babylon.

Chapter III

ignis fatuus

(foolish fire)

Begone, Dull Care!

"O, great owl of Bohemia, we thank thee for thy adjuration.
Well should we know our living flame
Of Fellowship can sear
The grasping claws of Care,
Throttle his impious screams
And send his cowering carcass
From this Grove.
Begone, detested Care, Begone!"

**—Slightly different version of the Cremation of Care ritual,
as published in *The Bohemian Grove and Other Retreats*
by G. William Domhoff, 1974.**

Exactly when the Cremation of Care ceremony came into being at Bohemian Grove is unknown. Some sources say that 1910 marked the first ceremonial burial of the cares of the world during the Grove midsummer encampment. But the printed program I received at the Grove in 2000 billed the spectacle as the "121st Annual Cremation of Care," which would imply that the first such ritual took place in 1879. In any case, it is certain that by 1913, Care was being cremated during the first weekend of the Grove camp, roughly around July 15, and that tradition has remained the same to the present day.

The Cremation of Care Ceremony was produced as a stage play in 1920, wherein a High Priest standing before a huge altar is confronted by Dull Care wrapped in chains. Care is not yet dead because Bacchus, the only warrior Care fears, is truly dead. This twist was written into the play most likely as a reference to recent alcohol prohibition, as the 18th Amendment had just passed in 1919. This ceremony has been rewritten on several occasions, changing with the times, but the theme is always the same. The only way to dispose of Dull Care once and for all is to sacrifice him in the bonfire, which can only be properly lighted with the Lamp of Fellowship. The Eternal Flame of Fellowship sits at the base of a giant 40-plus foot tall owl statue, called the "Owl of Bohemia."

"Dull Care" is still dispatched yearly in a fiery death that symbolizes the initiation of Bohemian fellowship. In recent years, Dull Care's cremation has become one of the Bohemians' more infamous activities due to published descriptions by the mainstream media, and the release of our shocking exclusive footage of the ritual itself captured on tape. A complete transcript of the Cremation of Care ceremony, just as Alex Jones and I filmed it, appears later in this chapter. You can also watch it for yourself in our documentary film, *Dark Secrets: Inside Bohemian Grove*. Free sample clips are available in streaming video on Alex Jones' website, *www.infowars.com*.

Mary Moore's Bohemian Grove Action Network has been raising questions about this bizarre ritual for years. During the protests outside the Grove, some activists held symbolic anti-Cremation Of Care ceremonies that challenged the Bohemians for not "caring about something." These whimsical rituals are called the "Resurrection of Care" by demonstrators, and can become quite animated, with protesters donning long black robes and chanting incantations over a witch's cauldron. We can only assume the protesters' goal in performing this pseudo-witchcraft is to simply "fight fire with fire."

Bohemian Club member and official historian Al Baxter addresses this issue in his 1986 unpublished paper, "Witness in the Woods." Baxter claims the cremation ceremony is meant "to set aside the nagging and often unworthy preoccupations which inhibit openness and warm sympathy for human affairs generally and for works of artistic and moral creativity in particular."

THE OWL OF BOHEMIA

*"Ye shall make you no idols nor graven image, neither rear you up a standing image, neither shall ye set up any **image of stone** in your land, to bow down unto it: for I am the Lord your God."*

—Leviticus 26:1

Bohemia's symbol is an owl, which has been in use since the first year the Club started. Club members collect owl statues, figurines, jewelry—anything with an owl on it. You'll see them walking around the Grove wearing polo shirts embroidered with owls, owl belt buckles, owl bolo ties, owl cufflinks, owl rings—all of which can be purchased in the Bohemian Grove gift shop. The owl is found on all Bohemian materials from matchbook covers and doormats to the most elaborate Club publications. (Interestingly enough, the owl also makes an appearance in the logo of the National Press Club, and is also to be found lurking in the artwork found on the U.S. Federal Reserve Notes, if you look carefully.)

To Bohemians, the owl has come to symbolize the wisdom of life and companionship that allows humans to struggle with and survive the cares and frustration of the world. A forty foot concrete (or stone, sources vary) owl stands at the head of the lake in the Grove. Built to serve as a ceremonial site for traditional Bohemian rituals, the Owl of Bohemia is used yearly for the Cremation of Care Ceremony.

But before the Owl, the Bohos used to worship a different idol: a huge statue of Buddha! No kidding. According to the National Park Service, which controls the lands surrounding Bohemian Grove as part of the Muir Woods National Monument, the 70-foot Buddha statue was constructed of Plaster of Paris and was built in the late 1880s.

The Buddha was modeled after the Daibutsu of Kamkura, and a photo of it was recently found in the archives of the National Park Service (see photo next page). The statue gradually deteriorated over time, and by the 1920's there was very little of it left. Around 1929, the Bohemians thought it wise to replace Buddha with the owl statue that still stands by the Lake today.

*Before the giant owl statue was built, an even taller idol stood in its' place:
this Plaster of Paris Buddha stood over 70 feet tall, nearly double the height of the
owl that crowns the altar today. In this recently rediscovered 1880s photograph,
a group of Bohemians pose in the belly of the Buddha.
(National Park Service/Muir Woods National Monument Archives)*

The Great Owl of the Bohemian Grove has been identified as representing Moloch, the chief god of the Ammonites who lived in Ammon, an eastern section of Canaan. This form of worship spread to a few other cities in the region, including Tyre and Carthage, where, for example during a siege of the city in 307 B.C., two hundred boys of the best families were burned to death in sacrifice to Moloch. Some sources claim that "passing through the fire" meant being quickly passed through flames, which would not harm the child, as a means of dedicating the child to the god. However, there is archeological evidence of actual child sacrifice in areas corresponding to Moloch-worship.

The Great Owl of Bohemia presides over a recent Cremation of Care ceremony.
Note the fire in the "belly of the beast," and the Bohemians dressed
as "priests" in long hooded robes.
(Photo courtesy of Mary Moore, Bohemian Grove Action Network)

Does the Owl symbolize Molech as some claim? Maybe not—Moloch was not a God worshipped in ancient Babylon. Although there are many biblical references to Molech in the Bible, none of them describe this strange god being represented by an owl or as being an owl-faced God. Whereas the Grove's owl is made of solid rock, the bronze Molech was hollow. Technically, Owl worship, as it is practiced in the Grove, is somewhat different from Molech worship. However, there is no shortage of evidence that the rituals conducted at Bohemian Grove are derived from the rituals of ancient Babylon, Sumer, Canaan, Phoenicia, and Carthage.

The source of this information came to Alex from an interview with Professor Texe Marrs, a retired USAF officer who keeps an extensive library on theology and the occult. Marrs himself has produced an audiotape lecture series called *The Wicked Men of the Bohemian Grove*. In our documentary film *Dark Secrets—Inside Bohemian Grove*, Marrs explains:

"Of course we can go back in history—all the way back to ancient Egypt, Babylon or Greece, Rome—and I think you're going to see sort of the roots of the Bohemian Grove. But particularly in the Illuminati era, originating during the French revolutionary days; you know, there we had the actual order of the Illuminati—Adam Weishaupt and all his evil philosophers, let's just call them; Voltaire and the others—and that has come up all the way to today. Hitler of course was a Bohemian. I think it's more Babylon mystery religion. All of the elements are there. Of course, even the owl is a symbol of ancient mystery Babylon. The owl was worshipped by the ancient Egyptians and by the Babylonians. And it's interesting to me that many of the members of Bohemian Grove have in their homes, as I understand it, small figurines of owls. And I believe they actually worship those owls as a symbol of the deity, the Great Goddess of Babylon. And of course, here again we have the counterfeit of Christ sacrificed on the cross. I mean all of those things…there has to be, in my belief, an occultist, a deep occultist, who designed each of the elements of this ceremony. It wasn't just a bunch of guys getting together in a bar, and saying, "Hey, let's have a good time; the Cremation of Care, and why don't we do this or that." I believe it was purposely designed—each element in its term for what they did. No doubt about it."

Note that he does not even mention Molech in the above quote, nor does he equate Molech or Moloch with an owl. In fact, his statement of the owl representing the great goddess of Babylon (Ishtar) is more accurate. So where did this "Moloch Theory" come from? How did the Biblical Moloch wind up back in ancient Babylon, where history records no evidence of a God by that name being worshipped by the Babylonians?

The only published source I could find that makes a connection between the Bohemian Grove and Molech worship was an article from a local community newspaper, the *Santa Rosa Sun* (July, 1993). The *Sun* reported on the Cult of Canaan and the legend of Moloch in place at Bohemian Grove:

> These cults were based on human sacrifice. Why would a 20th century elite resort reproduce these ancient Caananite cult ceremonies? At the minimum, it demonstrates an attraction to the ceremonial practices of the cult, i.e. adoration of destruction, blood, barbarity and sacrifice of children.

THE CULT OF MOLOCH

The New World Order that the plutocrats are attempting to bring to birth is far more Babylonian and pagan than Christian. And that should come as alarming news to America, a nation clearly founded upon Christian ideals. Let's take a closer look at what the Bible has to say regarding Molech:

BIBLICAL REFERENCES TO MOLECH
Old Testament References to Bel or Molech

Leviticus 18:21

And thou shalt not let any of thy seed pass through [the fire] to Molech, neither shalt thou profane the name of thy God: I [am] the LORD.

Leviticus 20:2

Again, thou shalt say to the children of Israel, Whosoever [he be] of the children of Israel, or of the strangers that sojourn in Israel, that giveth [any] of his seed unto Molech; he shall surely be put to death: the people of the land shall stone him with stones.

Leviticus 20:3

And I will set my face against that man, and will cut him off from among his people; because he hath given of his seed unto Molech, to defile my sanctuary, and to profane my holy name.

Leviticus 20:4

And if the people of the land do any ways hide their eyes from the man, when he giveth of his seed unto Molech, and kill him not:

Leviticus 20:5

Then I will set my face against that man, and against his family, and will cut him off, and all that go a whoring after him, to commit whoredom with Molech, from among their people.

1 Kings 11:6,7

So Solomon did evil in the eyes of the LORD; he did not follow the LORD completely, as David his father had done. On a hill east of Jerusalem, Solomon built a high place for Chemosh the detestable god of Moab, and for Molech the detestable god of the Ammonites.

2 Kings 23:10

And he defiled Topheth, which [is] in the valley of the children of Hinnom, that no man might make his son or his daughter to pass through the fire to Molech.

Isaiah 46:1

Bel boweth down, Nebo stoopeth, their idols were upon the beasts, and upon the cattle: your carriages [were] heavy loaden; [they are] a burden to the weary [beast].

Jeremiah 32:35

And they built the high places of Baal, which [are] in the valley of the son of Hinnom, to cause their sons and their daughters to pass through [the fire] unto Molech; which I commanded them not, neither came it into my mind, that they should do this abomination, to cause Judah to sin.

Jeremiah 50:2

Declare ye among the nations, and publish, and set up a standard; publish, [and] conceal not: say, Babylon is taken, Bel is confounded, Merodach is broken in pieces; her idols are confounded, her images are broken in pieces.

Jeremiah 51:44

And I will punish Bel in Babylon, and I will bring forth out of his mouth that which he hath swallowed up: and the nations shall not flow together any more unto him: yea, the wall of Babylon shall fall.

In *Paradise Lost,* John Milton described Moloch as follows:

"First Moloch, horrid king, besmirched with blood
Of human sacrifice, and parents' tears,
Though, for the noise of drums and timbrels loud,
Their children's cries unheard, that passed through fire
To his grim idol."

Molech was an ancient fire deity, of a common type worshipped throughout Canaan generally, and Phoenicia particularly. Under various names, depending upon the city or country, Molech is essentially identical with Chemosh of Moab, and probably Melqart of Tyre. The general name for this type of fire god used throughout Palestine was Baal, meaning 'lord.' Molech was the national deity of the country of Ammon, east of the Jordan, or the Ammonites. Molech was also worshipped by the Israelites on many occasions, much to the distress of the prophets.

The name Molech presents many problems to the interpreters of the original texts. The word means king, and there several variations, using the familiar terminations *om* and *am*. Hence, the words are also rendered as Milcom, or Malcam, and are then proper names. It is possible that Melqart is another such variation. In short, it is difficult to decide if Molech is a simple appellative meaning king, and therefore a variation of lord, or is in fact a proper name.

The word Topheth stands for the everlasting fires of hell was once "the king's music grove" where the image of Molech stood. There, they burned babies in the red-hot arms of the idol with tabrets or tambourines, harps and all kinds of musical instruments. The screams pleased Molech who then gave the priests a secret message, which was translated out of the screams.

Like the Owl of Bohemia, the ancient Ammonite idol Molech was a towering larger-than-life edifice. Molech worship consisted of the ritualized sacrifice of the first-born infant son of every Ammonite newlywed family. Building a fire in the belly of the beast until the flames poured out of the mouth, the high priest mounted a scaffold and tossed the first-born male child into an aperture in Molech's chest, to the incantation of drums and droned liturgy of the priests of Molech. The mock human sacrifice ritual at Bohemian Grove also has incantations of drums and droned liturgies by men dressed in priest-like gowns.

A casket christened "Dull Care" and borne, like the passing of Arthur, in a boat across the lake could be a symbol, also, not only of "cares of the world," but of caring itself. The denizens of the Grove, as a collective body, are the ruling class and upper echelon bagmen who make and orchestrate war—the modern Molech.

During this part of the ceremony, I took special notice of the musical selections (usually played live by the Grove's house orchestra, or recorded on tape) chosen to accompany the action. All of the chosen works have occult overtones, often written by composers (like Ludwig Van Beethoven, a high-level Freemason having many close ties to the Bavarian Illuminati) known to be practiced in high ritual magick. Most prominently featured in the ritual I attended was Edvard Grieg's *Peer Gynt Suite no. 1*, (Opus 46) particularly *Morning Mood*, *Aase's Death*, and *In The Hall of the Mountain King*, which is heard as the boatmen cross the lake. *The Abduction of the Bride* is also employed from *Peer Gynt Suite no. 2* (Opus 55). Although often read as a children's tale, Henrik Ibsen's classic story *Peer Gynt* could be considered the *Harry Potter* of the 19th Century. Peer Gynt is an anti-hero who traverses the magical worlds of Morocco and Egypt, leading the reader through a fantasy complete with trolls, witches, and of course, a powerful Mountain King.

This may all seem confusing at first, but I am hoping that sharing my research with you in this chapter will provide you ample evidence that the dark rituals performed at the Bohemian Grove are ultimately derived from Babylon and its offspring—Canaan, Phoenicia, and Carthage. I will also attempt to unravel the mystery surrounding the identity of the Great Owl.

Although I have ruled out the Great Owl as a statue of Moloch, the evidence of a connection between the Bohemian Grove and Babylon is a clue to its true identity. In addition, one of the prayers used during the Cremation of Care ritual at the Grove provides another key piece of evidence:

"O thou, great symbol of all mortal wisdom, Owl of Bohemia, we do beseech thee, grant us thy counsel."

The owl throughout occult history usually is a symbol of a female entity, such as Athena, a.k.a. Ishtar or Isis, a prominent member of the Babylonian and related pantheons, known among other things as the goddess of wisdom.

80

Considered the mascot of Athens, the owl was even named for the goddess Athena, scientific name: Athene noctua.

These birds were abundant in ancient Greece. Athenian coins bore the likeness of Athena on one side and an owl on the other. Indeed, these coins were called "owls." Also remember the tradition of King Arthur's Merlin, who was always depicted with an owl on his shoulder? The owl is the unrivaled symbol of intelligence and wisdom. Gender ambiguity in the ancient Mediterranean world where the goddess Ishtar was honored by a cult festival characterized by cross-dressing also sounds a lot like what goes on every year at the Grove. Ishtar, another cultural descendant of Athena, was the most important female deity in the Middle East before the rise of monotheistic religions.

All the evidence seems to be pointing towards the Bohemian Grove's ritual being a contemporary manifestation of the ancient Cult of Isis. Among many other titles, Ishtar was known as "The Lightbringer," "Light of the World," "Exalted Light of Heaven," and "Torch of Heaven and Earth." Ishtar is also known as Venus, and many theologians see Ishtar as the female counterpart of Lucifer, who is also referred to as "the Lightbringer."

The statue of her in New York Harbor, which is known as the Statue of Liberty (designed by a French Freemason), carries a torch and a book, symbolizing intelligence and information, two components of wisdom. Many believe that her torch is also a symbol of a future role of Lucifer controlling America. Note the statue's similarity to the Colossus of Rhodes, which was dedicated to Ishtar's brother, Shamash/Helios, the Sun God (which is also a designation for luciferic beings).

In the final analysis, the Great Owl of Bohemia symbolizes the Cult of Isis, by symbolizing all four of its gods: Ishtar, Lucifer, and by virtue of the associated flames representing abandonment to Lucifer-stimulated desires, Dionysus and the "greater Moloch," Satan.

Bohemian Club literature boasts that the Cremation of Care ceremony derives from "Druid rites, medieval Christian liturgy, the Book of Common Prayer, Shakespearean drama, and nineteenth-century American lodge rites." Is this the straight goods, or is it sugar—coated PR covering a darker sacrificial rite, terrifying even on a symbolic level? The question has now been raised—how do we know that is only an effigy that is being burned and not an actual human body?

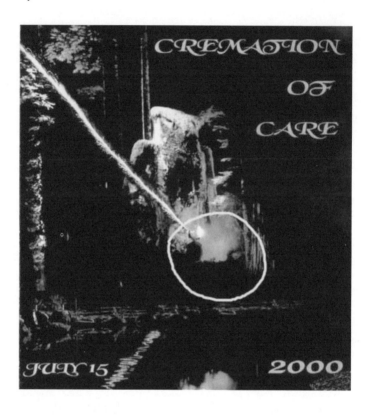

This is the official program for the 121 st Annual Cremation of Care ceremony, which Alex and I secretly filmed in the summer of 2000. The circle shown here (just beneath the owl) highlights the silhouette of a small human-like body, like that of a child, burning in effigy.

Bizarre as it sounds; the very idea sounds like something out of a horror movie. It brings to mind *The Wicker Man*, made in 1973. In this supposedly fictional tale, a policeman goes to Summer Isle, off the coast of England, to investigate a missing child, only to discover an entire community completely dominated by an amoral, bloodthirsty cult of Druidic pagans. The Druids are plotting to sacrifice the girl on May Day, placing her inside a giant effigy called "The Wicker Man", which is then set on fire.

While *The Wicker Man* was fictional, the historical depiction of children being sacrificed to Moloch has been portrayed in film many times. Perhaps the most breathtaking restoration of these ritual events was in the groundbreaking 1914 silent film *Cabiria*. Italian director Giovanni Pastrone's innovative techniques in this film inspired American director D.W. Griffith to make his legendary epic *Intolerance* about the fall of Babylon.

Another well-known depiction of the Molochian rites can be found in Fritz Lang's 1927 silent masterpiece, *Metropolis*. In the film, Freder witnesses a horrifying industrial accident in which the giant machine morphs into Molech, gobbling up the slave workers into its' fiery jaws. The film also deals effectively with themes of a modern, mechanized German city where all citizens are mind-controlled slave laborers; banished to the underground, where they toil endlessly to produce the commodities needed by their rulers in the glittering city above. The citizen slaves are put to work building a new Tower of Babel, intended to be the crowning glory of this modern Babylon. Predating George Orwell's *1984* (published in 1949) by 22 years, Lang's *Metropolis* foresees the future in a way that is both uncanny and amazingly accurate. Surely this piece of so-called "science fiction" must have been an inspiration for Orwell's later work, which expands upon this original concept.

THE DRUIDS

Who were the Druids? It appears they were Celts, a mixed breed of bloodlines. According to Julius Caesar, Druids exercised great authority and held extreme power over nations long before the birth of Christ. Druids lived in forests and caves, and possessed vast knowledge of geometry and natural philosophy. Religious instructors, teachers of children, priests, judges and interpreters of laws, their knowledge of the stars and medicine added to their prestige. They may have been related to the Chaldean magicians or perhaps Jewish Kabbalists.

The word Druid is generally considered to be derived from "DRU," which means Oak Tree, although its etymology may also be found in the Gaelic word Druidh, *"a wise man"* or *"magician."* Druid priests usually wore a ritual costume symbolizing the heavens, our solar system, the 13th constellation, the sun and moon, quite similar, in fact, to those worn by the priests and acolytes in the Grove's "Cremation of Care".

Their temples, wherein the sacred fire was preserved, were generally situated on the tops of hills and mountains, and in dense groves of oaks. The adytum or cave of the mysteries was called a Cromlech, and was used as the sacred altar of regeneration. To some, the "Cromlech" altar the Druids used sounds very similar to the "Molech" owl altar at Bohemian Grove.

The Druids venerated the mistletoe when growing on the oak, a tree that they esteemed sacred. Trees, particularly groves of trees, are associated with Zeus, and the worship of that god. Human sacrifice was one of the characteristic rites. Their gods were the same as worshipped by the Greeks and Romans, but bore different names. Only sons of famous families could enter training for the order, and the same practice still exists today. In fact, the Grove in and of itself is an indication of a Druid heritage. Although information on Druidism is sketchy because of the eradication of the Sun Mysteries from civilization beginning in the fourth century A.D., there are some sources which trace them back to Phoenicia and the Babylonian pantheon. Political and religious suppression forced the Druids to go underground. Many thought that the religion had disappeared, but it survived, handed down within families and villages to resurface again in the early eighteenth century.

The phrase "dull care" is derived from an old English ditty entitled *Begone Dull Care:*

> *Begone, dull care!*
> *I prithee begone from me;*
> *Begone, dull care!*
> *Thou and I can never agree.*
> *Long while thou hast been tarrying here,*
> *And fain thou wouldst me kill;*
> *But [in] faith, dull care,*
> *Thou never shalt have thy will.*
>
> *Too much care*
> *Will make a young man grey;*
> *Too much care*
> *Will turn an old man to clay.*

My wife shall dance, and I shall sing,
So merrily pass the day;
For I hold it is the wisest thing,
To drive dull care away.
Hence, dull care,
I'll none of thy company;
Hence, dull care,
Thou art no pair for me.

We'll hunt the wild boar through the wold,
So merrily pass the day;
And then at night, o'er a cheerful bowl,
We'll drive dull care away.

One thing that Alex and I couldn't help but notice was the seemingly orgasmic enjoyment the Bohemians gathered from watching Dull Care cremated in this strange ritual. We weren't the first to take note of this. When *Spy* magazine's Philip Weiss observed the ceremony in 1989, he reported this conversation between two young (30-something) Bohos in the crowd: "My friends don't understand this," one said to his friend. "I know that if they could see it, they would see how terrific it is. It's like great sex…it's *more* than it's cracked up to be. You can't describe it."

The Bohemian Club wrote to British filmmaker Jon Ronson after viewing *Dark Secrets—Inside Bohemian Grove*. Their official response to our film was:

> "The Cremation of Care is a musical and verse pageant heralding a two-week midsummer escape from business cares, and celebrating nature and good fellowship…As a grand-scale stage drama, it may be a bit overdrawn, but it's about as innocent as anything could be."

Innocent? Read the transcript of the entire ceremony reprinted here and decide for yourself.

Complete Transcript of the 121st Annual Cremation of Care Ceremony
As filmed by Alex Jones and Mike Hanson on July 15, 2000

(The ritual begins with a processional of priests marching slowly towards the stage while the second movement of Beethoven's 7th Symphony plays. This process takes about ten minutes. Once the Bohemians are in their places onstage, one of the acolytes sounds a bell, calling all to order.)

Video still of the Cremation of Care from our hidden camera.

High Priest *(wearing white robe, center stage):*

"The Owl is in his leafy temple. Let all within the grove be reverent before him. Lift up your heads, oh ye trees, and be lifted up ye everlasting spires—for behold! Here is Bohemia's shrine! And holy are the pillars of this house."

(Bell sounds again.)

(Voice calling from the chorus, from behind the high priest):

"Weaving spiders come not here!"

(Procession of seven hooded, robed men carrying torches enter.)

High Priest:

"Hail, Bohemians!

With the ripple of waters, the song of birds…such music as inspires the sinking soul…do we invite you to midsummers' joy. The sky above is blue and sown with stars, the forest floor is heaped with fragrant grit. *(Author's note: this is likely a thinly-veiled reference to the strange urination ritual of the Bohemians)* The evening's cool kiss is yours. The campfires glow…the birth of rosy-fingered dawn. Shake off your sorrows with the city's dust…and cast to the winds the cares of life!

But memories bring back the well-loved names of gallant friends who knew and loved this Grove. Dear boon companions of long ago. Aye! Let them join us in this ritual! And not a place be empty in our midst.

All his battles to hold…in the grey autumn of the world or the springtime in your heart…attend our tale. Gather ye forest folk! And cast your spell over these mortals! Touch their world-blind eyes with carrion…open their eyes to fancy. Follow the memories of yesterday…and seal the gates of sorrow.

It is a dream…and yet, not all a dream. Dull Care, in all his works, harbored it. As vanished Babylon and goodly Tyre. And moss rends the stones of Babylon. For beauty is eternal…and we bow to beauty everlasting.

For lasting happiness, we turn to one alone, and she surrounds you now! Great Nature. Refuge of the weary heart. And only found her breasts that had been bruised. She has cool hands for every fevered brow…and dreadless silence for the troubled soul. Her counsels are most wise. She healeth well, having such ministries as calm and sleep. She is ever faithful. Other friends may fail. But seek ye her in any quiet place…smiling, she will rise and give to you her kiss.

So must ye come as children. Little children that believe don't ever doubt her beauty or her faith, nor deem her tenderness can change or die."

(From the orchestra pit, the organist begins to play a slow funeral dirge as the robed men take their places onstage for the ritual.)

"Bohemians and Priests! The desperate call of heavy hearts is answered! By the power of your fellowship, Dull Care is slain! His body has been brought yonder to our funeral pyre to the joyous pipings of a funeral march. Our funeral pyre awaits the corpse of Care!"

(A boat containing the aforementioned "corpse" begins to cross the lake, moving towards the stage as the Bohemians eagerly await.)

High Priest *(speaks to Dull Care):*

"O, Thou, thus ferried across the shadowy tide…in all the ancient majesty of death.

Dull Care, enemy of beauty. Not for thee…forgiveness, or the restful grave. Fire shall have its' will of Thee! And all the winds make merry with Thy dust!"

(Priest calls to torchmen)

"Bring fire!"

(The torchmen come forward to the altar. Cheers and applause erupt from the assembled crowd of Bohemians. Seconds later, the torchmen flee as Dull Care lets loose with wild, wicked laughter.)

Dull Care speaks:

"Fools! Fools! Fools! When will ye learn that me ye cannot slay?

Year after year, ye burn me in this Grove, lifting your puny shouts of triumph to the stars. When again ye turn your faces to the marketplace—do you not find me waiting, as of old?

Fools! Fools! Fools to dream ye conquer Care!"

High Priest: "Say Thee, mocking spirit! It is not all a dream. We know Thou waitest for us when this, our sylvan holiday has ended. We shall meet Thee and fight Thee as of old…and some of us will prevail against Thee. And some Thou shalt destroy.

But this too we know: year after year, within this happy Grove, our fellowship bans Thee for a space. Thine malevolence which would pursue us here has lost its power under these friendly trees. So shall we burn Thee once again this night?

And with the flames that eat thine effigy, we shall read the sign: Midsummer sets us free!"

(More cheers, screams, applause from the audience.)

Dull Care: "Ye shall burn me once again? *(hysterical laughter)* Not with these flames…which hither ye have brought from regions where *I* reign. Ye fools and Priests! I spit upon your fire!"

High Priest: *(turning to the 45-foot stone owl)* "Oh, Owl! Prince of all mortal wisdom…Owl of Bohemia, we beseech Thee! Grant us Thy counsel."

(Music starts to play, the owl-God is illuminated with fiery light, and sings:)

(Song)

> *No fire…No fire…No fire…*
> *Unless it be kindled in the world where Care is*
> *Nourished on the hates of men*
> *And drive him from this Grove.*
>
> *One flame alone must light this fire*
> *One flame alone must light this fire*
> *At last, within the Lamp of Fellowship*
> *Upon the altar of Bohemia.*

High Priest: "O, great owl of Bohemia, we thank thee for thy adjuration."

(Fire is brought from the Lamp of Fellowship, the eternal flame)

> "Be gone, detested Care, be gone!
> Once more, we banish Thee!
> Be gone, Dull Care!
> Fire shall have its' will of Thee!

Be gone, Dull Care!
And all the winds make merry with Thy dust!

Hail Fellowship's eternal flame!
Once again—Midsummer sets us free!

(Funeral pyre is lit with torch, fires ignite all around the lake. Crowd cheers again as Dull Care is finally cremated and forever banished.)

The fiery grand finale of the Cremation of Care.
(Video still from our film, "Dark Secrets: Inside Bohemian Grove.")

Chapter IV

Magister mundi sum!

(I am the master of the universe!)

Inside the Grove

"Hail Bohemians!
With the ripple of waters, the song of birds...such music as inspires the sinking
soul...do we invite you to midsummer's joy."

—High Priest's greeting in the Grove's Cremation of Care ritual.

To get to the Bohemian Grove, you cross the bridge over the Russian River and take the second left, which is called the Bohemian Highway. Signs sternly warn off trespassers, and the Grove is vigorously guarded during the entire encampment. Visitors must have invitations and sign in and out; cooks and other workers have to wear ID badges at all times. Once Alex and I managed to bluff our way inside, we just tried our best to look like the other Bohemians, walking with an air of self-importance as we took a good look around.

There is a 24-hour transportation system called "The Owl" shuttle. These open air trucks with rear seating for about twenty adults cruise back and forth on the paved roads, allowing for men to get on or disembark at their convenience, making getting from one end of the Grove to another relatively quick and efficient. It is a little over a mile between the entrance to the last camps out on River Road.

Once inside the front gates, we encountered a sort of central administrative area (most Grove maps refer to it as the "Civic Center") which includes the Bar and Grill, Post Office and Grove Store. Immediately we noticed that nearly everyone was smoking a cigar. The men take pride in their cigars. The carrying of a cigar clip is a common practice at both the Grove and the City Club. In fact, the Grove gift Shop even sells specialized cigar clips with the Club's Owl logo on them for the serious smoking enthusiast.

While the Grove's public areas afford a communal atmosphere for the Grovers to socialize, the real action goes on in the private confines of the individual camps. I have included in the Appendix section of this book a complete list of camp names, as well as a full 2010 membership list that also gives the camp affiliation of each club member. This in itself will be a fascinating study for serious Grove researchers. By gaining knowledge of who-camps-out-with-who, the bigger picture of this network of power (and more importantly, how it works) begins to emerge. We tried to check out as many individual camp-sites as we could, although there were some we dared not walk into without an invitation.

A typical camp at the Bohemian Grove has some sort of entryway that depicts the camp name. Pig'n Whistle has a ceramic group of suckling pigs at its' entrance. Toyland has a soft light behind a toy soldier figure in a glass case. Many camps have fences that set apart camp boundaries and ensure privacy to the men inside.

One camp entryway was set through two redwood trees wide enough for two adults to pass. Between the trees was an old wooden sign adorned by a human skull. The words "Je Suis Lafitte" were hand-painted on the sign. Translated from French, this means, "I am Lafitte," a reference to the famous pirate of the French Revolution. Knowing the Bohemians' penchant for adorning their campsites with historical antiquities, I naturally assumed that someone had paid a hefty price for this ominous signage that probably once belonged to Jean Lafitte himself. As for the skull...well, we can only guess as to where that came from.

There is a wide old tree stump displayed that shows its history by the rings growing out from its core. It reads something like this: "At the year 800, Charlemagne was crowned emperor. At 853, the first book was printed in China." The ring marking 935: "text of the Koran finalized". At 1300: "Aztec civilization in Mexico." The growth ring signaling 1595: "Shakespeare completes *Romeo and Juliet*". And so it goes, a piece of redwood stump providing a fascinating history lesson, from Joan of Arc burned at the stake in 1431 to Leonardo da Vinci completing the Mona Lisa in 1506 to Mozart born in 1756 to gold being discovered in California in 1848 to Hitler invading Poland in 1939 to the end of World War II. Amazing what you can learn from a tree.

At the base of a particularly majestic 301-foot tall redwood, a plaque reads: "I LOVE THIS TREE AS THE MOST SOUND, UPRIGHT AND STATELY REDWOOD IN THE GROVE. LET MY FRIENDS REMEMBER ME BY IT WHEN I AM GONE." By the sounds of this heartfelt declaration from a former Grover, I can only assume that the way he wants his fellow Bohos to "remember" him is to urinate on his favorite tree. *Strange.*

The oldest tree in this forest is 1,400 years old. It is 89 meters high. The tall redwoods provide adequate all-day cover from the California sunlight, keeping the camps in a constant state of semi-darkness; campfires burn both day and night. Most camps have a wall around them to prevent others from seeing what goes on inside. The camps are about 100 feet wide, with wooden platforms on which campers set up sleeping cots. The wealthier camps feature redwood cabins. No one seems to worry about rain spoiling the party—somewhat miraculously in fact; it never rains when the Grove summer camp is on. Must be some pretty effective magic these guys are working.

The patron saint of the Grove is St. John of Nepomuk, who lost his head around 1393 A.D. for keeping the Queen's confession of adultery secret from King Wenceslas IV. St. John certainly knew how to keep a secret. A statue of him, with his index finger held up to his lips, signaling secrecy, stands near The Lake in the Grove.

The Lake, as it is called on the Grove map, is about 100 feet wide and 400 feet long. The Lake was originally built in the mid-1920s, and relined with earth and concrete in 1981. An artificial waterfall tumbles into it, and water lilies float in natural-looking patterns across the water. A light mist rises off the Lake giving it a mythic middle-ages quality. A bandstand in front of the giant concrete owl sits on the south shore of the Lake, and is used for concerts and ceremonies during Grove sessions. When the camp is in session a fully-staffed fire department is on the scene, just in case the Cremation of Care ceremony fireworks display should get a little out of hand, as has actually happened on a few occasions. Two staff doctors and two emergency medical technicians man the Grove's fully equipped medical center.

A typical day at the Grove starts with juice, fruit and pastry snacks, prepared and laid out by the camp stewards, and a copy of the *San Francisco Chronicle* available for each camp member. In some camps gin fizzes start the day, although generally alcohol consumption is fairly limited before noon. A small number of men are out jogging or taking brisk walks, but most of these power brokers decide to sleep in an extra hour or two, usually to quell a hangover.

Breakfast at the dining circle runs from 7:00 a.m. to 11:00 a.m. with seating available at long picnic tables linking 26 men together to encourage interaction and conversation. Members may order specialty items such as eggs Benedict, or pick an entree from the main listings such as baked trout or a mushroom omelet. Red-coated waitpersons, both men and women, bring out platters of ham, bacon, sausage, pastries, fresh fruits, along with lots of California orange juice.

After breakfast men can wander back to camp, go off for trap and skeet shooting, take a perimeter ride around the Grove in the Owl Shuttle, or attend a scheduled museum talk at 10:30 a.m. Museum talks are a post-World War II tradition, eventually emerging into daily programs and Grove nature tours known as "walkie-talkies". Past summer encampment museum topics have included everything from Endangered Species in Somalia to Marble Carving, from Nuclear Disaster to Population Growth. In 1993, the museum also addressed "Desert Storm's Aftermath in the Gulf" and the curiously titled "Eye On/In Iraq."

While the majority of museum talks focus on topics concerning the natural environment, such as lessons on the history of the Grove's redwood trees and exhibits on logging in the nineteenth century, clearly not all of the subjects are environmentally friendly. In 1992 John Lehman, former Deputy Director of the U.S. Arms Control and Disarmament Agency, spoke on "Smart Weapons". For the years 1989, 1991, 1992, and 1993 there were fifty-seven listed museum talks at the Grove. While military and space science topics only make up about 10% of the total number of museum talks, business, technology and biology constitute another 40%.

Daily at noon there is an organ or band concert as a prelude to the Lakeside Chat speakers who usually give a thirty-minute talk at 12:30. Arguably, the Lakeside Chats are the most important aspect of what goes on inside the Grove; matters of public interest are discussed and perhaps even decided here through the collective consensus-building process. More on the Lakeside Chats will be covered extensively in a later chapter because of their mostly political content. For now I'll just say that these Lakeside Chats often feature prominent Bohemians or well-known guests, from former presidents to foreign prime ministers and business leaders, along with a few scattered celebrities for entertainment value.

The Grove dining circle, 1915.

After the Chat, Bohemians are off to their camps for lunch. This is a time when personal invitations are frequently given to friends and associates at the Grove to join a camp for lunch. Lunches are usually cooked and served by the camp stewards. Early afternoon is the time of day that many Bohemians begin to drink alcohol. Wine was served in the dining hall and the various gatherings I witnessed, and mixed drinks and beer were readily available. As no money exchanges hands at the Grove, if you are a guest in a camp for lunch or a party, all the food and alcohol is paid for by camp members. And naturally, the libations are the finest money can buy. But these men do a lot more than just sip a little wine with meals. In fact, heavy drinking is one of the unwritten rules of the Grove—everyone is expected to be at least a little tipsy, if not outright drunk by afternoon. The games begin at 7 a.m., when camp valets bring campers gin fizzes in bed. Guzzling continues throughout the afternoon and by evening, everybody is pretty loose.

Mid to late afternoon at the Grove is time for camp to camp visiting or a walk to the Russian River for a swim. On occasion there is a late afternoon museum program or organized walkie-talkie, but these are fairly intermittent. Camp visits are one of the principal activities at the Grove, and the hospitality mat is always out.

Dr. Peter Phillips, who came to the Grove as an invited guest, notes in his Ph.D. dissertation, *A Relative Advantage*: "I visited seven camps for extended periods during my days at the Grove. On each occasion I had the name of a camp member to ask for and a superficial reason for the visit. In each camp I was warmly greeted, usually by the camp captain, and introduced to each member of the camp. I was immediately offered a drink and often a cigar and invited to join the campfire circle or on-going discussion."

Spy magazine reporter Philip Weiss had a similarly hospitable experience. When he stopped into Valhalla camp one afternoon, he joined a group of Bohemians who were drinking their own home-brewed beer particular to the Valhalla camp. A stage show was in progress on an elaborate but makeshift platform in front of a giant redwood tree, on which was hung a framed 19th century engraving. "The scene was permeated by a kind of Nazi kitsch Black Forest Imagery," he writes, "and the setting seemed very Wagnerian—though the music was sometimes undercut by the soft drumming of tinkling urine off the edge of the porch, where the beer drinkers went one after the other. Then the beer brewer himself came out to sing *The Road to Mandalay*; the song based on Kipling's poem. He was a goateed giant with massive shoulders and a beer gut."

Rudyard Kipling, romantic colonist and example of the conquering masculine spirit, is, naturally, one of the Grove's literary heroes. In fact, the Grove's most exclusive campsite, Mandalay Camp (home to Kissinger, Ford) takes its name from the poem. Weiss writes that *The Road to Mandalay* is "a triumphant white-man's-burden song. The brewer finished tearfully, his arms high above his head, fists clenched: *'Take me back to Mandalay-ah.'*

"Amid wild applause," Weiss observed, "one man removed a heavily chewed cigar to say, 'If that don't send a chill up your spine, you ain't a Bohemian.'"

As a sidebar to his *Spy* magazine piece, Weiss included "A Completely Authentic 1989 Bohemian Grove Joke Book," a collection of tasteless jokes he overheard during his stay at the Grove. I will include a few of them here, just to illustrate the ridiculously juvenile (and often twisted) humor these grown men actually find funny:

> A Bohemian at dinner holds up a wine bottle filled with a yellowish liquid and reads the label in puzzlement: "*Chateau de pissoir.*"
>
> **—From the *Owl Hoots* cartoons at the Camp Fire Circle.**

> "A man stumbles home early one morning. His angry wife yanks open the door and he lurches onto the floor. Getting up, he says, 'I think I'll skip my prepared remarks and take your questions now.'"
>
> **—From Associated Press President Louis Boccardi's Lakeside Talk.**

> "A ten-year-old boy is fornicating with his nine-year-old sister. 'Gee, you're almost as good as Ma,' he says. 'Really?' she says. 'That's what Pa says.'"
>
> **—Juvenile joke told at Land's End camp.**

> "You're as young as the women you feel."
>
> **—Quote from the Low Jinks theatrical performance.**

> "Take care when you unsheathe your sword—it can pierce a young lady's...heart."
>
> **—Advice from one character to another in the Grove Play.**

> "A lot of years have been going by for me. You know, there are three things that begin to happen as the years pile up. First, you begin to forget things. [Pause] I can't remember the other two."
>
> **—From Ronald Reagan's Lakeside Talk 1989.**

Walking through the Grove at night is quite an experience. Music, songs, and baritone laughter fill the forest. Lights twinkling through trees and bushes scattered up the hillsides give the Grove an enchanted forest quality. Official Bohemian Club historian Al Baxter said in a June 3, 1994 interview with Dr.

Peter Phillips (author of *A Relative Advantage*) that certain areas in the Grove have a shrine-like quality that some Japanese visitors have compared to sacred forested sites in Japan.

All of this, of course, is for the exclusive use of members and guests. The Grove has an ample staff of security guards to discourage uninvited intruders into their private retreat. The Bohemian Club has had a summer encampment at the Grove every year since 1899, even during World War II when formal encampments were canceled; hundreds of men would still make the pilgrimage to the Grove for a two-week summer visit.

Camp members may reserve use of their camp for weekends and special events any time of the year. But other than the two-week midsummer encampment during July and August, and a few special weekend events (Spring Jinks, and Spring Picnic) the Grove sits mostly empty, maintained by several permanent staff who live on the grounds.

THE CAMPS

Former President Richard M. Nixon was a member of the Cave Man camp, the right-wing coven where he chatted around the campfire with Ronald Reagan's domestic policy advisor Martin Anderson, Emil Mosbacher and grain merchant Dwayne Andreas, among other bigwigs. Meanwhile, Ronald Reagan himself camped just down the hill at Owl's Nest, along with his old Hollywood friend, actor Eddie Albert and the chairmen of United Airlines, United California Bank, Dart Industries, Carter-Hawley-Hale Stores, Dean Witter Reynolds and Company, and Pauley Petroleum, plus retired chieftains from General Dynamics.

Al Haig slumbered in Toyland, while Caspar Weinberger and William P. Clark hunkered down at Isle of Aves. A camp simply called Woof boasts James A. Baker III and Merv Griffin. Allen Drury sleeps at the Totem Inn camp; Prentis Cobb Hale at Zaca camp. David Rockefeller was a member of the Stowaway Camp, and John Kluge belonged to the camp with perhaps the strangest name of all, Wohwohno.

The Wayside Log camp is the spot where Herman Wouk and Oscar Lewis slept. Former California governor Pat Brown (Jerry Brown's father) camped at Sheldrake Lodge; legendary entertainer Art Linkletter at Dragons camp.

Dragons camp was also home to A.P. Giannini, founder of the Bank of Italy (later renamed Bank of America). Bing Crosby serenaded his fellow Bohemians at Moonshiners camp.

The Bushes call the Hill Billies camp home, as did Walter Cronkite, William F. Buckley Jr. and Christopher Buckley,—so did astronaut Frank Borman. Hill Billies also has a strong core of top business executives, and the corporate parallels between the Bush and Reagan camps become very clear upon closer inspection. At Owl's Nest, Reagan camped out with the chairman of American Airlines, while over at Hill Billies, his vice-president George Bush Sr. was rubbing shoulders with the president of Eastern Airlines. Reagan's camp has the chair of United California Bank, Hill Billies boasted Alden W. Clausen, the president of Bank of America (and President Jimmy Carter's nominee to head the World Bank). Hill Billies also houses directors from General Motors, Southern Pacific, Westinghouse Electric, B.F. Goodrich, Morgan Guaranty Trust, Mutual Life Insurance, Metromedia, and Superior Oil.

But the most elite camp at the Grove sits perched atop the tallest hill, overlooking the reckless abandon below. Mandalay is the campsite where you'll find Henry Kissinger, former president Gerald Ford, Nicholas Brady, George P. Shultz; William French Smith and former IBM head honcho Thomas Watson Jr. While the sleeping quarters at Mandalay are called "Condemned row," the corporate connections found within reflect anything but a condemnation of doing business at the Grove. Past and present chairmen and presidents of General Electric, Bankers Trust, Bank of America, Bechtel Construction, Wells Fargo Bank, and Southern California Edison have been members of Mandalay camp over the years.

Former President Ford was a close friend of Bohemian Leonard K. Firestone of the tire-manufacturing dynasty, and was Mr. Firestone's guest at Mandalay camp several times before becoming a full-fledged Bohemian Club member himself in 1977. Although Ford wisely waited to join the club until after his presidential term was over, he continued to quietly exert his influence over political matters from within the cozy confines of the Grove as an advisor to the next Republican president, Ronald Reagan.

During the Reagan years, Mandalay camp was subject to pointed media critique for being well-stocked with Ronald Reagan's closest friends and advisors, or as some have quipped, the president's "California cabinet." William

French Smith, for example, had served as a director of Pacific Lighting, Pacific Telephone, Pacific Mutual Life, and Jorgensen Steel. Smith's corporate connections are nearly overshadowed by his academic ones; he was an U.C. regent, a member of the executive committee of the California Round-table, and a member of the advisory board for the Center for Strategic Studies at Georgetown University.

George Shultz, during the years he served as a top Reagan advisor, was concurrently serving terms as a director of Morgan Guaranty Trust, Sears Roebuck & Co., the Alfred P. Sloan Foundation, and the Council on Foreign Relations (CFR). The CFR and Bohemian Club membership lists reflect a lot of the same names. By a recent comparison, I was able to count about 40 Bohemians who are also CFR members.

It goes without saying that the presence of all these powerful politicos, businessmen and entertainment luminaries requires an extraordinary amount of enforced discretion and security on the inside. Even the Grove guest list, which once floated around freely, has in recent years been posted only in a locked glass museum case during daylight hours. The list is removed from the case every night to prevent curious staffers or undercover journalists from absconding with a copy.

Although Republicans usually far outnumber Democrats at the Grove, a careful study of available guest lists from past years indicates that the Grove is not exclusively for GOP dignitaries. For example, Secretary of the Treasury G. William Miller was a guest in 1979, staying at Mandalay Camp courtesy of Edmund Littlefield, retired chair of Utah Mining and Construction. Sol Linowitz, President Carter's top negotiator on the Panama Canal Treaty and the Egypt-Israel talks, was also at the Grove that year as a guest of Glenn T. Seaborg, former chairman of the Atomic Energy Commission, at Wayside Log Camp. The only confirmed Bohemian in Carter's Cabinet was Secretary of Defense Harold Brown, who in 1980 hosted Secretary of Energy Charles W. Duncan as his guest at Lost Angels Camp.

Another fascinating way to document the histories of individual camps at Bohemian Grove is to study the photo collections that are available in various California archives. Although cameras are not permitted in public areas of the Grove, they are allowed inside single campsites. Many camps keep annual photo albums of members eating, making music or cocktailing together.

These photo albums can become the basis of privately published camp histories that are written for the camp members and Bohemian Club archives. Such books have become quite rare on the collectors market, as there were usually less than 500 copies individually printed of each volume. Books are available detailing the histories of the Lost Angels, Mandalay, Silverado Squatters, Isle of Aves, and Midway camps, among others.

Each camp's history gives a listing of all its members and a brief overview of how and who formed the camp. Other areas covered are personal histories of certain members. Bragging about important celebrities who have visited is also a regular feature. "We have entertained some of the most celebrated men in the world at our Lost Angels Camp." (*Lost Angels Camp: The First 50 Years: 1908–1958*)

Camps used to have memberships that tended to emphasize certain professional or business associations. For example, of Pleasant Isle of Aves' twenty-nine members between 1904 and 1964, all but two were in some way affiliated with U.C. Berkeley. Midway Camp, in the 1930s, was made up of executives from the Pacific Insurance Company, and Tie Binders were, appropriately enough, all railroad men. Silverado Squatters Camp's history includes two university presidents, a Deputy Director of the U.S. Treasury, a U.S. Supreme Court Justice, a Security Exchange commissioner, and a Deputy Secretary of Defense.

Camps like to have distinctive images. These often include a specialty food or alcoholic drink; for example, Jungle Camp's famous mint juleps, or Owl's Nest's gin-fizz breakfast. Other camps' claims-to-fame are historical artifacts, or specialty art pieces. Camps are the centerpiece of a member's identity at the Grove. One of the first exchanges of information in conversation is what camp a person is from. A 1979 publication entitled *The Camps*, gives a great deal of information about the specialties of each camp at the Grove, most of which have to do with alcoholic refreshments. A few of the more intoxicating examples are the infamous Nembutal Fizz served only at Fore Peak camp, the wine and cheese party to commemorate Bastille Day at Interlude Camp, El Toro II Camp's Magnificent Mai Tai, the all-time Abbott auxiliary martini machine at Pow Wow Camp, and the strong imported German beer served exclusively at (where else?) Moonshiners Camp.

Grove camps are packed with cherished historical artifacts mostly donated from former Bohemians. Roaring Camp has the original bar from Bohemian Jack London's home, while at Ye Merrie Yowls Camp, the bar is the former altar from the Catholic Church in nearby Forrestville. Last Chance Camp owes its name to its legendary swinging doors, the originals from San Francisco's Last Chance Saloon. Sahara Camp is so named because it was the only camp at the Grove that was dry during prohibition.

Hideaway Camp houses a classic oil painting of a nude woman, where artists add one gray hair per year. Thalia Camp has the original stop signal from the corner of Powell and Post Streets in San Francisco. For the scholar, Halcyon Camp features the Grove's finest library of classics, and for the decidedly less Bohemian, the Dog House Camp hosts the annual "Beer and Beans" party after every Cremation of Care.

Camp captains are responsible for financial control and general management of the camp. This can include issuing work order requests to the Grove committee for camp maintenance, purchasing supplies and food and supervising valets. Captains coordinate the invitation of new Club members to join a camp, a process not unlike a fraternity rush on a university campus. It may take Club members several seasons before they actually connect with a camp that invites them to join. New members stay in Bromley Camp near the main gate.

Camp stewards or valets are an important part of Bohemian culture. About two-thirds of the camps have valets, and these men may serve a particular camp for decades. Valets address all camp members and guests formally using Mr. and their surname. Camp members address valets by their first names, thus maintaining the formal employer/employee status. Valets are responsible for the comfort and welfare of camp members. They mix and serve drinks, prepare lunches, and snacks, and are generally available to assist members with special needs.

Mandalay may well be the most "posh" camp at the Grove, employing six valets. Mandalay has a fairly small bar, but a beautiful deck and camp clubhouse. The inside area flooring is polished hardwood, and there is adequate room for a formal dinner seating for 50–75 men. In book shelves along the River Road wall are camp scrapbooks, showing pictures of Mandalay Camp members going back fifty years. George Bush's picture along with Henry Kissinger and George Schultz was in the 1991 album.

Most camps have a clubhouse building that holds a bar and a kitchen including a sheltered area adequate to seat the camp members during inclement weather (although this is apparently never necessary). There is an outside deck area large enough for hosting parties of 50–100 men. A campfire pit or fireplace is a featured part in the clubhouse area and fires are set every evening. Many camps have a piano for spontaneous sing-alongs and campfire cheer. Camps tend to display various former Bohemian posters and event announcements, especially those sired or written by camp members. Some camps have pin-up pictures of women in various states of undress.

Member sleeping quarters in the Grove can be as simple as four-man tent cabins to spartan motel-size private rooms. Almost all construction is of redwood, so that a rustic forest theme is present throughout the Grove. Sixty-three years of Grove additions and improvements have resulted in elaborate redwood staircases, winding forest trails, several miles of paved roads, a central dining area that seats over 1,500, a large campfire circle, art studio, museum, civic center, bar and cafe, and two magnificent outdoor theaters.

Camps have hot water showers in their central restrooms, and interconnecting trails between central clubhouses and various other buildings or tents. There is often construction of new buildings in progress as the Grove continues to grow. Even campsite improvements incite controversy, it seems. According to the September 11, 1987 *San Francisco Chronicle*, Bohemian Grove was investigated by the Sonoma County Assessor in 1987 and was found to have done $300,000 worth of improvement since 1975 without the benefit of construction permits. The Club admitted its error and blamed a transition in personnel for its mistake.

THE STAFF

Grove employees are of all ages and come from various social and ethnic backgrounds. They wear a uniform consisting of a white shirt, black pants, closed-toed shoes, and a red smock is also provided. There are many union workers from San Francisco, and some have been there for 20 or 30 years now, clearly happy with their jobs. Free room and board in this lovely natural environment is certainly a perk of the job. Many staffers live in bunkhouses during the whole encampment.

Most kitchen workers do split shifts, such as a 7 to 11 AM breakfast, then 5 to 9 PM dinners. They "punch in" at a little shed near the employee parking lot, then board the red "owl shuttle", which carts them into the campground. They are limited to the parking lot and the dining circle, allowed nowhere in between. It is strictly prohibited for employees to walk back to their cars while on duty. Employees are not allowed to take any leftover food from the tables, although some have admitted to smuggling out a few edibles underneath their smocks. Dinner and breakfast are served for the employees before each shift starts. It's not the same food as the members were served, but employees say it is well made and nutritious at least.

Not all of the help was happy with the Bohemians, though. In August 1987, Local 2 of the Hotel Employees and Restaurant Employees Union held several public demonstrations while attempting to negotiate a new contract for its members who worked at the Bohemian Club's San Francisco headquarters. Collective bargaining talks between the city's largest union and the exclusive men's club wore on for nearly two months. The union regards the Bohemian Club as the most prestigious of the private clubs and the one with the most aggressive management.

So the union responded with equally aggressive bargaining tactics. They sent multi-racial delegations of union members, males and females of different age groups, to the offices of individual Bohemian Club members in San Francisco to explain the contract proposals put forth by the club and why they were not acceptable to the union. Delegates would call on one or two Bohemians per workday, sitting in their office lobby and asking for a brief personal meeting. Responses varied. Some club members listened respectfully, some argued with them, a few refused to meet with union delegates at all.

The Local 2 also held a "Boho Safari" through a wealthy Pacific Heights neighborhood in San Francisco, stopping in front of the residences of Bohemian Club members. Several of the homes had assessed values of over a million dollars. On Labor Day, the union held a sit-in at the club's Taylor Street headquarters. Thirty-three people were arrested and cited for trespassing.

The points of contention with the union boiled down to four basic workers' rights issues: first, major reductions in employer participation in worker health, welfare, and pension fund plans, particularly in medical benefits for retirees. Second, the club wanted to do away with the seniority system of scheduling, layoffs, and promotion; third, the club was demanding the right to subcontract out any and all work; fourth, a wage cut that for waiters would mean nearly a ten dollar per-hour loss in wages. Bohemian Club waiters' wages are higher than those of waiters at public restaurants because of the club's no tipping policy. In addition, an attempt by the club to lump negotiations for a new contract for workers at the club's Bohemian Grove country retreat together with the city workers' contract negotiations resulted in unfair labor practice complaints being filed.

ISOLATED OR INSULATED?

Many of us have some difficulty imagining how all of these powerful businessmen can truly enjoy themselves for two weeks in this remote locale, where they are cut off from all contact with the outside world. For men who usually spend their days glued to television, radio, cell phones and the internet, it's hard to fathom them without all of these precious power toys.

Until very recently, the Grove was out of the reception area of cell phones, leaving these men with only one solution for conducting urgent business: a bank of 16 pay phones located in the middle of the redwoods. While on assignment for *Spy* magazine in 1989, journalist Philip Weiss observed Henry Kissinger (who cut in front of 12 other men in line to use the phone) engaged in a rather humorous conversation with someone he only referred to as "sweetie" and "sunshine."

"We had jazz concert," Kissinger said. "We had rope trick. This morning we went bird-watching."

Kissinger dropped names of his fellow campers, presumably to impress "sunshine": U.S. Treasury Secretary Nick Brady and his brother, L.A. Times publisher Tom Johnson, foreign dignitaries like Indian Shankar Bajpai, Roald Sagdeyev from the Soviet Supreme Council of People's Deputies, and French prime minister Michel Rocard, who was visiting the Grove secretly that year.

"Oh, Rocard is having a *ball*," Kissinger laughed over the phone. But "…I told him, 'Do anything you want, hide in the bushes—just don't let them see you.'"

The public certainly was not aware that the Prime Minister of France was making a speech at the Bohemian Grove, and in this rare instance, most of the Grovers themselves were not informed who the unannounced "special guest speaker" would be at the 1989 Lakeside Talks. *Spy* magazine's Weiss attended the speech and recorded Rocard's stunningly arrogant admission for posterity: "Because you are such an astonishing group of men," the Prime Minister said, "I can speak privately."

Which leads us to the subject of Weaving Spiders. Don't be fooled. They DO come here.

Chapter V

scandalum magnatum

(scandal of magnates)

Weaving Spiders

"Thou dost protest too much, methinks."

—William Shakespeare
Hamlet, Act III, Scene 2
(paraphrased)

The Bohemian Club's motto, "Weaving spiders, come not here", first appeared on a Club announcement in 1875. This was taken from Shakespeare's *A Midsummer Night's Dream,* and was intended as a reminder to all Bohemians that conducting or soliciting business at Club functions was strictly prohibited.

Bohemian Club members solemnly deny that their forest preserve is a forum for behind-the-scenes intrigue and dealmaking. One veteran member told reporter Jack Anderson for a 1981 *Parade* Magazine article; "I like to get away from that stuff. I don't go there to do it."

The Grove does offer a secluded hideaway to political and financial leaders who wish to shed the problems and pressures of their daily lives. Here, they can speak freely without fear of being quoted and drink as heavily as they wish without finding an embarrassing photo in the next day's paper. Released from the inhibitions that constrain their public lives, they come to the Grove to sing and play, tell bawdy stories, dress up in drag, and generally make fools of themselves without fear of retribution. As one former Grove employee wryly observed, "Those guys are drinking morning, noon and night. They're too looped to discuss business."

Dr. Peter Phillips spent several days at the Grove in the mid-1990s while researching his dissertation *A Relative Advantage.* While he agreed overall that the "weaving spiders" rule is still enforced somewhat, he also was careful to note that business dealings *did* go on despite this rule—only with extreme discretion.

Phillips wrote: "One time when I was speaking with a San Francisco attorney at the Grove, I asked him if I could have his card and perhaps call him later. His response was that we were not supposed to trade cards, but he went ahead and handed me one when he thought others were not looking. While at the Grove I heard a story about a guest who violated the no business tradition by soliciting other camp members for an investment. Late in the night several Club members allegedly rousted him from his bunk and unceremoniously escorted him to the front gate."

Yet, views articulated at the Grove have been known to affect public policy. For example, at the 1979 encampment, Gerald Ford unloosed an attack on consumer advocates that far surpassed the tepid words the former president had used in public settings. But perhaps the most striking example of the elite Grovers' prior knowledge of future events is a speech given at the 1981 camp by the late nuclear scientist Dr. Edward Teller (aka "father of the H-bomb"). In this Lakeside Talk, he accurately predicted that the United States would go to war in the Persian Gulf—ten years prior to our first incursion into Iraq.

Over the past two decades, exhaustive research on Bohemian Club members has been done by Bohemian Grove Action Network activist and photographer, Kerry Richardson. Richardson is always on hand to photograph the fantastic array of private jets that fly into nearby Sonoma County airport each July, and many of these photographs are available to the public on his web site. Richardson, like other area residents, was curious about the big green jet seen at the county airport during the Bohemian Grove encampment in the early and mid 1980s. After doing some more research, he discovered the plane was registered to the cement manufacturer Lone Star Industries and it transported that company's Chief Executive Officer (CEO) James E. Stewart who is affiliated with the "Wohwohno" camp.

In 1989, Malcolm Forbes and Caspar Weinberger traveled to the Grove on Forbes' jet, which had Forbes' motto, "Capitalist Tool" printed on its tail. Weinberger, the former U.S. Secretary of Defense and member of the Grove's "Isle of Aves" camp, was working as Publisher of *Forbes* magazine at the time.

Other corporate CEO private birds parked at the Sonoma Airport each summer include the UNOCAL (Union Oil Company) four-engine hot rod that was used by UNOCAL CEO and Bohemian Fred Hartley. During the 1997 Grove encampment, Richardson snapped a photo of the IBM Corporation's Gulfstream G-4 jet parked next to Exxon Corporation's G-4. That's over $56 million dollars worth of iron and steel, sitting empty on the tarmac.

Two airports are used to bring in the bigwigs: Sonoma County Airport, north of Santa Rosa on Hwy. 101, and Santa Rosa Air Center, nearest the Bohemian Grove. This is a private airfield that is not open to the public. It was built during WWII as a training base for P-32 pilots, and deactivated in 1952. After the war, it was leased to private companies. There are no buildings over two stories in the entire area, and no control tower. The FBI has an office in the Federal building downtown, and FEMA has a radio station at the airport. Only a handful of small planes sneak out of the closed base each day, and for a base of this size to remain closed is very interesting in itself. The planes take off in the evening and do not turn on their lights until they are hundreds of feet into the air. The Santa Rosa *Press Democrat* ran an article on April 22, 1993 about the federal government selling 70 acres of property just to the east of the airport. However, when one reads closely, the land was going to be offered to a host of Federal agencies. The property was "being used by FEMA." The close vicinity of this secret activity to the elite's campground at Bohemian Grove makes this one for closer inspection by the public.

THE BUSINESS OF BOHEMIA

Private business is the dominant career interest of Bohemian Club members. With such strong business interests and elite corporate connections the question arises, are Bohemians weaving spiders or just a bunch of fun-loving old farts on summer vacation?

The answer to this question is always hotly debated, both outside the Grove gates and within. It seems to me that the economic and political elites took the Bohemian Club over more than a century ago, and eventually took the focus of the club from the principles upon which it was founded (celebrating the arts). Naturally, Club members adamantly defend their rights to do as they please within the confines of the Grove and warn fellow Bohos strongly against business dealings in the City Club or at the Grove. However, there is mounting evidence that suggests these efforts are only intended to be superficially observed.

By matching a recent membership list with the names of corporate CEOs and other power brokers found in books like "Who's Who," I found that at least 150 Bohemians hold nearly 300 directorships in the top 1000 U.S. corporations. Of these, I spotted several corporations with more than one Bohemian serving as directors. These include Bank of America, PG&E (Pacific Gas and Electric). AT&T, Ford Motor Company and General Motors. As most Club members are Californians, it should come as no surprise that most of these corporations are headquartered on the West Coast. For the past quarter-century Bohemia has had a consistent 25–30% of the top U.S. corporations represented at their summer encampments.

Over that same span of time, there was also a marked drop in guests from the top 100 non-California corporations. One possible explanation for this decline could be a 1987 ruling by State of California's Franchise Tax Board discontinuing the practice of allowing individuals or corporations to deduct their dues and expenses for a private men's clubs on their State income tax returns. Having to pay for a party out of your own (or the company's) pocket may well have been incentive enough to drive some longtime Bohemians away. Nowadays, the Bohemian Club is quite adamant about adhering to this law, and has adopted a strict policy of not accepting any business checks for dues and expenses. In the early winter of 1994, a member was expelled from the Club for deducting club expenses on his income taxes.

Apparently, before the law was changed, the Bohemians did get a little carried away with writing off their Club expenses. According to a report in the June 16, 1987 *Capitol Reporter*, an inter-office memo from a prominent Los Angeles Republican lawyer requesting reimbursement for private men's club dues and expenses was presented before the State Franchise Tax Board:

> December 30, 1975
> To: Management Committee
> Subject: Club Membership
>
> There are a total of three clubs for which I propose to seek reimbursement for dues paid during the year 1976, which I am a member; the Bohemian Club in San Francisco, the Links Club in New York, and California Club in Los Angeles.
>
> One—Bohemian Club
>
> This club, as you know, is one of the most prestigious in America and is particularly helpful for entertaining guests and visiting with members at the summer encampment. As examples, I have had, in the past, guests such as Thomas V. Evans, Esquire, of the firm of Mudge, Rose, Gunthie and Alexander in New York; Reese Meller, Senior Vice President and General

Counsel of Richmond Corporation, an insurance company in Virginia; Robert H. Finch, Esquire, while he was Secretary of Health, Education, and Welfare, William Rogers, former Secretary of State…

I also use the downtown Club when I am in San Francisco, but only for business lunches or cocktails. I pay and will request reimbursement for non-resident dues and also my proportionate share of the Lost Angels Camp as I have in the past…"

Just at the Lost Angels Camp alone, you'll find representatives of the following global corporations: Atlantic Richfield, Avery Dennison Corporation, Colgate-Palmolive, Calfed, CBS Broadcasting, Great Western Financial, IBM, MCA Entertainment (now part of the conglomerate Universal/Vivendi Entertainment Group), Mattel Incorporated, Media General Inc., Northrop Corporation, Philip Morris, Pacific Enterprises, Rockwell International, Sears & Roebuck, SCE Corporation, Security Pacific, Times Mirror Company, Union Bank, Union Electric Company, and Wells Fargo Bank. By the way, that's not even the complete list. There's more. I only included here the names you might easily recognize!

And so it goes. Do the Bohemians really expect us to believe that a prominent Republican attorney invites cabinet officials, corporate chieftains and foundation directors to share the same intimate camp site in the redwoods, and all these gentlemen are going to do is talk about music and the arts?

Overall the corporate data shows that the Bohemian Club has been and continues to be highly interconnected with both U.S. and California corporations. After World War II the Bohemian Clubs' connection with national corporate elites grew significantly. Those numbers dropped off slightly from 1970–1990, but started growing again in the '90s as the Silicon Valley "new rich" technology wizards begin to join the fold.

Dr. Peter Phillips makes the point clear in his aptly titled doctoral dissertation on the Bohemian Club, *A Relative Advantage*:

It has been fairly well known that Bohemia is structurally inter-linked with the American business community, but less well-developed is a historical and qualitative interpretation of how the men in this network use it for business advantages.

In addition to this, many men cannot resist the temptation to discuss specific business deals in the privacy of paired or small friendship groups. While the culture of the Grove forbids solicitation and economic dealing, the vastness of the Grove makes private discussions between individuals easily possible. This behavior is qualitatively observable to a listener sitting on a Grove bench catching snippets of conversations of passing small groups of Bohemians. Walking at a leisurely pace men engrossed in a specific business discussion tend to ignore other Bohemians passing by or within hearing distance of their conversation. This phenomena gave me an opportunity to briefly overhear several paired business conversations at various locations in the Grove during the Spring Jinks.

Paired conversation pieces from three sets of Bohemian Grove men, June, 1994:

"Would G.E. come in on the deal? Only with new prototypes and a 500K investment, in a target area of the 7th largest area base."

"The bond market was flat, and the guy signed early. I guess that is why he is so fucking rich."

"The Asian mentality doesn't comprehend paying for financial advice. Do they expect to get it for free?"

Granted this is only a few brief conversations in crowds of Bohemians, but they have led me to believe that men tend to observe Grove conventions in large groups, but succumb to their primary career interests with friends or associates in paired settings.

The former C.E.O. of a major defense contractor participated in a conversation with *(Bohemian Club historian)* Al Baxter and myself on this topic of business activities at the Grove. He frankly admitted, "Being at the Grove is a business advantage for me." He went on to say that, "I don't come to the Grove first off for business, but the guys you meet definitely give you an advantage."

To better illustrate that point, let's take the example of one of the Bohemian Club's most legendary members, John Neylan, who is perhaps best known to Californians. Neylan is one of the easier case studies because his personal archives are available for public inspection at Berkeley, and his files are packed with information regarding his years as a Bohemian, an affiliation of which he was most proud.

John Francis Neylan was a long-term legal advisor to the Hearst Newspapers, a U.C. Regent, Director of National City Bank of New York, and a big time player in Republican Party politics. Neylan joined the Bohemian Club in 1932 and used the Club network for many of his socio-political activities without shame or apologies.

Neylan's dinner parties were as legendary as the man himself; an invitation to one of his private luncheons or suppers was highly coveted, and a sure sign that one had "made it" in elite San Francisco circles. Over a 23-year period, Neylan hosted 26 such parties, and nearly 50% of the attendees were fellow Bohemians. At a 1943 formal dinner honoring Nelson A. Rockefeller, 73 people attended, 26 of whom were Bohemians. In August 1952, Mr. Neylan honored Bernard Baruch at a party of 50 attendees. Half of them were Bohos. A 1957 event to honor Herman Phleger boasted 30 Bohemians out of a total attendance of 44 men. That's nearly 70 percent. It's safe to say that if you were a member of the Bohemian Club, your chances were much better of getting an invitation than if you were not.

This leads to the understanding of how personal networks bonded in the Bohemian experience came to exist. Neylan had contacts throughout the Bay Area, yet repeatedly he invited a disproportionate number of Bohemians to attend his special all-male dinner parties. Thus, it stands to reason that these men do have a particular advantage over other businessmen of their class, in terms of access to the "right people," if nothing else. And through the longtime friendships cemented at the Grove and functions outside the Club, such as Neylan's famed dinner parties, these selected few will naturally call upon each other first when a favor is needed, or when a new contract is to be awarded.

POLICY FOR SALE

Numerous studies that have been conducted on policy councils over the past 30 years clearly show that policy councils tend to be dominated by large corporate interests, and that there is an interactive network of members among the top ten policy councils in the U.S. In fact, the most central policy councils in this interlocking network are the usual suspects—The Business Roundtable, Business Council, and the dreaded Council of Foreign Relations, or CFR.

As to be expected, Bohemians take an active part in national policy councils. The numbers may fluctuate as the decades pass, but as a general rule, Bohemians consistently hold anywhere from 10–25% of positions on the board of directors for these top policy centers. That makes the Bohemian Club one of the top four most interconnected elite men's clubs in the country.

The California-based Hoover Institution has the largest and probably the longest overlap with the San Francisco Bohemian Club, with about half of their Board of Overseers being active Bohemians on average. President Herbert Hoover was a Bohemian before he founded the Hoover Library on War, Revolution, and Peace in 1919. Up through WWII, the Hoover Library was primarily for research purposes and was administered directly as a part of Stanford University, with faculty and administrators exclusively making up the board of directors. Facing financial difficulties, the Hoover Institution formed a corporate-based advisory board in the 1960s. Then things began to change rapidly. By 1971 the Hoover board of overseers read like an elite *Who's Who* of corporate America, with over half of the directors holding positions in top U.S. corporations or important legal firms including: Chemical Bank, Lockheed-Martin, Hewlett-Packard, GE, Mobil Oil, Standard Oil, U.S. Steel, and the Chicago Tribune.

In 1991 the Hoover Institution sponsored former Prime Minister of Britain Margaret Thatcher's first speech after stepping down as Prime Minister. The American Enterprise Institute, Heritage Foundation, the Manhattan Institute and the National Review were all co-sponsors of Thatcher's visit to Stanford.

The Hoover Institution and the Bohemian Club are natural historical extensions of each other. Currently popular weekend Lakeside Chat topics and Hoover Institution research areas are very similar, which would be expected from organizations with common economic interests. And to this day, the majority of Hoover Institution heavies belong to Caveman Camp, which was former president Hoover's old stomping ground. Sharing a camp together at the Grove gives Bohemian directors of major U.S. policy councils ample opportunity to discuss current affairs and policy issues. Additionally, about half of all the camps at the Grove have at least one member who serves on a foundation board, thus giving immediate foundation access to half of Bohemia.

An earlier example of a national research/policy institute formed through connections within the Bohemian Club was the Stanford Research Institute

(S.R.I.). S.R.I. was originally organized at the Bohemian Grove in 1945 at a meeting in the Semper Virens Camp. Three Bohemians had discussed the idea for S.R.I. for several years: Robert Swain, Philip Leighton, and Dudley Swim, who had frequently used the Grove as a place for conversation on the idea. S.R.I. is literally a sub-camp of the Bohemian Club with eleven Club members serving on S.R.I.'s Board for the past quarter century.

Today, S.R.I. is a world level organization that forms policy recommendations at national, state and international levels. S.R.I. subcontracts with governments and private corporations for various scientific research projects. According to their own documents, some of S.R.I.'s research areas include biomedical integration, economic policy simulators, NAFTA, treatment of hazardous waste, and, even as early as 1991, S.R.I. was looking into "Technology and Anti-Terrorist Strategies for Airlines." That's a decade before Middle Eastern terrorists hijacked American commercial planes and flew them into the World Trade Center and Pentagon on September 11, 2001. But back in 1991, most Americans could never conceive of such an event. Apparently, the folks at S.R.I. knew more on this subject than the rest of us, and were planning ahead for risk and disaster management, at least for government and the aviation industry.

IN THEIR OWN WORDS

These examples of personal policy planning intimacies begin to give us an understanding of how these policy development sessions really work. The Bohemian Club certainly serves as one of the centralized places for the formation of policy-making among socio-economic elites. For example, in his book *Turmoil and Triumph*, Bohemian George Shultz talks about his years in the Reagan Administration, and names 26 Bohemians as friends and co-conspirators in the text.

Former German Chancellor Helmut Schmidt came to the Grove in 1979 as the guest of George Shultz. In his autobiography *Men and Powers*, Schmidt wrote "this weekend gave me one of the most astounding experiences I ever had in the United States." He went on to describe the "boyish romanticism" of the Bohemian atmosphere that to him contained all the "dash characteristic of television Westerns."

"This weekend allowed me an illustrative glimpse of America's elite," wrote Schmidt, who was all too eager to return for a second visit a few years later. In his memoirs, the former chancellor gushes with admiration as he drops the names of celebrities he met at the Grove. There was violinist Isaac Stern, writer Herman Wouk, banker Peter Peterson, and industrialist David Packard, whom Schmidt admits knowing ten years earlier when Packard (of Hewlett-Packard Corporation) had been deputy secretary of defense under Melvin Laird. Schmidt seems quite taken with the relaxed camaraderie of the Grove, adding that "altogether I cannot imagine a greater contrast to the somewhat cool and stylish New England atmosphere in the Council on Foreign Relations or the River Club in New York."

One of the Club's most elite longtime members is Steven Bechtel Jr., a name very familiar to most Californians and Washington watchdogs as head of the Bechtel Group. Founded by his grandfather Warren Bechtel near the turn of the last century, and owned by the Bechtel family every since, the Bechtel Group was at one time the largest engineering and construction company in the world. Bechtel had business and political connections stretching from Saudi Arabia to Indonesia to Washington and back again. It had built coal mines in Peru, copper mines in South Africa, synthetic fuel plants in New Zealand, nuclear power stations in India, a subway system in Washington, D.C., factories in California, hospitals, hotels, airports and industrial structures the world over. In the Middle East, Bechtel's refineries and pipelines helped to make OPEC possible. In Libya, where Bechtel had been one of the last American companies to depart, its' creations inadvertently had generated the revenues that would help finance the regime of Muhammar Qaddafi. In the United States, where it had been influencing presidents since Herbert Hoover (Warren's personal friend and fellow engineer), Bechtel had built many of the roads and bridges that had opened the West, and the dams, such as Hoover Dam, that had brought it life.

The book *Friends In High Places: The Bechtel Group* tells the remarkable story of Bechtel's career in business and world politics, and talks about the Bohemian Club a great deal. In fact, Chapter One of this book is entitled *The Grove*, and opens with Bechtel's 1982 visit to the midsummer encampment. That same year, Bechtel Group reported revenues of $13.6 billion, placing it as the 20th largest corporation in America. Yet, Bechtel Group was not listed on the *Fortune* 500 list, or on any public exchange. It was a private company, one of the largest in the world, and that too was the way Steven Bechtel, Jr. preferred it. He had no patience for troublesome stockholders or filings with the SEC, and even less for the prying scrutiny of the public and the press. "There's no reason for the public to hear of us," he once arrogantly said to a reporter. "We're not selling anything to the public."

Instead, Bechtel did his selling to companies and to governments, quietly and out of public view; in boardrooms, on golf courses, in royal palaces and prime ministers' residences, and of course, at his favorite spot, the Bohemian Grove. For Steve Bechtel and the power-brokers like him, Bohemian Grove was the ultimate getaway, the grown-up equivalent of summer camp. But the real business of the Grove, as Bechtel freely admitted, was *business*. Not business by contract (which was strictly forbidden by Grove rules), but business by sheer association, by men getting to know and like each other. "Once you've spent three days with someone in an informal situation," explained John D. Ehrlichman, who attended Grove encampments while a key aide to President Richard Nixon, "you have a relationship—a relationship that opens doors and makes it easier to pick up the phone."

Few understood that fact better than Steve Bechtel Jr., who, like his father before him, had been coming to the Grove all his adult life. Nothing could keep him from this annual encampment. For it was friends like those at the Grove—friends in high places—who, as much as anything, had made the Bechtel Group the master builder that it was. They had provided the contacts and the contracts, they had opened doors, which, in turn, opened other doors. They had smoothed the way, endorsed, facilitated, and on occasion, skirted the law. It was they, and the Bechtel Corporations' shrewd courtship of them, who had made everything possible.

Because of those friends, anonymous Steve Bechtel was a big presence at the Grove. A man whose very appearance generated awed and admiring whispers. He belonged to Mandalay, the most prestigious camp in all the Grove kingdom, as had his father, Steven D. Bechtel, Sr., alongside old friends like former Bechtel Group president and Secretary of State designate George P. Shultz, who that year was bringing former west German chancellor Helmut Schmidt as his personal guest. Bechtel's other Mandalay campmates included former IBM chairman and U.S. Ambassador to the Soviet Union, Thomas J.

Watson, Jr. (and his father before him). The Thomas Watsons are another multigenerational Bohemian family and longtime friends of the Bechtels.

In his autobiography, *Father, Son & Co.—My Life at IBM And Beyond*, Thomas J. Watson, Jr. devotes several pages to his Bohemian Grove experiences. On pages 440–441, Watson Jr. recounts many public speaking engagements against the proliferation of nuclear weapons, including a speech he made at the Grove that same year. He referred to the Bohemians as a "tough audience"—no surprise considering the Grove was the birthplace of the atom bomb! The Grove was packed full of men who have made tremendous fortunes from nuclear arms, and the very idea of disarmament wouldn't go over well with this crowd. Watson writes:

> "My first chance to win the hearts and minds of influential people came in 1982, when I was asked to give a speech at the Bohemian Grove...It's not the kind of scene I like, because it requires lots of meeting and talking with strangers. But when I was young my father had told me that the Grove was a gorgeous place and that I should go if I had the opportunity, because I would never find that kind of atmosphere anywhere else.

> "Someone put me up for membership in 1957, the year after my father died. But unless you had a special in, it took about twenty years to get to the head of the waiting list, so I ended up going as the guest of Dad's old friend Lowell Thomas. I went to the Grove as a guest seven or eight times while I ran IBM, but I didn't actually join until I came back from Moscow in 1981. The following summer came an invitation to give a speech...When I got up to speak I could see before me in the audience such dignitaries as Henry Kissinger.

> "It was my big chance to pitch bilateral reduction of nuclear arms, and I gave it everything I had. Like any good salesman I was really sure that I could win them over. My thinking had developed in the year since my Harvard speech, and I felt confident that my ideas on national security were comprehensive and realistic enough to make sense even to veteran policymakers. Not only could I demonstrate why we had to reduce our blind dependence on atomic weapons, but I was able to paint a picture of how the United States might defend its interests without them. I took the position that, given the strength of the Soviet military, we couldn't cut back our nuclear arsenal without beefing up conventional forces—even if this meant reinstating the draft and raising taxes. Then I suggested that antinuclear protesters had a point—they were ordinary Americans applying common sense to the fact that we had more nuclear weapons than we needed. I told the Bohemians what I had learned as head of the General Advisory Com-

mittee—that nuclear strategy, like any national issue, benefits from open public debate.

"There was plenty of applause when I finished, but I was looking for something more—maybe people jumping up and sending cables to Reagan, or turning to the senators in the audience and saying, "Watson's right! What are we going to do about it?" Of course that didn't happen. Later that afternoon I overheard a conversation between two Bohemians. "Did you listen to Watson?" said the first.

"No," said the second. "How was it?"

"It was terrific, absolutely terrific."

"I was just starting to swell with pride when the second Bohemian asked, "Well, did you learn anything you didn't already know?" And there was no reply. I felt as though I'd been dropping pebbles down a well."

LAKESIDE CHATS

Although Watson's Lakeside Chat didn't bring the results he was hoping for, other selected speakers have indeed had great success in getting their ideas over to the Bohemian crowd. When *Spy* magazine's Philip Weiss successfully infiltrated the Grove in 1989, he witnessed a Lakeside Talk given by General John Chain, commander of the Strategic Air Command, in which he pleaded with his fellow Bohemians to give him the necessary appropriations for the Stealth B-2 bomber:

"I am a warrior, and that's how I come to you today," said General Chain. "I need the B-2."

Naturally, the General was speaking to the right crowd. The money was approved.

Weiss also observed that during his Lakeside Talk, "Henry Kissinger made a bathroom pun on the name of his friend Lee Kuan Yew, who was also in attendance—the sort of joke that the people of Singapore, whom Lee rules with such authoritarian zeal, are not free to make in public."

Kissinger's special secret guest at the Grove that year was French prime minister Michel Rocard. In his Lakeside Talk, Rocard (who is known as a right-wing socialist), overtly laid out to the elite Bohos the still-covert plan for a European

Union. Nearly a decade before the EU became a reality, Rocard, with seemingly psychic powers of prediction, outlined to the letter, exactly what would happen in the future: Europe would eliminate trade barriers, establish a central currency (the Euro), and a central government. He even predicted that Great Britain would be the only nation that would resist, but that the UK would eventually "get on the train when it is leaving the station." That was indeed the case; only it was Prime Minister Tony Blair who put up the play-fight instead of Margaret Thatcher, as Rocard had said in his Grove speech.

The French prime minister's 1989 visit to the Grove went totally unreported by the American and French press—they had been informed that the prime minister was on his boat off the coast of Brittany during the last two weeks of July. The public would have no knowledge of it today had *Spy* magazine's Philip Weiss's article gone unpublished. The press did, however, get an advance tip about German chancellor Helmut Schmidt's visit to the Grove in 1982; reporters literally followed his car to the front gates.

When Sonoma State University professor Dr. Peter Phillips visited the Bohemian Grove as a guest, he witnessed a few of the Lakeside Chats and recorded his observations in *A Relative Advantage*: "On Saturday, June 4, 1994 the Lakeside Chat was given by a political science professor from U.C., Berkeley. The chat was entitled "Violent Weakness", which focused on how increasing violence in society was weakening our social institutions...The speaker claimed that to avert further deterioration, we need to recognize that "elites based on merit and skill are important to society" (loud clapping). "Any elite that fails to define itself will fail to survive...We need boundaries and values set and clear! We need an American centered foreign policy...and a President who understands foreign policy." He went on to conclude that we cannot allow the "unqualified" masses to carry out policy, but that elites must set values that can be translated into "standards of authority". This speech was forcefully given and was received with an enthusiastic standing ovation by most members. I asked a dozen men after the speech how they felt about it. One said it was too simplistic, and another said it should be discussed more, but the others all gave it strong approval. In three camps I visited after the chat it was inevitably one of the topics of discussion."

From Dr. Phillips' observations above, we can safely conclude that despite the efforts at collective consensus building the Lakeside Chats are designed to construct, not all Bohemians agree on every issue. One particular case in point occurred in 1993. William Simon, former Secretary of the Treasury under President Ford, gave a Lakeside Chat during which he delivered some scathing remarks about George H. W. Bush while the freshly defeated President was in the audience. The *San Francisco Chronicle* columnist Robert Novak reported on August 9, 1993 that Bush had walked out of the chat in disgust.

Bohemians love to discuss and debate various political topics at the Grove. Contact with the pinnacles of power, presidents, foreign dignitaries, cabinet officials, and intellectual giants in an informal off-the-record discussion format, gives Bohemians a heady sense of sharing ideas at the top-most level. Intellectually, Bohemians can agree or disagree with the specific issues of the chats, but overall, the Lakeside Chats are a shared process that enhances a sense that all of these men are brothers, fighting together in opposition to perceived common threats.

Below are some highlights of Lakeside Chats given over the past two decades, courtesy of Mary Moore's Bohemian Grove Action Network:

LAKESIDE CHATS, 1980–2003

DATE	SPEAKER	TOPIC
2003		
July 12	CHRIS MATTHEWS (Bohemian, MSNBC Anchor)	"American Exceptionalism"
July 18	CHARLIE ROSE (PBS News Anchor)	"The View From The Table"
July 19	GEORGE P. SHULTZ (Hoover Institute Fellow)	"A Changed World"
July 23	IAN MACKINLAY (Bohemian and Architect)	"9/11—Did The Terrorists Expect the World Trade Centers to Fall?"

2002		
July 16	FRED STARR (Policy Institute Chairman)	"Any Good News from Afghanastan & Central Asia?"
2001		
July 15	DANIEL KAMMEN (Prof. of Energy Unv. of Calif. Berkeley)	"The Coming Energy Transition"
July 19	RICHARD MULLER (Prof. Physics Unv. of Calif. Berkeley)	"Military Secrets of the Ocean, Atmosphere & UFOs
2000		
July 18	JAMES R. LILLEY, Former Ambassador to China & Korea	"China, Taiwan & the U.S. in the 21st Century"
July 21	MARTIN ANDERSON, Senior Fellow, Hoover Institution	"Status of Missile Defense"
July 22	JOHN MAJOR, Former Prime Minister of England	"World View"
July 29	HENRY KISSINGER, Former Secretary of State in Reagan Administration	"Do We Need a Foreign Policy?"
1999		
July 16	DAVID BRODER, Author & Syndicated Columnist	"Direct Democracy—Curse or Blessing?"
July 20	JOHN SPENCER	"Africa—Are We Wasting Our Time?"
July 21	FRANK POPOFF, Chairman of the Board of DOW Corporation	"Environmental Journey"

1998		
July 17	WILLIAM PERRY, former Secretary of Defense	"Preventive Defense & American Security...21st Century"
July 18	LOU GERSTNER, Chairman & CEO of IBM Corporation	"The Networked World: Are We Ready For It?"
August 1	JAMES A. BAKER III, Former Secretary of State in Reagan Administration	"The Imperative of American Leadership"
1997		
July 11	AMB. JAMES WOOLSEY, former CIA Director	"Rogues, Terrorists...: National Security in the Next Century"
July 15	CHRISTOPHER DeMUTH	"The Triumph of the Market & the Politics of Affluence"
July 25	ANTONIN SCALIA, Sitting Justice-U.S. Supreme Court	"CHURCH, STATE & THE CONSTITUTION"
1996		
July 13	GOV. PETE WILSON, Governor of California	"Keeping Faith With Leland Stanford"
July 16	DAVID M. KENNEDY, Author & U.S. History Professor	"Can the U.S. Still Afford to be a Nation of Immigrants?"
1995		
July 20	ROBERT NOVAK, Conservative Columnist	"Behind the Beltway-How the GOP is transforming Washington's Tribal Society"
July 21	ALEX J. MANDL (Executive VP AT&T)	"Communications & Weaving Spiders—the Complex Web of Futuristic communications"

July 22	NEWT GINGRICH, Speaker of the U.S. House of Representatives	Topic Unknown
July 29	GEORGE BUSH SR., Former President of the USA	"Reflections: Past, Present and Future"
1993		
July 17	CASPAR W. WEINBERGER, (former Secretary of Defense)	"The World and Mr. Clinton"
July 28	CHARLES W. HOSTLER	"Desert Storm's Aftermath"
1992		
July 18	RICHARD NIXON, Past resident of USA	Topic Unknown
July 22	GEN. VERNON WALTERS, involved in CIA coup in Chile	"Integration of the European Economic Community"
July 24	PRINCE BANDAR BIN SULTAN	"Middle East Peace Process"
1991		
July 20	JOHN LEHMAN, Secretary of the Navy in Reagan Administration	"Smart Weapons"
July 20	HELMUT SCHMIDT, Former Chancellor of Germany	"The Enormous Problems of the 21st Century"
July 22	ELLLIOT RICHARDSON, Secretary of Defense/Attorney General in Nixon Administration	"Defining a New World Order"

July 26	RICHARD CHENEY, Secretary of Defense in Bush Sr. Administration, current Vice President of the United States.	"Major Defense Problems of the 21st Century"
July 17	GEORGE SHULTZ, Secretary of State in Reagan administration	"Agenda for America"
1989		
July 14	FRANK BORMAN (Astronaut)	"The Future of the U.S. in Manned Space Flight"
July 22	MICHEL ROCARD, Prime Minister of France	"Europe: 1992…"
July 28	MALCOLM FORBES, Industrialist	"Who's On First?"
1986		
July 17	SIDNEY D. DRELL	"Arms Control and Star Wars"
July 19	WILLIAM H. WEBSTER, Director of the FBI	"Spies and Terrorists: Confronting the Enemies Within"
July 21	ALEX HALEY, Author of *Roots*	"Why Am I Here?"
July 25	DAVID PACKARD, Co-founder of Hewlett Packard	"A Presidential Commission"
1983		
July 17	EDMUND W. LITTLEFIELD (CEO General Electric/Utah Mining)	"Enjoying the Corporate Climb"
July 21	A.W. CLAUSEN (CEO Bank of America/President: World Bank)	"The Global Economy—Time to Get Out of the Woods"

July 25	ADM. ROBERT FOLEY	"World Naval Power"
1981		
July 16	MARVIN L. GOLD-BERGER	"Space War-Fact vs. Fancy"
July 17	CASPER WEIN-BERGER, Secretary of Defense: Reagan Administration	"Rearming America"
1980		
July 24	GEORGE LENC-ZOWSKI	"The Persian Gulf Crisis"
July 25	FRED HARTLEY, CEO Union Oil	"Oil"
July 26	EDWARD TELLER, Scientist & Father of the H bomb	"Nuclear Energy"
August 1	FERDINAND GRAF VON GALEN	"World Bank and International Monetary Systems"

These are only a *few* examples, culled from Lakeside Chats of particular interest to the general public. This list was taken from the official Schedule of Events published yearly by the Bohemian Club. Unfortunately, the year that Alex and I went into the Grove, we did not get to witness any of the Lakeside Chats. As you can see from the official schedule below, we didn't miss much on July 15.

BOHEMIAN GROVE SUMMER ENCAMPMENT —July 14–30, 2000
SCHEDULE OF EVENTS

Friday, July 14	Art Linkletter	"Successful Aging-Getting the Most Out of the Rest of Your Life"

Saturday, July 15	Ken Jowitt	"Communists, Democracy and Golf"
Sunday, July 16	John M. Barry, Writer & Scholar	"The Power of Rivers and Men: The Mississippi Flood, Presidential Politics and Herbert Hoover"
Tuesday, July 18	James R. Lilley, Former Ambassador to China and Korea	"China, Taiwan & the U.S. in the 21st Century"
Wednesday, July 19	William Davidow, Author & Venture Capitalist	"The Internet, Interconnections, Instability and Policy"
Friday, July 21	Martin Anderson, Senior Fellow, Hoover Institution	"Status of Missile Defense"
Saturday, July 22	John Major, Former Prime Minister of UK	"World View"
Sunday, July 23	Nathan Myhrvold, Former Chief Technology Officer, Microsoft Corp.	"The Technology Revolution—You Ain't Seen Nothing Yet"
Tuesday, July 25	Seth Shustak, Astronomer, SETI Institute	"Are We Alone in the Universe?"
Thursday, July 27	Jesse Choper	"The Supreme Court's Renewal of States' Rights"
Friday, July 28:	David M. Kennedy, History Professor, Stanford University	"A Tale of Three Cities: How the United States Won World War II"

Saturday, July 29	Henry Kissinger, Bohemian	"Do We Need a Foreign Policy?"

Also present during the 2000 encampment was ex-president (and longtime Grover) George Bush Sr. His son's vice presidential choice Richard Cheney was on the guest list that year, and was reportedly selected as the VP candidate at the Grove. Because of the Grove summer camp falling right in the midst of George W. Bush's presidential campaign, he apparently did not put in an appearance at the Grove that year. At least, the official sources tell us he was not there. It's hard to know for certain. Politicians are known to visit the Grove secretly, then flatly deny it later.

The 1999 encampment began with strong rumors that George Bush Sr. along with sons George Jr., candidate for president of the United States and then-governor of Texas, and Jeb, current governor of Florida, were coming at some time during the two week festivities. This rumor came to the Bohemian Grove Action Network from several anonymous callers as well Mary Moore's usual sources and was backed up by *Santa Rosa Press Democrat* reporter Bleys Rose using his own sources. When the paper finally did a very small article on the gathering, Rose prefaced his words with "reports abound" before he informed his readers of the impending visit of the Bushes, Sr. & Jr. This turned out to be a wise move on his part.

Suzanne Bohan from the *Sacramento Bee* did not use such precautionary language; she reported it as fact, which promptly got her in trouble with the Bush Jr. campaign. Almost immediately after her August 2 story appeared in the Metro section of the *Bee,* she received a call from a campaign manager denying his presence at the gathering and demanding a retraction. She then contacted the Bohemian Grove Action Network as well as the *Press Democrat,* looking for an eyewitness to a Bush—*any* Bush-sighting. This is when all the sources started back-pedaling, afraid to ruffle such important feathers. In the end, no one would come forward to confirm the rumor.

Mary Moore also got a couple of calls from Bob Mulholland of the state Democratic Party who was interested in whether Bush Jr. was there. Apparently Bush had turned down an offer from LA RAZA of Texas to speak at their convention telling them that he was going to be on retreat in Maine (during the exact time of the Bohemian Grove gathering in July). When LA RAZA (a Hispanic activist organization) found out he was planning to stand them up, they wanted an explanation. We'll probably never know for sure what happened, but to me it is very strange indeed that suddenly a trip to the Grove is something that a presidential candidate needs to dodge and disclaim. This is the place after all that Reagan and Nixon had their famous meeting to decide who would run for president first. If nothing out of the ordinary goes on at the Grove, and the boys are just "being boys", then why all the intense secrecy? Methinks the Bohos protest too much, if indeed the Grove is just an excuse to take a vacation from business and the cares of the outside world.

So, is it "Much Ado About Nothing", as Shakespeare once wrote? That may be what the Bohemians would like to have us believe, but the historical record proves otherwise.

Chapter VI

Imperium

(absolute power)

"The Ultimate Aphrodisiac"
A Political History of the Bohemian Club

"Anyone can be president of the United States, but few can have any hope of becoming president of the Bohemian Club."

**—President Richard Nixon's telegram to the Bohemian Club
upon being pressured by the media to cancel
his Grove visit, summer, 1971.**

Henry Kissinger once said, "power is the ultimate aphrodisiac." If that's true, then the Bohemian Club crowd must be one helluva horny bunch. The Grove has been the seat of Republican politics at the presidential level ever since the turn of the last century. This is the place where power-drunk future leaders are chosen and groomed for America's highest office.

One early example of this insider networking takes place in 1927, when Herbert Hoover was sitting by his tent at Cave Man Camp just as President Calvin Coolidge (also a Bohemian) made his announcement that he did not plan to run again in the 1928 election. At that moment, Hoover's bid for the presidency began in earnest. "Within an hour," wrote Hoover in his memoirs, "a hundred men—publishers, editors, public officials, and others from all over the country who were at the Grove—came to my camp demanding that I announce my candidacy."

Let's do lunch: Ernest O. Lawrence lunching with future U.S. President Dwight Eisenhower (center) and former U.S. President Herbert Hoover (head of table, right) at Bohemian Grove, July 23, 1950.
(Photo: Lawrence Berkeley National Laboratory Collection)

Dwight Eisenhower gave a premier political address at the Grove in 1950, setting himself on the path to the presidency. Ike was made an honorary member of the Bohemian Club that same year. Before the talk, Ike had lunch at Cave Man Camp with Herbert Hoover (see photograph above). Among those present was Richard Nixon, who long remembered Ike's rousing speech, and wrote about the strong impression Eisenhower made on the Grovers in his own memoirs:

> "After Eisenhower's speech we went back to Cave Man Camp and sat around the campfire appraising it. Everyone liked Eisenhower, but the feeling was that he had a long way to go before he had the experience, the depth, and the understanding to be President. But it struck me forcibly that Eisenhower's personality and personal mystique had deeply impressed the skeptical and critical Cave Man audience."

Of course, just making a great speech at the Grove was certainly no ironclad guarantee that one would become President of the United States. One such case would be Presidential hopeful Nelson Rockefeller, then governor of New York, who flew into the Grove for a Lakeside Chat in 1963. To his great dismay, Rockefeller's schmoozing at the Grove didn't win him the GOP nomination (the nod went to Arizona Senator Barry Goldwater). Another well-known close call happened just a few years later in 1967; Nixon and Reagan sat down informally at the Grove to work a political deal wherein Reagan agreed to run only if Nixon faltered.

Indeed, Nixon's campaign was launched from the Bohemian Grove that year by means of his Lakeside Talk. He later wrote that this was "the speech that gave me the most pleasure and satisfaction of my political career." He acknowledged that his Lakeside Talk had, "in many important ways marked the first milestone on my road to the Presidency." He quite rightly called it "an unparalleled opportunity to reach some of the most important and influential men, not just from California, but from across the country."

Richard Nixon has had an interesting on-again/off-again relationship with the Bohemian Club over the years. Nixon did not visit the Grove for the last several years of his life due to an internal spat with the club's board of directors. Apparently, the club was offended by his decision to resign the Presidency during the Watergate scandal in 1974. For Dick "I-am-not-a-quitter" Nixon, quitting was very un-Bohemian behavior. The Bohos felt betrayed, after so many decades of helping to place Nixon into positions of power. Just as the Bohemians were quick to take credit for his political success, they backed away from his failure just as rapidly. In the former president's own words, they didn't have Dick Nixon to "kick around anymore."

During happier times, Nixon was a Boho favorite. Even before Nixon ascended to the national political stage, he was clearly part of the Grove's inner circle. Bohemian connections were also a prominent part of Republican Party leader and U.C. Trustee John Francis Neylan's political network. Neylan wrote to Richard Nixon on July 24, 1950: "I'm sorry I missed you during your visit to Mandalay Camp at the Grove. Some of my fellow members told me they had a very delightful visit with you. I shall be very glad to be helpful...on your return trip to San Francisco."

This letter was sent only a few months after giving a "generous donation" to Nixon's Senate campaign. In a letter from Nixon's campaign headquarters dated May 24, 1950, Mr. Neylan is "buttered up" nicely by David Parkhurst Smith: "...Your contribution for Nixon is in my opinion an excellent investment....He will become an outstanding leader in the United States Senate dedicated to free enterprise and to stopping the present rapid trend towards complete Socialism with its' attendant confiscatory taxes..."

While he was vice president in 1953, Nixon hosted a special ceremony in honor of Herbert Hoover's 40-year anniversary as a Bohemian. The party was not held in California, though the club paid to have many actual redwood branches from the Grove shipped directly to New York's Waldorf-Astoria hotel for "atmosphere." Later, when Nixon was President, the press caught wind of his scheduled Lakeside Talk at the Grove in 1971. This was one of the first times the media called attention to the fact that a sitting President would be giving a secret speech that his constituents were not allowed to hear. As a result of the brouhaha, Nixon was forced to cancel his talk and did not put in an appearance at the Cave Man Camp that year, much to the Bohemians' dismay.

When Gerald Ford became the heir apparent, Nixon was faltering, and Leonard Firestone invited Ford to the Grove for his first visit. Ford was able to meet approximately 150 top-level Republican corporate leaders in a matter of two days. In 1977, Bohemian Loyal McLaren recalled how they pulled it off:

> I had a call from Leonard Firestone, who was having Mr. Ford as a guest at his camp, and he wanted to know about rounding the thing out, to give him an interesting time and enable him to meet as many people, useful people as possible. So I thought the thing to do was to have some rather small parties at two or three of the different camps...The first night they had Ford at Mandalay. And the next day we had a luncheon at our camp (Stowaway) and then a sort of brunch at another camp, and finally on the last day they went to the Hoover camp (Caveman) where of course, there are a lot of Republican politicians.

After the embarrassing demise of Nixon, and Ford faded away, the Bohemians found their next GOP Great White Hope in the late Ronald Wilson Reagan. "Uncle Ronnie" was a member of Owl's Nest Camp, joining in 1975, just two months after leaving the office of California governor. He had given a Lakeside Talk the previous year, while still serving as governor. Back then, no one outside the Bohemian Grove would have been able to imagine Reagan as a serious candidate for president of the United States. A Hollywood movie actor as our commander in chief? *Get serious*, many said, *he doesn't stand a chance.* The naysayers were hushed when Ronald Reagan was indeed elected president in a 1980 landslide victory, going on to serve two terms in the White House.

And it wouldn't be the last time a Hollywood actor with lofty political aspirations was recruited at the Grove. At the most recent summer encampment in 2003, during the heat of Governor Gray Davis's recall, the name of Grove favorite Arnold Schwarzenegger was echoing loudly through the redwoods. According to a July 23, 2003 article in the *San Francisco Chronicle*, "the state Republican hierarchy—especially those close to former Gov. Pete Wilson—would favor Schwarzenegger. At least that's the word that came out of the Bohemian Grove this past weekend, where a number of state and national GOPers, including presidential adviser Karl Rove, happened to have gathered at a club getaway."

Less than two weeks later, Schwarzenegger formally announced his gubernatorial candidacy to the public, but to the insiders at Bohemian Grove, this was already old news. Early additions to his campaign team of advisers include Warren Buffett and Bohemian George Shultz. Not surprisingly, the Bohemian old boys network pulled the right strings, and Schwarzenegger was elected as governor of California in October 2003. As for the future, we can only guess, but I predict that whether or not he wins a second term as governor, Schwarzenegger is the man to watch. He is definitely being groomed for much bigger roles than *The Terminator*.

During the years of his presidency (1980–1988), Ronald Reagan wisely avoided visiting the Grove himself, although most of his cabinet and high level administration officials were always there. And like most of his Republican predecessors, he could hardly wait to get back to the Grove once his presidential term was over. Hollywood Ronnie was back at Bohemian Grove the following year.

At the 1989 Grove summer camp, *Spy* magazine's Philip Weiss reported the former president's activities, even managing to pass himself off as a Grover long enough to meet Reagan face-to-face and ask him a few carefully-worded questions. To find him, Weiss simply followed the tinkling sound of "whorehouse piano music" wafting down Kitchen Hill Road; a waiter had tipped him off that Reagan "likes that kind of music."

Upon arriving at Owl's Nest, Weiss walked past the giant wooden owl statue at the door and made his way to the bar, where he noted that even the ice buckets at the Grove are topped with tilting owl heads. He asked a Secret Service guy if he could meet the former president, and he was escorted right over to where Uncle Ronnie sat, engaged in conversation with a few friends. Weiss said that Reagan "projects an automatic, almost druggy congeniality." When the undercover reporter asked Reagan to confirm the oft-repeated story of how it was decided at the Grove that he wouldn't attempt to challenge Nixon for the 1968 Republican nomination, Reagan's genial reply was: "Yes, yes, that's true."

Reagan even gave a very special Lakeside Talk at the Grove that year. To the delight of the assembled Bohemians, the former president called for greater regulation of the media. "You know, the press conferences were adversarial bouts," Reagan said, reflecting on his years in office. "They were there to trap me into something or other." Little did he know that he was being "trapped" by the media even as he spoke—by a little tape recorder hidden in Weiss' pocket. During his administration, the press certainly "trapped" Reagan on one occasion relative to the Bohemian Grove. I'm talking about the William Casey debacle, of course, which brought both the Bohemian Club and the Reagan administration a great deal of unwanted publicity.

It all started when William Casey's name appeared on the Grove guest lists for both 1980 and 1981. Images of the Grove Guest List with William Casey's name and address listed for 1980 and 1981 are available from the National Archives. At the time of the 1980 Grove encampment, Casey was managing Reagan's presidential campaign. By 1981, Reagan was President and Casey was his new Director of the Central Intelligence Agency. At the Grove in 1981, John McCone, who had been the CIA Director from 1961 to 1965, hosted Casey.

But it was Casey's visit to the Bohemian Grove in 1980 that drew the attention of investigators from both the United States Senate and the House of Representatives. In the summer of 1980, Darrell Trent, an economic and domestic policy advisor for the Reagan campaign, hosted Casey at the Grove's Parsonage camp. Yet, it wasn't until 1992, more than ten years after the fact, that the Senate and House investigators were interested in establishing Casey's daily whereabouts during the summer and fall of 1980, including the exact days of Casey's 1980 visit to the Grove. It was a difficult task because Casey was deceased and his passport and some of his calendar pages from that period were mysteriously missing.

This story might have gone away quietly if not for the efforts of one lone journalist. Robert Parry had worked as an investigative reporter for the Associated Press from 1980 to 1987 and his reporting included breaking stories about the activities of Oliver North, the covert war in Nicaragua, and the Iran-Contra scandal. From 1987 to 1990, Parry was a correspondent for *Newsweek* magazine. In 1990 he was approached by the Public Broadcasting System's *Frontline* documentary television show to do an investigation of allegations regarding an "October Surprise."

Several sources at that time were suggesting that a deal had been cut between the Reagan presidential campaign and certain Iranians to insure that American hostages being held in Iran would not be released prior to the November 1980 U.S. Presidential election. Then-President Carter had been unable to obtain release of 52 hostages seized by Iranian militants at the U.S. Embassy in Tehran in 1979. It was alleged that the Reagan campaign was interested in avoiding a pre-election October surprise release of the hostages that might help boost Carter's popularity and help him win reelection. (Eventually, the hostages were released on the day of Reagan's inauguration.) The "October Surprise" allegations included a date specific allegation that William Casey met with an Iranian cleric in Madrid, Spain on July 27–28, 1980.

Parry's book *Trick or Treason* is an account of the investigation he undertook for *Frontline* that eventually resulted in two broadcasts. Starting in August 1990, the story took Parry into a sort of nether world of arms merchants, federal prisoners, former intelligence agents and government officials. With producer Robert Ross, he traveled extensively in the United States, Europe, and the Middle East to tape interviews. Published in 1993, *Trick or Treason* includes Parry's observations and analysis of the Congressional October Surprise investigations.

Among the conclusions of the 1993 House October Surprise Task Force report that rejected the October Surprise allegations was that the Madrid meeting could not have happened because William Casey had an alibi. They said he was at the Bohemian Grove on one of the days the meeting was alleged to have occurred.

Parry's second book on the subject, *The October Surprise X-Files*, was published in 1996 and is based on documents from the files of the House October Surprise Task Force. Late in 1994, Parry obtained permission to review the files, which were being stored in boxes in an unused ladies room at the Rayburn House Office Building in Washington, DC. He approached several publications about writing a story on the new material, but was rebuffed. Parry writes that "no editor, it seemed, wanted to jeopardize his or her reputation by challenging the powerful taboo that the October Surprise story had become. Even left-of-center publications recoiled at the idea. The documents clearly challenged the findings of the House task force which had collected them."

Parry takes specific issue with the "Bohemian Grove alibi" incorporated in the report of the House task force. Parry's texts make it clear that the Bohemian Club cooperated with the congressional investigation, allowing Congress access to official club records, even including Casey's personal bar tabs. Club members submitted to interviews with FBI agents. A Parsonage camp member shared his own diary entries that helped Parry establish which dates Casey attended the Grove encampment. If Casey had been at the Grove July 26 and 27 of 1980, it would debunk an important element of the October Surprise allegations.

The House Task Force put Casey at the Grove the weekend of July 26 and 27, and the task force Chairman Lee Hamilton cited that alibi in his op-ed piece in the Sunday, January 24, 1993 *New York Times* titled "Case Closed." Yet the committee's own evidence placed Casey at the Grove the following weekend, from Aug. 1 to Aug. 3, 1980. Robert Parry, while preparing the *Frontline* documentaries (which were broadcast *before* the congressional investigations were undertaken) had already reached the conclusion that Casey had been at the Grove the first weekend in August. Parry devotes around seven pages in *Trick or Treason* to a close examination of the alibi put forth by the House task force, and his criticism stings:

"So the new question was, how could a staff of experienced lawyers and investigators accept this...There seemed to be only two plausible answers; either the House investigators were very stupid or they were very biased. But nobody could be that dumb. So the only possible conclusion was that the House task force was willing to twist any evidence to disprove the October Surprise allegations. Evidence that fit that bias, no matter how flimsy or contradicted, was accepted; any that went the other way, no matter how strong, was thrown out."

"I AM NOT A QUITTER"

While it is extremely rare for any Bohemian to leave the Club (after waiting 15–20 years just to get in, who would want to quit?), not all high-level Republicans are content to remain in the Bohemian Club. Perhaps it was a sudden attack of conscience that made David Gergen (then-counselor to President Clinton) resign from the Bohemian Club in June of 1993. His resignation came only three days after Gergen said he would not run around naked at the Bohemian Grove summer camp. Curiously, he also resigned his positions in the Trilateral Commission and the Council on Foreign Relations, as well as 14 other interest groups, charities and public boards at the exact same time. Did Gergen have an epiphany? Did he see the "vast right-wing conspiracy" he was taking part in?

No, said White House spokeswoman Dee Dee Myers. She told the *Washington Times* that Gergen's surprise resignations took place strictly as a matter of custom for presidential advisors, but that it was not mandated by Clinton administration policy. Mr. Gergen's resignation from the Bohemian Club opened up a spot for another eager candidate from the waiting list of over 3,000 names. Gergen himself had waited 13 years, and had only gained full membership a few months previously. Bohemian Club officials would not confirm his resignation to the media, since club policy allows mention of a member's name only after his death.

Although Newt Gingrich has long been a favorite of GOP elites, he apparently never even bothered to join the Bohemian Club, although he did make a very hush-hush appearance as a guest on one occasion. Press reports confirm that the former Speaker of the House of Representatives flew into the Sonoma County Airport Friday afternoon, July 21, 1995, during the heat of the Grove midsummer encampment. A check of the FAA aircraft registry indicated that the plane Gingrich arrived on was registered to the United States Tobacco Company. He schmoozed, kissed babies, shook hands, signed autographs, and even posed for a few pictures. Gingrich was traveling with one of his congressional allies, Republican Representative David Dreier of California. Gingrich gave a last-minute unscheduled speech at the Grove. The topic of this talk has never been announced—to this day, Bohemian lips are still sealed about it.

FRIENDS IN HIGH PLACES

Bohemians regularly invite government men and politicians to attend the Grove encampments. The Grovers have traditionally invited a large number of guests from the East Coast to attend their midsummer encampment to be "entertained" (and, we might presume, quite royally so). Washington DC was second only to New York as the city most likely to have guests at the Grove.

If we combine the U.S. government officials who are members and the government guests the results are that attendees at the Grove consistently include thirty-one to thirty-two of the top political figures in the United States, with a strong emphasis on Republicans. This remains true even when the administration is Democratic, such as in the Clinton years.

I want to include here the startling results of an independent analysis done by Sonoma State University sociology professor Dr. Peter Phillips to illustrate just how many top level positions within our government are held by Bohemians. While researching his doctoral dissertation, *A Relative Advantage*, Phillips built a database that included the names of all the top political appointees in the United States government listed in U.S. government manuals for 1991 who were also Bohemian Club members. He then looked up the names of all active Bohemians in the 1971 index from the same source. Government officials were matched against the active Club members for 1971 and 1991 to determine exactly how many Club members held high-level government positions.

Dr. Phillips built a similar database for important government officials who are *not* members of the Bohemian Club, but came to the Grove as guests. His research covers a 23-year period, from 1970–1993, and clearly shows us that the Grove guest lists can prove every bit, if not more enticing, than the regular membership lists.

142

High Level Positions Held by Bohemian Club Members in U.S. Government

1971

1. President
2. Deputy Secretary of Defense
3. Deputy Under-Secretary, Dept. of the Interior
4. Associate Justice of the Supreme Court
5. Rear Admiral, U.S.N.
6. Director: Office of Science and Technology
7. Member: National Science Board
8. U.S. Circuit Judge: 9th District
9. Trustee: JFK Center for Performing Arts
10. Chairman: JFK Center for Performing Arts
11. Member: National Science Board
12. Deputy Asst. Secretary of State Dept., Asian-Pacific Affairs
13. Asst. Deputy-Data Management, Veterans Administration

1991

1. President
2. Secretary of Treasury
3. Postmaster General
4. Chairman: U.S. Postal Service
5. Director: National Railway Passenger Corp.
6. Director: Federal Justice Center
7. Board Member: U.S. Institute of Peace
8. Director: Museum of National History
9. Director: Pension Benefit Guaranty Corp.
10. Secretary of Smithsonian Institution
11. Director of Finance: Dept. of Treasury

Government Officials Invited As Guests To The Bohemian Grove

1970

1. Secretary of Interior
2. Secretary of the Treasury
3. Secretary of Defense
4. Secretary of State
5. Chairman: U.S. Export-Import Bank
6. Chairman: Joint Chiefs of Staff
7. Director: U.S. Information Agency
8. Chief of Protocol: Dept. of State
9. Asst. to the President: Domestic Affairs
10. Asst. to the President
11. Asst. to the President: National Security
12. Deputy Director: Office Management and Budget
13. Board Member: Smithsonian Institute
14. Under Secretary: H.E.W.
15. Commissioner: Federal Trade Commission
16. Associate Administrator Operations: Dept. of Transportation

1991–93

1. Secretary of Defense
2. Chief of Protocol, Dept. of State
3. Senator from Wyoming
4. Representative from Tenn.
5. Representative from WA
6. Representative from CA
7. Ambassador to Denmark
8. Ambassador to Great Britain
9. Ambassador to Bahrain/Canberra
10. Asst. Secretary, Dept. of Defense
11. Under Secretary for Mgmt: Dept. of State
12. Administrator of EPA
13. Director of Foreign Service Institute, Dept. of State
14. Librarian of Congress
15. Asst. Secretary of Navy: Financial Mngt
16. Officer of Federal Reserve Bank: SF
17. Director: Federal Maritime Commission
18. Board Member, National Railroad Passenger Corp.

1970	1991–93
17. Deputy Associate Admin., Planning: National Aeronautics & Space Administration	19. Chairman: J.F.K. Center for Performing Arts
18. Asst. Admin., Industrial Affairs: National Aeronautics & Space Administration	20. Chief Economist: Office of Thrift Supervision
	21. Military Asst. to Secretary of Defense

THE SECRET WAR ROOM OF WWII

Before and during WWII, California received more money from Army and Navy defense contracts than any other state in the union. Defense money was an important stimulus to the San Francisco Bay Area economy and the promotion of this continued business was important to a number of important people. Ernest O. Lawrence, physicist at U.C., Berkeley, was actively involved in facilitating Bay Area military spending, ultimately drumming up support for his nuclear research projects.

According to the Lawrence Archives at Berkeley, Lawrence hosted an overnight party at the Bohemian Grove in honor of Admiral A.H. Van Keuren, Assistant Chief Bureau of Ships U.S. Navy, who had responsibility for all shipbuilding contracts. The date was October of 1941, and the guest list included a host of bigwigs from the University of California mixing with top naval brass. There was Robert Sproul, University of California President, James Corky, Office of Controller, U.C., H.E. Bolton, U.C. Professor, William Donald and Don Cooksy of the U.C. Radiation Lab, Mauro P. O'Brian from U.C. Engineering, and U.C. Dean Charles Lipman. Representing the U.S. Navy were Rear Admiral John Greenside, Commandant of 12th Naval District, Rear Admiral Wilhelm L. Friedland, Mare Island Navy Yard, and the Admiral's son. Joseph Moore Jr., President of Moores Dry Docks was also present, as was Captain H.M. Gleason, Manager of Naval Construction for Moore.

This cozy private gathering held at the Grove's river clubhouse combined one of the leading shipbuilders in the Bay Area with the Navy's key person in charge of naval contracts and the top officials at U.C. Berkeley. This party apparently got quite friendly, and the manager of shipbuilding for Moores became a first name acquaintance with the Chief of Naval Shipbuilding. Lawrence was actively involved with other major defense contractors throughout his life, by serving as a consultant to and later on the board of directors of Monsanto, and working as a consultant to General Electric from 1928 to 1958.

The October 1941 meeting at the Grove with Admiral A.H. Van Keuren, Assistant Chief Bureau of Ships, U.S. Navy, is quite interesting for it's close proximity to the attack on Pearl Harbor. At the time, Pacific Fleet commanders were incensed at President Roosevelt's recent decision to move the entire fleet of ships to Pearl Harbor. This may have been a key secret meeting before U.S.'s entry into WWII, at Bohemian Grove, with naval brass and shipbuilders, the latter of whom stood to make a fortune in government contracts for the war effort.

An article in the *New American*, published June 4, 2001, strongly suggests that the President and his top advisors not only had prior knowledge of the attack on Pearl Harbor, they did nothing to stop it because they intended to use the war for political and financial gain. In *Pearl Harbor: The Facts Behind The Fiction*, James Perloff writes:

> After meeting with President Roosevelt on October 16, 1941, Secretary of War Henry Stimson wrote in his diary: "We face the delicate question of the diplomatic fencing to be done so as to be sure Japan is put into the wrong and makes the first bad move—overt move." On November 25th, the day before the ultimatum was sent to Japan's ambassadors, Stimson wrote in his diary: "The question was how we should maneuver them [the Japanese] into the position of firing the first shot...."

> The bait offered Japan was our Pacific Fleet. In 1940, Admiral J.O. Richardson, the fleet's commander, flew to Washington to protest FDR's decision to permanently base the fleet in Hawaii instead of its normal berthing on the U.S. West Coast. The admiral had sound reasons: Pearl Harbor was vulnerable to attack, being approachable from any direction; it could not be effectively rigged with nets and baffles to defend against torpedo planes; and in Hawaii it would be hard to supply and train crews for his undermanned vessels. Pearl Harbor also lacked adequate fuel supplies and dry

docks, and keeping men far from their families would create morale problems. The argument became heated. Said Richardson: "I came away with
the impression that, despite his spoken word, the President was fully determined to put the United States into the war if Great Britain could hold out
until he was reelected."

Richardson was quickly relieved of command. Replacing him was Admiral
Husband E. Kimmel. Kimmel also informed Roosevelt of Pearl Harbor's
deficiencies, but accepted placement there, trusting that Washington
would notify him of any intelligence pointing to attack. This proved to be
misplaced trust. As Washington watched Japan preparing to assault Pearl
Harbor, Admiral Kimmel, as well as his Army counterpart in Hawaii,
General Walter C. Short, were completely sealed off from the information
pipeline.

It appears that Bohemian Grove played a bigger role in the events of World
War II than has previously been realized. Ernest Lawrence's use of the
Grove's river clubhouse for a Manhattan Project planning meeting in September of 1942 is well documented. Bohemians make no effort to deny that this
important historical moment took place at the Grove; in fact, they rather enjoy
telling the story around the campfire. They publish it in their internal history
books with a sense of pride.

Less well known is who exactly attended this meeting. The Club library notes
the following in attendance at the Grove meetings of September 13–14, 1942:

James B. Conant, President of Harvard University
E.O. Lawrence, U.C. Radiation Lab
Donald Cooksey, U.C. Radiation Lab
Robert L. Thornton, U.C. Radiation Lab
Robert Oppenheimer, U.C. Physics Department
Arthur H. Compton, Dean, Dept.. of Physical Science, University of Chicago
(also consultant to General Electric)
Lt. Col. Kenneth Nichols, U.S. Army
Major Thomas Crenshaw, U.S. Army
Lyman Briggs, Director, Natl Bureau of Standards
Eger V. Murphree, Chemist, Director of Standard Oil Company

The atom bomb made this particular meeting at the Grove world famous, but
it was not an isolated case of business and government war planning through
Bohemian Club facilities. This was but one in a long series of historical busi-

ness-related activities done in the context of a Bohemian corporate family net-work. In actual fact, it's safe to say that Bohemian Grove serves as the West Coast Headquarters of the "military-industrial complex" President Eisenhower warned us about in his farewell address. Ike was more than qualified to speak of what he knew to be true about the Grove—after all, he *was* present at most of these key strategic secret meetings.

U.N.-AMERICAN

One of the foremost political events in which the Bohemian political network played a significant role was the United Nations Conference of International Organization (UNCIO), April 25th to June 26, 1945 in San Francisco. This was the original formation meeting for the United Nations, with delegates from fifty nations attending. Receptions for UNCIO delegates and key dignitaries were held at the Bohemian Club on May 17, May 29, June 4, and June 5.

Towards the end of the U.N. conference, the Bohemian Club invited all delegates to a program at the Grove. The U.S. Navy provided bus transportation to the Grove. The U.S. Army furnished enlisted personnel to assist with cooking, waiting tables, bar tending, and any help that was needed. The Air Force even put on a special air show for the visiting dignitaries. How ironic that we, the American people, actually pay our armed forces to entertain foreign diplomats and economic elites at a party that we could not gain entrance to. We are cordially *not* invited, even if we foot the bill.

The Club was quite proud that Bohemians Earl Warren, then-Governor of California, played a big role in greeting the U.N. delegates. Earl Warren was a proud Bohemian from 1941 until his death in 1974. As State Attorney General, Governor, and U.S. Supreme Court Justice, he used the Club formally and informally for many political activities.

Earl Warren references the Bohemian Club politically in his memoirs twice. In 1951, while Governor, he was considering a run for the presidency when General Eisenhower came to the Grove midsummer encampment for a little informal politicking. Warren writes that "the general was a guest and very popular," and that Eisenhower reportedly "asked people if they thought he could obtain both party nominations."

ONE BIG HAPPY GLOBAL FAMILY

While the Grove has primarily been known as a retreat for American politicians and economic elites, that is not always the case. In fact, many foreign leaders and diplomats have been invited to the Grove as guests through the years. While visiting the encampment, these men are treated like Kings. Or perhaps like Queens, depending upon whether or not they choose to don the traditional drag outfit! Here are just a few of the most important historical examples:

On November 1, 1938, U.C Trustee John Francis Neylan was called upon by Bohemian friend William Chadbourne, who had stayed with him at Mandalay only three months earlier, to assist with coordinating the visit of Alexander Kerensky to the Bohemian Club. Kerensky had been Prime Minister of Russia after the fall of the Czar and before the rise of Lenin, and was then gearing up for a lecture tour of the USA. Neylan made sure that Kerensky would have all the "privileges" of the Bohemian Club while visiting San Francisco. Neylan and Ernest Lawrence were also close friends and Bohemian buddies. Neylan was often involved in promoting various political agendas through the Club.

Bohemians Loyal McLaren and Harry Collier, were co-captains of the Stowaway Camp, where Eisenhower stayed in 1951. McLaren and Eisenhower became quite "congenial", as they both liked to play bridge. In 1953 McLaren invited Eisenhower back to the Grove but he was unable to attend. Eisenhower did reciprocate however, by inviting McLaren to a black tie "stag dinner", at the White House in January of 1954, that was meant to serve as a thank you to heavy Republican contributors. Later that year McLaren got a telephone call from the White House asking him to arrange for the Prime Minister of Pakistan to be received at the Grove that summer. McLaren took responsibility for hosting the Prime Minister at Stowaway Camp and even arranged for him to give a Lakeside Chat (*McLaren Memoirs*, 1977).

Loyal McLaren also wrote about when Britain's Prince Philip visited the Grove:

> Before leaving London for a visit to California in November, 1962, Prince Philip wrote to Jack Merrill, an old friend and expressed a desire to visit the Bohemian Grove…Since the weather was unpredictable at this time of the year; we decided it would be safer to hold the party inside the grill and bar

building...we restricted the invitation to former presidents of the club, committee chairmen, and groups of our highly talented entertainers...At luncheon...Charlie Kendrick delivered the speech of welcome. However, the show was stolen by Prince Philip, who made a most amusing but salty speech in keeping with the traditions of Bohemia.

Another famous (or more recently, *infamous*) royal prince the Grove has entertained is none other than controversial Saudi Arabian Prince Bandar bin Sultan. In November, 2002, the FBI launched an investigation into how funds from the private bank of Prince Bandar's wife found their way indirectly to two of the September 11 suicide hijackers. Khalid al-Midhar and Nawaf al-Hazmi were part of the team of hijackers who apparently overtook Flight 77 and crashed it into the Pentagon.

But why should we be surprised that Saudi Arabia provided funds to the terrorists? As we now know, the Bush and Saudi Royal families are old friends and business partners; even partying together at the Bohemian Grove in 1992. Bush Jr. is particularly close to Prince Bandar, and has hosted him at the ranch in Crawford, Texas. After September 11, Prince Bandar helped to evacuate the bin Laden family members from the United States, along with President Bush's help and cooperation.

While this chapter has focused mostly upon the Bohemian Grove's impact upon American government, I felt it necessary to include some of the better known visits from foreign leaders and diplomats just to illustrate the point that clearly, the Grove's influence reaches far beyond our borders. I will close this chapter with the one person (surprisingly, a woman) who may be the Grove's most eminent guest in the club's entire 130-year history—the Queen of England herself.

In January 1983, the Queen and her consort toured the United States. There seemed to be no apparent reason for her visit, other than the honor bestowed upon her by the Bohemian Club during the final evening of her stay. On February 3, a five-minute segment of the Grove celebration in honor of the Queen was aired on all three major television networks. It was, for most average Americans, the first time they had ever even heard of the Bohemian Grove. It was also the first time the general public had the opportunity to glimpse the bizarre occult rites that went on in the redwoods.

The televised event began with a view of the Queen sitting atop a pyramid onstage before a huge crowd of assembled Bohemians. Two dancers entered the stage wearing huge hats hanging from cables. The cone of the first hat was representative of a walled city with a pyramid, or ziggurat, towering in the middle, obviously portraying ancient Babylon.

At the base of the pyramid two doors continuously flapped open and closed displaying a large picture of Prince Charles and Princess Diana. As the dancer and hat moved stage right, a second dancer entered from stage left. The cone on the second dancer's hat portrayed the city of London, with Big Ben towering in the center. When both dancers centered themselves, with the brims of the huge hats reaching from one end of the stage to the other, a voice cried out, "Oh, Queen, you have traversed the ages from Babylon to London!"

Ever so slightly, and without smiling, Queen Elizabeth nodded her agreement.

Chapter VII

dramatis personae

(characters of the play)

"Strange Bedfellows"
The Art of Politics at Bohemian Grove

"Politics acquaints a man with strange bedfellows."

—**William Shakespeare,** *The Tempest*

What makes the Bohemian Club unique above most all other American elite men's clubs and secret societies is their tremendous emphasis on the "Bohemian" aspect of the club's name. Art, drama, politics and power all intersect here in the Northern California redwoods amongst an atmosphere of ancient Druid nature rituals and pagan fire ceremonies. Granted, it seems like an unlikely setting for the men who rule the world to confer and revel in secret, but facts are stubborn things.

We've all heard the saying "politics makes strange bedfellows." This phrase dates back hundreds of years. The earliest reference seems to come from Shakespeare, the Bohemian Grove's patron saint of drama. In Act 2, Scene 2 of *The Tempest*, Trinculo, a court jester, makes the remark in jest. While the line has been adapted to "politics" in more recent years, Shakespeare originally wrote it as "misery acquaints a man with strange bedfellows." The "politics" maxim seems to be correctly ascribed to Charles Dudley Warner, a 19th century Connecticut newspaperman. (Warner was also a neighbor of Bohemian Club member Mark Twain, and his collaborator on *The Gilded Age.*) Ah, misery…politics…what's the difference?

In order to understand social interaction at the Bohemian Club, it is important to have an understanding of Bohemian traditions in the theater, music, literature and popular culture. This includes not just the ceremonial activities of Bohemia, but their spiritual and emotional content as well. In the next two chapters, I will try to illustrate the common thread that binds art, politics, and elite business powers throughout modern history, uniting factions of society who would otherwise be likely enemies. That unifying thread is the occult.

BOHEMIA

When we refer to Bohemia, we are not necessarily referring to a spot on the map. Bohemia is more of a state of mind. It represents the mutual supportive companionship of artists and intellectuals. Bohemia is a land without geography; but its capital is Paris. Its inhabitants are nowadays spread among many nations, but in the 19th century, Paris was the intellectual and artistic capital of the world. Two high periods of bohemian creativity were just before the 1848 Revolution and during the 34-year period often referred to as "The Banquet Years" or "La Belle Epoche," from roughly 1885 through the outbreak of the First World War in 1914.

The influence of Bohemia has not only been felt in the arts, but also in political and social movements. Within its frontiers Bohemia contained not only artists, sculptors, and men of letters, but elements of vocal opposition to the establishment. Crowns might tumble, nations made and lost, but ever since 1789 social upheaval has been a fact of modern life. Almost as worrisome to the monarchies of Western Europe was the progressive outrageousness of the revolutionary opposition, led by Bohemians.

The social revolutionaries adapted for their own purposes some of the Bohemian critique of society, but the rebellion of the Bohemian underground was much more a rejection of the world that monarchs had built than a protest against injustice. The most influential rebellions were those whose leaders had a strong interest in the occult. In fact, the "Occult Revival" of 19th century Paris was closely bound with the more artistic or literary levels of Bohemia.

During "La Belle Epoche," and into the early 20th century, these occult ideals continued to spread across the continents, catching fire in mainstream society. Ouija boards were common parlor games for the elite, as were the casting of runes and the reading of Tarot cards. Madame Blavatsky's Theosophical Society counted the rich and famous amongst its membership, spurring interest within the masses to learn more about astrology, palmistry, geomancy, eastern religions, magic, secret societies, and many more apparently dissimilar beliefs. Any strange, unorthodox, but semi-religious belief became part of the occult complex in those years, making the true belief system of Bohemia nearly undetectable underneath the hodgepodge of contrasting ideologies.

The term "Bohemian", in a 20th Century cultural context, refers to the various cults that adopted a libertine attitude and lifestyle based upon communalism. The origin of the term is from the ancient prehistory tribal peoples that inhabited the area known as Bohemia. These ancient people worshipped trees in communal tribal groupings. The original Bohemians were "green people," the forest people, or "tree huggers." They practiced a religious pagan worship of the "souls of trees".

When Adolf Hitler was a young art student in Leitz, circa 1905, he was "living a Bohemian lifestyle", as described in most published accounts. Similar to the Pythagorean socialist experimental cults that existed in the mountains of the Sudetaen, Adolf Hitler became a socialist, and an activist. During his years in Vienna most biographers describe him as a person of the streets, a young Bohemian, an artist. Hitler in *Mein Kampf* describes this as the most difficult time of his life. He was not yet a political leader, but rather known around Vienna more as a sort of poet.

These Bohemians attempted to create a New World based upon Pythagoras with a mixture of Marx, and the study of mystical religions from the East. The Spartacans were more in line with the works of Hegel, while the German Vril Society (precursors to the Nazis) zeroed in on the similarities of the Pythagoreans and the mythical Germanic tribes, even to the extent of the resurrection of pagan symbols of that mythical culture, in particular the Swastika. It is the combination of the German myths and reminiscences about Alexander the Great and the Aryan tribes of Afghanistan that make the overall Bohemian, New Palestine, New Pythagorean, New Arcadian or Hellenic Greco movements in their entirety so interesting. This mystical undercurrent certainly gave momentum to the Pan Germanic based political movement called for in Hitler's *Mein Kampf*.

In America, the late 19th and early 20th centuries were the period in which Bohemianism became fashionable. Similar to today's New Age movement, the Bohemians had become an amusing tourist attraction in New York's Greenwich Village and also in San Francisco, a city that has always been known for progressive social attitudes. It was a time when the cultural values of the Victorian era were being refuted. What a perfect time and place for the San Francisco Bohemian Club to flourish.

The Astor Hotel on Sacramento Street in San Francisco served as the club-house for the first Bohemians. Organized in 1873, the Bohemian Club was originally established as a gathering place for a few bored local newspaper reporters and their friends, mostly fellow writers and artists, to relax and perhaps brainstorm new creative ideas together in a collective (and terrifically alcohol-fueled) environment. That original mission is now all but forgotten within the confines of the Bohemian Club; except, of course, for the alcohol. Bohemians still love telling the story of when the notoriously homosexual English playwright Oscar Wilde was entertained at the Bohemian Club in 1882, and how he drunk his guests under the table. No matter what other kinds of silliness may go on at the Grove, Bohemians take their drinking very, *very* seriously.

But let us not be fooled into believing that the Bohemian Club is simply an overpriced Elks Lodge with one hell of a well-stocked bar. Men of such power and rank would not make this club such a priority in their lives if it were just a frat party. They've got better things to do, like run the world, for example. Are we really convinced that these leaders of nations and industry actually *stop* running the world for a few days while they're "banishing Dull Care" at the Grove? Of course not. The world would presumably stop turning if our leaders took a vacation, right? So the answer must be that these men are indeed still running the world from inside the Bohemian Grove.

Something has sustained this Club for 130 years. *Something* has emerged within the Bohemian Club that draws world class applicants willing to wait fifteen years to get in. Perhaps some members join for business purposes, or the seeking of political connections, or even just the social status of being a Bohemian. Yet, there must be more here than networking and status that sustains the intense loyalty and a fierce sense of "oneness" so often expressed by Bohemian Club members.

While love of the arts in all its varying forms may have been the original stated purpose for the founding of the Bohemian Club, surely that alone cannot be the glue that has held this group together through generations of Bohemians. Or is it more likely that the Bohemian Club was at one time hijacked by big businessmen and political heavyweights that gradually thwarted the original artistic mission of the Club? To find the answer, we must look back at the Bohemians' humble beginnings and work our way forward.

BIRTH OF THE BOHOS

After the Civil War, the era of Westward Expansion was in full swing, and the city of San Francisco had become the major metropolis of the West Coast. In almost all phases of economic expansion, San Francisco by 1866 had been booming for more than a decade. No longer a supply station and recreation center for the motley gold miners, but an emerging major urban center, San Francisco enjoyed a population explosion and building boom that had been going strong for years. Brick and stone business establishments several stories high, opera and theater houses, picturesque dwellings perched on steep slopes, government and financial centers (including a branch of the U.S. Mint), and even paved streets were features of the "new" San Francisco.

People of every description poured into the Bay Area, but what made this relocation and settling unusual was the extraordinary number of artists and writers who arrived during this era. Far from the aftermath of the Civil War in the north, the humiliating ordeal of Reconstruction in the south, and the riots of eastern industrialization, San Francisco, with its early lead on post-war prosperity, enjoyed flush times with a unique emphasis on culture.

In the late 1860s San Francisco was already becoming a hotbed for artists and writers. Many have called this city the birthplace for what would come to be called the "local color" movement in American literature. Practically every writer associated with early western local color at least made an appearance in San Francisco. While in San Francisco, most of these writers knew each other, and came to regard themselves as the circle or group that formed the cutting edge of a new kind of American writing.

Surely the dominant figure of this emerging literary movement was young Bohemian Francis Bret Harte. For *The Californian*, a literary newspaper of the mid-1860s, Harte wrote a number of pieces about San Francisco that were pointed satire, often mixed with humor. Several of these examples were actually folklore, a reporting of local customs and beliefs, such as "The Legend of Devil's Point" (1864), or "A Legend of the Cliff House" (1865), or "Early California Superstitions" (1865). In the local color decade of 1865 to 1875, he would rise from local fame (and sometimes infamy) as a satirist, poet, editor, and short story writer to become the most celebrated figure of current American literature, before slipping away into a sad obscurity.

Another "one of the boys" who appeared in San Francisco during this era was Samuel L. Clemens, who would emerge from the West as Mark Twain. It is only poetic justice that Sam Clemens garnered his famous *nom de plume* not in the service of captaining a riverboat, but in the world of western local color. Scholar Paul Fatout learned from old timer George W. Cassidy and other sources that "Mark Twain" (which literally means, "allow two free drinks") was a reference to the "on credit" drinking contests Clemens held with a number of opponents in Virginia City's Old Corner saloon.

After a time Mark Twain hurled one pointed barb too many in his local newspaper column, and he left Virginia City under a certain amount of pressure from his journalistic peers and other victims of his pointed prose. Already, he was a perfect candidate for membership in the yet-to-be-founded Bohemian Club. In addition to being a Freemason, Twain was also a member of the occult Society for Psychical Research.

Clemens moved to San Francisco in May of 1864, having recognized the city's literary potential on a visit the previous year. Clemens found a home with *The Californian*. For this imaginative literary newspaper, he developed his eye for local color by writing ten articles every week throughout the fall of 1864. With these pieces for *The Californian*, Clemens came directly under Bret Harte's tutelage. While Harte led local color fiction in the direction of literary respectability, Mark Twain in 1872 published the greatest work of satiric local color, *Roughing It*. By this time Mark Twain had gained even more respectability, if not fame, than Bret Harte.

Mark Twain used the techniques he learned in writing western local color fiction to help create his great masterpieces, *Tom Sawyer* (1876) and *Adventures of Huckleberry Finn* (1885), as well as his other celebrated novels and stories. Two other younger San Francisco writers—both very colorful and at opposite ends of the literary spectrum—used their experiences in the city to gain fame in England. These two men were Bohemians Joaquin Miller and Ambrose Bierce.

Miller proved to be a sensation in London. Tom Hood got Miller's lush *Pacific Poems* and prolix *Songs of the Sierras* into print, but it was on the stage that Miller really achieved popularity. Dressed in the outlandish garb fellow writer Ina Coolbrith had suggested—a ten gallon hat, riding boots, spurs, and a sealskin coat with real gold nuggets for buttons—Joaquin fascinated the English with marvelous tales of his adventures in the west. Although he gained a certain measure of fame as a popular poet, his poetry never received much but scorn from serious literary critics.

As an older man, Joaquin moved to the hills of Oakland, and became something of a professional "character," and indeed, there was always an aura of the innocent flower child about him. In his final years, Joaquin abandoned writing poetry in favor of entertaining lady admirers at his cottage and planting eucalyptus trees around San Francisco Bay.

Ambrose Bierce cut quite a different figure. Ever sneering at Victorian poetry and all lofty sentiments, Bierce was a journalist who could wield a bitter, abusive prose that maintained the rhetorical stance of vituperative, frontal attack. In 1868, he took over the "Town Crier" column of the *NewsLetter*, a San Francisco newspaper that welcomed his relentless attacks and satiric jests. Odd as it may seem, Bierce got along famously with Bret Harte.

Bierce was part of the literary contingent that left San Francisco in the early 1870s. His satires, increasing in their skill and bite, were very well received in England, where three books of his satiric sketches on California were published. Like Miller, but unlike Harte and Clemens, a now famous Bierce returned to San Francisco, the area which he so often claimed treated him with alienation and estrangement. As a satiric journalist in the corrupt "Gilded Age" of the 1880s and '90s, Bierce was not wanting for material. During these years, he attacked virtually everything, from Denis Kearney's Workingmen's Party to the local Humane Society. Having offended practically everyone by the turn of the century, Bierce, despite his brilliance, came to be regarded by many as a crank. He disappeared in 1914, trying, at age seventy-one, to join up with Pancho Villa's band of bandits. He departed for Mexico after completing his classic collection of bitter definitions, *The Devil's Dictionary*.

Mark Twain, now recognized as unquestionably the group's greatest writer, was on the way to fulfilling his potential, and should be regarded as the second key figure in the San Francisco circle. These men were the leading lights of local color, and all of them found an audience for their work in freewheeling San Francisco. What more perfect place was there for these men to gather together informally than the Bohemian Club?

Right about this time, the Bohemian Club began to take shape in downtown San Francisco. The Bohemian Club's founding was a literary event that marked the continuation and expansion of the San Francisco literary circle. Perhaps the most significant and far-reaching examples in the 1870s and '80s of this expanding circle were the works of nature writers Clarence King and John Muir. A rather bizarre non-stop talker and mountain climber, King in 1872 published *Mountaineering in the Sierra Nevada*, a collection of short pieces that was very popular.

John Muir, who in the early 1890s founded the Sierra Club and became known as the "Father of our National Parks," was the first widely read western writer with a mystical, ecological vision. Far more than even King, Muir explored the Sierra Nevada wilderness areas, coming to the deep belief that wild country must be preserved for its intrinsic value. Muir was the original "tree-hugger" and environmentalist, whose philosophy of pagan earth worship combined with a flair for the literary, made him a perfect addition to the Bohemian Grove crowd.

Speaking of eccentrics, no discussion of the early Bohemian Club literary legend would be complete without mentioning Jack London. We've all heard the legend of Jack London the adventurer and pioneer, Jack London the hard-hitting, hard-drinking, hard-living individualist. All the favorite clichés that have been used to describe the spirit of the American west were incarnated in the London persona, and his public image was as spectacular as that of any of his fictional heroes.

Portrait of Jack London at Bohemian Grove, 1904
(Photo: the Bancroft Library, UC Berkeley)

Jack London's father was an itinerant astrologer, his mother a spiritualist. Jack was born out of wedlock, for his father had deserted his mother when he learned she was pregnant. He recollected his early years as clouded by poverty, solitude, insecurity, and deprivation—emotional as well as financial. Jack's first stories were published when he was only 16, and he embarked upon a stellar literary career; he was an ace war correspondent and world-famous novelist before he was thirty, and became the first author ever to earn a million dollars from his writings.

But there was a darker facet of London's persona. He eventually escaped to the countryside to battle physical illness and depression, relocating to the hamlet of Glen Ellen, in the Sonoma Valley, sixty miles north of San Francisco. He lovingly called this area "The Valley of the Moon." He also lived in close proximity to the Bohemian Grove, making it easier for him to travel to his beloved club's summer retreat, an event he rarely missed. Even late in life, when his health was very frail, he always made a special effort to get to the Grove. He had spent several months in Hawaii in 1915 and 1916, hoping to recapture his lost health in that benevolent climate; but his body continued to deteriorate. He returned home from Hawaii in July of 1916, just in time to attend the Bohemian Club High Jinks one last time.

London was also an unapologetic socialist and fervent naturalist whose work often reflected these beliefs. The back-to-the-land theme is explicitly dramatized in *The Acorn-Planter*, the Bohemian Grove play which London began writing on Christmas Day, 1914. Written as a Grove Play for the Bohemian Club's Jinks, it was never staged at the Grove because of difficulties in setting the play to music.

The play is a mythopoeic fantasy beginning in which California is seen throughout as the new Garden of Eden, *"A sunny land, a rich and fruitful land,/ The warm and golden...land."* Red Cloud, though killed by the Sun Men, is resurrected; and *"In place of war's alarms, peaceful days;/Above the warrior's grave the golden grain/Turns deserts grim and stark to laughing lands."* The play ends on a strong note of affirmation as *"The New Day dawns,/The day of brotherhood,/The day of man!"*

MEN OF TALENT

By the 1880's, at the latest, businessmen had joined the Club in large numbers. Original Bohemians found that admitting men of wealth (called "men of use" by the original Bohos) helped pay the expenses for the club's "men of talent." Club membership rose rapidly from 182 members in 1874 to over 550 in 1887. Early Club rosters do not show any difference between artist members and those who joined as "supporters" of the arts. The 1887 roster has an interesting combination of literary figures and San Francisco businessmen including: social radical Henry George, four members of the Crocker banking family, William Randolph Hearst, Bay Area shipbuilder Arthur W. Moore, and fourteen Army and Navy officers. Honorary members included Oliver Wendell Holmes, Mark Twain and Joaquin Miller. The Club rapidly outgrew the Astor Hotel, and by 1877 had moved to a building at 430 Pine Street in San Francisco.

The Bohemian Club was clearly off to a strong start, already boasting many of San Francisco's most noted writers on their membership list. Even before the corporate chieftains and politicos arrived years later, the Bohemian Club was drawing plenty of attention to itself with notices in local newspapers. In those days, if Ambrose Bierce, Daniel O'Connell, and Henry George were in a room together, that was *news*. Mark Twain and Bret Harte were even bigger celebrities, and in the next generation Jack London and Frank Norris also made headlines due to their association with the already prestigious Bohemian Club. But the club's most notable creativity was among its members who worked in the visual arts. The roll call of artists who joined the Bohemian Club in its first few years constitutes a list of painters who are today recognized as important mid-nineteenth century American artists.

The Bohemian monopoly on artistic talent continued through the turn-of-the-century period as a second generation of Bohemian artists, a number of them California-born, returned from European study to Northern California. These younger painters were joined by a generation of sculptors, designers, architects, and writers—most of them active in the Bohemian Club.

Art historians agree that the Bohemian Club's strongest period ranges from the 1870s to about 1915. Some famous artists who were club members include Samuel Marsden Brookes, Norton Bush, Giuseppe Cadenasso, Maynard Dixon, Paul Frenzeny, Percy Grey, Thomas Hill, Christian Jorgensen, William Keith, Lorenzo Latimer, Xavier Martinez, Gottardo Piazzoni, Granville Redman, William Ritschel, Julian Rix, H. E. Smith, Jules Tavernier, Frank van Sloun, Virgil Williams, and Theodore Wores.

Since the club's inception, the Bohemians have exerted a great deal of influence (some argue that a better word is "control") over the Bay Area Visual Arts scene. Indeed, the club has always counted the area's most prominent painters and sculptors amongst their membership, and, not surprisingly, these are the artists who tend to receive the most prestigious and highly paid commissions in San Francisco. One example would be Charles Stafford Duncan (1892–1952).

A painter and printmaker, Duncan was born in Hutchinson, Kansas, studied at the Mark Hopkins Institute (now the California Institute of Fine Arts) and was a member of the San Francisco Art Association, the California Society of Etchers, and the Bohemian Club. Duncan's awards included the SFAA Gold Medal and the Bohemian Club's James D. Phelan Prize in 1927, the SFAA's Anne Bremmer Prize and the Pacific Southwest Exposition's Gold Medal in 1928 and the California Palace of the Legion of Honor's William L. Gerstle Prize in 1930. One of his most stunning and unusual works can be seen easily enough today by visiting the basement women's smoking room at Oakland's Paramount Theatre.

When Stafford created the mural in 1931, few women smoked in public, so they were relegated to a basement room. The walls are all painted black, a shiny black lacquer, accented by vermilion bands above the high baseboard and at the cornice, and by three bands of the same color dividing each corner horizontally into quarters, making the whole room look like the inside of an oriental fortune-telling parlor. Half-figures by Duncan are centered on each sidewall. One represents a girl in a yellow dress holding a red comic mask and a green tragic mask. There are shooting stars behind her head. The mural is filled with celestial and mystical symbolism throughout. The black walls contrast sharply with bright red carpet, strangely illuminated by the reflection of the gold-finished ceiling.

It is through having some of the world's most distinguished artists as members that the Bohemian Club has played a central role in making San Francisco the center of West Coast art. To understand the importance of the visual arts to the Bohemian Club, we must go back to a time when post-Gold Rush California was developing its culture. As noted Bohemian historian Kevin Starr puts it, "The 1870s were emerging as a golden age of landscape painting in the Far West, and the Athens of this golden age was San Francisco."

Dr. Starr graduated from the University of San Francisco and holds a Ph.D. in American Literature from Harvard University and a Master of Library Science from U. C. Berkeley. He is the author of numerous highly acclaimed books and articles on California history and is also a member of the Bohemian Club. Naturally, his scholarly treatises about the club all have a favorable bent, as do those written by the Bohemian Club's resident historian Al Baxter. Still, Bohemian Club members are the only ones who truly have the access needed to trace an accurate and thorough history of the club; most of the club's membership lists, histories, records and documentation are kept private, as are many of their activities. In this sense, the internal histories contain invaluable information to other researchers and authors, and I would recommend these books to anyone attempting to do serious historical research on the Bohemian Club. These internal histories were for the most part privately published, and quite rare to find on the collectors market. However, many are available for viewing in the club archives at Berkeley.

EVERYBODY IS A STAR

Back in 1887, the entrance fee for joining the Club was a hearty $100 and the dues were $3.00 a month, quite a bit of cash in those times. By 1930 it had risen to a $500 initiation fee and $15 a month dues. In the 1990s, the initiation fee for a regular member was $10,000 with $120 a month dues. Associate Members (artists, writers, and musicians) are generally admitted without a fee as "men of talent," and only pay half of the monthly dues.

In the early days of the Bohemian Club, activities included poetry recitations, performances by musicians, lectures and frequent plays. Regular entertainment became known as a "Jinks," named after a Scottish drinking game. A "Jinks" had a master of ceremonies known as a Sire who was in charge of orchestrating the program. These positions were filled on a rotational basis, so numerous men could become involved in Club theatricals.

Today Bohemians still maintain an active annual calendar of events. Currently the Club has an event almost every Thursday night of the year. These consist of various types of musical, theater, comedy, or variety shows sired by different individuals each week. Generally, these mid-week shindigs attract between 300–400 Club members. Postcards announcing Club events, often art pieces in themselves, are mailed out weekly to encourage attendance. The Club holds nearly 200 scheduled events a year.

"It is like being a Sunday painter." Bohemian Al Baxter told Dr. Peter Phillips in a 1994 interview for Phillips' dissertation, *A Relative Advantage.* "It's great for the amateur artist. Maybe he is not good enough to go pro or takes over Dad's business, but still has a yen as a tenor…So the Bohemia is made for this population…A guy writes funny skits, plays the cello and wants to do chamber music…They can have a little show and invite their friends…it's for their own private amusement."

To be a good Bohemian you are expected not only to participate in plays, workshops, and seminars, but also to take your turn at actually writing or organizing activities. For example, those with musical talent get together frequently at weekday lunches to "jam" informally. One of these jam nights was humorously titled "Can't Anyone Here Play?" in a 1971 Bohemian Club program of events. The music played might range from classical to jazz or rock, depending on the musicians and types of instruments available. And there are always plenty of instruments available; the Grove employs a full time orchestra, and also keeps a beautiful grand piano at the encampment year-round. At noon every day, an organ concert is given, followed by a distinguished orator standing beside a lake covered with water lilies straight out of a Monet painting, reciting verse. Meanwhile, someone else on another stage might be talking about "The Music and Poetry of the Harlem Renaissance."

The Club has a long history of various special events that date back to early Club years. These annual traditions become meaningful in members' lives. This allows an emergence of a personal sentimentality that has been described as the "Spirit of Bohemia". Over the years, numerous Bohemians have written and talked about this spirit. In 1977, Kevin Starr said, "...*the Bohemian Club fights the mechanization or the routinization of modern life. In a charming, naive way it asks the worldly-wise...successful American men to feel vulnerable again...Pleasure, true pleasure...has a way of doing that, of bringing to life old, lost dreams about art, beauty, and friendship.*"

The Bohemian Grove has been a major contributing factor to the Club's international reputation. The ownership and exclusive use of a private ancient redwood grove has placed the Bohemian Club in a unique position among elite men's' clubs of the world. The maintenance of a stylistically traditional city clubhouse rooted in the anachronism of a 19th century English gentlemen's club has also contributed to its distinction. To members, the Bohemian Club and Grove stand as time-honored sentinels against the crassness of a modern age. As men pass and the next generation matures, the sacredness of these private spaces multiplies. Members share in the belief that a man's honor recorded in Club history is as immortal as the sacred redwoods themselves.

BOHEMIAN RHAPSODY

In 1878, several dozen Bohemians held a Jinks in the forest in Sonoma County near what is now known as Camp Taylor. This was the start of a long Bohemian tradition of making the pilgrimage to the Sonoma County redwoods during July and August of each year for the annual midsummer encampment. In 1880, the Club conducted their first Hi-Jinks at nearby Duncan Mills. By 1882, Bohemians were doing regular midsummer weekend campouts under the stars at various locations in Sonoma County. They rented what is now known as the Bohemian Grove from the Sonoma Lumber Company between the years of 1893–1899.

Sonoma County was heavily logged during the latter part of the 19th century. The completion of the transcontinental railroad made this possible, and railroad spurs were built into vast areas along the Russian River where clear cutting was a common practice. Bohemians would ride the trains from Marin County to the remaining forested sites for overnight camping.

Sonoma Lumber Company had preserved a particularly beautiful grove of old growth redwoods in the hopes of greater profits at a later date. It was this 160-acre property surrounded by clear-cut lands that the Bohemian Club arranged to purchase from D. L. Westover in 1901. Cutting of redwood was forbidden and John McLaren, superintendent of Golden Gate Park in those days, was invited to plan the trails, the reforestation, and to install the water pressure system at the Grove. Over the past century, that original tract of land has grown as the Club continues to buy up all of the available surrounding property. The Bohemian Grove now consists of 2,712 acres.

But even in those formative years, there were plenty of people who resented the exclusiveness of the Bohemian Club. Residents of nearby Guerneville protested the Club's private use of one of the last old growth redwood groves in the area and petitioned for a public road through the property. Local families had enjoyed use of the land for years as a place for picnics, swimming, and for their children to play. They did not appreciate this recreation spot being made off-limits to them. Private property rights prevailed, however, and the Grove has been maintained exclusively for Club use up to the present day.

Initially the Bohemian Grove was kept in a mostly natural state, with members erecting tents along the valley floor for long weekends. By 1914 members were extending weekend campouts to three weekends over two weeks, and more permanent cabin structures were constructed around the property, many of which still stand today.

The Club grew rapidly before World War I and had a membership of 1,259 in 1914. Clearly, the Bohemian Club had accomplished something unique among elite men's clubs by combining a city-based club with a rural retreat. This particular rural-urban combination earned the Bohemian Club a worldwide reputation as a gathering place of the power elite, attracting business, political and cultural leaders for a romp in the redwoods. By World War I, the Bohemian Club had emerged as a premier elite men's club, with a flourishing arts and literary program and a one-of-a-kind private redwood grove. Early Bohemians liked to publicize their prominence by releasing news reports of important guests attending the Grove or Club functions. In fact the Club was so famous that in 1921 the United States Shipping Board allowed a tanker built by Moore Shipping in Oakland to be named The Bohemian Club. A full Club ceremony was held at the launching, with the Club chorus singing as the ship slid down the ramp.

The *San Francisco Chronicle* is an excellent source for tracking notable visitors to Bohemia. The paper boasted with great civic pride the names of famous entertainers who came to visit the popular Grove summer encampment. From Charlie Chaplin and Douglas Fairbanks clowning on the Grove stage in 1922 to Sir Hamilton Hart, conductor of the London Symphony Orchestra appearing with the Grove musicians in 1931, the *Chronicle* printed all the celebrity comings-and-goings for their readers to devour. Novelist Thomas Beer came to the Grove in 1926, Ossip Gasrilowitsch, famed pianist with the Detroit Symphony Orchestra visited in 1927, humorist Will Rogers in 1928, and motion picture director Edmund Goulding in 1929.

From the club's earliest years up through the 1930s, the San Francisco press afforded regular coverage of the annual encampment in glowing, reverent tones. An example of this type of reporting can be found in the Society Column of the *San Francisco Chronicle*, July 28, 1922:

> *"Among the celebrities [at the Grove] is that noted builder of public parks, Frederick Law Olmsted, who helped to plan the beautifying of such cities as Washington, Boston, Cleveland, and so on. He is president of the American Society of Landscape Architects and head of the Sage Foundation Homes and is on the United States Housing Corporation that did such ideal things during the war. Mr. Olmsted is in the party that H.T. Cory is entertaining.*

> *...Among the big guns in the William H. Crocker camp is Dr. Henry Smith Pritchett, president of the Carnegie Foundation for Teaching, a trustee of the Carnegie foundation of the Metropolitan Museum...*

> *Another who stars among Who's Who in America is Ray Long, the popular editor of the Red Book, the Blue Book, the Green Book and other magazines not exactly in the chromatic scale but equally popular and important, such as that highbrow International Magazine, and so on. George Horace Lorimer of the Saturday*

Evening Post, with Mrs. Lorimer and their children, the latter in town, is among the big editorial guns at the grove.

Charlie Chaplin of the funny feet ought to look awfully well up there on the benches and logs of the grove, and one wonders if Douglas Fairbanks, who is also there, is practicing jumping from treetop to treetop or something like that. It would be hard to visualize either of them in a quiescent unstrenuous mood.

...Lieutenant-Commander Frederick C. McMillan of Washington, DC, on duty with the Paymaster-General of the Navy, is visiting with his friends at the Bohemian Grove. Admiral David Potter, chief of the Bureau of Supplies and Accounts of the Navy, is here renewing friendships at the Grove...Commander Virgil J. Dixon is with friends at the Bohemian Grove for a week or longer.

One is really overcome with the idea of all those notables up there admiring California, being one of us, having a gloriously good time just the same as the plain everyday human. The list is indefinably long and overwhelming with its scintillating greatness.

They come from Europe, Australia, from every State in the Union. Even Paris has sent several who really had the heart to leave that gay city for the majestic beauty of the redwood camp on the Russian River.

And just fancy, probably many San Franciscans have never even seen this enchanting spot within a few hours travel from here and within the limits of a $10 weekend outing from this city.

One of the most delightful things about the crowd up there is that while there are millionaires galore and big financiers, every one, including themselves, can forget this role about them and see them as "one of the boys." Generals and admirals, with a number of colonels and captains, their gold braid at home, are probably having the time of their young lives—one hopes so, anyway."

And so goes the typical coverage of the Bohemian Club's summer camp from an obedient and obviously star-struck local press in the 1920s. Of course, all that media attention would soon disappear—quietly—within the next decade as the Grovers instituted a press blackout that is still the standard operating procedure to this day.

Many visiting celebrities to the Grove made use of the adjacent Northwood Golf course, built in 1926 as a complement to the Bohemian Grove. A walking bridge gave club members easy access to the course designed by Jack Neville, a Bohemian who also designed the famed golf course at Pebble Beach.

Northwood is the world's only course with redwoods lining all nine holes. Some of the celebrities who have played here over the years include Arnold Palmer, Adolph Menjou, Douglas Fairbanks Sr., Bing Crosby, and the late Bob Hope. Lowell Thomas, nationally renowned news and travel commentator (perhaps best known for introducing us to the real Lawrence of Arabia during WWI), used to broadcast his radio show from Northwood while he was in town for the Grove's annual midsummer encampment.

Prohibition dealt a major blow to the hard-drinking club's festivities in the 1920s by closing the central Grove bar. The communal big party atmosphere of the Grove changed during this time, as club members were forced to adjourn to their private camps to indulge in a few sips of bootleg liquor they had smuggled in.

During the Coolidge years, the Bohemian Club's waiting list appeared for the first time, and it soon grew to ridiculous lengths as more and more "men of use" clamored to join up. By 1927, most of the Grove's nearly 2,800 acres had been purchased for $99,500. The Bohos now had all the privacy and space they required to do whatever they pleased without scrutiny.

HI AND LO JINKS

While theatrical traditions at the Grove started with a humble "Jinks" in the redwood forest, the productions have grown considerably more sophisticated through the years. But one thing remains constant—there is still live entertainment every night at the Grove, as there has been from the earliest days. During weekdays the programs range from an orchestral concert to campfire variety shows. It is the weekend evenings when the full stage productions and Broadway style shows are performed. The second Saturday is the Low Jinks, which has become, by tradition, a rollicking farce designed to create a good below-the-belt laugh. The 1993 Low Jinks was entitled *Sherwood Estates*, and was described in the program of events as "a recently discovered episode of Robin Hood and His Merry Men". The 1980 production was entitled *Forever Chastity*, a comedy involving a princess and a Gypsy in the mythical 16th century kingdom of Buxomburg. Male members in drag impersonating female characters delivered most of the big laughs.

The actors are all generally Bohemians, although on occasion a special guest may be featured as a star attraction. The Low Jinks is performed in the Field Circle, which is a steep outdoor amphitheater (located nearest the Pink Onion camp, noted for its pink bedsheets), with a full professional quality stage and the towering redwoods as a backdrop. The 1989 Jinks was called *Sculpture Culture*, revolving around a character named Rex Greed, an effeminate gallery owner who sells toilets as art. He tries to convince a fellow artist that the latest trend is sculptures made of garbage. One such sculpture was of a female torso whose breasts and buttocks had both been re-attached to the front. This "work of art" later ended up as a permanent fixture at Faraway Camp. She was renamed the "statue of Piece," and was displayed up against a wall with a fern leaf wedged between her buttocks. She made an appearance in the *Owl Hoots* cartoons the next day, in which one of the Bohemians remarked she would be "fun to dance with."

Men in drag played all of the female roles, and every time they paraded across the stage, the crowd went nuts. A mental picture of this might look like one of the floorshows in *La Cage Aux Follies*. The female roles were obviously written to be demeaning to the fairer sex, with characters like Bubbles Boobenheim (a showgirl) and all of the secretaries in the play were cast with fat Bohemians. After one character in the show referred to the secretaries as "heifers," the audience chimed in with a hearty "moo." If you're not into racist or sexist jokes (such as this tasteless punch line from Rex Greed: "The only difference between rape and rapture is *salesmanship*."), better avoid the Low Jinks altogether.

When it comes to the decidedly lowbrow Low Jinks, the play is *not* the thing. The thin plots and bathroom humor of these theatricals indicate that nobody here is looking to win a Tony Award. It's the star power that makes the plays worthwhile. You never know who is going to make a cameo onstage. Even in a lame show like *Sculpture Culture*, the highlight wasn't Bubbles Boobenheim; it was the surprise appearance of Grovers Peter O'Malley and Bob Lurie, respective owners of the Los Angeles Dodgers and the San Francisco Giants, in full baseball uniform.

Another surprise cameo featured a man walking out of an elevator onstage wearing a rubber Henry Kissinger mask. One of the "heifers" asked him, "can

I help you?" The man then pulled off his mask, revealing that he really *was* Henry Kissinger.

He spoke only one line, but it made the crowd explode in cheers: "I am here because I have always been convinced that The Low Jinks is the ultimate aphrodisiac."

Observing the 1989 Low Jinks show, *Spy* magazine's Weiss wrote: "At such times, among strong leaders, deep in the forest—the Grove takes on a certain Germanic *ubermenschlich* feeling." This is probably not exactly the type of publicity the Bohos were hoping for—is it any wonder that the press is cordially *not* invited to camp?

Prior to the media blackout imposed on the Grove in the 1930s, events (particularly theatrical ones) at the Grove received a great deal of publicity from the local newspapers. Researchers can learn much about the Grove's history from simply studying news coverage of the day. One example from the July 20, 1922 edition of the *San Francisco Chronicle* speaks glowingly of the Grove's annual "Jinks."

> *"There was a rollicking time last Saturday evening at the opening of the camp for 1922. The feature of the evening was a dinner, followed by an inimitable campfire program, such as only the Bohemians can present.*

> *Next Saturday will be a gala occasion. First there will be the elaborate ceremony, "The Cremation of Care." The principal parts will be taken by Harry Perry as The King, Frank Corbucier as the Chancellor, Boyd Oliver as the Priest, Fred Myrtle, the Merchant, and Care, played by Wilbur Hall.*

> *Following that will be unfurled the misadventures of "Rosie Crucian, or the Bohemian Girl," which will be given under the direction of David Eisenbach. On the following morning there will be a band concert at 11 o'clock.*

(**Author's note:** "Rosie Crucian" dates back to the days of Elizabethan England, using the old English spelling for the occult Rosicrucian society.)

> *Thursday evening, July 27, in the field circle of the grove, an entertainment will be given by the Bohemian Club Little Symphony Orchestra, directed by Alex Saslavsky. The presentation of the "Semi-Centennial High Jinks," written by Haig Patigian, with two musical numbers especially contributed to the program by Henry Hadley and Wallace A. Sabin, has been set for the following evening.*

The Grove Play, "The Rout of the Philistines," will be staged on Saturday evening, July 29. This play was written by Charles G. Norris and its music composed by Nino Marcelli. It will be presented under the direction of Reginald Travers…

The 1922 Jinks will end the next day with a concert by Nino Marcelli."

THE GROVE PLAY

The last Friday night of the encampment is the annual Grove Play. Since the dawn of the 20th Century, an original play has been performed on the Grove stage each summer. The tradition continues to this day, and remains one of the high points of the annual summer encampment. These plays, known as the "Midsummer High Jinks" before 1912, are written each year exclusively for this one-time presentation. Grove plays are theatrical extravaganzas that cost tens of thousands of dollars to produce and can involve up to two hundred actors.

Cast of the 1915 Grove Play, "Apollo."
Jack London is in the center of the back row.
(Photo Jack London Archives, Bancroft Library)

The 1980 Grove play *Olympus* was an adaptation of the Greek myth of Cronus and Zeus supplemented with fireworks, smoke bombs, a light show, and a cast of more than 100. One can only wonder if Bohemian Ronald Reagan ever starred in a Grove play. He certainly has more acting experience than most club members do, although entertainers such as Jose Ferrer, Eddie Albert, Merv Griffin, George Gobel, and Art Linkletter have donated their talents to productions on the Grove stage.

Much like the Low Jinks, the Grove Play also contains its share of sexual innuendo, some of it very overt, indeed. For example, a poster advertising the 1989 Grove Play, *Pompeii*, featured a giant erection underneath a toga. The set for the play included a wall inscription in Latin (*semper rigidus*) meaning "Always Hard."

War and conquest are also recurring themes in Grove Plays. For example, the 1992 Grove Play, *Cristoforo Colombo*, memorialized the 500th anniversary of the morning Columbus set sail from Spain to discover and conquer the Americas. The 1993 Grove Play, *Oin Shihuang-Di, The First Emperor*, is described in the official Bohemian Grove program as follows: "Taoist priests prophesies the imminent attack of the six warring states...Victory will depend on one lowly foot soldier...Prince Feng attempts to murder his brother...Emperor builds his mausoleum to include 7000 warriors and Empress Liang and ten concubines."

Bohemian Kevin Starr, remarking on the special spiritual significance of the Grove Play, said, "The Grove play might last for only an hour, but that hour is an important one...Its memory of its own past and its references to the menial aspects of human experience are symbolically presented with breath taking intensity. Ironically, the Grove play, our best defense against accusations of triviality, our best expression of identity...is an essential moment in the yearly Bohemian cycle...because these plays so affirm the club's deepest identity, they are worth the expense of production..."

Grove plays are indeed costly, elaborate spectacles. The general public is not invited nor allowed to see these for-members-only shows. One could well make an issue of the expense, the exclusivity, and the irony of a play about poor people presented to economic and social elites. Because Grove plays are often specially written and produced for a single performance at the Grove, and are never seen before the public, it is difficult to trace the titles of some works. Few public sources are available. The best resources are club histories kept at the California Historical Society, University of California Bancroft Library, and the California State Library.

On the theatrical side, the Mandeville Special Collections Library at the University of California, San Diego, yielded one particular historical treasure: an album of photographs and ephemera, apparently collected by George G. Clark to document his stay at the Bohemian Club in August of 1923. Included are many rare photographs of the Bohemian Grove and its guests, and photographs of the Grove play *Semper Virens*.

Semper Virens is also the name of a camp within the Grove. In translation from the Latin, this means "always prepared," "ever ready," or "ever living." Probably not coincidentally, the Semper Virens Masonic Lodge (Six Rivers Lodge #106, California F&AM) was founded that same year of 1923 and named for the majestic coastal redwood tree, *Sequoia Semper Virens*, found in abundance at the Grove.

Although these plays are especially written, produced, and performed for club members, and are usually never performed again, a few of the more famous plays have been published in book form through the years, such as the 1940 Grove Play. Written by Benjamin Allen Purrington, *Saul—A Grove Play* was obviously a musical spectacular, with music composed by Charles Hart.

Although his name is hardly recognized today outside of literary circles, poet, playwright and Bohemian Witter Bynner was as well known early in the 20th Century as his friends Carl Sandberg, D.H. Lawrence and Edna St. Vincent Millay. Bynner (1881–1968) was also a translator of several foreign languages, essayist, and editor. He was an early supporter of O. Henry, Ezra Pound and Langston Hughes, helping them to get their first works widely published. Bynner was also openly homosexual.

Born in 1881, he went to Harvard with Wallace Stevens and Franklin Delano Roosevelt. Upon graduation, went to *McClure's* Magazine, where he arranged to bring O. Henry to the staff. Bynner was committed to Walt Whitman's sense of democracy as a brotherhood; in fact he worshipped Whitman, both as his literary and political hero. He was also an avid FDR supporter. Bynner felt Americans should "tolerate communism" if the US was to be a "true democracy".

He went to teach at UC Berkeley in 1918, refusing to fight in WWI. He was in the Bohemian Club and was about to write the 1920 Grove Play for his men's group when he was caught up in a bitter controversy over his support of the release of conscientious war objectors from prison. Local civic leaders threatened him and the issue was all in the newspapers. Due to all this, he abandoned the play—and Berkeley—for good.

Another reason for his swift departure from UC Berkeley involved a "quiet scandal" where he had been caught serving alcohol to freshmen in his rooms. He admitted to the university authorities it was true, and agreed that this was incorrect behavior for a professor. Because of Bynner's social status, the university brass decided to let the matter drop, probably fearing the scandal that would undoubtedly erupt once it was discovered that Professor Bynner was doing more with these young men than just having a few beers alone in his room. Perhaps he should have considered entertaining the young men at the Grove instead, where such activity would not have been considered quite so out of line.

THAT'S ENTERTAINMENT

Music also plays a pivotal role in the Bohemian Club. Many famous musicians attend the Grove camp each summer. A full-time orchestra is employed by the Bohemian Club, most of whom live in residence at the Grove and participate in concerts year-round. Some are professionals, some amateurs. Each year a number of the campers leave the Grove and go to the local elementary school in Monte Rio, the small town where the Grove is located. They put on a variety show open to the public, with money from ticket sales benefiting local schools. The 1987 benefit performance featured a Mariachi band of Bohemian clubbers called "Los Amigos." Among the performers in past years at the benefit were tenor Dennis Day and comedian-storyteller Art Linkletter.

Linkletter is a perennial favorite, both onstage at the Grove and at these annual Monte Rio benefit shows. Millions of radio listeners and television viewers have listened and watched Linkletter, and many consider him to be the world's greatest senior entertainer. Most Americans remember him as the host and creator of the popular TV show *House Party* (which ran for 25 years on CBS) and *Kids Say the Darndest Things* in the 1950s. He is now 90 years old and still hard at work. But perhaps even more illustrious than his entertainment career are Linkletter's personal, political and business interests.

He served on President Nixon's National Advisory Council for Drug Abuse Prevention; on the Presidential Commission to Improve Reading in the U.S., on President Reagan's Commission on Fitness and Physical Education; he was also Ambassador to Australia and named Commissioner General to the 150th Australian Anniversary Celebration. As both Linkletter and Nixon were proud Bohemian Club members together, it is fair to assume that their working relationship may have naturally evolved from the friendship they cultivated at the Grove.

Equally successful as a businessman, Linkletter has served on many Boards of Directors including MGM, Western Airlines, Kaiser Hospitals, and the French Foundation for Alzheimer's Disease, to name a few. As Chairman of the Board of Linkletter Enterprises, he oversees companies involved in the building and management of public storehouses, office buildings, cow-calf operations, real estate development, cattle and sheep stations in Australia, and various oil enterprises around the world.

In retrospect, the much-loved *Kids Say The Darndest Things* books and TV series may present a few troubling aspects, as pertains to the rumors of child sexual abuse and even accusations of child sacrifice taking place at the Bohemian Grove. The series gave Linkletter unprecedented access to young children, obtaining full cooperation from schools in recruiting kids and bringing them to Hollywood.

Linkletter reveals how this happened in an interview with *The New Sun* Newspaper:

> *"I went down and talked to the board of education to see if I could get kids from the grammar schools. They said, "If you hire a teacher—we'll provide you with a teacher—we'll go to all the schools and you have nothing to do with who the kids are. None of them are to be told what to say. You have a good reputation so we presume you won't be exploiting them or doing things with the kids." Taking children out of school to a commercial program in Hollywood was not an easy thing to convince a suspicious board of education...because everyone is trying to get into the schools one way or the other. So, I got the kids, and of course over 26 years I interviewed 27,000 children, all from 5–10 years old, which kept them under the difficult age of being smart alecs."*

Interesting words from a man known as perhaps the greatest commercial exploiter of kids in the 20th century.

Another favorite performer at Bohemian Grove is John Creighton Murray. Only a few years younger than Linkletter, Murray is classified as an all-time great violinist. When Murray played the classic *Ave Maria* for the Monte Rio audience, there was complete silence among the listeners, "as if he had cast a magic spell upon the entire crowd," said one local news account. The Bohemian Club annual benefit shows feature more famous entertainers on stage than any other show including those in Las Vegas, Hollywood and New York.

To summarize, the men who go to Bohemian Grove today are the same men who produce our major television shows and movies. They are the Hollywood elite. These are the men we have to blame for producing so much of this drivel, this non-issue TV, this mindless garbage that they are feeding our society now. It's easy to see where some of our societal problems are coming from just by looking at what they're putting on TV. Garbage in, garbage out—that's what's going on in our music, our video games, our movies. It's not just an American problem. Entertainment worldwide has sunk to a whole new low.

These people are trying to dumb us down, dumb our children down, and keep us distracted with lots of *Judge Judy*, *Cops*, and *Monday Night Football*. They know that by providing us plenty of gladiatorial diversions, we will be suitably placated. They don't want us thinking for ourselves, they don't want us talking about the Federal Reserve or the United Nations. They don't want us having the time or even the desire to research history or analyze the news we get. They don't want us to be talking about the Bush and Bin Laden families' long business partnership, and the big oil deals that are *really* motivating our foreign policy in the middle east.

That is precisely why power elites have always wanted to control popular entertainment—they see it as a useful tool for propaganda, suppressing independent thought and building consensus among the general public. The Bohemian Grove, with it's intermingling of top-name entertainers, big business tycoons and high level politicians, has proven an invaluable asset to the New World Order's agenda for a mind-controlled population.

Even more appalling is the knowledge that such a great deal of our arts and entertainment is filled with hidden occult meanings and symbolism. As the next chapter illustrates, this clever and secret (except to initiates) infiltration of our popular culture is, and always has been intended to bring about a certain magical result; to exert a powerful influence over the minds and belief systems of the masses.

Chapter VIII

Maireann a sgriobsar

(History cannot be denied)

A Midsummer Night's Dream
Mysticism in Art

"The Illuminati of the race are the custodians of Ageless Wisdom, dispensers of the truth that sets men free. There, unrecognized and unknown to the multitude, is that company of exalted Beings called Elder Brothers, who release into the world from time to time through suitable and qualified human instrumentalities, revelations most needed for their development.

It is to them we must look for the mighty creative impulse that manifested in Europe as the Renaissance and found its primary English expression in the brilliant literary lights of the Elizabethan Era—the greatest of which was Shakespeare. Thus Shakespeare becomes a link in a chain of inspired mediators through whom the race of men have come into possession of an ever-increasing knowledge of the divine Mysteries."

—From the Rosicrucian Fellowship International Headquarters Website.

While we can all read a book, hear a beautiful piece of music, or watch a play and be wholly entertained by only what is intended for us on the surface, anyone possessing keys to their deeper import discerns an added wealth of wisdom. For true authorship of works bearing the name of a Shakespeare or Goethe, a Beethoven or Mozart, one must peer behind the veil that conceals the Guardians of the Mysteries.

It is important to remember that the partnership between politics, business powers, and the entertainment industry is not strictly a 20th Century phenomenon. Because the connection between the occult and the arts is well-documented throughout history, it explains why these powerful men would naturally be attracted to a place like Bohemian Grove. Not only are they there to celebrate art, but perhaps more accurately, they are there to worship the same Pagan gods and esoteric symbols celebrated in the works of art themselves. For, as this chapter attempts to point out, most of the great artists, authors, playwrights, and composers of the past were also Freemasons and Illuminists.

A very early (and decidedly Pagan) Cremation of Care ceremony, circa 1915, featuring a live human offering instead of an effigy. Before the Cremation of Care became a mammoth stage spectacle, it was a somewhat small and informal gathering. Another key difference is that rather than 12 hooded acolytes, this ritual has only one High Priest. I have no earthly idea what the drawing in the lower left-hand corner is depicting. My best guess is the figure represents Dull Care, bound nude in a manner that is suggestively homoerotic.

SHAKESPEARE: FATHER OF FREEMASONRY?

The Bohemian Club's motto, "Weaving spiders, come not here", first appeared on a Club announcement in 1875. This quote was borrowed from Shakespeare, the Grove's patron saint of theatre. The motto was intended to speak to the inappropriateness of conducting or soliciting business at Club functions. But the *real* reasons for the apparent Shakespeare-worship practiced at the Grove probably has a lot more to do with the bard's own political and occult beliefs than mere enjoyment of his literary talents.

No one familiar with esoteric doctrines can have any question as to Shakespeare's familiarity with the wisdom of the illuminated. Those who believe that Shakespeare was merely a pen name for Sir Francis Bacon (1561–1626, known to many as "the Secret Bard") also assert that Shakespeare was the "Father of Freemasonry," as Bacon is widely acknowledged to be.

Occult studies of magic, black and white, are given illuminating treatment in *Richard III* and *The Tempest*, respectively. The spiritual significances of the winter and summer solstices are unfolded in *The Winter's Tale* and *A Midsummer Night's Dream*. Under the veil of fancy and frolic, the latter is a virtual transcription of the mystic marriage ritual as enacted in the Eleusinian Mysteries—in keeping with which the locale of the drama is a wood near Athens. Magical potions, charms, forest fairies and the supernatural all intertwine in Shakespeare's *A Midsummer's Night Dream*. This play is especially cherished by Bohemian Club members, serving as a virtual backdrop for the redwood rituals of midsummer. Indeed, the Grove's motto of "Weaving spiders come not here..." is taken from *A Midsummer Night's Dream*.

One of the strongest components of the "Father of Freemasonry" theory about Shakespeare is Alfred Dodd, editor of several volumes of Shakespeare's Sonnets. He also wrote a remarkable examination of the plays and poems, and makes a convincing case that these works were saturated in Masonry, that Shakespeare was a Freemason and that he was even the original founder of the secret fraternity.

While the roots of Freemasonry can be traced back to Germany—a group calling themselves the *Steinmetzen* (Stone Masons) existed as far back as the year 1080—speculative Freemasonry was born in Elizabethan England. Shakespeare took an active part in its genesis. The story is told in the *Great Shakespeare Folio of 1623*, which has been called "the greatest Masonic Book in the world". The System was buried in secret and left to grow in the dark for a hundred years. Dodd asserts that the emergence of the Masons in 1723 was a *planned* emergence, the centenary of the 1623 Folio. For Dodd and many other Masonic historians, William Shakespeare was not only a Freemason; he was the *father* and *founder* of the fraternity, the Writer of the Rituals.

These historical facts alone should be intriguing to students of Freemasonry. The birth of 'modern' Freemasonry is thereby subtly linked to Shakespeare, and it was in Shakespeare's time that the origins of modern speculative Freemasonry would seem to lie. Most importantly, the Shakespeare plays and poems bear abundant evidence of Masonic knowledge of Masonic customs, terms and teachings that could only have been known to a Mason of high degree. Indeed, the whole canon of Shakespeare plays and poems embodies both the philosophy and the degrees of initiation of Freemasonry, expressed in various allegories that are akin to and hint at the Masonic mysteries.

Elizabethan England was anything but a free society. Like Continental Europe at the time, the authority of the Monarchies and the Church was undisputed. Sovereigns held the power of life or death over their subjects. Authorities encouraged informers—spies—to hand in heretics and political radicals, who were then tortured into confessions before their executions. England was split over religion, and its coming renaissance was but a flicker in the minds of a tiny learned elite. It was a time of new ideas, change and excitement. Elizabeth I (1533–1603, queen from 1558) reigned at the height of the influence of the Renaissance. The Renaissance (1350–1600) was not merely an artistic movement in continental Europe. New ideas were fostered in the areas of astrology, alchemy, and magic.

It was also a golden age for theatre. The great playwrights William Shakespeare, Christopher Marlowe and Ben Jonson were all living at this same time. And all of them reflect an Elizabethan pre-occupation with magic, although they did not always embrace these new ideas in their work. Ben Jonson's play *The Alchemist* reveals a distinct wariness toward men who dabbled in the occult arts. In his play *Dr. Faustus*, Marlowe warns us of the dark power inherent in magic. Faustus sells his soul to the devil in return for knowledge and worldly success, but his dream is eventually shattered. For Marlowe, magic is a downright dangerous practice.

There is one other particularly interesting example of how Freemasons were tolerated and allowed to operate somewhat openly under Queen Elizabeth's rule. In The *New Book of Constitutions,* Anderson recounts how Elizabeth, "being jealous of all secret Assemblies", sent "an armed Force to break up" the Freemason's Grand Lodge at York on St. John's Day, 1561. But Sir Thomas Sackville, Lord Buckhurst, the Grand Master, *"took Care to make some of the Chief Men sent Free-Masons, who then joining in that Communication, made a very honorable Report to the Queen; and she never more attempted to dislodge or disturb them…"* again.

One can hardly impart the intellectual and spiritual climate of Shakespeare's England without a mention of John Dee. The career of John Dee (1527–1608) illustrates the way in which what we now distinguish as magic and science were not so separate in the Renaissance. Dee, Queen Elizabeth's astrologer, was a distinguished mathematician, pursuing research in geography and the reformation of the calendar. At the same time, he was a believer in the mystic power of numbers, and experimented with spiritualism, using an assistant and a crystal ball to talk with the archangels Michael, Gabriel, and Raphael. As well as deciding on which day she should be crowned, Dee became, in effect, a secret agent for her, uncovering plots to destroy the growing English navy, and developing cryptograms for communicating official secrets.

Dee was of Welsh origin—and proud of it—but the Welsh had a reputation for dabbling in the occult, a fact that contributed to his contemporary reputation. Dee was a devout Christian, but he was thought by many in his own time to be a magus. Since astrology was still part of the medical mainstream, however, many of his views were far from eccentric. There is some suggestion that Dee, or others like him, may have been the model for a few of Shakespeare's characters, most notably Prospero in *The Tempest*.

Occult Neo Platonism's dealings with the supernatural proved suicidal. The magical theory and practice, so easily seen as diabolism, was the exposed underbelly. Bruno was burned at the stake in Rome in 1600 and Dee was discredited, and died rejected and destitute in 1608 (Francis Yates believes *The Tempest* was written in his defense). While Shakespeare was still alive, the occult movement had retreated into various more or less secret societies and brotherhoods strongly colored by the Masons and Rosicrucians.

In the time of William Shakespeare there was also a strong belief in the existence of the supernatural. Thus, the supernatural is another recurring aspect in many of Shakespeare's plays. In two such plays, *Hamlet* and *Macbeth*, the supernatural is an integral part of the structure of the plot. In *Hamlet*, the supernatural (his father's ghost) is the guiding force behind Hamlet. The supernatural occurs four times during the course of *Macbeth*. It occurs in all the appearances of the witches, in the appearance of Banquo's ghost, in the apparitions with their prophecies, and in the "air-drawn" dagger that guides Macbeth towards his victim.

It appears that Shakespeare was greatly infatuated with astrology; his plays mirror the debate of his time between those who believed that the macrocosm of the stars influenced the microcosm of human life, and those who dismissed astrology as "excellent foppery." The phrase comes from Edmund in *King Lear*, who comments on his father's tendency to blame human evil on the stars. In *Julius Caesar* too there is a debate about the influence of the stars, with Cassius arguing for human responsibility: *"The fault, dear Brutus, is not in our stars. But in ourselves, that we are underlings."*

Richard III also casts a dark mystical aura; supernatural elements are intrinsic to this play. Dreams, ghosts, and curses—these supernatural elements all have a natural place in *Richard III*, for they weave together the fascinating horror in the storyline and ensure that the tyranny of a mortal man will not reign in the end.

The works of Shakespeare, like the music of Beethoven, Mozart and Wagner, Goethe's *Faust*, Dante's *Divine Comedy*, and a few other books of comparable rank, are designed for esoteric as well as exoteric absorption. In the minds of their creators, they are direct communications from planetary centers of Divine Wisdom.

In the case of Shakespeare, the source was the Western Wisdom School of the Rosy Cross. To the esotericist, no other evidence of this is required than the works themselves. But specific signatures, cryptically conveyed, are also present in the dramas. In *Love's Labour's Lost*, a whole scene is devoted to revealing the Rosicrucian connection; but it is so ingeniously involved in the banter of words that only those possessing the keys to its veiled meanings will read it correctly.

Shakespeare has been called "The Rosicrucian Mask." The long history of freemasonry, the English crown, and the theatre is well documented, even in Shakespeare's time. And the tradition continues today at Bohemian Grove, with the 1980s appearance of the Queen Elizabeth on the Grove stage for a very special royal "command performance".

There's no doubt that Shakespeare, whether he was a peasant playwright from Stratford-on-Avon, Sir Francis Bacon, the son of Queen Elizabeth I, or part of some vast conspiracy of time-traveling aliens, has had a tremendous impact upon Western culture for hundreds of years. Like the master magician Prospero in *The Tempest*, Shakespeare himself was adept in orchestrating powerful energies to his will.

BEETHOVEN AND THE BAVARIAN ILLUMINATI

Just as Shakespeare is the patron saint of the theatre at Bohemian Grove, Beethoven is the Grove's patron saint of music. It is Beethoven's 7th *Symphony* that is traditionally played during the Cremation of Care ritual, the mystical equinox of the Bohemians' summer fire festival. Why Beethoven? A closer look at Ludwig van Beethoven's historical life reveals a brilliant, tormented, and perhaps marked man with many clear ties to the original Bavarian Illuminati.

During Beethoven's formative years in Bonn, Germany, he came into contact with a number of "freethinkers", notably Count Waldstein, who were members of a radical sect called the Illuminati. This fact is well documented in most credible biographies of the composer. Bonn was a "University City" in which ideas freely circulated during the years leading up to the French Revolution; translations of works by the major French writers of the Enlightenment were freely available. It was in Bonn that Beethoven began his lifelong habit of reading widely. His music was profoundly influenced by literature, especially Shakespeare. He even composed his *Piano Sonata No. 17* in admiration of Shakespeare's *The Tempest*.

Christian Gottlob Neefe, a composer, organist, and conductor, was Beethoven's composition instructor in Bonn from 1781 to 1792. Neefe nurtured Beethoven's genius. It is also possible that he steered Beethoven's thoughts toward the esoteric. Neefe was a Mason and, perhaps more important, had been involved in a branch of the Illuminati. Neefe encouraged Beethoven's interest in Enlightenment ideas of freedom and brotherhood, which would inspire Beethoven throughout his life and achieve their most powerful expression in the magnificent Ninth Symphony.

Beethoven developed an interest in "oriental mysteries" through reading the Idealist philosophers Schelling and Schlegel, both of whom were heavily influenced by mythology. When he came across an inscription in *The Paintings of Egypt*, by J. F. Champollion (who decoded the Rosetta Stone), Beethoven copied it, had it framed, and hung it over his desk. It read: *"I am that which is. I am everything that was and is and shall be. No mortal has raised my veil. HE is himself alone, and to this only one all things owe their existence."* Later these verses found their way into Masonic ritual.

The role of the Illuminati in Beethoven's life is so important to his art that I quote here a telling passage from Maynard Solomon's *Beethoven* biography:

"Despite the receptivity to Enlightenment ideas, advanced and radical thinkers were constantly on the alert for signs of repression. A Freemason's lodge had been founded in 1776 but it soon disappeared, perhaps because (the Empress) Maria Theresa had suppressed Freemasonry within the Austrian territories. Its place was taken by a secret, anticlerical Order of Illuminati, founded in 1781, which combined Enlightenment notions of 'progress through reason' with quasi-Masonic ritual. Its members included many who were associated with Beethoven... The order was uncovered and suppressed in Bavaria—its headquarters—in 1784-85, and the Bonn Illuminati, fearing a prohibition, dissolved their group in favor of a less dangerous forum, the Lese-Gesellschaft (Reading Society), which was founded in 1787 by thirteen 'friends of literature', who included most of the former Illuminati. Soon its membership numbered 100..."

Among these were Franz Ries, Court musician, family friend and violin tutor to Beethoven (his son Ferdinand in turn became a pupil of the composer in Vienna); the revolutionary Professor Eulogius Schneider and the aforementioned Count Ferdinand Ernst Gabriel Waldstein und Wartemberg von Dux, Knight of the Teutonic Order. It should not come as a surprise that many aristocrats numbered among the political radicals of the period. These "enlightened" or "illuminated" elites saw reform as essential to prevent violent revolution and looked to a "good prince" to bring about change.

Beethoven retained his passion for revolutionary politics throughout his life, and the evidence for this surfaces frequently in his music. The influence of the group of Illuminists with whom Beethoven associated thus resulted in the young composer's admiration for the reformist emperor Joseph II, who provided the first embodiment of the 'hero' in Beethoven's music, in 1790, in *the Cantata on The Death of Joseph II*. The libretto was written by a local poet Severin Anton Averdok for a memorial service held by the Reading & Recreation Society of Bonn (*i.e. the Illuminati*).

Although the Illuminati only existed openly for six years, the secret society continued its' operations underground, under many different organizational names. A chapter of the *Order of Illuminati* also existed in Vienna, in a disguised form, of course, and it has been suggested that the Lichnowskys (Beethoven's closest royal patrons for many years) were members of it. This linkage explains Beethoven's access to the highest levels of Viennese society from his arrival in the capital. It also explains his financial independence, the result of three aristocrats (including Prince Karl Lichnowsky) collaborating to provide him with an income. It also explains the continuing presence in Beethoven's music of a subtext of revolutionary politics. We now take this for granted as an element of Beethoven's eccentric character. But Vienna was the center of the Hapsburg Empire, and the most conservative capital in Europe. People were frequently arrested and imprisoned for being less outspoken than Beethoven was.

Beethoven's passion for radical politics, which was ignited in Bonn, later became entangled in a love affair with one of Vienna's three most beautiful women, the Princess Lichnowsky herself. She would go on to become both the inspiration for many of his greatest early works; all of which have romantic, heroic themes. The first piece Beethoven dedicated to the Princess Marie-Christiane Lichnowsky is the Variations on *See the Conquering Hero Comes* from Handel's *Judas Maccabeus*. The work was written in 1796 while Beethoven was still in residence with the Lichnowskys.

Their affair was illumined by intelligence and humor, and the seal was set on his music, ensuring that politics, philosophy, metaphysics, music and sex were forever enmeshed inextricably. Two of his most famous piano sonatas, the Opus 26 and the Opus 13, the *Pathetique* (composed 1798), were dedicated to Marie-Christiane's husband, Prince Lichnowsky, suggesting a rather unusual arrangement between these three. Beethoven was lodged as a guest in the Lichnowsky's home during his first few years in Vienna, his room just across the hall from the couple's bedroom inside the palace. They were the first to recognize his genius, funded the publication of his Opus 1 (the first three Piano Trios) and "induced the entire nobility to support him," according to Maynard Solomon's biography of Beethoven.

The *Symphony No. 3 in E flat* was originally dedicated to Napoleon Bonaparte, but later became known as the *Eroica*. Upon learning that Napoleon had crowned himself Emperor (thus betraying the ideals of the Enlightenment), the composer removed the dedication in a fury. Up until that time, Beethoven had been a very vocal supporter of Napoleon, an ardent Republican, and Beethoven was shocked at the tyrant Napoleon had become. Tearing out the title page of his *new Symphony in E flat*, and scratching out Bonaparte's name so hard that he ripped the paper, Beethoven raged: *"Is he then nothing more than an ordinary human being? Now he, too, will trample on all the rights of man and indulge only his ambitions. He will exalt himself above all others and become a greater tyrant than anyone!"*

In 1808, Beethoven composed his Fantasia for piano, chorus and orchestra (also known as the *Choral Fantasy*), which was later recycled as the theme for *the Ode to Joy* in the Ninth Symphony. The content of the verse in both the *Fantasia* and the *Ode to Joy* is undeniably similar, and in each we find, in poetic code, a statement of the ideals of the 18th century Enlightenment, carefully phrased to avoid political censorship.

We must first consider that Schiller's first intention in writing his verse was to call it *Ode to Freedom*. The word "Joy" was substituted to avoid political censorship, since the words "Freedom" and "Liberty" were now revolutionary terms.

Lyrics from the *Ode to Joy* by Friedrich von Schiller:

> *Praise to Joy, The God Descended,*
> *Daughter of Elysium,*
> *Ray of mirth and rapture blended*
> *Goddess to thy shrine we come.*

The radical message in Schiller's verse is clear. He not only advocates freedom (joy) but, by invoking subversive pagan imagery (through goddess worship) alludes to the secular goddess 'Liberty,' whose image was already a revolutionary icon, and whose statue today stands in New York Harbor, a gift to the US from the French Freemasons. She is the "Daughter of Elysium", the Greek name for Paradise. Being a "God descended" means that she will bring Paradise to earth.

During the Romantic age, when Republicanism was rising against the old world order of Europe, music and art were celebrated as weapons in the battle against tyranny. Secret police were present in the audience at the premier of Beethoven's Ninth Symphony to ensure that no treason was sung. It was, but they didn't notice. The message was cleverly veiled.

Beethoven himself was admittedly fascinated with occult sciences such as numerology, and his fascination with "power numbers" and inserting coded messages in the numeric musical alphabet into his works are well proven. And Beethoven's own life numbers contained some very interesting clues; the numbers nine and eleven seem to have a recurring and powerful presence in his life and destiny. His full name has the numerological value of the number nine. Ludwig has six numbers, Van, 3 numbers. Add them and you have nine. His last name, Beethoven has 9 letters. The sum of his name is 18. In the practice of numerology, two-digit numbers are always reduced to a single digit. This is done by adding the two numbers together. In this case, 8+1=9, so the number nine represents not only his first and middle names, but his last name as well. It also represents the numerological value of the exact date of his death. This is quite unusual.

By numerological calculations, Beethoven's life number was 11. A person's life number tells us a great deal about their personality, much as a person's zodiac sign does. It is well-known that the number 11 is considered sacred in esoteric circles and especially freemasonry, where it forms part of the Masonic triangle, at 11, 22, and 33 degrees.

The date of Beethoven's death (March 26, 1827) also adds up to the number 11 (3+2+6=11), and the year of his death adds up to the number 9 (1+8+2+7=18. Reduce to single digit by adding 1+8=9), both powerful numbers in his life and also to "enlightened" freemasons. A Masonic obelisk sits atop Beethoven's grave, a sort of miniature Washington monument.

It is also interesting to note that Beethoven's final symphony was the Ninth Symphony, which was heavily laced with hidden Masonic symbolism. There is an old superstition amongst classical composers that they will die after writing their Ninth Symphony—which in several cases proved strangely true, such as that of Gustav Mahler. Mahler was a neurotic who was obsessed with death. He even consulted Freud about his superstitions. In particular, he was terrified of completing his Ninth Symphony, because Beethoven, Schubert and Bruckner had all died after penning their Ninth. So when he wrote his Ninth Symphony, he attempted to dodge fate by skipping the cursed number nine and calling it *Symphony No. 10* instead! This only seemed to speed the dreaded "curse of the Ninth Symphony"—Mahler died soon thereafter, before his Ninth was ever performed.

Speaking of bizarre superstitions, it may be worth noting that some new conspiracy theories have come to light in recent years alleging that Beethoven did not die of natural causes as previously reported. Some believe that Beethoven's Illuminati "friends" eventually turned on him, and silenced him for his political views. First, through withdrawing their patronage, driving him into poverty and discrediting him in the public eye. Second, by slowly poisoning him over a long period of time, leading to his subsequent mental instability and painful physical ailments that lead to his death. In a recent book by Gail S. Altman, *Fatal Links: the Curious Deaths of Beethoven and the Two Napoleons,* (Anubian Press) the author, a Beethoven scholar for 45 years, raises suspicions that ironically, Beethoven may have suffered the same fate of his one-time hero, Napoleon.

While it may sound fantastic at first, remember the assassination of John Lennon. The former Beatle was a revolutionary musical and political icon who had the power to influence millions of young minds, arguably the Beethoven of his own time. His fatal shooting in December, 1980 by Mark David Chapman, a CIA-trained MK-Ultra "lone nut" gunman, conveniently eliminated Lennon, who had been on the federal government's secret "hit list" since the Nixon administration. Is it then such a stretch to consider that Beethoven may have also been "eliminated" for the progressive political messages in his music, silenced as John Lennon was?

It is indeed interesting to note that the date of John Lennon's assassination—December 8, 1980—also has the numerological value of 11. (12/8/ 1980. 12+8=20 [2]. 1+9+8+0=18 [1+8=9]. 2+9=**11**.)

THAT OLD BLACK MAGIC

Fantasy and occult themes have always been very prevalent in classical music. To give just a few better-known examples, let us look at some of the musical works performed by the Bohemian Grove house orchestra through the years.

On the subject of forest creatures, there is *Ballad of the Gnomes* by Ottorino Respighi. This piece of music has been described as "an orgy of sexual abuse", as the fantasy tale involves a group of female gnomes who capture and subjugate a group of male gnomes to extremes of torture and rape.

Another Grove favorite is one of Percy Grainger's most poignant works; *My Robin is to the Greenwood Gone*. Not an ode to that popular garden bird of Christmas folklore, but a lament for the fall of Paganism to the Christian usurpers of the middle ages. The "Robin" of the tune refers to Robin Goodfellow, the spirit of all nature and green places, perhaps better known as the gentle but sometimes mischievous player of the pipes, the Greek god "Pan".

Sergei Vasilyevich Rachmaninoff's symphonic poem *The Isle of the Dead* tells the tale of the ghostly ferryman transporting the coffin of the deceased, accompanied by a single silent mourner garbed in white, moving slowly across the still waters towards that place from which there is no return. It should come as no surprise that this piece is the one usually played at the Grove's Cremation of Care ceremony, as the bound body is brought across the lake by the hooded boatmen.

Felix Mendelssohn composed the overture to Shakespeare's *A Midsummer Night's Dream,* the Bohemian Club's favorite play, filled with forest fairies, magic and witchcraft. Speaking of witchcraft, there is *Dreams of a Witches' Sabbat,* the fifth and final movement from *The Symphonie Fantastique* by Hector Berlioz. The fourth and fifth movements both revolve around opium-induced dream sequences in which a man imagines he sees his recently deceased beloved surrounded by spectres and all the monsters of Hell, dancing to a demonic melody. The dance develops into a satanic orgy in a forest clearing where witches dance around her coffin, which is eventually offered up to the Devil. Insanity and chaos magick reign supreme.

Death is a strangely important theme in classical composition, often with dark undertones. An example of that would be Charles-Camille Saint-Saens' grisly piece *Dance Macabre.* In this piece, two skeletons rise from their graves at midnight, and waltz together to the music played by Death on his fiddle. And Franz Liszt composed a dance to honor the Prince of Darkness himself: *The Mephisto Waltz No. 1.*

Think of Gods, Heroes, Giants, Demons and Dwarfs, and Wagner's *Ring Cycle* automatically comes to mind. This mammoth operatic extravaganza which lasts just over fourteen hours comprises of four operas: *Das Rheingold, Die Walkure, Siegfried and Gotterdammerung.* Perhaps the best known piece from the entire cycle is the ever popular *Ride of the Valkyrie'*, played as Brunhilde and her eight sisters, all the daughters of Wotan, ride carrying the souls of slain heroes to everlasting triumph and merrymaking in the mythical heaven of Valhalla. This sort of Wotan-worship was sacred not only to Richard Wagner, but also to the rising Nazi party in Germany, who adopted his music to suit their "cause" of racial purity and "might makes right."

To further define and clarify the connection between occult and supernatural themes in the classical music so revered at the Grove, we must understand the mindset and spiritual beliefs of the composers themselves. Why do these themes keep showing up time and again in these composers's works? The answer, as will be shown below, is that most of the composers were freemasons and occultists in their private lives.

Wolfgang Amadeus Mozart was a Freemason and quite possibly an Illuminist. In late 18th century Vienna, esoterica was all the rage. Freemasonry was popular, as were dark intrigues, like the secret Order of the Illuminati, which combined rituals and initiations with radical politics. Indeed, the Baron Swieten, a patron of both Mozart and Beethoven and a collaborator with Franz Joseph Haydn (also a Mason), was involved in an alleged Illuminati plot in 1791, the year of Mozart's death. Like Beethoven, many of Mozart's other friends and colleagues were members of the Illuminati. And although there is no evidence that Mozart himself was involved, he would certainly have found the egalitarian ideals of the society's founder, Adam Weishaupt, a worthy cause.

Mozart became a Mason in 1784, joining Lodge Benevolence in Vienna, which would later be renamed New Crowned Hope. Other members included "the Magnificent" Prince Nicolaus Esterhazy, Haydn's famous patron. Mozart was certainly not the first to combine an interest in music with a taste for esotericism. Indeed, the link between music and esotericism goes back at least as far as the sixth century BCE, when the Greek sage Pythagoras discovered the laws of harmony and developed a mystical brotherhood around them.

Mozart took to Masonry with a passion, introducing Masonic elements into many of his works, and writing music specifically for Masonic affairs, like his moving *Masonic Funeral Music*. His final three symphonies form a triptych of Masonic initiation symbolism. But his greatest Masonic work is his opera *The Magic Flute* (1791), which centers on the archetypal struggle between Darkness and Light.

Masonic, Egyptian, and hermetic elements crowd the work—too many to elucidate here—but by the time Mozart wrote it, Freemasonry was on the defensive. The Illuminati had been suppressed in Bavaria, and Mozart had to muffle his esoteric themes in the innocuous fabric of a fairy tale. Nevertheless, much of the message got through, and one wonders if it is just by chance that Prague, the city that loved Mozart most, was the age-old home of alchemists, Rosicrucians, astrologers, and esotericists?

In this chapter, the esoteric fascinations of Shakespeare, Beethoven, Mozart and Wagner, whose works are celebrated and performed frequently on the Bohemian Grove's private stage, have been firmly established. Now it is easy to understand that the Bohemians' interest in these artists is likely much more than just musical or literary, and that the artistic focus of the Club serves as a perfect cover for its true occult nature. Just as the old Reading and Recreation Society in Bonn were the Illuminati in disguise, the Bohemians continue this age-old tradition at the Grove.

Chapter IX

Diabolus fecit, ut id facerem!

(The devil made me do it!)

"Midsummer Sets Us Free!"
The Bohemian Bacchanalia

"THE PRODUCTIVE DRUNK IS THE BANE OF ALL MORALISTS."

—Motto of the Grove's Sundodgers Camp.

This powerful chapter should be prefaced with a warning. It contains adult language, graphic sexual and violent content, and is not suitable for minors or those with easily upset stomachs! I have chosen to include this disturbing material in my book because what follows are eyewitness accounts of the activities that have gone on within the Grove. While these things may not be pleasant to think about, one cannot have a full understanding of the subject if this information is omitted. So if you're strong enough, read on. But be cautioned—this chapter leaves little to the imagination.

These are the secrets of the redwoods. And I am about to reveal them to you.

Imagine for a moment that you are one of the richest and most powerful men in the world. Picture yourself having everything money can buy, surrounded by every luxury and comfort. Let's say you venture to the Bohemian Grove each summer for two weeks of rest and relaxation amongst friends of your social caste. But just like most summer camps, "roughing it" in the wild loses its' luster after the first couple of days. So what to do then? One must find new ways to pass the time and stave off boredom somehow, right? The Bohos find their salvation in the time-honored tradition of "whiskey and wimmen," although as you will find out here, the sexual partners they choose are not always female.

But before we delve too deeply into that subject, let's start with something a bit more tame and at least legal (This, by the way, will be the only *legal* activity discussed in this entire chapter!). If you imbibe, this would be a good time to get up off the couch and pour yourself a stout cocktail. You're going to need it to dull the shock of the revelations that await you later in this chapter!

"DEMON" DRINK

Alcohol is definitely a major part of Bohemia and is available 24 hours a day at any camp bar. The brands of alcohol consumed are all premium or exotic liquors and San Francisco's Anchor Steam Beer is often on tap. Most of the individual camps have concocted some special drink or other that becomes their trademark. Probably the most infamous example is the "Nembutal Fizz," a specialty of Fore Peak camp.

As far as can be established, the so-called "Nembutal Fizz" is actually a stout blend of hot rum and hot chocolate. This drink is rumored to contain a powerful white powder barbiturate provided by a Bohemian executive from a major drug company. A doctor member of the club suggested the name many years ago, and the tradition he started is still honored today at Fore Peak Camp. It's not unusual to see one of the campers dressed in a doctor's lab coat with the name "Dr. Nembutal" stitched on it, a stethoscope around his neck. The drink has become so popular at the Grove, Bohos from every camp make a point to stop in at Fore Peak and consume at least one Nembutal Fizz during each annual encampment.

Perhaps the most seductive aspect of the Bohemian Grove is the open civility and hospitality of members. Dinner is probably the biggest social affair of each day at camp, and the meal is often preceded by a concert on the Grove's mammoth pipe organ. For 50 years of the Bohemian Club's existence, this was the second largest outdoor organ in the world. Dedicated in 1920, the organ contains 1,300 pipes up to sixteen feet in length, covering a range of eight octaves. Designed for outdoor use, it is stored away in a heated building with exact humidity controls during the off-season.

When the evening organ recital has ended, Grovers return to the dining circle for a full course meal. Dinners are livelier with the Jinks Band playing music. By this time, the effect of the day's alcohol is evident, loosening tongues and dropping defenses. The humor becomes far more ribald as the night progresses, and the drunker one is, the more one can presumably appreciate the non-stop barrage of locker room banter. Jokes at the Grove range from clever poems, dirty limericks and twists on words to gross misogynist or homophobic tales.

The conservative political bent of the club is sometimes most obvious in the types of jests members enjoy, whether at the dinner table or in smaller camp gatherings, where they feel much more at ease to speak freely. Language in the private camps includes a lot of four-letter words and some sexist, racist slurs disguised as humor. When Dr. Peter Phillips visited the Grove as a guest, he observed this behavior in only one of seven camps, and his conclusion was that this type of behavior is not the norm here; rather the exception. In his dissertation *A Relative Advantage*, he also observed that, "Clinton jokes were probably the most common humor among members in 1994. Judging from the frequency and on occasion strong angry tone of jokes about the President, I think that it is safe to say that there are few people at the Grove who like Bill Clinton, or if they do they are extremely quiet about it."

Four years later, the Clinton humor at the Grove would reflect every Monica Lewinski joke in the book. Perhaps a few new ones were invented here. Maybe the Bohos had gained a new respect for President Clinton; while at the same time many of them were sitting on the very committee designed to impeach him for his sexual offense. Privately, however, since he had been caught with his pants down in the oval office, the Grovers may have decided that Bill was "an allright guy" after all. Even if they still didn't like him, the Bohos certainly had a lot of low laughs at his expense.

It stands to reason that Bill Clinton's callous treatment of Ms. Lewinsky would likely raise the Bohemians' estimation of him as "one of the guys." In fact, the humiliation and disrespect of women is an integral part of Grove culture. Whether the Bohos are mocking feminine beauty by dressing up in crude drag, cracking sexist jokes around the campfire, or pinching the derriere' of a particularly attractive waitress as she passes by, it is clear that women are considered little more than objects to them.

Strangely ironic for an occult organization that worships a feminine goddess entity in their rituals to have such a low opinion of women, isn't it? These men gather before the owl idol representing Ishtar and invoke the magic powers of the female goddess; they celebrate her reproductive and regenerative ability to make all things in the forest new. The same men who ask for the Spirit of Bohemia's blessing upon them each year in the annual Cremation of Care ceremony are the same drunken fools you will find a few hours later engaged in an orgy with a group of prostitutes. Try to make sense of *that* logic.

SEX AT THE GROVE: PORN AND PROSTITUTES

Our story of the porn/prostitution connection to Bohemian Grove begins at the famous (or rather, infamous) Mitchell Brothers O'Farrell Theatre in the Tenderloin red-light district of San Francisco. For years, rumor has been that the Mitchell Brothers were the Grove's main supplier of strippers and high-class call girls from their legendary talent roster, and that they would then in turn tape their own girls engaged in sexual acts with the Bohos. In this chapter, I will bring forward new eyewitness testimony from four former Mitchell Brothers dancers who were prostituted to the Bohemians and pornographically filmed at the Grove. But before we hear from them, let me take just a minute to give tell you the fascinating and often twisted tale of the Mitchell Brothers "empire of smut," just to give you some idea of who we're dealing with.

Brothers and business partners Jim and Artie Mitchell were fraternal pornographers who just happened to make one of the most legendary films in porn history. The Mitchell brothers were called "visionaries of one-handed entertainment." In 1969, they opened the "cleanest" dirty-movie house in the Tenderloin, the O'Farrell Theatre. Three years later, they released the X-rated film *Behind the Green Door* (interestingly enough, the 'plot' of this film involves a young woman who is kidnapped and forced to perform in a bizarre live sex club) starring an apple-cheeked former Ivory Snow model named Marilyn Chambers. The brothers spent $60,000 and made $20 million.

The film was instantly a porno classic. The publicity generated ensconced the Mitchells in the pantheon of adult entertainment alongside figures like Larry Flynt and Hugh Hefner. In 1975 their adult theatre chain had expanded to 11 locations. Lawsuits brought by communities to keep them out, as well as police raids and even copyright disputes, kept the Mitchells in court the entire time their porn empire grew. In 1985, Mitchell veteran Marilyn Chambers was arrested for prostitution at the theatre; the brothers themselves were accused of pimping and went to court again.

By the late '80s the O'Farrell Theatre had become a world-class flesh temple featuring films and live sex acts where women gyrated, jiggled and convulsed to packed houses day and night. The talent included one Honeysuckle Divine, celebrated for playing a trumpet with her vagina. As word spread, some local elected officials at nearby City Hall were outraged. Especially then-Mayor Diane Feinstein, who detested the porn industry. Police raids became a regular occurrence in the Tenderloin and especially the O'Farrell Theatre. Eventually, it was Feinstein who lost the battle; she learned the proverbial lesson of politics—some people just can't be brought down. The Mitchell Brothers were well-protected. Having powerful friends at the Bohemian Grove, the brothers were quickly able to take the matter far over the Mayor of San Francisco's head. Case closed.

Feinstein's career did not suffer; she is currently U.S. senator from California. The O'Farrell remains in business, but the brothers' story is tragic. During a 1991 drug-fueled argument, Jim shot and killed Artie. Convicted of voluntary manslaughter, he served only three years and was released from San Quentin. Even after Artie Mitchell's death and Jim's imprisonment, problems kept coming for the Mitchell Brothers Theatre. In 1994, the club was exposed by Bay Area activist (who works for the legalization of prostitution) Carol Leigh in two documentary films. She filmed a "strippers strike" outside the club that made headlines all over San Francisco and heaped even more bad press on Jim Mitchell and friends. These ladies were loudly protesting labor violations and mistreatment by Mitchell Brothers.

In the meantime, the politics of porn were shifting. On July 28, 1999, the *Green Door* girl, by then nearly 50, returned to the O'Farrell stage. Mayor Willie Brown proclaimed it Marilyn Chambers Day in San Francisco. The Mitchell's' rise as porn czars and the murder of Artie Mitchell are chronicled in the 2000 *Showtime* cable film *Rated X* starring brothers Charlie Sheen and Emilio Estevez. Today, Mitchell Brothers O'Farrell Theatre is nationally noted as "The Carnegie Hall of Sex."

That doesn't mean that the problems are over for Mitchell Brothers. In September, 2000, former dancer Kathleen Pacello sued Jim Mitchell, having the courage to say what most people knew what had been covertly going on for years at the club—that the Mitchells *were* prostituting their girls. Pacello says she was raped by a patron while working there, and that the management urges the dancers to commit acts of prostitution. She was fired, she says, when she reported the rape and complained that the booths for "one-on-one sessions" were unsafe for the dancers.

In a July 3, 1999 article for *Salon.com*, journalist Annalee Newitz visited various strip clubs around San Francisco to write a story on the feminine response (or lack of it) to "gentleman's clubs." She writes:

> *"Although we'd grown accustomed to being the only women in the audience at a strip club, something about the Mitchell Brothers Theater was different. The only bathroom for women had to be opened with a key by a clerk at the front desk. We'd been in far sleazier clubs, but there was a strange, menacing atmosphere here that we hadn't felt before."*

"Even the music at Mitchell Brothers was unsettling." Newitz observed. *"While most strip clubs we'd seen had featured pop music, here every song was slow and soulful. The Eagles' "Hotel California" played while strippers writhed, groveled and posed—never dancing."* Probably not coincidentally, *Hotel California* is a song that Cathy O'Brien says was used for "programming" mind-controlled sex slaves in the Bohemian Grove chapter of her book, *TRANCE-Formation of America*.

As part of her "research," the journalist was given spending cash to buy lap dances with. When she and a dancer named June were alone in a plush Mitchell Brothers booth, she quickly discovered why the activity in *this* club seemed so secretive. She noticed a tidy rack next to her that contained condoms, lubricant, and rubber gloves. Newitz reveals what happened next:

> *"So you want a dance, right?" asked June when I gave her a twenty. "I haven't done a dance in a long time. This isn't really a strip club—it's a sex club."*
>
> *"You mean women here normally do more..." I trailed off uncertainly, not wanting to say the wrong thing.*
>
> *"Yes, some of the women here will have sex," she replied matter-of-factly.*

The four Mitchell Brothers dancers I interviewed for this book confirmed that this was certainly the accepted "unofficial" policy at the club, and that the girls were expected to "perform" sexually for patrons. They were also often called upon to do private shows for the Bohemian Club crowd regularly. These ladies knew plenty, and possessed the photographic evidence to prove what they say happened at the Grove is true. The women were understandably opposed to having these photographs published, and you will not find them here. But as the situations described below will indicate, the photographs and video they hold depict some pretty strange, obscene, and definitely illegal behavior on the part of the Bohemians. "It's bizarre," said Nina, one of the dancers. "Absolutely mind-boggling."

These four ladies used to dance at Mitchell Brothers Theatre a couple of years ago. All of them are stunning beauties in ages ranging between 21 and 25 years. For their protection, we will not use their real names here. Let's just call them Nina, Amber, Trixie, and Marilyn.

One night, while working at Mitchell Brothers Theatre, two of the girls were approached by a few men after the show. They were asked if they would like to do a private party at the Bohemian Grove. A reasonable amount of cash was flashed, and the girls took the bait. However, they asked the girls to sign contracts stating that they never performed at the Bohemian Grove before the fact. A written denial was required of them in advance, which they thought was very unusual. We cannot reveal how much they were paid, but it is safe to say these dancers are accustomed to making $2,000 per night each on a regular basis.

Friends had tried to warn the ladies not to accept the contract, warning them that doing a private party at the Grove might involve more than they bargained for. The girls laughed it off, disregarding the advice, and did agree to do the private party a week later.

The first night of the private party, the girls were entertaining a crowd of about 40 men, and they noticed that all of them men were wearing matching rings in the shape of an owl. They were offered drinks at the bar by the men, but with a condition: "if you want a drink, you'll have to take your pants off." Amber, who is African-American, was very offended by this demand. She questioned him why it was necessary to remove her pants, and the man just glared at her. He then instructed the bartender not to serve her at all.

Later, when Amber was making conversation with another man in the lounge, the same Grover who had refused her service at the bar looked over at them and put his hands up in the air. With his hands in the air, the man loudly said the word "NO!" The whole room went silent and everybody immediately sat down. The girls thought this was very weird behavior. Now the girls are thinking, "what the hell have we gotten ourselves into? This is a *very* strange party."

The party eventually resumed, and the girls performed their stage act for the appreciative Grovers, who tipped handsomely and paid for several lap dances.

They also made quite a bit of extra cash from various Grovers who wanted to purchase their company for the night.

The next morning, the girls were treated to a full spa treatment, facials, massages, swimming in the river, and other pleasant diversions during the day. All seemed to be fun and they felt fairly safe, except Nina did receive an invitation to go boating alone with one of the men. She did not feel good about going anywhere alone with him, as the girls had been forewarned never to go anywhere within the Grove where there were no witnesses. Amber answered for her, "My girls don't go anywhere without me," she told him.

That night they did another show for a crowd of about 100 men. They also noticed that they were not the only hired entertainers; another three strippers had arrived to perform for the Bohemians. They did not know the other girls personally, but recognized them as dancers from another club in San Francisco. When the girls went up to change for the show, they noticed a briefcase in the room that had apparently been left behind by one of the Grovers. Curiosity got the better of them, and they peeked inside. What they found shocked them. Inside was an owl mask, a long black robe with a gold hood, ritual gear, and a long butcher's knife that was very old and rusty.

When Trixie opened the briefcase, she said she definitely felt a very negative energy literally coming out of the case, and that the objects themselves, particularly the knife, felt ominous. "The knife looked like it had been used to kill before," she said. "It was old and very ornate in its design, with old stains on the blade. Whether it was rust or blood stains, I don't know."

Trixie became so alarmed, she refused to stay another minute, even though their act had been contracted for a three-day appearance at the Grove. But remembering the strange owl rings the men wore, the warnings she'd heard about the ritual abuse, and finally finding this briefcase full of bizarre gear made her decide that the best plan of action was to just get out of there as fast as possible. She became physically, violently ill within a few hours and had to be taken to a local hospital, where she spent the night.

By this time, all of the girls had changed their minds and agreed that they too should leave. They asked the Bohemians to pay them for their services, that they were tired and just wanted to go home. But the club did not agree, saying that the girls had been hired for a three-day engagement, and that's what they expected to receive. They were told that if they wanted to leave a day early, that was fine, but they would not be paid for the work they had already done. In fact, they would not get paid at all.

The girls quickly fled the Grove. As payment, the girls helped themselves to a laptop computer that one of the men had left lying around. Upon their safe return to the city, the girls had a computer expert examine and copy the contents of the hard drive. They were stunned to discover pictures of the dancers engaging in sexual acts with the men, apparently filmed with a hidden camera. In addition, they found photos of extremely brutal group sex scenes that looked more like rapes to them, many involving what appeared to be children.

To the best of their knowledge, these photos were taken at the Bohemian Grove and kept in a private collection along with several original pornographic movies found on the computer. In the films and photos, the men were wearing hoods or masks over their faces, cleverly making it impossible to know their identities.

SEXUAL ABUSE

In more recent years, troubling new information has come to light in the testimony of CIA Mind Control survivors involving sexual abuse they suffered at the Bohemian Grove. According to these reports (some of which are included here), the types of abusive perversions they were subjected to at the Grove make the much-ballyhooed Abu Ghraib torture photos look tame by comparison.

By now, the whole world has seen the shocking photographs of the sexual abuse, rape and murder of Iraqi prisoners by U.S. troops. These disturbing photos have rightly fueled outrage in the Arab world and escalated the war beyond proportions formerly imaginable. But what I am telling you now is that this type of behavior is not "isolated" amongst a few "rogue soldiers" in our military, nor is this type of abuse a new phenomenon. In fact, this has been the classified, unofficial policy of our military intelligence and CIA for decades. And this brutish treatment was not reserved for enemy combatants during wartime, either; no, these tactics were used on patriotic American citizens—innocent civilians!—Without their consent.

For those unfamiliar with the U.S. Government's Mind Control experiments, I will give you a brief overview of the MK-Ultra and Project Monarch programs here, along with some substantiating evidence that this type of state-sanctioned "research" involving unsuspecting humans as "guinea pigs" has many historical precedents.

Over the years, I have spent thousands of hours studying the Illuminati, Freemasonry, and the occult in general. The centerpiece of these organizations is the trauma-based mind control that they carry out. Without the ability to carry out this sophisticated type of mind-control using MPD (Multiple Personality Disorder), drugs, hypnosis and electronics and other control methodologies, these organizations would fail to keep their dark evil deeds secret. When one of the former mind-control programmers of the Church of Scientology was asked about MPD, he said, "It's the name of the game of mind control."

The basic techniques of mind control were developed in German, Scottish, Italian, and English Illuminati families and have been done for centuries. Some of these techniques even date back to the ancient mystery religions of Egypt and Babylon. The Nazis are known to have studied hermetic Egyptian texts in their mind control research. The records and rituals of the generational Illuminati bloodlines are very well guarded secrets. Intelligence agencies such as MI-6 began investigating these mind-control techniques early this century, but their records have been routinely destroyed and tampered with. There are some survivors and professionals who know that the British used programmed trauma-based MPD (DID) agents in WWI.

Traugott Konstantin Oesterreich (1880–1949), who was professor of philosophy at Tubingen University, Germany, studied MPD and demonic possession and wrote a classic study of it in 1921 entitled *Possession Demonical & Other*, which was translated into English in 1930. His classic work on this subject provides documented cases, which reveal that the basic trauma-based mind control was going on in Germany, France & Belgium long before the 20th century.

Oesterreich's research in the early 1900s was the type of research that the Nazi mind-control programmers were very aware of. In the 1920s and 30s, the Germans and Italians under the Nazi and Fascist governments began to do serious scientific research into trauma-based mind control. Under the auspices of the Kaiser Wilhelm Medical Institute in Berlin, Joseph Mengele conducted mind-control research on thousands of other hapless victims. Himmler supervised genetic research. After the war, the Nazi research records were confiscated by the Allies and are still classified. We also imported many of the top

Nazi scientists to continue this important "research" for the US in the now-infamous Operation Paperclip.

In the book *Trance Formation of America—The True Life Story of a CIA Mind Control Slave* by Cathy O'Brien and Mark Phillips, a former mind control abuse victim reveals her experiences at the Bohemian Grove. Cathy O'Brien was "trained" from her youth to act as a CIA mind control subject and sex slave. Eventually, she became a "presidential model," programmed to service the needs of VIPs, visiting dignitaries, world leaders, and a list of American presidents from Gerald Ford to George H.W. Bush to Ronald Reagan, Bohemians one and all.

In her published memoirs, O'Brien writes of her visits to the Bohemian Grove, secretly approved by top insiders. Her programmed mission was to take part in porn films shot at the Grove, and to entertain in the various secret live sex rooms located within the massive property. Her entrance to the Grove was secured by Michael Dante', whom she claims was President Reagan's personal pornographer. Aside from producing porn according to Reagan's own (well known) perversions and instructions, Dante' was present during many key international government gatherings, according to O'Brien. She says she was often prostituted to various government leaders, and that Dante' had hidden cameras filming these perverse sexual acts, apparently for future black mail leverage. These videos were scandalous in proportion and were usually ordered by Reagan himself. O'Brien recalls that Dante' turned over the master tapes to Reagan, and always covertly kept copies to protect himself. Dante' had converted a small room of his Beverly Hills mansion into a security vault, where he kept copies of the international blackmail porn tapes under lock and key.

Among these internationally scandalous tapes are numerous videos covertly produced at the supposedly secure sex playground in northern California, Bohemian Grove. According to Cathy O'Brien, Dante's high-tech undetectable cameras used fiber optics, and fish eye lenses that were placed in each of the elite club's numerous sexual perversion theme rooms. "My knowledge of these cameras was due to the strategically compromising positions of the political perpetrators I was prostituted to in the various kinky theme rooms." O'Brien writes in her book. "I was programmed and equipped to function in all rooms at Bohemian Grove in order to compromise specific government targets according to their personal perversions. *'Anything, anytime, anywhere with anyone'* was my mode of operation at the Grove."

"I do not purport to understand the full function of this political cesspool playground, as my perception was limited to my own realm of experience," she says. "My perception is that Bohemian Grove serves those ushering in the New World Order through mind control, and consists primarily of the highest Mafia and U.S. Government officials. I do not use the term "highest" loosely, as copious quantities of drugs were consumed there. Project Monarch mind control slaves were routinely abused there to fulfill the primary purpose of the club—purveying perversion."

O'Brien observed that the only room inside Bohemian Grove where business discussions were permitted was the small, dark lounge referred to as the Underground. (The lounge's wooden sign was carved to read: UN DER-GROUND pertaining to implementing the New World Order via the United Nations.) While sex slaves were not routinely permitted in the Underground for security reasons, O'Brien saw impromptu performances on the club's small stage from Bill Clinton, George H.W. Bush, the late Lee Atwater, Boxcar Willie and Lee Greenwood.

But Cathy O'Brien was *not* having a good time at the Grove. She writes:

> *"My purpose at the Grove was sexual in nature, and therefore my perceptions were limited to a sex slave's viewpoint. As an effective means of control to ensure undetected proliferation of their perverse indulgences, slaves such as myself were subjected to ritualistic trauma. I knew each breath I took could be my last, as the threat of death lurked in every shadow. Slaves of advancing age or with failing programming were sacrificially murdered "at random" in the wooded grounds of Bohemian Grove, and I felt it was "simply a matter of time until it would be me." Rituals were held at a giant concrete owl monument on the banks of, ironically enough, the Russian River. These occultish sex rituals stemmed from the scientific belief that mind controlled slaves required severe trauma to ensure compartmentalization of the memory, and not from any spiritual motivation.*

> *My own threat of death was instilled when I witnessed the sacrificial death of a young, dark haired victim at which time I was instructed to perform sexually "as though my life depended on it." I was told, "...the next sacrifice victim could be you. Anytime you least expect it; the owl will consume you. Prepare yourself, and stay prepared." Being "prepared" equated to being totally suggestible, i.e. "on my toes" awaiting their command.*

The club offered a "Necrophilia" theme room to its members. I was so heavily drugged and programmed when used in the necrophilia room, that the threat of actually "slipping through death's door" and being sacrificed "before I knew it" did not affect me. My whole existence was balanced precariously on the edge of death as a matter of routine anyway…My necrophilia room experience was only for the purpose of providing Dante' a compromising film of a targeted member anyway.

Other perversion theme rooms at the Bohemian Club included what I heard Ford refer to as the "Dark Room." When he not so cleverly said, "Let's go to the Dark Room and see what develops," I understood from experience that he was interested in indulging his perverse obsession for pornography. In the Dark Room, members had sex with the same mind controlled slave they were viewing in porn on a big screen television.

There was a triangular glass display centered in a main throughway where I was locked in with various trained animals, including snakes. Members walking by watched illicit acts of bestiality, women with women, mothers with daughters, kids with kids, or any other unlimited perverse visual display.

I was once brutally assaulted by Dick Cheney in the Leather Room, which was designed like a dark, black leather-lined train berth. As I crawled through the leather flaps covering the narrow entrance, I heard Cheney play on the word "berth/birth" as the soft blackness engulfed me. With the small opening covered, the blinding darkness enhanced the sense of touch and provided an option of anonymity. Cheney jokingly claimed that I "blew his cover" when I recognized his all-too-familiar voice and abnormally large penis size.

There was a room of shackles and tortures, black lights and strobes, an opium den, ritualistic sex altars, a chapel, group orgy rooms including water beds, poster beds, and "kitten" houses. I was used as a "rag doll" in the "toy store" and as a urinal in the "golden arches" room."

(*TRANCE-Formation of America* book excerpt © 1995, Cathy O'Brien and Mark Phillips.)

As an interesting footnote and update to Cathy O'Brien's personal story, I should point out that in 1995, A Lakeside Chat was given by a Mr. Fred Crews at the Grove. His topic was "The Recovered Memory Movement". That, of course, is the movement of incest and mind-controlled MK-ULTRA survivors who years later identify and then stand up to their abusers.

Over the past decade, many former CIA mind control victims have broken their programming and come forward with published accounts of the abuse they suffered at the hands of their "handlers." In addition to Cathy O'Brien's shocking book *Trance-Formation of America*, another memoir, published by MK-ULTRA survivor and former self-described "presidential sex toy" Brice Taylor describes "secretive meetings with the owl" at Bohemian Grove.

On page 223 of *Thanks for the Memories*, Brice Taylor writes about traveling to the Grove with her "handler," Henry Kissinger. She says he plied her with psychedelic mushroom drugs and programmed her brain with fairy tales about a magical redwood forest where she would be a beautiful princess who has a "special" connection to the forest animals. She was told to make friends with the great owl, who would watch over her and keep her safe. This fairy tale was intended to cover and scramble the real memory of what else was going on at Bohemian Grove.

"MERRY MEN" OF THE FOREST

Allegations have floated around the Grove for over a hundred years that many of these men, considered "straight as an arrow" to the outside world, actually use the Grove as a private spot to exercise their own hidden gay streak. In fact, a close examination of the Bohemian Club's own written histories and promotional materials reveal vague homosexual overtones in nearly all of the club's official published literature, dating back more than 100 years. The late-19th and early 20th Century Grove annals refer to "slender, young Bohemians, clad in economical bathing suits."

Even in the Cremation of Care ceremony, they speak of how a man's heart is divided between "reality" and "fantasy," how it is "necessary to escape to another world of fellowship among men". How on earth are we supposed to interpret this remark?

When *Spy* magazine's Philip Weiss observed the Cremation of Care ceremony in 1989, he noted that the main priest wore a pink-and-green satin costume, while a hamadryad appeared in a gold spangled bodysuit dripping with rhinestones. They spoke of "fairy unguents" that would free men to pursue "warm fellowship."

"I was reminded," Weiss reflected upon the obvious homoerotic references in the ceremony, "of something Herman Wouk wrote about the Grove: '*Men can decently love each other; they always have, but women never quite understand.*'"

Men gathered together around the campfire, summer Hi-Jinks of 1911.
(Photo by Jack London. Bancroft Library.)

Weiss also took note of the open chumminess between these men; hugging, kissing, walking with their arms around each other's waists, lying on the grass together in small groups. It goes without saying that even if these men are heterosexual and just happen to be *really close friends*, exhibiting this kind of behavior in public would certainly cast doubts upon their public image as respected, conservative Christian family men. The very physical aspect of this "male bonding" at the Grove can't be overlooked.

Then, there is the "drag culture" so prevalent at the Grove. The Bohos don women's clothing and enact female roles in Grove plays out of necessity, sure, as there are no women around. But the troublesome fact is that these men seem to *enjoy it so much*. They are encouraged by the wild cheers of the audience each time a man steps out onto the Grove stage in drag, and Bohemians can frequently be overheard admiring their cross-dressing comrades' choice of lingerie or fishnet stockings!

For most of the club's history, it was well-known that the homosexual members of the club could find a "date" for the evening amongst the handsome and eager young men who would gather on River Road outside the Grove entrance. While AIDS has certainly curbed the freewheeling atmosphere of the Grove's River Road pickup scene that the *San Francisco Chronicle*'s Herb Caen used to write so much about, gay activity still goes on at the Grove—only now the Bohos are much more circumspect about it.

Discreetly, single men are often invited back to various camps for "private parties." Male escorts or dancers might be brought in as guests to "entertain" the gay Grovers. Several male Grove employees have come forward in recent years with their own personal stories of being propositioned by Bohemians. But perhaps the most shocking allegation of all that has come out of the Grove in recent years is the story told by a then-teenage boy named Paul Bonacci.

SCREAMING BLOODY MURDER

Paul Bonacci was an eyewitness to the ritual rape and murder of a young boy at the Bohemian Grove in the summer of 1984. Former Nebraska State Senator John DeCamp's book, *The Franklin Cover-Up*, includes Paul Bonacci's testimony about being forced to participate (at gunpoint) in a homosexual snuff film where another teenager was actually *murdered* by men Bonacci believes were members of the Bohemian Club.

The boy took meticulous notes on everything he witnessed in his diary, which has since been examined by numerous forensic experts and was determined to be genuine. His entries were not forged or penned at some later date. While Bonacci's story may be the most difficult of all to believe, the details he gives about the surroundings—the exact location, the men in hooded red and black robes, the giant moss-covered owl altar—are simply too accurate to ignore altogether.

No teenage boy could possibly know these intimate details about the Grove unless he had actually been there. Even more, Bonacci had never even heard of the Bohemian Grove at the time he was taken there to "entertain" the Bohos years ago. In the fall of 1992, Paul was shown a black and white photo of the Grove's moss covered owl statue and quickly identified it as the site of the July 1984 snuff film described in DeCamp's book. This is not a game or the fanciful imaginings of a child. This is the cold-blooded ritual murder of a human being!

Even more difficult to ignore is the fact that Bonacci's tale jives with that of Cathy O'Brien, who was forced to participate in a similar snuff film where she witnessed the murder of another young woman at the Grove. Paul Bonacci and Cathy O'Brien have never met. They do not know each other. Their experiences happened several years apart. Yet, they tell nearly the same story.

But don't take my word for it. I want you to read the evidence for yourself and make up your own mind about these horrifying accusations. In the "Personal Stories" section of this book, I have included a recent interview with *Franklin Cover-Up* author and investigator John DeCamp in which he gives more details about this fascinating web of intrigue that entails a whole lot more than just sick sexual practices. He names the guilty parties, comes forward with numerous documented facts and details, and reads the Bohemian Grove passage *verbatim* from Paul Bonacci's original diary.

Bonacci's diaries and testimony have been available to the authorities for 12 years now, and to this date, no official investigation has been done. In my opinion, this is a travesty of justice. The only way his claims can be proven or disproved once and for all is for a fair and unbiased jury to hear this case for what it is—1st degree murder.

And it happened at the Bohemian Grove.

Selected Photographs for
Bohemian Grove

Some of the cast members of the pagan ritual drama, 1909

214

A negro (today called African American) youth is strapped to a stretcher at the 1909 encampment. Was this young man an actual, live sacrificial victim to the great owl deity, or was this simply part of the grand drama?

Cremation of Care ritual, 1907.

As speaker of the House of Representatives, Newt Gingrich attended and spoke at one of the Bohemian Grove encampments.

German Chancellor Helmut Schmidt, pictured here on the cover of Time magazine, wrote in his memoirs, Men and Power, of his visit to the Bohemian Grove.

President George W. Bush and his father, also President, at the Bohemian Grove.

Immediately following a press conference, President George W. Bush stunned onlookers by grasping and kissing the bald head of a man named Jeff Gannon. Gannon had been given White House press credentials by Bush officials, but is was later revealed that he was a male prostitute who also frequently visited the White House in the wee hours of the morning. Equally shocking, a few investigators alleged that Gannon had been sexually abused at the Bohemian Grove as a young boy.

Among the most important persons to attend the Bohemian Grove conclaves were these Presidents of the United States: Herbert Hoover, William Howard Taft, Jimmy Carter, Ronald Reagan, George W. Bush, George H. W. Bush.

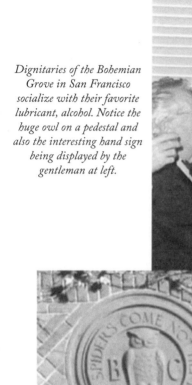

Dignitaries of the Bohemian Grove in San Francisco socialize with their favorite lubricant, alcohol. Notice the huge owl on a pedestal and also the interesting hand sign being displayed by the gentleman at left.

The Bohemian Club logo, laid out in red brick masonry.

Some believe that the owl deity at the Bohemian Grove to whom victims are sacrificed is a representation of the ancient Hebrew god, Moloch. In the book of Amos of the Old Testament, and in the book of Acts in the New Testament we are informed that the ancient Hebrews worshipped this evil fire god, Moloch and literally sacrificed their children to this monstrous idol.

II

PERSONAL STORIES

Chapter X

fortes fortuna adiuvat

(fortune favors the brave)

"Forgive Those Who Trespass..."
How We Got Into the Grove

We left Austin on Thursday, July 13, taking the 10:15 a.m. flight out of town. After landing in San Francisco, Alex, his wife Violet, and I traveled through the city, across the Golden Gate Bridge, into Northern California. From there, we went north to Santa Rosa, going west on Highway 12, the gateway to Bohemian Grove.

We were to meet up with the British media at a local hotel in the town of Occidental. Pulling into the parking lot of the Occidental Lodge, we saw that Jon Ronson and his crew were already waiting for us, ready to get started. We held our first planning and strategy meeting that night.

(Below is an excerpt from *Dark Secrets—Inside Bohemian Grove*, recording that meeting in the hotel room. Here, we are devising how to get inside the Grove, along with Alex, Violet, Jon Ronson and his two cameramen.)

Alex Jones (AJ): I want to hang out in the woods till it gets dark.
Jon Ronson (JR): I've...got a map. You guys want to look at that?
AJ: My question is: what do they do if they catch you in there?
JR: They have you killed? (Joking)
Mike Hanson (MH): I doubt that! (Laughs).
JR: I don't know...
Violet Nichols-Jones (VN): What about me, because I'm a woman. I can't really sneak in, can I?
JR: You can't really. You...you've got to stay.
VN: I've gotta stay? I've gotta stay behind in the spooky Occidental Lodge? (Laughs)
AJ: My only question is: is there a fence all the way around the property?
JR: No, just trees.
AJ: OK, here's the big question: what farmers or ranchers are living here that are going to blow my ass off when they see me sneaking across their property? If there's a road, I can find a way to insert myself into this, with Hanson. Also, I need to know about the Cremation of Care, what day they're supposed to do it, where this pond is?
JR: July 15th—at dusk.
AJ: That would mean that this will actually take some more planning, 'cause I didn't have these maps like you guys did—I'll need to know where I'm supposed to get in here. Where there's a road, where...

(One of the BBC crew): Well, this guy tonight will give you a really good briefing.

JR: Yeah...this guy knows everything.

AJ: So, you think you can trust him?

JR: Yeah...(laughs, smiles)...yeah.

AJ: (Joking) I'm not gonna end up tied down to a pentagram with Henry Kissinger's fat belly hanging over me while he's naked with a big dagger, am I? I just wanted to make sure...that's a joke. (Laughing) Or Governor Bush running around in a pink tutu, foaming at the mouth, with a purple wig on, am I? (The whole room breaks up laughing) Supposedly, I hear that's what they do.

JR: I think they do these things, but the question is: why?

AJ: These power brokers, who bomb innocent countries, slaughter people, and pump the food chain full of garbage, and just everything else they do—it's probably something fun for them. They really get off on being bad little boys.

JR: They rule the world! I mean, to some people this is "the secret room."

AJ: Well...I mean, certainly in the whole class system, it's the pleasures of class. And how one class has the power to have something different. And to me, from my research of the Bohemian Grove—you guys have obviously done more—I've read a lot of mainstream articles, alternative articles, talked to people, talked to some guests; and really people go in there to do whatever they want to do. So, it's probably a bunch of old men sitting around fishing, right?

Ronson: (to Violet) Do you think Alex's temperament is such that he'll be able to maintain the stealth needed to undertake this operation?

Violet: Well, I think Alex is not only a great activist and a great broadcaster, but he's also a great actor. So as long as he's able to think of what he's doing as acting—like if he has to infiltrate as a, you know, a guy carrying a golf bag—it'll be great.

Ronson: You're definitely not dangerous...you're not going to do anything stupid this weekend?

Alex: Well...I mean dangerous...dangerous to myself? Are these people dangerous? They certainly may be. But I'm completely non-violent when it comes to just going out there and trying to get the information. That's what I'm trying to do. I mean, I'm an activist first and foremost, but also a journalist in that I'll make some jokes and speculate occasionally 'cause I'm a radio show talk-host. But when I say something that I believe I have to be on-target about it. But...dangerous? I'm definitely dangerous to corrupt bureaucrats and their financial bosses that would like to control the American people and the planet.

Mike: We need to clear this up. He said, "are you dangerous"? You know, the thing is, you're *not* dangerous. You're defending freedom for our children and grandchildren. You need to clear that up for the cameras. Cause that's kind of, you know…a misleading question. (To Ronson) He's not dangerous. But it's the difference between being dangerous and protecting your freedom.

JR: But not in a violent way.

AJ: Not in a violent way. And if…for anyone that doubts we're in global government now, or entering it, we now have the UN criminal court—they're saying if sixty countries ratify it, then it doesn't matter if America doesn't sign on. UN Secretary General Kofi Annan claims he has the power to enter any country anytime he wishes. We've all read that in the papers, you see it on television. So, I'm fighting this global government. And long before global government came out in the open in the last 4 or 5 years, they were conditioning the public that anybody that talks about global government is a kook, a weirdo, a terrorist, a racist. And now they're out on the nightly news saying global government's here, you better accept it; we're getting rid of juries all across the planet; the IMF and the World Bank basically run things now; the WTO decides what you can buy and sell and trade on the international market.

But see, they've pre-conditioned us that it doesn't exist. They've pre-conditioned us that anybody that talks about this stuff and who is against it is a kook or a racist, because it doesn't exist. And then, everybody's decided that, "well I'm gonna be culturally cool; I wanna be in style, I wanna be accepted". So even when they're airing the news admitting it, telling us how great it is, they've already pre-positioned it psychologically that it's not acceptable, it's not kosher to discuss it. You see the tactic they're using there?

Five years ago I would laugh when I heard about black helicopters. I would say, "I'm about taxes, I'm about corruption, I'm about, you know, getting local control back, I'm about State's rights—everything's going…coming under Federal control". I'm a pretty mainstream, what you call so-called Conservative. Then I saw the light when black helicopters started going into North Carolina, started going into Florida. They fired into an all-night restaurant in Miami—just training, firing bullets into where people were eating. They started burning buildings; police chiefs started throwing them out of their towns, like they did in San Antonio. All this started happening, and I said, "Whoa, this is real!" And then I realized that *I* was pre-conditioned, even as a so-called Conservative person who understood that the media lies. I didn't realize how thick the propaganda was: that they pre-condition us before they release something on us, that it number one doesn't exist in our minds, the classic double-think; but that it can pre-exist at the same time because they say it does, and it's "good". So it's really George Orwell's doublethink. And one has to have it to stay sane in this world. Well I refuse to be part of it. I mean the news everyday: "Black helicopters are a joke; they're stupid"; the culture, commercials, movies. At the same time almost every month in this country they're attacking and terrorizing some town with burning buildings and.... terror!

I don't want to be part of their sick, control-freak system. I don't like these degenerate, in-bred, New-World-Order-crowd people. They're not going to run *my* life, they're not gonna control *me*. And I'm gonna try to expose them. And I think I've had some success doing that. I know this: the Henry Kissingers, the George Bushes, those people—*these* are dangerous individuals. They've proven they're dangerous. They have no problem controlling and destroying entire societies.

Ronson: I just wanted to make sure that you weren't going to actually push any of them in the river, or throw them into the Owl...?

Alex: No, I...I see most of these, most of these elitist individuals and snobs; I see them as pathetic. And it's really, a gross analogy but I'll use it: when I see a whole bunch of dog turds being laid all over this society, I don't run around stomping on them because I don't want to get it on my feet; I just say...I say to the general public, "Let's clean these up, and let's tell these people they can't do this anymore, that they can't shit on us". That's really what I'm saying. You can't shit on us anymore. I just want 'em to stop shitting on us.

JR: (pulling out a map of the Bohemian Grove, showing Alex): This is the amphitheater, this is where they have the Lakeside Talks. It's where George Bush gives those talks, people like that; from this stage. Look, that's the Lake...and there's the owl shrine.

AJ: Let me get a shot of this. Now, what is this river...the Russian River? Now see, here's the shrine of the Devil Owl, which they even admit has its roots in like, Babylon, and the Druids. So all over the world this weird owl shows up. Some cultures they've thrown children inside this thing...inside the bowels of the burning owl; that's historical. We've all read in the Bible about throwing your children to idols, uh, inside their belly. So, I...it's weird behavior, definitely. So it needs to be investigated. Plus it gets the adrenaline up. Thrill seekers have to have more. Right here's the shrine—can you zoom in on that, Mike?

(While I took a close-up shot of the map, Alex continued his impassioned rant to Ronson's crew.)

Then we get into the whole semantical debate about "is there a left and a right?" To me there really isn't; there's command and control on one end and anarchy on the other, and it ought to be in the middle in the real spectrum. Certainly gotta have some control in a complex society and civilization, but all the developments I see are pretty bad toward dehumanization. And now you have the UN demanding everybody sign on to this Interna-

tional Criminal Court; then they're telling the U.S. if we don't sign on it won't matter—if sixty countries ratify, we'll be under its control. I mean we're here; we're in global government now. Then they say they're going to have some World Court in the Netherlands where they'll take anybody they want to be tried. In fact, I was reading some of the talks that they've given, and that they've released; that the Bohemian Grove has discussed. It's all population control, and world courts; we're talking twenty years ago. So definitely some stuff going on here that's pretty important. But is it the ultimate elitist retreat? I would imagine that those...we don't even know the names of. This is probably just one more steering committee where they bring in a lot of underlings and high-level corporate chieftains that really aren't upper, top echelon; make them feel important, then implement some new type of strategy. From the stories I've heard of things that happened, I mean it is pretty well documented that people run around naked, they have orgies—they go into town and visit hookers—and these are our world leaders. I've got a serious problem with that. Just by the very nature of how this...to me Bohemian Grove is probably a way to compromise people. You want to be in the New World Order club, it's like a big kid fraternity; and just like a fraternity you have to do weird things for initiation. Here you probably have to do weird things. I've got a problem with governors, presidents, prime ministers, corporate chieftains running around and doing this, when they have so much power over what happens in the public domain. They have a responsibility to disclose what they're doing. So, I think it is important like you were saying, to somehow try and maintain some security without being way out in the open, because they'll call in a bunch of security. I mean, George W. Bush is going to be at the Grove this year, so security will be tight. I hear he really enjoys himself here. (Laughs)
JR: I think Henry Kissinger will be here this year, too.
AJ: Well, if I've got a stink detector we'll be able to find out where he's at. It's like everything evil you can imagine, Kissinger's always involved in it.
JR: But, aren't you a Republican, Alex? (Facetiously) You don't like Bush and Kissinger?
AJ: I'm not a Republican! The point I keep making is this whole Republican/Democrat deal is complete garbage...people always go back to that stuff. Probably in your country you've got Labour and you've got the Tories over there, and it's all the same people behind closed doors. It's just a big joke. And your...your leadership, our leadership—it's all the same people. You do see a fight going on, but it's two different management teams in the same system. Bidding for control. That's why I call them the CEO jobs of Slavery Incorporated.
JR: Are you worried for Alex, Violet?
VN: Um, I do worry because Alex gets so impassioned by what he's doing, that sometimes I'm afraid that he might be a little bit, you know, reckless; or maybe a little bit too fearless. I worry about Alex when he drives down

the street to come home, you know. It's just that I used to worry about him when he had a…he'd come home every night from the same radio studio at the time in the same car. And, you know I'd worry about him sometimes when he's late getting back from the studio and he doesn't give me a call. I mean, you know, he is putting himself out there, but I think the fact that he's in the public eye as much as he is really, you know, keeps him safe to a certain degree. So, maybe something like this is…yeah, you know, people might not necessarily know where he is, right now. You know, people that listen to the radio, whatever. So this might be a little more risky. It's a little creepy at night up here in the woods, you know.

The closest town to the Bohemian Grove is the tiny community of Monte Rio (population 1200). The forest surrounding the area is so thick; streetlights stay on both day and night, giving the whole place consistently gray, even somewhat spooky atmosphere. When the fog rolled in after dark, the surroundings began to look more like the Transylvania set from an old Dracula movie! A perfect setting for the sorts of activities we had heard were going on in the Grove.

The next morning, we went off on our own to interview the locals and get their thoughts on the Bohemian Grove. What amazed us was how painfully uninformed they were. We spoke to people of all ages, genders, races, and religions, trying to conduct an informal survey that was as accurate as possible. I have included some of these interviews below, verbatim, so you can see for yourself how much the average Sonoma County resident knows of the Grove.

Alex and I first approached a middle-aged man who appeared to be former military, wearing a Camp Meeker T-shirt.

Alex Jones (AJ): How you doing, sir?
Unidentified Man (UM): OK.
AJ: You from Camp Meeker? I noticed that on your T-shirt.
UM: Yeah.
AJ: Oh! I'm Alex Jones. I make documentaries. I'm just curious: what do you think about Bohemian Grove?
UM: I used to work there.
AJ: You used to work there?
UM: Yeah.
AJ: And now you work at Camp Meeker.
UM: No, I don't work…see, I live at Camp Meeker.
AJ: Oh, you live there.

UM: Yeah.
AJ: Well that's great. Uh, did you ever watch the Cremation of Care?
UM: Uhh...ummm.... No. No.
AJ: What'd ya do at the...
UM: I just worked there.
AJ: But you never saw them march around in the red robes?
UM: No, no! (Laughs)
AJ: Oh, really? That doesn't go on?
(Man becomes uncomfortable. Makes his excuses to end interview quickly, walks away)
AJ: (Laughs) OK.

Alex and I then spoke to two young men, probably in their late teens, in a store parking lot:

AJ: What have you guys heard about Bohemian Grove?
Unidentified Man 1: Oh, I don't know. A bunch of rich people there.
AJ: Have you ever heard about the 40-foot stone owl and the mock-human sacrifice?
UM1: Uh, I heard about a little of that, yeah.
AJ (speaking to passenger in the car): So what have you heard about them?
Unidentified Man 2: Oh, I just read something about it in the paper; I don't know, some people don't like it. They protested it or something.
AJ: But what about the 40-foot stone owl and the mock-human sacrifice? You say you heard something about that?
UM1: Well, just what I read about in the paper.
AJ: Oh, the paper admitted that.
UM1: Well...no, I don't know it they admitted it. They just said that people go protest it. Supposedly happens. Sounds kinda weird.
AJ: Does sound weird to me.
UM2: Yeah. Why? You guys...what are you guys...what are you guys doing? TV show or something?
AJ: We're just having fun.
UM2: Oh, yeah?
AJ: This isn't like *Children of the Corn* or anything, is it?
UM2: Oh, no. Nothing like that. But uh...I don't know. Supposedly a lot of people go there. Some kind of weird event. I don't know.
AJ: What would you say if we told you that they sacrificed a human in effigy in a box to a 40-foot stone owl in black and red and silver cloaks?
UM2: Sounds kinda different.
AJ: Do you think it's good to have...do you think it's good to have so-called world leaders secretly engaging in Pagan activities?
UM2: Uhhh...I can't say it's that great, no.

AJ: Why would you have a problem with that?

UM2: Well, I don't know. It could be all right. Depends on how you look at it.

AJ: Kind of a relativist world view, huh?

UM2: Yeah.

AJ: Gotta sacrifice Care to the winds, huh?

UM2: Well, I don't know. Could just be for fun, or it could really be weird.

Another local, a young man, early '20s, sitting on his front porch with some friends:

AJ: Sir, what have you heard about the Bohemian Grove, where our world leaders meet?

Unidentified Man 1: They run around naked. Run around naked and freak out.

AJ: Have you heard that?

UM1: Yeah. Absolutely. Actually, to tell you the truth, here's a funny story.

AJ: OK, go ahead.

UM1: No, no….it's the truth. A couple of years ago, I was down the road, just down "yar", past Camp Meeker, and I was stopped with a friend of mine…

AJ: Camp Meeker's right outside Bohemian Grove.

UM1: That's an affirmative. (Smiles) And we were standing on the road, and uh…we were stopped there because we were just having a cigarette, hanging out, taking a break. And these Secret Service men actually pulled up behind us and asked us what we were doing, why we were there. This is true. They were like, "what are you guys doing, where are you at, why are you parked here, what's going on"? And asked us a whole bunch of questions: what our names were, what we were affiliated with, where we lived, all kinds of stuff. They interrogated us.

AJ: Did you answer their questions?

UM1: Totally!

(One of the man's friends speaks up)

UM2: I don't know. They're always here. There's like, big fat rich guys with prostitutes there.

AJ: Really?

UM2: Yeah.

AJ: What about the Owl, and the rituals?

UM2: Uh, I don't know anything about it.

AJ: Never heard about the rituals?

UM2: Rituals. Uh….

AJ: Ritual killing of a human sacrifice, of a human.

UM2: Nope. Never heard of it.

AJ: What would you think if that were going on?

UM1: I'd think it was pretty weird. Wouldn't be that surprised. I mean, it is our government after all.
AJ: Hey, thanks for talking to us, bud. Hey, I like your shirt. The Declaration of Independence.
UM1: Yeah.
AJ: We're talking about the Bohemian Grove, and trying to see what locals think about it; how it's all secret, and all these "fat cats" there, and the supposed strange rituals that go on. All right, man. Take care.

Alex and I then approached two old hippie types, a man and woman, original San Francisco 1960s "flower children" who had moved north to Sonoma County to escape city life.

AJ: Excuse me, sir—Are you a local?
Unidentified Male: No, but she is.
AJ: What do you think about the Bohemian Grove?
Unidentified Female (UF): Uh…well, uh…it provides a lot of jobs to the people around here.
AJ: They offer a lot of employment?
UF: Uh huh.
UM: What's going on there? What kind of rituals do they do there?
AJ: I don't know. We're talking to locals about what the rumors are.
UM: What are the rumors?
AJ: About a big 40-foot stone owl, and simulated human sacrifice.
UF: Oh, no! (Laughs) Oh, I don't know about that! It's politicians that come…that vacation there.
AJ: It'd be really weird for politicians if they were acting like they were sacrificing people, wouldn't it?
UM: Ah, no…You can't trust politicians.
AJ: Oh, really? They might be doing it, huh?
UM: They might, yeah. (Everybody laughs). They're politicians, you know? (Laughs).
AJ: I hear ya, bud. Hey, good talking to you. Appreciate ya. You guys take care.
UM: Good luck.
AJ: Hey, those are pretty flowers!
UM: These are sweet peas.

The next man we spoke to was an older gentleman, probably about retirement age.

AJ: We're just asking locals what they think of the Bohemian Grove.
UM: The Bohemian Grove's a wonderful place.

AJ: Have you been there?
UM: Yeah, I've been in there a bunch of times.
AJ: What'd you do, work there?
UM: Worked there, yeah. And you know when it's the most wonderful-est time? It's when nobody's there.
AJ: Oh, it's a beautiful area?
UM: Yeah, very beautiful. Big trees...
AJ: Have you ever been there for the Cremation of Care?
UM: No.
AJ: So you've never been there for the rituals.
UM: No.
AJ: You ever heard about them?
UM: Yeah.
AJ: What have you heard they do, sir?
UM: Nothing. They've got this tree that looks like an owl.
AJ: Tree that looks like an owl?
UM: Tree, or rock, or just carving, or...it's where the stage is.
AJ: But have you heard what they do there in that, during that...
UM: No, I have no idea what they do there.
AJ: What would you say if we told you they burn a human being in effigy; they don't really do it, they burn it in effigy?
UM: I don't know what that means.
AJ: Well, they have a dummy that looks like a person under a black blanket, and they take it up there and burn it.
UM: Well, I don't know.
AJ: Pretty weird.
UM: Huh?
AJ: Pretty weird.
UM: Yeah, I've never seen that.
AJ: How long have you lived around here?
UM: I don't know...how old am I? Twenty, forty years?
AJ: Really, huh? Your whole life.
UM: Yeah.

We walked into "Vital Roots," an organic deli/coffeehouse and struck up a conversation with the counter clerk, a young male. Two other females of about middle age soon joined in on camera:

AJ: How long has "Vital Roots" been here?
UM: Couple of years.
AJ: Couple of years?
Unidentified Female 1: This is about Bohemian Grove?
AJ: Yeah.

Unidentified Female 2: Lot of politicians, lot of bigwigs, making a lot of big decisions.

AJ: Oh, really? Do you think it's good that they get together in secret and make all these so-called decisions?

UF2: Do I think it's good?

AJ: Yeah.

UF2: No, of course not.

AJ: What about the rituals? Have you heard anything about the rituals that go on?

UF2: No. There's all kinds of rumors about rituals that go on there.

AJ: What types of rumors have you heard?

UF2: I…. Don't make me go there! (Laughs)

AJ: Well, we're just talking to some locals about it…

UF2: Uh huh. Well, I really don't know that much about it. You know, it's just what I've read in books about it. There are books out about it.

AJ: Oh, you've read books on it, huh?

UF2: I have a book that was published in 1956 that was written about some of the rituals…

AJ: Because now it's been going on for 120-plus years

UF2: Yeah.

AJ: I think they said it's the 120—something anniversary. What would you say if I told you there's a 40-foot stone owl, and that they burn a human being in effigy; not in real life, but in effigy?

UF2: I wouldn't believe it.

AJ: You wouldn't believe it?

UF2: Nah. I think it's a bunch of garbage.

AJ: So you doubt there's a stone owl, and you doubt that they…

UF2: Well, I wouldn't doubt there's a stone owl; maybe there's a stone owl. But I wouldn't think…that's kind of…you know, rumors is rumors. What the word implies. Pretty much.

AJ: Just a conspiracy.

UF2: Yeah. Just a bunch of hearsay.

AJ: Pure conspiracy theory.

UF: Yeah, whatever.

Probably the best-informed individual we managed to find was a local auto mechanic who worked at a service station near the Grove:

AJ: How long have you lived around here?

Unidentified Man: Approximately, on and off, 32 years.

AJ: Oh, really? So most of your life?

UM: Uh huh.

AJ: Uh, what have you heard about the Bohemian Grove?

UM: It's where all of the, like, FBI and the…you're just talking about THE Bohemian Grove?
AJ: Yeah.
UM: Yeah, it's like the um…"Elite" and Presidential retreat.
AJ: Have you heard about the rituals?
UM: No, I haven't. Well, the people who have more money than the rest of us in the world are a bit…different. They're stingy. They want to hoard it all for themselves. And they think they're gonna go to Heaven. They're not. Because they're not doing what Jesus told them to do.
AJ: What would you say if I told you that they sacrifice a human in effigy before a giant 45—to 50-foot stone owl?
UM: I would say that that's probably why they're going to Hell.
AJ: Really? Have you ever heard about that?
UM: No.
AJ: You've lived here your whole life?
UM: Uh huh.
AJ: Where were you born?
UM: San Francisco.
AJ: It's a beautiful town. You've got the Grove just about 10 miles down the road. Have you talked to people that have worked there?
UM: Uh, no I haven't. I don't even know anybody that works down there, to tell you the truth. Um, I know people that have gone down there. Couple of years ago when Schwartzkopf and Colin Powell…they were all down there doing big presentational speeches, and whatnot. I've heard about that. And Presidents that have gone there for their retreat, and whatnot. What I've heard it's also an "elite" men's club only. Women haven't been able to, or allowed to work there except for the past few years, which they're only kept in the parking lot. They're valet parkers. That's the only job women can have there, 'cause of whatever goes on in there.
AJ: What if I told you that it's true that they burn a human being in effigy to a giant owl god that they start worshipping the owl, and talking about how it gives them power? What do think about that?
UM: I would say they are in grand delusion. And they need to give some of their money away.
AJ: You're saying that they're on a power trip.
UM: Totally.
AJ: But what is this burning a person? This is ancient. Did you know that thousands of years ago different societies would have large, metal, hollow owls, and that they'd throw children into them?
UM: Well, I would say they were quite Satanic. Or, on another level, if you will, more…*demented*. Very sick.
AJ: But these people, we're talking about men who control billions of dollars. And we're talking about governmental control. Is it bad to have something that's secret-elite and pagan at the same time?

UM: Yeah. Sounds like Satan's building his cult. Satan is building his army.

That afternoon, we also met with a local Grove "expert," whom we'll call Rick The Lawyer. Mary Moore of the Bohemian Grove Action Network had suggested Rick to the British TV crew as someone experienced with the different methods of getting into and around the Grove property. Rick is not a conspiracy theorist. He infiltrated the place because he was curious after hearing so much local gossip about the Grove. Here is a partial transcript of that meeting:

Alex: Tomorrow, what time do they have the Cremation of Care, or the Owl ceremony?
Rick: That's typically right at dusk. It'll start when it's still sort of light out and by the time it's over it's dark.
Alex: Have you ever witnessed that?
Rick: Uh huh. Yeah.
Alex: What do they do?
Rick: There's a real large...it looks like probably a redwood tree that was cut off, and they've built things on top of that that get...you know, the fire goes up and they do all these things. And then there's sort of a, I suppose a Druid type of ceremonial altar out in front of it that they do things at.
Alex:...Druid ceremonial altar?
Rick: Well, it has that look about it—very old, very pagan.
Alex (looking at map): So basically, you would come in—I want to get this absolutely concrete...
Ronson: Are you still thinking about going by the terrain?
Alex: Well, now that...see, that's why I wanted to talk to him. If these are those big hills we're talking about, you're gonna have cliffs and all this kind of stuff, that'll be...
Rick: Coming in this way...you could kill yourself. Especially if you go out that way. But of course if you came this way, you could just walk out that way.
Alex: Why don't we just walk in here? (Pointing to main entrance on the map)
Rick: There arc going to bc 1 or 2 guys, sitting by the side of this road, in a camp chair, looking bored and uninterested. And you're just gonna say...just nod to them as you walk in. That's it.
Ronson: Now what about clothes?
Alex: How would you get in?
Rick: I'd walk in wearing this shirt and a pair of khakis, and I...I'd just walk in, from Monte Rio.

Ronson: Preppy jeans?

Rick: Yeah. Preppy…preppy clothes.

Alex: Jeans won't fly…

Rick: I'm trying to remember whether or not I've seen people wearing jeans. You're going to blend in better with khakis—casual cotton pants—than you would with jeans. You don't have to wear a cap. Really. It's not necessary. But, on the other hand, if you do wear one, nobody's going to pay any attention to it.

Alex: What about me wearing flip-flops, or something, or sandals?

Rick: Sandals would be fine. Flip-flops might not be a good idea. Sandals, running shoes, loafers, you know. I would guess that what you don't do is you don't stand out. Certainly the crowd at the Grove is—even the ones who are in their 20's probably, and those are fairly rare-they don't dress young.

Alex: So basically you would come in—I want to get this absolutely concrete—this is…

Rick: We'll go there.

Ronson: Let's take a drive, then.

After scouting the Grove's exterior with Rick and visiting the local mall where we purchased the appropriate "preppy clothes," Alex and I were finally ready enter the forbidden redwood grove. We tried to retire early, get a good rest to feel better prepared, but I honestly don't think anybody on that trip could sleep at all. We all seemed to be preoccupied with all the possible scenarios of what might happen to us if something—*anything*—went wrong tomorrow.

Chapter XI

persona (non) grata

(an unwelcome person)

"Here is Bohemia's Shrine…"
Captured On Tape!

It was now the afternoon of July 15, 2000. Alex and I were about to attempt the first—ever-successful infiltration of the Bohemian Grove with cameras. Others had tried and failed. No one has ever actually made it in and out with video evidence. We knew the odds were clearly against us.

After careful planning, we decided the best tactic would be to insert ourselves about a half mile from the main entrance, into the heavily wooded area; entering the gorge by stealth and getting into the main parking lot. From there we would pose as Bohemian Club members, thus entering the inner sanctum of the New World Order.

On the drive there, we discussed contingency plans with Jon Ronson and Violet; concocting a cover story for ourselves in case we got "busted" by security:

Alex: If our cover's blown, we'll just say, "Hey, we're going", and say, "No, no, no; we'll be over here". And then just be nice, just start walking away. If they start following us, just say, "Listen, you better get away from me", and a few other choice words, then we'll just get in the woods; get away for a few minutes, and then come back out. They'll never know.
Ronson: "You better get away from me"—that sounds like a threat. I don't think you should threaten them.
Alex: No, but I'm gonna tell 'em to get away from me. But it's not gonna be a problem, because we're gonna be slick! There's not gonna be any problems. (Grins)

We turned our car onto the Bohemian Highway, approaching the Grove property line. As we neared our destination, a ball of nervous energy began to well up in my gut. Alex kept talking nervously, probably to diffuse his own trepidation about the task we were about to take on:

Alex: Well, here we go…the moment of truth. We're driving now; it's a Saturday night here in Occidental. The Bohemian Grove is between Occidental and Monte Rio, both small towns. We're gonna try to just infiltrate, by just acting as if we're members of the Grove. We're walking straight through;

we've assumed fake names. Mike of course is David Hancock, and I'm Mike Richardson.

British Cameraman: What do you do for a living, Mike?

Mike: I don't think that's been decided yet.

Alex: Yeah, we better decide that right now. I'm a documentary filmmaker, which is true. And we'll just say that Mike is also in the media; Mike is a writer. He's the famous writer, David Hancock. Whoever that is.

Mike: What if somebody asks some of the book titles?

Alex: Mike, don't hesitate.

Mike: *The Blue Lagoon*...(thinking)...*The Black Lagoon*! I wrote that in 1984; it was my first one. (Laughter)

Alex: Right! You're David Hancock, and I'm Mike Richardson. *(Trying to memorize the names repeats them again)* David Hancock, Mike Richardson! OK, got it.

Mike Richardson and David Hancock
(a.k.a. Alex Jones and Mike Hanson!)

Violet dropped us off several yards away from the main entrance, and we made plans to meet back at the hotel later tonight. She gave us one last look and said, "be careful." When Violet asked me what she should do if we didn't return, I told her to simply pray for us.

When we went over the barbed—wire fence, I just kept saying in my mind…"God, help us. Protect us. Make us invisible." Just like a lot of people, I try to make deals with God when I'm afraid or backed into a corner! You see, I never thought we'd even get on the property—that's what I was thinking the whole time. I want to make that clear. I never thought we'd get *ten feet* on the property before we would get caught and either taken to jail, or thrown out like so many other journalists have been. And I never thought in my wildest dreams we would ever get that far.

So when we *did* get in about ten feet, we quickly discovered that this place was full of poison oak or vines that looked like poison oak. It was like a moat-type thing; and we were wearing these nice shoes that we had just bought at the mall—well, so much for the new shoes.

I was so scared—literally *so scared*—that I thought I was gonna have a heart attack. My thoughts went back to my friend George Humphrey, who had told me about his experience getting caught trying to sneak into the Grove once before. All the stories I'd heard of past failures befalling journalists who had undertaken this mission now came back to me. But Alex was leading the way, tramping through the dense underbrush of poison oak, and he was making the most noise that I've ever heard!

It reminded me of when I used to go hunting with my grandpa; he always told me the main thing is when you're hunting raccoon at night is that you have to be very quiet. Don't step on any sticks or anything like that. Alex Jones stepped on *every* stick and every thing that made noise that I wasn't sure whether to laugh out loud or run for my life. Naturally, I was nervous about making too much noise because I was told there were listening devices all over this place. That's what George Humphrey had told me, and I'd heard it from other people too. I mean, it was a *lot* of noise we were making, walking through those woods. Every leaf and twig crunched loudly under our feet. And Alex was telling me all the way "Hurry, Hurry". Not only was he making a lot of noise, he was talking all this time, telling me stuff, discussing our plans loud enough for any nearby microphone to detect.

Then he would go through the branches, and they would swing around and hit me in the face and in the body. And it was real difficult for me going second, walking behind Alex because I kept getting slapped in the face going through this forest! And you almost had to step on the branches that had fallen out of the trees, because you would sink down in the...well, it looked like quicksand or Louisiana marshland. It probably was not quicksand, but it was just real, real soft and wet in a lot of places. You really didn't want to step in the moat parts of it because you might sink in. And all I could seem to worry about at this moment was how my muddy new shoes would be a dead giveaway that I didn't belong here, once I got inside the Grove camp.

When we got to a point where we could see, after about 30 minutes of hiking, we got to the first parking lot where they were; I guess where the employees or something had parked their cars. We got into where the employees' parking lot was, and we didn't really see anything. Then we snuck over to where, I guess where the Bohemian people parked their cars. By the time we got up into the main parking lot where all the bigwigs go in and out of the Grove, I was *really* nervous.

Mike: We're in.
Alex: Well, we're not actually inside yet, Mike.
Mike: Well, we're in the parking lot. (*Hilarious—at this point, I felt like it was such a blessing just to get into the parking lot! OK, mission accomplished. Can we go home now?*)

I just wanted to turn around and run. I think Alex had to just kinda stop me and tell me to calm down because I was literally scared half to death! And truly, I was praying the whole time we were in there. I just didn't like this situation *at all*. I did not feel safe here, and was incredibly worried that Alex and I would wind up in some backwoods, small town jail, or else tied up in California court for years. Then, there was yet another, far more greusome option; the bizarre tales of murder and human sacrifice rituals that I didn't even want to think about. And it took every bit of strength for me not to just turn around and run, like I was running away from an armed bank-robber or a mad dog. It just took every ounce of energy and courage that I had, to just not turn around and run back the way I came.

When we got up on the parking lot where the Bohemians parked their cars, I decided that I had better start acting like I'm supposed to be here, or we would surely get caught. That's what I said over and over in my mind to prop myself up. When we got up into the flat asphalt lot, I saw the security guards, or the Sheriff's department, or whoever's guarding this place, right away. It just so happened that right when we came in—must have been "the luck of the draw" or either it was the grace of God—but right when we came out of the woods into the Bohemian parking lot, the guard shack was empty. The guy had either gone off to the restroom, or was out walking his rounds. When he came back, I saw him. So I quickly grabbed a Mercedes-Benz doorknob like I was getting out of it. I was literally touching the doorknob like it was my car. And he looked right at us when I got, saw me standing by the car, and really didn't pay that much attention to us because we just looked like a couple of guys standing by our car, having a conversation.

Then I noticed two older gentleman nearby, sort of looking at us and giving us a very friendly smile, and I had remembered from my studies of this place that the Grovers bring a lot of men in there for homosexual activity. So it just clicked in my mind, "well maybe I'd better run over and act like I'm with these two older men. We'd blend right in here!" So that's exactly what I did, and Alex followed suit. I walked over to them and engaged in some small talk with one of these men. I even patted him on the shoulder like an old friend, and said, "how are you doing this year?" and this type of stuff, and the man was actually really nice to me. I'm sure he was just being polite—after all, it seemed like *I* knew *him*, but inside his mind, I'm sure he was trying like crazy to remember where and when we'd met before.

About that time, I noticed the shuttle bus was coming. The Bohemians call it "The Owl." I've never seen any kind of truck quite like this in my life. But they had a few of them, at least I saw about four driving around. And they all looked the same, all with the same Bohemian Club owl logo on the side of the truck. To the best of my knowledge, they're some kind of old 1940s style jeeps or something like a 6x6 command car, but they were convertible tops. To me, they actually looked like old Army trucks or jeeps that the military had gotten rid of because they were outdated. They looked official to me. We noticed that the men we were talking to weren't walking toward the Bohemian Grove gates; that they were waiting for a shuttle to drive them inside, and Alex says, "well maybe we should wait for the bus, too". Of course, I wasn't going to leave the side of our two new "friends"—I knew that they were either our

Bohemian Grove: Cult Of Conspiracy

ticket in or out. It made sense to me that these two old men were our best bet to get into the Grove safely and without arousing any suspicion.

So, when we were on the shuttle bus, still talking with these two men when all of a sudden, out of nowhere, this guy just asks," How much did you pay for your ROBE?" And I remember it really shocked me when he asked that question. I was taken completely off my guard and all my pre-scripted small talk flew right out of my head. I specifically remember the one old man, who asked his buddy how much he paid for his ceremonial robe, and Alex had misunderstood him and said, "how much did you pay for the ROAD?" Then I spoke up and clarified, "No, how much did you pay for the robe, he said how much did you pay for the ROBE?"

Of course, I was making the best conversation I knew how to, talking to these two old guys like I had known them for years, bluffing like crazy. Alex was kind of "hush hush" and circumspect about it, choosing not to say much. When I get nervous, I start talking, and I don't quit talking. It's my way of coping. And I think Alex does the opposite: when he gets nervous, he just kind of shuts up. First of all, I knew that these two old men were either going to get us in or get us out of this thing ALIVE. So I latched on to them like I literally was their "boyfriend". And I stuck with this old man, and of course Alex stuck with me. I did take the bull by the horns because I knew that these two old men were our way in, or they were going to soon figure out that we weren't Grovers, and have us tossed out by security.

I don't know how we would have gotten into that place if it hadn't been for these two old men. When I say "old", I'd mean around sixty-five or something like that. He was telling us, and this other guy, how beautiful this place was, and all this kind of stuff, as we rode up to the main gates. He said there used to be a redwood tree in Bohemian Grove so big, you could literally drive a car through its' trunk. When we were ready to get off of the "Owl" bus, the driver gave me a real dirty look. Now, I'm kind of a mind reader, I'm kind of psychic—and I *knew* what he was thinking. He looked at me and his eyes said, "Oh, God, you dirty little person!" He probably thought in his mind that we were sleeping with these two old men, because I'm sure he sees that sort of thing happens here all the time. So he figured that Alex and I were "hooked up"…that they had us as escorts or something for these old men, because why else would two old men like that be hanging out with two young men like us? (Alex is in his late twenties; I'm in my mid-thirties.)

Of course we were dressed up real nice, in casual clothes. I had on real expensive (albeit muddy!) loafers and khaki pants, paired with a standard "preppy" checkerboard-pattern button-down shirt. I was still scared to death on the inside, but at least I looked the part on the outside. I also knew that it was survival of the fittest at this point, so I was ready to be the best actor I could be, knowing that this would have to be the performance of my lifetime—or else!

We had a small, hidden pager-cam clipped onto a navy blue shoulder bag we were carrying with us. That's what we did when we went through the woods, and when we were on the bus I was afraid they were going to notice it, so I just guarded that bag for dear life. My biggest concern the entire time was making sure that nobody saw this pager-cam, or the bigger camera we had stashed inside the bag, covered only by some extra clothing and a towel.

Another point I want to make is that a lot of the people who work at the Grove don't even get to go over to where the Owl is. That's a whole separate part from where they work and they are confined to a certain area. We talked to some Grove employees who don't even know that the owl statue is there. They don't even know there's a 40-foot stone owl in the place where they work! They probably think this is just a resort or retreat. That's the impression that I got. It seemed to me like most of the Grove employees don't question the moves of the Bohemians; after all, these men are used to being in charge. A worker who wants to keep his job would not dare to speak frankly and risk angering a top cabinet official or CEO. They could be fired on the spot.

About 10 minutes later, Alex and I came to the next checkpoint, and they did stop us this time. I was even afraid to turn around and look at the guards, but one of them walked right up to us and looked us over real good. He came around the Owl shuttle bus and looked at everybody, and he said something to the two old men we were sitting with. Then, to my relief, he just waved us on and smiled as we drove away.

At the third checkpoint, the guard didn't even stop us—he just waved at us, and we waved back, of course. I think the guard knew one of the old men in the bus; the man next to me recognized him and shouted, "Watch my car", to the guard. The guard gave him a nod, like "no problem." To tell the absolute truth, this old man looked pretty evil, too, at least to me. He had long, gray hair and looked like a warlock. He almost sounded like the voice of the High Priest in the ritual. Of course, he had to be one of them if he's bringing a robe. No matter—more important things were on our minds—we had just successfully passed through security, and were now officially inside the Grove compound. We had finally made it!

When we got a few feet inside the gates, the shuttle bus dropped us off. Of course, I was not ready to let loose of these two men because I still felt at that time that I was in some danger, and if I let these two old men out of my sight that I thought that we would either be caught or not be able to find our way around inside. So when we got off the bus, one of the old men got his bag and started walking toward the civic center area. Hell, I stuck to this guy like glue and tried to make all the conversation I could. Of course Alex came along too, but I definitely went in trying to follow this guy. At a certain point the man actually ditched me, because I'm sure he thought I was becoming a pest, and I probably was! I mean I don't know *what* he thought we were doing, but he kind of ditched off to the right, leaving Alex and I to explore independently.

I knew we were finally safe to go off on our own now. We walked down a woodsy trail, following the distant sound of classical piano music until we reached River Road, the Grove's main thoroughfare. Rounding the corner, the first thing we saw was an old man with a beer in one hand and his penis in the other, urinating against a tree. While we thought his manners left a lot to be desired, it reminded us of something…we'd been in the woods for hours…uh, where's the nearest bathroom?

Of course, at this time I was so scared that *I* actually had to pee like a racehorse. It was just unreal how bad I needed to go at this point because I was so scared…you know how you get when you're afraid, it almost makes you want to pee in your pants? I'm sure Alex was feeling the same way; we both desperately needed to use the restroom. Now, we'd both been raised properly, so of course we weren't just going to urinate against a tree like we saw that other man do. So we ducked into this over-sized, large cabin that looked like it was some kind of ritzy restaurant, looking for a restroom. When we asked where the bathrooms were, the camp stewards glared at us like we were crazy to ask for such a thing. Why didn't we go in the woods like everybody else? We didn't understand.

Of course, we later found out that this strange public urination ritual was a grand old tradition here in the redwoods. We didn't realize it at the time—Alex and I just thought it was about the strangest thing we'd ever seen. Even more puzzling, we saw signs actually posted on some of the ancient trees that said: "GENTLEMEN PLEASE! NO PEE PEE HERE!"

It probably goes without saying that the Bohos routinely ignored the signs. Maybe it's all some kind of elaborate inside joke I still don't get, but to the best of my knowledge, this is the most gloried-in ritual of the Grove; the freedom of powerful men to pee wherever they like, such is their divine birthright. Other expert researchers I've talked to believe that it also has something to do with the power-rush of man over nature. The Grovers peeing on sacred redwood trees particularly offends environmental activists. To them, it's just a simple matter of disrespect for Mother Nature.

This place we had stepped into looked like a big log cabin—kind of like one of these resorts over in Montana or like the Yellowstone Park type thing—you would see a grand cabin, or clubhouse near the entrance. When we went in there, there was a waitstaff in there wearing white aprons that looked like they were ready to serve food, but nobody was eating. We could hear this Scottish bagpipe music filtering through the whole place. You can hear that on the film we made. They had the fireplace going. I thought that was kind of odd because it really wasn't cold or anything. It was the middle of July, about 85 degrees outside that day. Too hot for a campfire!

First things first—we immediately headed for the restroom, and of course by this time Alex was leading the way. When we got to the restroom, I figured I better put the camera bag down somewhere. I knew I still had the pager-cam going so I didn't want to, you know, be too conspicuous if somebody should happen to walk in. I was carrying the bag over my shoulder like a purse, and then I had the pager clipped onto the bag. We had another, larger camera (a Canon XL) inside the bag, wrapped up in a bunch of newspapers, with a can of shaving cream, a change of clothes piled on top of it. I just needed to do an equipment check in a private place. Seeing the stalls, I decided that would be the best spot. I just hoped they didn't have surveillance cameras in there!

Amazingly, I had *some* of my mental faculties about me—my wisdom—even though I was terrified of being in this situation and wondering to myself why I agreed to even come here in the first place. I was still thinking, "how am I gonna get out of here?", and, "am I ever gonna see family and friends again after this?" Because after hearing those two old men talking about how much they paid for their robes, I didn't know *what* was going to happen later tonight.

I asked Alex at one point; "Do we have to have robes? I mean, aren't we gonna be out of place if we don't have robes?" I just kept asking Alex questions, and of course Alex didn't know anymore about this place than I did, so it was just kind of a way for me to get through the whole thing, to keep blabbering about anything at all, going through the motions and pretending everything was normal. So, when we were finished taking care of business, I picked up the camera bag and we got out of there. It was time to explore.

Alex and I decided the best way to look like we belonged there was to just keep walking, so we strolled through the grounds and had a good look at things. I remember us going over to the other side of the lake and noticed a man was following us, dressed in uniform. I became terrified again, and was ready to make a run for it if need be. Alex actually had to grab me and say," No, do NOT run." He told me to "be friendly to this guy, and if he asks you any questions, just play it by ear." So we both tried to look outwardly calm and kept walking towards the stone owl idol. We had to see for ourselves if this thing was for real. We just strolled on, minding our own business, and once we were sure this security guard wasn't going to bother us, we finally came to a halt. Alex told me to point the bag towards the Owl and get pictures of it. We have video of the owl statue taken during daylight, and this is how we got it. We were standing across the Lake from the Owl, and could easily tell this stone idol was 40-50 feet tall in relation to the 100-foot redwoods trees that surrounded it.

Then we walked right up to the Owl and touched it. We stood at the altar of the Owl, and I got a few close-ups of the statue. But when you're up close to it...really, I didn't even understand what this Owl was yet. Before this journey inside the Grove, I had heard Alex and other people talk about "burning the Owl", you know, like they burn the whole Owl. That's not what they do; they burn the effigy of a person at the ALTAR of the Owl.

There's an altar at the bottom of the Owl, and when you're up around it, you can tell it's an altar. But the funny thing about it is that this Owl statue up close looks like it's a million years old. It has moss all over it, and appeared to

248

me as if it were built of stone or rock. It actually only *looks* ancient, but the fact is that it has been in place there since 1928. Apparently, the Bohemians had it made to look like it's been there for thousands of years.

We were alone at this point, and felt free to take video of the area. There was no one else around that Owl at all—no employees or anything else. Of course, we were still inwardly terrified. I couldn't sit still. I told Alex, "we gotta keep walking, we gotta do something", because I felt uneasy staying in one spot too long. I was so paranoid that I thought surveillance cameras were watching us; I was looking in every tree to see if I could find microphones in the trees or whatever. I'm sure they are there; I'm *positive* they are there, but they are well hidden from sight.

We walked by quite a few of the camp areas and they had owls and skulls and other macabre symbols on display. We got some video of the camp sign that says "Je Suis Lafitte," which must be a reference to the legendary French pirate Lafitte, and what appears to be a real human skull adorns the sign. When we got to the end of River Road, we saw a small building that kind of looked like an outhouse at first glance. We went down this path that led us to a stunning overlook of the Russian River. Alex wanted me to take the video camera out of the bag and shoot some footage of the scenery. I told him I thought that would be too risky, to just stand there with a camera right out in the open, and that I didn't feel comfortable about it. Alex said, "Come on, Mike—hand me the camera. I'll do it."

He took the camera out of the bag and started taking video. Our pager cam only had an hour on the battery, which had gone dead by this time. So Alex took the other video camera out and shot video of the river and the big carpeted floatee where the Bohemians lay out and get a suntan. I should probably mention here that this "carpet" on the floatee was actually a very expensive Persian rug, not some cheap indoor-outdoor carpeting. Nobody was swimming that day because the water was too cold. The area was completely quiet—no signs of people around.

I was supposed to be the lookout to alert Alex if anybody was coming around the bend. I sat on a bench a few yards away and kept my eyes peeled for other campers or a security guard on patrol. Sure enough, Alex was just about caught red-handed actually filming when a Sonoma County sheriff (or perhaps a deputy) came around the corner, and of course I just about turned white as a ghost. I thought, "Oh, my God, this is it; we're gonna get caught. It's all over now. We're done."

The Sheriff walked up to us and luckily, he thought we were looking through binoculars. Apparently, he hadn't noticed Alex was holding a video camera. It was taking a big chance, but Alex asked him if he wanted a look, flashing a friendly smile and handing him the "binoculars." Of course, he didn't take us up on the offer, but it was a pleasant way to make conversation with the Sheriff and make him feel more at ease with us. I remember babbling nervously about the weather. I kept saying to Alex, "Oh, no, I won't go swimming today with you. It's too cold." The guy probably thought that I was with Alex as his "date," and Alex told the guy a bunch of nonsense. It was something else. We had a lot of laughs about it later, but at the time, my heart was racing and I had *no* sense of humor left.

The Sheriff finally left us alone again, and I exhaled deeply, thinking, *"Whew—that was a close one."* After the guy left, I was actually about ready to jump off that cliff into the Russian River, and try to swim my way out of there! I just didn't feel safe in this place at all. Something felt wrong. It was actually like this Sheriff knew what we were up to somehow. When we came out of the overlook area, we walked back by that same small building we had seen coming in, and observed banks of TV monitors inside that showed view of the various surveillance cameras located around the property. So, that's how the friendly Sheriff knew what we were doing up on the cliff with our camera. We got out of there FAST, before he could round up some help and come back for us!

When we got back up in the woods to the main areas, the Grovers were partying like crazy. There was quite a bit of liquor being served, and everyone we saw looked pretty looped. We ducked into one of the camps—I was too nervous to even notice the name—where they were having a big party, and I was thinking, "Oh, we're gonna be safe here; you know, there's so many people, we'll just blend right in." Right when we walked into the camp area, a man walked right up to us, seeming to come out of nowhere, and said, "Hi! Who are you all?" Oh, God, the panic I felt at this moment was *unreal*. But before I could speak up and tell the guy my fake name, Alex got so startled by the situation he goofed and gave the man MY fake name instead of his! And of course, I was totally knocked off base by that, so I just sat there and didn't have anything to say! Then, the man looked at me and asked, "Who are you?" Well, Alex had already given my fake name! I stammered, "Uhhhh…" and finally just ended up using my real name. What the hell. I was too stunned to think of anything else, anyway—my mind had just gone completely blank.

Our host was actually very friendly inside the camp. He led us over to the bar and told us to "get anything you want to drink." He was *real* nice, so was everyone else we met, as a matter of fact. So we mingled a little while, and of course, we didn't stay very long because we didn't know what to expect. We had hoped to maybe eavesdrop on a few conversations, curious to hear what the men were talking about, but the music and drunken laughter was so loud, it was impossible to hear much of anything. By now, it was starting to get a little dark outside; sunset was approaching, and the Bohemians were all starting to assemble in the dining area. We thought this would be a good time to look around undetected while the Grovers were all off having dinner.

Besides, we would have been very out of place in the dining hall. We didn't know anyone; there wouldn't be a placemat for us. Each table had a camp name where members could gather, but obviously, we were not affiliated with any of the camps. I thought to myself, "Oh, God, we're not gonna have anywhere to eat, because they all know each other in there. Where are we supposed to sit if everybody is in their little groups?" We saw the Bohemians starting to assemble in the dining circle, called to their places by a dinner bell in the shape of an Owl. Big surprise there.

So we started working our way up to the very top of the mountain, taking a path that led us past many of the more elite camps. Seems like the further up the mountain you go, the richer the camps get. Some of the camps I saw even had grand pianos and rock fireplaces, although we couldn't see much more of the interior because most of the camps are fenced.

Of course, we don't have a campsite, so we hiked all the way up to the top of the mountain and staked out a good vantage point where we could see the Bohemians at dinner and shot some video of that. It's a very communal ritual, they way they all go to supper together likea big family. It was really kind of weird. You know, like when you're in the Boy Scouts or when I was in the Army, nobody ever goes *everywhere* together; there's always one or two people who don't feel like eating and they stay behind or something. The dinner hour is obviously an important time for the Grovers. And tonight was special indeed—this was the big feast before the annual Cremation of Care ritual.

Alex and I were the only ones up in that area, up in the mountains. It was very quiet where we were. But we could hear them down there cheering and singing and doing all sorts of things while they were having dinner. You can hear it on the video, because it was really loud. The sound carried that far up the mountain to where we could hear it. After shooting the festivities for a few minutes, we decided we had better do another equipment check somewhere before the ceremony started at dusk.

We had to find a private spot again; somewhere that afforded a little light to see what we were doing. It was too dark to see outdoors now. The sun had disappeared over the horizon. So what we did was we snuck into one of the camps, which was pretty risky in my opinion, but Alex wanted to try it. We needed to have a knife in order to cut a hole in the bag for the camera lens.

We made our way into this very elaborate camp, one of the wealthier ones, obviously; it was very richly furnished. By this point, I was actually starting to gain some more confidence, if not false bravado. Might we actually get away with this? I was still fairly nervous being up in someone's private camp, knowing that someone could find us there, but we'd been bluffing our way through pretty well so far. We'd just act like we were drunk, tell them we got lost and staggered into the wrong campsite.

We made a hasty retreat from the camp once Alex had "borrowed" a knife from the bar, and adjourned to a bench outside, waiting for the Grovers to finish their meal and adjourn to the lakeside for the Cremation of Care. We figured we would just "blend in" with the Bohemians as they slowly filtered in for the big show. It felt like forever, the time that we had to wait, and of course, I grew increasingly anxious as each long minute ticked by. Every second having to sit there was like torture for me. It was the most intense agony I've ever been through in my life, because you never knew whether some security guard was gonna come out of the woods, or if there was a camera watching us, or if there were listening devices nearby, or whatever. You didn't ever know if they were just going to snag you at any moment. They could've just grabbed us. Which was a very good possibility in my mind at least, and I think in Alex's mind, too. But we sat there…and sat there…*and sat there.*

Finally it became fully dark, and we started walking slowly down toward the dining hall. I remember Alex making me keep watch, making sure that nobody was coming so that he could get a little more video. There was a point from the path where you could see down into the dining room, because the dining room didn't have a roof on it or anything; it just had lights hanging above the tables, strung between a bunch of tall trees.

There was a uniformed guard that we kept seeing walking by, and we took notice of him. Before we went up in the woods, we had seen this same guard once before, and he seemed to take notice of us, too. That's why we had to drop out of sight for a while because I think they were getting suspicious of us. We saw that guard one more time, that's when we ducked into the dining area. Of course, we couldn't sit down, there weren't any available chairs for us—the place was packed.

I walked to the back of the large dining area, and nobody really seemed to be paying any attention to me. Some of the staff looked at me, and seemed to be wondering why I didn't just take a seat somewhere and order dinner. I realized I had better think of something to do, because just walking around and around in circles made me look very out of place. Just then, I had a bright idea—I saw somebody's abandoned drink that was half full, so I grabbed the drink and I just carried it around like I was part of the group. I also picked up a few napkins from the tables that had the Bohemian Club logo and the owl on them as souvenirs.

We casually strolled back out on the main walking path, and were immediately confronted by the sight of old men relieving themselves on the trees again. They almost peed on our shoes as we walked by! And everybody was doing it, so by now, the whole place just reeked of urine. There was so much of it that it was literally running down the sidewalk.

The specific case that I remember is, when I went back out on the main walking path, I saw this old man—he must have been about 75 years old, with an odd-looking cap covering his gray hair—and he just pulled out his penis *right in front of me!* I was shocked beyond words; I remember he just whipped it out and start urinating right there. These men start talking to you while they're peeing, making idle conversation or telling jokes. Some of them took it like a religious experience; they weren't just peeing on the trees, they were *watering* the trees, like a hose, like going back and forth and then going off to the sides and doing it again. Some of them were a little discreet about it, but what astounded me were the older clubbers. For them, it was like a ritual or something for them that they had to show their penis to you. Like little boys act, you know? I don't know how else to describe that. I hate to have to get into graphic detail, but this is so bizarre, I have to put it on the record.

But the whole thing about it that confounds me so much is that they have plenty of bathrooms and porta-potties around the Grove that the men can use when the need strikes. They don't *need* to just pee all over the place. Most normal men just wouldn't do that in a civilized place, like on a city street in front of everybody. I spent several years in the army, and was already accustomed to seeing other men nude in the showers, but was still absolutely amazed by the behavior of these rich, powerful "gentlemen." Even when you go hunting, you don't just go right up and just start peeing that close to someone. You go off behind a tree, and you turn your body around where no one else can see. That's just good manners.

But enough of that—frankly, the smell was making Alex and I both sick to our stomachs. Even if they had offered us dinner, I honestly don't think we could have eaten a bite. About this time, we noticed the men were all getting through with dinner, and they were moving in lock-step towards the Owl. We figured we'd better get over there to the Lake, but we had one problem. The camera needed to be loaded with a new tape, it had to be turned on and the lens properly positioned through the hole we cut in the bag. So Alex and I went into this outdoor restroom. (By now, it should come as no surprise to you that we were the only occupants! Rule #1—if you want to be alone at Bohemian Grove, go to the bathroom.) Alex pointed to one of the stalls and told me," Go in there and change the tape out."

I was nervous because what if I, in the dark, did not turn this camera on? This camera had a funny thing about it: if you didn't do it just right, you didn't turn it on and it was doing something else besides filming. That was one mistake I sure didn't want to make tonight! I had to be very careful, taking extra time to do this right, because all I could think about was the sheer disappointment we would feel if I didn't get anything on film, blowing this mission and not getting another chance for a year. All I could think was, "Man, I do *not* want to have to do this a second time!"

As other people entered and exited the restroom to wash their hands (not to use the facilities), Alex was standing outside of the stall saying, "Hurry up, Bob," or whatever name he was calling me at that time. Of course, I was in there scrambling around trying to get this camera to work. And you know, I made damn sure it was working properly before I came out of the stall. This whole process took about ten minutes—I double-checked to ensure I had put a fresh one-hour tape in the camera, got the lens into position, propping it up to where it was sticking out of the hole in the bag and made sure it was recording!

Alex took control of the bag when I got out of the bathroom. We followed the crowd into the area where the ritual would soon take place. I recall looking over the huge crowd of assembled Bohemians, and it was just a sea of white faces, save for one. The only black man that I saw in there was handing out the programs. We were two of the last people to file in, and he gave us both a copy of the official Cremation of Care program. I was having a tough time trying to figure out if he was a member of the Club or not—he struck me more as an employee, not a Bohemian.

Of course, Alex and I went all the way around to the top of the hill because we wanted to be away from the crowd. I refused to have anyone behind me who could possibly see that I was filming. I wanted to be in the very back of the crowd, and be as inconspicuous as possible, which we managed to do.

I won't talk too much here about the ritual itself here because I've already covered the subject in a previous chapter, and also included a full transcript of the Cremation of Care ceremony as we recorded it that night. But one thing I do remember that's very interesting is when you see the explosion going off in the height of the Cremation of Care ceremony on our film, you can hear me let out an audible gasp. I almost fell backwards, the sudden loud noise scared me so bad! I rose up and just made the comment loud enough so everybody could hear me, just to cover, "Oh, they didn't do that last year!" Alex kind of hit me with his elbow and whispered in my ear, "How do you know they didn't do that last year? You weren't here!"

The commotion caused a few of the Bohemians to turn around and look at us, and I tried my best to distract them with a little conversation so that they wouldn't look too closely at Alex. It was so obvious to me that he was filming, so I was trying to cover the red light in the front by standing slightly ahead of him. The camera itself wasn't sticking out of the bag, but if anybody had really looked closely at the bag, they would have been able to see the red light through the hole. In my haste to load the camera earlier, I forgot to cover the red "record" light! It was kind of obvious—you have a bag on your shoulder and you're pointing it different ways, you know? So I think some people were getting kind of suspicious there toward the end.

Luckily for us, the Bohemians were too distracted by the elaborate fire ritual being carried out onstage to pay us much mind. I want to make the point that these people were actually raising their hands and worshipping this owl at certain points. I refused to worship an idol, because I think what God would do to you by worshipping the idol would be worse than what they could do to you even if you *did* end up on that altar up there. I could just not believe that this was going on and that our world leaders seemed to be delighting in it. The images that still haunt my mind most vividly are when the boatmen come across the Lake, and they had this body symbolizing Dull Care hollering as it was being killed, and they were burning it. I can still hear the screams as this raging bonfire consumed the effigy. And I'll never forget how these men were *oohing* and *ahhing*, like this was so *good* that they were killing Care. Old men in the audience were cackling wickedly about it. I found that shocking.

After the ceremony I started thinking *how in the hell are we going to get out of here?* I just kept asking God to please show us a way to get out of here fast because I felt it was really going to get even more bizarre after this ceremony; I was told by a lot of people that's when it really gets wild—you know, the sex parties and engaging in all sorts of drugs and alcohol and who knows what else. And I definitely didn't want to get involved in all that stuff. So I told Alex, "As soon as we get this on film, we need to get the hell OUT OF HERE and get out quick!"

Fortunately, when it was over with we jumped into the crowd of people and then we took a right turn and ended up going out of a servants entry. We found ourselves on a road that ended up at this first guard shack somehow. I don't how in the world we got out of there, to tell you the truth. My survival instincts were kicking in, and I just ran until I couldn't run anymore.

When we got on the other side of the guard shack we ran down the main road to where we had first come in, and walked a couple of miles up the road until we saw Jon Ronson and his crew waiting for us. We all went back to the hotel and started making copies of the tapes immediately. We weren't sure if the county sheriff was going to come knocking on our door any minute, so we wanted to make copies first thing and get them to the British. Everybody gathered around the TV set, eager to see the video we had taken such risks to get:

Alex (*viewing the tape, explaining the action to Violet*): We're standing in a big crowd and they keep getting in front of us. I'm trying to guess, holding this bag with this camera here, what's the best way to get the owl?

Mike: We're lucky. Nobody's ever gotten out with that footage at all.

Alex: Yeah. The problem is we just improvised. We just cut a hole in the bag and stuck the camera up in there. And we had...the camera stuck up right there, and I'd be standing there going (*gestures*)...like that. But it gets better. There's a lot of light later.

(Audio from "Cremation of Care" tape plays)

Violet: That's scary! God! They're wearing black robes. They're *terrifying*. How bizarre is *that*? A bunch of old men in black robes in the middle of nowhere.

Mike: They're worshipping...like an Owl god.

Alex: Yeah, this is all pretty disgusting.

Ronson: Mike, in a nutshell: do you think that what you saw was unholy?

Mike: Well, it's very strange to me that these people are supposed to be running uh...so-called "America", and the world, and they're up there doing this?

Ronson: Mike, you seem freaked out.

Mike: Oh, I *am*. Well, I get so tired of these people telling lies to the people...we know the Davidians so well, and I know that they're good people...they're saying the Branch Davidians are cultists? Well, THIS looks like a cult to me! Look at them!

Alex: Mike is absolutely right though. These people point their fingers all day and call people extremists or cult members or whatever, for their religious beliefs. This was a pagan ceremony, worshipping the earth, and then engaging in human sacrifice; that is, *mock* human sacrifice.

Ronson: Aren't they just saying that for 2 weeks, "We don't have to worry about anything"?

Alex: Yeah, but they're also worshipping the great Owl god and burning someone in effigy and torturing them. And as they're burning, they..."Ah, no! Ahhh!" You'll see it on the tape here. I mean, listen to these guys laughing behind us—(imitates wicked laughter). I mean, you got all these old guys going, "Burn him! Burn him!"

Mike: They're cheering for this guy to be killed, to be sacrificed.

Ronson: But they're not killing a person.

Alex: We understand that they're not literally killing a person, but they're...

Mike: How do we know they're not killing a person?

Ronson: I don't think they're really...surely they're not really killing...they're...

Alex: Now, wait a minute; wait a minute. You've got a black...I mean, certainly you saw it...you've got Death—right here, look; here's the boat; look at it, right there!...You've got Death on this black boat bringing a pallet with...like a paper-mache person, obviously. It's got the feet, and the body, and the head under the deal, and they take it over and burn it for some idol, for some Owl god. It really looks like a demon; it's got like horns up there. They just call it an owl.

Mike: The whole place is full of owl statues and gods!

Ronson: What kind of things?

Mike: It's just...owls are everywhere. They're everywhere! There's like statues of owls everywhere.

Alex: You're walking along, and it's like 80 year old men peeing on trees going, "Here, let's pee!"

And then you see them pull their...they're peeing on a tree when there's a bathroom 5 feet away. Out in public, I mean on concrete paved roads, asphalt roads; "Here, let's pee!" "Sure, Bob!" And they're like showing everybody; "Ha, ha, I'm peeing on a tree!" and it's running down the street.

Mike: I'm not gonna lie—I was scared to death.

Ronson: What did you think might happen?

Mike: If we got caught? What would have happened?

Alex: Well, we could have been put up on that boat!

Mike: Yeah, you don't know what these people are. These people are sick!

Alex: A bunch of bizarre, Luciferian garbage. (*Audio*) Here we go...

Violet: That is just so satanic!

Alex: George Bush, Jr. is supposedly going out there next week, and his father admits he's been out there many times.

Mike: We're supposed to be a "Christian" culture. And our elected leaders are worshipping an Owl god! How do you think that would fly with the American people?

Alex: Yeah, I mean, you're not supposed to worship Jesus or something, or anything else. It's worship the Owl god.

Mike: (*Pointing to the 40-foot stone owl statue*) That's a big rock, Violet. That's a big rock. I've heard this talked about for years and years and years, but I've never seen any footage of it.

I remember hardly being able to sleep that night—the excitement of everything that had just happened to us, combined with a few nightmares of what *could* have happened, kept me tossing and turning for hours. The next morning, I actually felt compelled to seek out the nearest church I could find to just pray and to thank God for protecting us and guiding us through that whole ordeal.

The whole experience sneaking into the Bohemian Grove had been a true test of my faith, and I must tell you that when I went to the local church to pray the next morning, I had every intention of getting up before the congregation and exposing what I had seen the night before. When I got to the services in the little white church in Occidental, I sat in the back pew and watched the people for a while. But it looked like to me like some of the people were "in the know" at that church, so I didn't open my mouth. I didn't talk to one person inside that church. I came into the service late, and it was just like any other small town church, but the vibes I picked up there from some of the people just didn't feel right at all.

A lot of times when you go to a small church like that, it's a church with 35 people or so, maybe 40, and they'll introduce you and they have gifts or something that are there. And nobody said *anything*. It just wasn't a very friendly atmosphere. I sat like in the back and nobody said anything the whole service and I left before they all got up. My whole plan was to go there and expose what I had seen the night before because it had affected me so much. But it never did happen. I almost felt that God told me to keep my mouth shut, that this wasn't the right time and place to speak up. And I'm glad I didn't because no telling who would have gone back and told their friends at the Bohemian Club that we had trespassed on their private property.

My gut feeling was that there were people in that church that either knew about the Owl and the ceremony, or had connections to people that worked there and it probably would have gotten back to the Bohemians that we had videotape of their ritual, and that we were still in town. Speaking up now might jeopardize our entire mission. I decided that silence was the best policy—for now—at least until we had gotten ourselves and the precious videotape safely out of the state.

We all just wanted to get the hell out of northern California, even though we had two more days scheduled on our stay there. But I told Alex and Violet I didn't think it would be wise for us to stick around. We all agreed that we were in danger if we stayed in Occidental, so Alex and I decided to go back to San Francisco and stay in a hotel under assumed names until we got on our flight back home. The British were getting out of Dodge already anyway—as soon as they filmed one last segment with me in a local park, they were outta there! Ronson had wanted to get my thoughts about last night's events on tape:

> Mike: I've heard these stories for years being in the Patriot community, and...it's true.
>
> Ronson: What's true?
>
> Mike: They sacrifice a...they sacrifice *something* to an Owl god, is what I got out of it.
>
> Ronson: Weren't they just sacrificing all the troubles in the world.... for a holiday?

Mike: That's not what I got out of it!

Ronson: But wasn't it just a metaphor?

Mike: To me, it doesn't matter what it was. I know that there's rituals that go on. Let's just take, for instance, April 19th, 1995—the Oklahoma City bombing, and what happened at Waco April 19th, 1993—I think that's all part of it. That's my opinion. That's part of it. I think they're sacrificing in the real world too.

Ronson: Was this the New World Order?

Mike: Yes. Definitely. I looked the New World Order in the face out there.

Chapter XII

ad absurdum

(To the point of absurdity)

The Fallout
All *Hell* Breaks Loose

As soon as we got back to Austin, Alex was all over the airwaves with this incredible story—not just his own nationally-syndicated show, but he was a guest on many other radio broadcasts as well. I remember he went on Bo ("Rambo") Gritz's radio show, and Bo could hardly believe what he was hearing. I was sitting right there in the car with Alex when he did the interview with Bo Gritz over the phone. Like a lot of people, Bo was having a tough time dealing with the reality of what the Cremation of Care ceremony actually entailed. Didn't sound very conservative or Christian to him, either!

Alex and I started airing the raw footage we shot inside the Grove on local public access television the same week we got back from California. The citizens of Austin were the first people in history to see this rare film of the Cremation of Care ceremony, live on the airwaves of ACTV—months before the rest of the world saw the tape of what really goes inside this exclusive retreat of the power elite.

We managed to get the film (*Dark Secrets—Inside Bohemian Grove*) edited and produced in a couple of months, an all-time speed record for us. We did it really fast because we just wanted to get this tape out to the people as fast as possible. The public showed an incredible interest in this story, even if the mainstream press didn't.

The film made quite a splash initially. What surprised me most was how many complaints we got from Christians in the United States. Of course, we expected them to like it, but what we found was sometimes just the opposite. One guy even got so mad, he apparently smashed the tape and jumped up and down on it, crushing it into a million bits! And the reason he got so upset was because he thought Violet (Jones) was showing too much cleavage in this movie. I think we got a dozen or more complaints from people who thought Violet's sweater was too low-cut, which is the most ridiculous thing I'd ever heard! These people couldn't get beyond that enough to actually look at what's going on in the rest of the tape, they never even made it as far as the owl ceremony. I'm a Christian too, but that's really taking things too far. They shouldn't be so worried about Violet's cleavage—they need to be worried about the New World Order.

We had much better luck with the churches serving black communities, as far as where we found the most favorable reaction to the film. We went to some of the small Texas towns, and gave copies of the film to local churches, and the black churches were very interested in it, very open to it, compared to the predominantly white churches we visited. And the big mainstream Christian churches, most of them operating in major cities, turned us down flat when we offered them the tape. But the churches in predominantly black communities were very open and receptive to this; in fact, a couple of the churches asked me to get up and tell my own personal story about the Grove to their congregation, which I was glad to do.

I talked to a lot of these people afterwards, and found that as a general rule, the people living in black communities have a much better grasp on what's really going on than the white people do. I suppose it's just because black communities have always been targeted by the U.S. government—they recognize oppression when they see it because they've spent hundreds of years underneath the heels of jack-booted thugs—so the antics of their leaders at Bohemian Grove came as no great surprise to them. African-Americans understood and embraced our film right away.

THE REDCOATS (TURNCOATS)

The next controversy we had to deal with was the public reaction to how Jon Ronson portrayed us in his British film, *Secret Rulers of the World*. As for my opinion, I thought Ronson did an excellent job overall, at least in educating the British public on the importance of Bohemian Grove. At the time, most Britons were totally unaware of the Grove and probably figured that because it was located on another continent and involved mostly American leaders, what went on there was of no concern to them. Ronson's film changed that widespread impression in the UK, and for that fact alone, I am eternally grateful to him for making the documentary.

My only issue with the film is that I didn't like the way he left it. He showed Alex leading a group of protesters down at the Governor's Mansion. This was when G. W. Bush was still Governor of Texas, but he was in the midst of his 2000 election campaign for president and may have still been at the Grove himself when we did the protest that day! Bush wasn't even there, but we were out in front of the mansion carrying signs, calling him an occult practitioner, marching around and making our point. But because one of the protesters, Lance Cook, was wearing a long black robe and a George Bush Halloween mask, Jon Ronson used that footage to make us all look foolish. And that's where he left it in his documentary. That's the last scene. I thought that he was trying to minimize the seriousness of this issue and just make it look like a freak show to the viewers. We were trying to get attention to the fact that this was really going on, and because we used a little humor to make our point, Ronson took that humor out of context and tried to make us out as kooks.

Just for the record, here is the entire text of that protest, unedited, so that you may see it in the proper context as originally intended.

> Alex Jones: *(driving with me to the Governor's Mansion. This conversation took place in the car on our way to the protest with the video camera rolling.)* "Well, we're going to confront George Bush Jr. on Bohemian Grove today. They'd been announcing on CNN, MSNBC, on television last night and this morning, for the first time in history, they're admitting it: "the decision to select Dick Cheney as Bush's vice-presidential running-mate was made at Bohemian Grove. George Bush, Sr. the former president, and Colin Powell and others were there." So now they're just throwing it in everybody's face.
>
> George Bush is down here at the Governor's Mansion across the street from the Capitol, about to announce Dick Cheney as his vice-presidential running mate. We're gonna go blow the party for him and get the information out to people. We're not gonna stop—we're taking the counter-propaganda and throwing it right back in their faces. I want to make it clear that I'm neither Republican nor Democrat, but the facts speak for themselves: George Bush Sr., Jr., even their grandfather Prescott Bush, were all members of the Bohemian Club and the Skull and Bones Order. So we are just dropping by to...well, let them know that we're fully aware of their activities.
>
> *(Out in front of the Governor's Mansion, surrounded by reporters from local and national news stations, Alex starts yelling through a bullhorn at the secret service agents across the street.)*
>
> Alex: This is madness! This is how George Bush dresses up *(points to protester Lance Cook, who is wearing a George Bush Halloween mask and a long black hooded robe)*. Right here! We got him on tape doing it! This is how they dress up—right here! In red and black robes. This is how George Bush dresses when he's at the Bohemian Grove. This is how he dresses! Somebody put it on television! Absolutely disgusting. George Bush isn't a Con-

servative; he's not for family values, he is nothing but a Luciferian twit. *A Luciferian twit*, Bush! You may think you can feed on the human population, but we say NO to you!

We're on the march—the Empire's on the run! Long live the Constitution, and death to the New World Order! We stand firm…we stand firm for America, but this is *evil*, Bush. And we're gonna get this story out. We're gonna continue to push it, because the truth will not be hidden! The truth that you are part of a 3,000-plus year-old demonic cult for the owl God Molech from Babylon as well as Tyre. We have your High Priest admitting all this! We have it on videotape. It's documented! Bush is a Luciferian, a devil-worshipper!

We're not afraid of you! We're not afraid of your minions; in fact we're waking your minions up every day, with the hard-core evidence. We know your father met eleven times with Bill Clinton in '91. The whole thing was stage-managed. We understand you've been helping sell this country out, Bush. And we're going to expose you and your Luciferian rites! We're going to expose your criminal activities at Bohemian Grove. We have the videotape! This is a massive story. One of the stories of the Century! One of the stories of the Century! These Luciferian rites have been going on in northern California for 120 years! We went inside the Grove for the Cremation of Care. We witnessed the entire debacle. Many of these Secret Service agents you see out here today have been protecting these people, inside of this system!"

Although the film Alex and I got out of Bohemian Grove probably made some small dent in the minds of American voters in the 2000 presidential election, it clearly didn't prevent Bush from winning or, depending on what you believe, *stealing* the election.

I've only had one personal encounter with George W. Bush, and it was not a pleasant one. Alex and I were covering a press conference in 1998 when Bush was still governor of Texas, and Alex was arrested for asking him a question about the Council on Foreign Relations. I captured the entire incident on camera and this arrest can be seen in our documentary film, *America—Wake Up or Waco*. It was pretty weird seeing him in person, and I was up front in the press area, very close, just a few feet away from him, so I got a very close look at the man. He did look rather…reptilian, for lack of a better term. There was something decidedly cold-blooded about him. He did not have the warmth of a true Texan about him. A lot of people mistakenly believe that George Bush is a Texan. Far from it. He's lived in Texas for years, but the Bushes (including

W.) are from Kennebunkport, Maine, not Houston, Texas. The whole Bush family is East Coast establishment all the way.

ONE YEAR LATER

After our heavily publicized foray into the Bohemian Grove the previous year, security was stepped up considerably for the summer 2001 encampment. So were the protests. Mary Moore's annual Bohemian Grove Action Network protest at the gates of the Grove saw many more people in attendance that year, and among the demonstrators was our own Ed Hohmann, a reporter for *infowars.com*.

Ed traveled from Texas to San Francisco to cover the 2001 Grove midsummer encampment, and although he wisely chose *not* to attempt getting inside, he did gather video footage of the protests outside the main gates. Alex and I were on the air doing our live local TV show on July 21st, just as Ed was driving back into town. Ed phoned the studio and did a live interview with Alex about what he witnessed at the Bohemian Grove. Here are some excerpts from that broadcast:

> Alex (AJ): Ed, tell us what you saw when you were there.
>
> Ed (EH): First of all, the protest itself—they bused in hundreds of people, apparently from San Francisco and other areas. There were locals—not "local" locals, but people from the county, from Sonoma County and the surrounding towns there—as part of the protest. I did not find anyone at all from the actual town of Monte Rio—the *real* locals—that participated in the protest. I've seen some of the protests. I was present at many of the anti-Vietnam protests back in the '70's. And this thing up at Bohemian Grove last weekend was in some respects just the typical rent-a-crowd type. They'll protest anything and everything except for the fact that this is a dark, sinister Luciferian cult!
>
> AJ: And there's no world government. I mean, the Luciferian stuff's "kinda cool", they think. I mean, these people say Alex Jones is a kook—there's no occult ceremony going on in there! It's an urban legend.
>
> EH: (chuckles) Right. That was also interesting that most of the people there, most of the protesters had not even heard that anyone had managed to sneak in and take film of this ceremony inside. For the most part, the protest was just a bunch of Marxist, pro-Communist people, and others

that were protesting the fact that people inside the Grove were capitalists and filthy rich. That was about the extent of it.

AJ: But again, Ed, there's no such thing as "Communists", there was no Satanic ceremony, and they weren't doing one outside the Grove. And the sky is not blue.

EH: As far as what they did outside the Grove, they did wait until the major media left—Channel 4 from San Francisco, for example, who was there filming the protest itself—and most of the protesters had left and gotten on the buses and drove away. Then this core group of people sat down and formed a circle right at the gates of the Grove. Now, the lady in charge of this did a really good job of guiding the people into what started off as just a quiet little bit of meditation that no Christian could possibly have a problem with. Gradually, this High Priestess took the entire crowd deeper and deeper until it turned into what I saw as a full-blown occult ceremony. But the interesting thing about this core group is that they weren't actually "local" locals, and they were all...at least...well I wouldn't say all, but at least 80 percent of them were completely familiar with the aspects of that ceremony; calling in the Four Spirits of the Elements, forming the magic circle, the chants they used to conjure up power. The object of all this chanting was to put a spell into the road that the Grovers would drive across, cast another spell into the Grove and at the people inside, and then they opened the circle releasing the spirits. This is all the basic form of a standard witchcraft ceremony. And this lady...it was a lady and an elderly man that basically were, I suppose, the High Priest and the High Priestess there...that actually conducted the ceremony, guiding everyone in the performance of it. And this blew my mind to actually catch this on video, to see that they were doing this openly.

AJ: And I wondered why these people didn't want to help promote our film, the Grove protesters didn't want to talk about it, they didn't want it out for the public to see. They attacked me on syndicated radio shows. Now we know why, Ed. They themselves were doing a ritual very similar to what these world leaders are doing inside the Grove with the Cremation of Care.

EH: That's exactly right. I think the protesters call this ritual the "Resurrection of Care," which is supposed to be mocking the Grovers. And the whole protest, I believe, was a diversion. It felt staged to me in that when the major media came out to cover this story because they had heard there were things going on inside the Grove, they would instead focus on this weird group of protesters, who were definitely the oddballs. Just watch the video and you'll see the kind of people that were on there. It wasn't about the issues at all—it was more about these folks trying to be as bizarre as they can, to attract as much media coverage as they could get.

As Alex and Ed were talking on the phone, Ed was frantically driving to get to the television studio with the tape, hoping to air it live for the viewers. He was racing against the clock—our show ended at 6pm, it was now about 5:30, and Ed was stuck in rush-hour traffic. So he continued telling his story live over the phone, just to get the information out to the viewers as quickly as possible:

EH: Again, I suppose the most important thing about this protest was the fact that it's...there hadn't been a protest for 14 years, and that included both Republican and Democratic administrations. There was some talk...the locals reckoned that maybe because Bill Clinton was in power the last few years that maybe that was the reason they weren't protesting at the Grove. But, the timing of this had everything to do with the fact that the documentary that the British made from the film Alex and Mike shot last year, has now been aired in England and is about to air nationwide in this country. So, they've gotta do something to counter that. And by linking Alex in with these protesters—these Marxist, Communist, anti-capitalist protesters...it's an easy way to try and make Alex look bad, and to distract people from the message itself. They're too preoccupied with the messenger!

Ed finally pulled up in the studio parking lot, and ran in with the tape, handing it to me. "Hot off the presses." He smiled. As soon as I had the tape cued up and ready to go, I gave Alex the sign and he brought Ed Hohmann into the studio to join him live on camera:

AJ: Ed, we're going to have you on the show next week, when we'll have more time. We're gonna have this footage in its entirety for people. I want to air about 5 or 10 minutes of them praying and maybe releasing the spirits and turning the cauldron. This is just raw footage. I haven't even seen it yet. We've cued it up to a middle point, and are gonna air some of it for you, and then next week we'll have all the tidbits. But Ed, while he's cueing this up—and it's ready, Mike? My producer, Mike Hanson, says the tape is ready to go. OK, just to set this up for the viewers, Ed, tell them about the cauldron and the spirits and some of those things real quick.

EH: In the middle of the road, right at the gate of Bohemian Grove, there was a young lady sitting stirring a cauldron. And that cauldron was water from various parts of the world; "sacred places" is where they said it came from. And there were a few other things in there, I believe looked like flower petals and things, but I wasn't able to make that out exactly. Anyway, they stirred this cauldron with the water while the chanting and the entire ceremony went on. And when the ceremony was over with, they offered water; they made water available from that cauldron to anyone that wanted to take it with them to perform magic spells, that sort of thing. And the water that was left over they dumped in the middle of the road where the Grovers would have to drive over it, and hopefully their anti-capitalist spell would work on the Grovers.

AJ: And I'm sure they want an anti-capitalist spell to work inside. I mean this is world government, folks. The globalists are the financiers and foundations who have always funded movements such as communism because it serves their agenda to divide and conquer us. And these are the leaders of the world have a bunch of communists out there protesting *for* them, and the poor kids out there waving signs don't even realize how they are being manipulated. But just like the WTO protests—just like over in England with the riots, and now in Sweden—riot police shoot people in the back! Good protesters come out, the paid provocateurs and agitators show up, cause a riot, and then the troops get to come in and sweep people. Always running offense and defense for 'em. Left and right are the same thing, folks, to get you totally confused. We're gonna go to that tape. Stay with us, ladies and gentlemen. This is important information.

I began to roll the videotape. It started out innocently enough, showing a crowd of more than 60 people holding hands, standing in a circle and humming a long, low note ("Om") in unison. Most of them appeared to be old hippie types, wearing tie-dye clothing, carrying flowers and chanting. Every so often, Alex or Ed would ask me to stop the tape so that they could add commentary:

AJ: Now, the chanting has been going on for about an hour, folks. I've shown you the footage of the satanic ceremony inside; now you see the "white magic" people outside, and there's the witch stirring her cauldron in the middle. And we have close-ups of all of this—this is unedited—we've just cued up the tape. As you know, Ed literally just got back from California, rushing into the studio so that we could get this tape on the air for you today.

EH: What they're doing at this point is, they're placing their hands on the road and they're putting a spell into the road, but it's the energy that was created during the ceremony. They're focusing it through their hands into the road that the Grovers will have to drive over to get in and out of the Grove.

AJ: Now, again, it's a black cauldron and they also had an altar on the back of a truck. Oh, you see the pentagram they have drawn on the ground there. Again, these people think they're getting a bunch of power. Look, I don't care; you want to dance around a witch's cauldron with a lady stirring it, and draw pentagrams on the ground, and think you're gonna stop the world leaders who are confiscating our guns and building concentration camps, that's your choice. They're doing the same thing you're doing inside the Grove to a strange demon god, and then you criticize me, saying, "Oh, no, there's no demon god; you're imagining that, Alex." Oh, really? Well, now that you've seen video of the pagan ceremonies that go on both inside *and* outside the Grove, can you still say that in good conscience? My point is these men at Bohemian Grove are the world leaders that have the nuclear missiles, that own the banks, that run our country. Their aim is the entire world. They're putting face-scanning cameras up, folks. You'd *better* get concerned and real, real quick!

A local Gurneville newspaper's coverage of the 2003 Grove protests (*Grove Protests Mostly Low-Key* by Lee Meryl, Sr.) confirms that things are changing in Sonoma County, at least the general mood and tempo of the demonstrations. This year, for the first time since its' founding, Mary Moore has taken a back seat in the Bohemian Grove Action Network, leaving the organizing and rallying to new faces. In addition, new protests were organized this year by the liberal anti-war group "Not In Our Name." The anti-war group staged a community forum on July 12, 2003 at the Monte Rio Elementary School, followed by a "Fat Cats Festival and Parade," marching from Monte Rio to the gates of the Grove on July 19.

Protesters gather outside the Grove gates, 2001.
(Photo courtesy of Mare Moore, The Bohemian Grove Action Network)

With a family member battling cancer, Mary Moore found that the demands on her time were now too great to continue her leadership of BGAN, and began to turn over the reins to other groups. However, this year, unhappy with the change of name and concept of the festival and parade, she removed herself as an organizer, although she continued to support the demonstrations, and maintained the Bohemian Grove Action Network booth at the festival.

For Mary Moore, the new approach seems to trivialize the serious issues being discussed inside the Grove. "I support the work that is being done," Mary told a local reporter, "but disagree with the setting. There is nothing festive about it. Why can't we go back to the way we used to do it? A rally, if that's what they want, should be kept under an hour, with one or two key people speaking." Attendance was down at the protests this year, with only about 100 people showing up at the Grove gates to participate in the "resurrection of care." They were greeted by a tremendous number of police in riot gear, ready for action. Apparently, the cops were expecting a bigger, angrier crowd, and surely must have been disappointed at not having more demonstrators to drag away in handcuffs.

THE PHANTOM PATRIOT

In November 2001, a curious letter arrived at the *infowars.com* offices from someone who called himself "The Phantom Patriot." His real name was Richard McCaslin, a former U.S. Marine and Hollywood actor with a rather impressive resume of film and TV credits listed on the back of his enclosed 8x10 promotional photograph. McCaslin was also a cartoonist in his spare time, and had created a comic strip about the adventures of the "Phantom Patriot," a sort of caped crusader who saves America from the New World Order bad guys. Alex had seen a couple of his comics and thought them unique enough to merit a brief plug on our local public access television show. For our enjoyment and amusement, McCaslin had included more copies of his "Phantom Patriot" comics in the envelope, too.

The letter itself started out like any other piece of fan mail, the type we receive by the hundreds weekly at the office. But the writer had obviously taken a tremendous amount of care in penning this little homage, which read more and more like a personal manifesto. From the tone of the letter, it became clear to me that this was a person who was determined to get attention at any cost.

The letter was 6 pages, neatly handwritten on both front and back of the lined notebook paper. It read in part:

"Dear Alex,

Thank you for promoting my material on your show. Outside of public access, I have no way of knowing how much of an impact I'm creating in Austin and beyond. I have decided that it is time to extend my trust to you and a few others. Up until this time, no one has known my real identity. I'm a one-man operation.

...I'd like to explain why I operate the way I do. I guess you could consider this whole "Phantom Patriot" thing a "grassroots psy-op" against the New World Order. If you have ever read *The Moon Is A Harsh Mistress* (Robert Heinlein), and remember the Simon Jester character, then you probably understand. I've simply taken the concept to the next level.

My goal is to create a folk hero for the 21st Century; a living, breathing urban legend. It became obvious to me that the freedom movement in this country needed some kind of larger-than-life icon. Originally, I had thought about forming a group of people who would make appearances across the country as the "Phantom Patriot." Unfortunately, we both know what can happen when a "secret society" is created. I would probably have ended up with a bunch of white supremacist nutcases, or worse yet, being infiltrated by the Feds.

The only sure way to keep this operation on track was to simply do it myself. If caught, I'd obviously be labeled a "lone nut." However, as long as I didn't kill or kidnap anybody, or blow up any buildings, I might be perceived as a *"Robin Hood/Zorro"*-type figure. That was my intent, anyway. Yeah, I know—I've read way too many comic books. But you have to admit; the concept seems to be working, to a certain extent.

As you can see from my enclosed resume, I have the acting background to pull this off. However, let me clarify that this isn't a show business thing. I've wasted too many years pretending to be a hero. I wanted to do something for this country for real. This is just my unique way of doing it.

Sincerely,

Richard McCaslin"

At the time, we didn't see anything threatening or dangerous about the letter, and although we figured the guy was eccentric, he was most likely harmless. Yet, something in my gut told me to save that letter for some reason, and now I'm very glad I did. In retrospect, this letter turned out to be a pre-confessional from McCaslin, who was discreetly revealing his plans to do something really big, although we didn't know exactly what he had in mind—*yet*.

We found out soon enough. Just two months after he sent this letter to us, McCaslin did the unthinkable: he broke into the Bohemian Grove in January, 2002, reportedly heavily armed and dressed in his "Phantom Patriot" costume, staging a Lone-Nut invasion of the Grove property.

After forgetting batteries for his flashlight, the camouflaged superhero got lost in the dark among the giant redwoods and fell asleep in one of the camp cabins. The bemasked vigilante then allegedly decided to arson the Grove's dining facility. Local deputies supposedly performed an historic act of negotiation, disarming the heavily armed "terrorist" without a single shot, grenade, or missile being fired. The jailed "Phantom Patriot" then immediately held a press conference to name none other than Alex Jones as his inspiration to do this crazy thing! McCaslin claimed that after seeing our film *Dark Secrets: Inside Bohemian Grove*, he was so disturbed by the idea of ritual human sacrifice going on there, he resolved to do something about it.

McCaslin was sentenced to 11 years in prison, a sentence that was dramatically enhanced because he had donned a bulletproof vest and armed himself with automatic weaponry and explosives for the assault. Meanwhile, back at the *Infowars* ranch in South Austin, our phones were ringing off the hook with reporters from the mainstream media wanting some kind of comment from Alex.

Alex told the *Santa Rosa Press Democrat* that he was stunned by the incident, saying that it "sounds insane." Yet at the same time, he defended his claim that there might be real human sacrifices going on in the Grove. But the press was brutal. *The New York Times* did a hit piece on Alex, laying the entire blame for the unfortunate "Phantom Patriot" incident directly at his feet. That reasoning is about as imbalanced as someone going on a killing spree because they saw the movie *Halloween* and then blamed the film for their resulting actions. Who is guilty of the crime? The movie or the murderer?

Like the *Times'* coverage, none of the mainstream press bothered to mention that free video clips of the Cremation of Care ceremony are available at *infowars.com,* where readers can judge the accuracy of our reporting for themselves. None of the critics admitted to actually watching our video, *Dark Secrets: Inside Bohemian Grove,* before writing their 30-plus pages of accusatory reviews.

Even the local *Press-Democrat,* who are usually fairly critical in their coverage of the Grove, ran with headlines that screamed: "PHANTOM PATRIOT FEARED HUMAN SACRIFICES—In jailhouse interview, suspect says he sneaked into exclusive Bohemian Club prepared to kill!"

The story said that McCaslin had been planning a heavily armed assault on the Bohemian Grove for more than a year, believing "it would take something dramatic" to draw attention to human sacrifices he feared were being held there. During the jailhouse interview, the paper described 37 year-old McCaslin as being a "well-spoken, lucid and clean-shaven man" who said he just "wanted to make a point" by breaking into the Grove, but was prepared to kill people if necessary. He was being held in the mental health ward of the Sonoma County Jail at the time:

> "McCaslin, who calls himself the "Phantom Patriot," said he doesn't belong to any militia, the National Rifle Association or any religious group, fearing he'd be immediately pigeon-holed and not taken seriously.
>
> McCaslin said he thinks he is sane.
>
> "They might beg to differ," he said with a laugh, pointing his thumb behind him into the mental health ward."

(*Santa Rosa Press-Democrat,* January 22, 2002)

275

Reports vary as to what exact weaponry McCaslin was carrying the night he busted into the Bohemian Grove. The *Press-Democrat* reported that he was armed with a semiautomatic rifle/shotgun hybrid, a .45-caliber handgun, a crossbow, a 2-foot-long sword, a knife and a hand-made bomb launcher. Wearing a skeleton mask and Phantom Patriot costume, and carrying several of the weapons, he sneaked past the guard outposts into the Grove near the Russian River. He also carried a camouflage-colored Bible, poems he'd written and pamphlets about his motives and concerns. One pamphlet included a reference to an Old Testament verse from Leviticus above a crossed-out Bohemian Club insignia. He said he left the papers at the base of a huge owl "idol."

Luckily, this was the off-season, when very few club members are present at the Grove, or the situation could have escalated into something much more violent than it actually was. McCaslin did not get the "heavy resistance" he expected. In fact, not a single shot was fired, and nobody was hurt.

After his arrest, he reportedly told detectives that he had come to the Bohemian Grove to kill child molesters and those performing human sacrifices. "He planned on killing people," Sonoma County Sheriff's Sgt. Steve Brown told the *Press-Democrat*. "He planned on confronting people doing these weird things."

McCaslin told reporters that he got the idea from watching our film *Dark Secrets: Inside Bohemian Grove*, although he said the tape was fuzzy and didn't show any faces. He was referring to the Cremation of Care ceremony sequence. But he said he could make out the form of a wrapped infant, which he believed was real and alive, being sacrificed by fire on the altar of the great Owl of Bohemia.

A Marine in the early 1980s and a former stuntman at Six Flags amusement park in Texas, McCaslin isn't married and has no children. Otherwise, he said, he couldn't have taken on the act. "That wouldn't be responsible," he told reporters from the jail.

He said he legally bought the weapons over time. He said he considered the legal and personal consequences if he was caught, and what his prison time could be depending on the whether he killed someone. In July 2001, he made a reconnaissance mission to the Grove. He wanted to make sure it really existed and map his route in.

In late December 2001, McCaslin said he moved to Carson City, Nevada, from Austin, Texas. He got an apartment and spent a few weeks "blending in," finalizing his plans. Less than a month later, he drove his pickup to Sonoma County and parked in the dark woods near the Grove. After sneaking inside the grounds, McCaslin said he heard only a couple of voices and realized there was no one there but security.

Not wanting the trip to have been in vain, he said he went into the main dining hall, and using degreaser and some flammable materials, set an admittedly "poorly made fire."

"I'm not an arsonist," he told the *Press-Democrat*.

Richard McCaslin, aka "The Phantom Patriot"

The fire was doused by a sprinkler system, but the fire alarm alerted security. Sheriff's deputies and California Highway Patrol officers, called by Grove security guards, arrived and confronted McCaslin, who was still wearing the superhero outfit and carrying the MK-1 assault rifle-shotgun, loaded with 70mm shotgun slugs and a full 30-shell magazine of .223-caliber bullets. He also was wearing a bulletproof vest and a blue uniform similar to what police SWAT team members wear. On opposite shoulders, he wore patches of the Democrats' donkey and the Republican elephant mascots, each within crossed-out red circles.

McCaslin said he waited behind a tree, wondering whether the officers were "legitimate" or part of the "Bohemian conspiracy" that might be planning to kill him to cover up his efforts. When the officers did not shoot, McCaslin said he knew they were legitimate and then "took the hard way out," putting down his weapons and giving up peacefully. Sgt. Brown said the officers showed great restraint during the confrontation and were relieved when McCaslin put his gun down.

Detectives working the case described McCaslin as an "intelligent, well-read man who is a fan of American history and government actions". He has no prior criminal record, and although some of his beliefs may seem a bit bizarre, McCaslin did not appear to be mentally unstable.

"He thinks (Timothy) McVeigh was programmed by the government to blow up Oklahoma City," Sgt. Brown told reporters. "And that (Osama) bin Laden has a company that George Bush is a partner in. But he's not dumb. His beliefs are just a little different."

In a strange twist of events, secret service agents quickly flocked to the jail to "question" McCaslin. A story published a week later by the *Santa Rosa Press-Democrat* (February 1, 2002) revealed that the suspicious "ex-Secret Service agent" working at Grove misrepresented himself to McCaslin at the jail. The plot thickens.

Twice since his arrest, a former Secret Service agent who claimed to be part of the security detail at Bohemian Grove had apparently interrogated McCaslin in jail. The questioning prompted a complaint from McCaslin's public defender, and sheriff's officials said the agent, identified as Martin Allen, had misrepresented himself to gain privileged access to McCaslin in the county jail.

Assistant Sheriff Mike Costa said Allen identified himself as an active Secret Service agent to obtain visits without time constraints, a right typically granted to lawyers and law enforcement. Costa said Allen "took advantage of all the resources available to him in order to accomplish his mission, which was to see Mr. McCaslin for longer than the 30 minutes granted to him as a civilian." In fact, Allen questioned McCaslin for more than 4 hours under this privilege.

Jail officials say Allen flashed a Secret Service badge and whispered he was an agent before his visits to McCaslin. Once the subterfuge was discovered, Allen's visiting privileges were immediately revoked, Costa said. "His ID credentials should have 'retired' stamped across them," he told reporters. "He is not a peace officer. He's more or less like a private investigator."

It was then rumored that the Bohemian Club was quietly conducting its own investigation into how this "Phantom" managed to sneak past security into their private campsite. A spokesman for the Bohemian Club confirmed that Allen visited McCaslin in jail twice in one week to obtain information for an internal investigation of the break-in. As for Costa's statement that Allen misrepresented himself, Bohemian Club spokesman Mike Oggero said: "I think he told them who he is and gave them his background."

McCaslin's attorney, Deputy Public Defender Jeff Mitchell, said he was concerned that some of the information his client shared could be subpoenaed by prosecutors and used against him in court. "It presents some difficult legal issues," Mitchell said. "He's been asked everything by this person...Given all this conspiracy stuff that's floating around, it's very interesting."

Bohemian Club spokesman Oggero said the club didn't intend to share any information obtained by Allen with other agencies. "We have an ongoing commitment to do everything we can to provide a safe environment for our members, guests and staff," he told the *Press-Democrat*. "This is simply...a little research to make sure we're doing what we can to make the Grove safe."

When The "Phantom Patriot" case went to trial, McCaslin claimed he wanted to draw attention to alleged human sacrifices that he believed went on at the Grove. The jury, however, decided this proved criminal intent and that he was simply taking the law into his own hands. One juror told reporters (***Bohemian Grove Intruder Guilty***—Santa Rosa *Press Democrat*, April 17th 2002):

> "Our world is full of people that think God calls them to a greater purpose and that gives them an excuse. Unfortunately, he's an American terrorist."

A TEDDY BEAR'S PICNIC

As if things couldn't possibly get more absurd at this point, the fallout from our foray into Bohemian Grove became a true comedy of errors when comedian Harry Shearer (*This Is Spinal Tap, The Simpsons*) released his independent film, *Teddy Bears Picnic*, in the summer of 2002.

This scathing send-up of the Bohemian Grove featured an all-star cast, including Harry Shearer's old friend from the *Spinal Tap* days, Michael McKean. Also starring Fred Willard, Howard Hesseman, George Wendt, Alan Thicke, Morgan Fairchild, and Shearer himself, the movie won numerous awards at independent film festivals and was eventually picked up for international distribution by VisionBox Pictures. I particularly liked the advertising copy used to promote the film: "*For fifty-one weeks a year they run the country. For one week they run amok!*"

Jon Ronson interviewed Harry Shearer for his *Secret Rulers of the World* documentary, and got him to share some of his thoughts about Bohemian Grove. To Shearer, of course, this was all just comic fodder. "If they were really seriously about the task of running the world in a secret conspiracy," he said smugly, "I don't think they'd be doing so much drag."

Yet in the same interview, Shearer had to acknowledge that: "You don't have to be a conspiracy theorist to know that this is a get-together of very powerful guys. Whatever it is they're doing there—whether they're running the world, or just re-living their adolescence—they're a self-selected group of powerful, white, Christian Americans. I mean, I love the conspiracy theories because…these guys are the only real good narrative writers left in the English language. They do write really good, compelling narratives, but I just don't happen to think they're true. And they keep you spellbound, you know?"

Ronson then asked Harry Shearer if he thought the Bohemian Club was a secret society. "Is it?" Shearer laughed. "Yeah, but I mean, it's a secret society like the secret society I was inducted into at UCLA in my senior year is a secret society. It's a lot of meaningless mumbo-jumbo, and the main conspiracy is to take it seriously. Now that's the real conspiracy—"*OK, let's pretend we're not being absolutely silly!*"

In Shearer's film, the names are changed to protect the guilty and the not so innocent, naturally. The Bohemian Grove thus becomes Zambesi Glen, an exclusive, rustic retreat and summer home-away-from-home in the redwoods of Northern California. The members identities are thinly-veiled (it's easy to tell who's who if you know the key players involved)—but you get the impression that this is a group of insanely powerful, rich, untouchable, mostly old, always white, men who decide the fate of nations and networks, universities and law firms from inside their fiercely protected Glen.

Stripped of the niceties required by the presence of their mistresses, wives and daughters, while adhering to the retreat's motto "Have No Care Who Enter Here," these pillars of society really know how to cut loose. They drink heavily, swear profusely, gambol naked in the woods, urinate communally, perform secret rituals, hatch nefarious plots, sing badly and wear women's clothing. They dress up in long hooded black robes to celebrate the annual enactment of "The Killing of Time" ceremony, which takes place at the foot of a giant Pelican statue! But of course, we're *not* talking about the Bohemian Grove!

Unfortunately for the Glen's stalwart denizens, times are changing. Women-folk are now included in a special one-time-only luncheon and tour (although they must be out before dark), feminists protest noisily at the gate, the media makes sport of them, the ten year waiting list just doesn't seem long enough, and good help is getting harder and harder to find. Just when it appears that things couldn't get worse, Zambesi Glen's iron clad code of secrecy is breached and its very existence imperiled by a reporter who manages to sneak in and out of the Glen with a hidden camera.

Hey—wait a minute!—This story is starting to sound very familiar, isn't it?...

It was obvious to Alex and I that the film was referring to our infiltration of the Grove, even though Shearer changed the gender of the reporter from male to a female in order to protect himself legally. Even if he was taking our work and making a comedy of it, at least we knew our film had made an impression on him. If nothing else, it made us feel that the footage we took inside Bohemian Grove was well worth the risks involved in getting the story. Now, the story was getting out to *millions* of people—with a spoonful of laughter to help the bitter medicine of truth go down.

We can only hope that this was Harry Shearer's unspoken motive from the very beginning when making *Teddy Bears Picnic*. It must have been more than just a mere giggle for him, because Shearer wrote, directed and produced the film himself. *Teddy Bears Picnic* was a labor of love for Harry Shearer, and I would find it hard to believe that he would have invested so much of his own time, effort and money into making this film if he hadn't meant for it to provoke some serious thought as well as laughter.

At first, I must confess to being angry with Harry Shearer for making this movie. I naturally thought he was trying to make fools of all of us. After some time had passed, however, and I actually saw the film, I came to respect what he was trying to do after all. Alex and I were so close to the whole Bohemian Grove story that we were in danger of taking our work (and ourselves) too seriously. We had almost forgotten one critical truth—that the best weapon against evil is *laughter*.

That's an important thing to remember. In the end, I have to thank Harry Shearer for reminding me of this fact. Nothing robs a tyrant of his power faster than the sound of his "people" laughing uproariously at how ridiculous he is. *Look! The Emperor Wears No Clothes!*

Chapter XIII

Unitam logica falsa tuam philosophiam totam suffodiant

(May faulty logic undermine your entire philosophy)

JON RONSON

Jon Ronson is the English journalist who helped us infiltrate Bohemian Grove. He produced the "Secret Rulers of the World" documentary series, which aired on British Independent Television Channel Four in 2001. He is also author of the book "Them: Adventures with Extremists."

Ronson and I since had a parting of the ways due to my dissatisfaction with the way Alex and I were portrayed in his film and book. But what bothered me even more was the fact that his story kept changing; from a slight distortion of the truth, to telling some real whoppers! In fairness, however, I felt it necessary to include Ronson's point of view here as well, in his own words.

This March 24, 2002 interview he gave to C-SPAN's "Booknotes" program turned out to be quite controversial. In this interview, Ronson actually claimed that he went into the Bohemian Grove in 2000, a transparent attempt to take the credit for what Alex and I had done. The partial transcript below speaks for itself. Although this interview covered a vast array of subjects, I have excerpted only the portions relevant to the Bohemian Grove. The complete "Booknotes" transcript can be read in its' entirety on the C-span website at cspan.org.

BRIAN LAMB, HOST: Jon Ronson, the book is called *Them: Adventures With Extremists*. Where did you get this idea?

JON RONSON, AUTHOR: I spent a year with an Islamic fundamentalist leader in London called Omar Bakhri Mohammed. And it was just going to be a newspaper article, actually. And he was so unlike one's mental picture of a Muslim extremist. He was kind of buffoonish and silly and burlesque. I thought, "That's so interesting. He's not like—he's not the one-dimensional demon we're—we're led to believe." I thought—I wondered if other extremists would be like that.

So then I spent a lot of time with a Klan leader who was giving his Klan an image makeover. He kind of figured that the Klan had a bad image, so he wanted to, you know, ban the "N" word and ban the robes and the hoods and the cross-burnings and—and replace those things with personality seminars, teaching—teaching their Klansmen to be—you know, to work out whether they're melancholics or sanguines, and so on. So again, he was very unlike my mental picture of a—of a Ku Klux Klan leader, this guy. He was nebbishy. He reminded me of Woody Allen. And I thought there was an irony there.

So then I figured, well, maybe there's a—there's a whole book in these unexpected portraits of extremist leaders, and I thought it would be funny and—and there'd be an interesting narrative. And I thought that maybe it would be an interesting way of trying to see our world through their eyes because all the extremists in the book are people who are living among us. They're trying to overthrow our way of life from within. So I thought maybe—maybe the "them" could be us, as well as them.

LAMB: Where else did you go, before we get into the individual stories?

RONSON: Kind of all around the world. Maybe 50 percent of the book is set in the States. There's a couple of British chapters.

LAMB: About the Bohemian Grove.

RONSON: Oh, yeah! You see, this is…

(LAUGHTER)

RONSON: How could I forget that? This is—this is a group—again, all the conspiracy theorists said that not only is this—is there this shadowy cabal, but once a year they go to a clearing in a forest in northern California and undertake an owl-burning ceremony, where men like Henry Kissinger attend this berobed torchlight procession which culminates in a human effigy being thrown into the fiery belly of a giant owl. So I kind of figured, "Well, that can't be true." You know, "I'm going to have to somehow infiltrate Bohemian Grove and find out if this is true."

So my plan was to—well—it was an ill-thought-out plan. I was going to shimmy up a mountain and find it, you know, find it amongst the redwoods. And then I was told, well, if I did that, I'd get myself killed and—not, I should add, by the Bohemians but by the terrain. And someone told me that the way to infiltrate Bohemian Grove is to pretend to be a Grover, to go to Eddie Bauer and get some chinos, you know, some cashmere sweaters, and just walk up the drive, giving the security guard an "I rule the world" kind of wave, which is what I did. And sure enough, I infiltrated the—the camp and witnessed this owl-burning ceremony.

LAMB: Where is the Bohemian Grove?

RONSON: It's halfway between Occidental and Monte Rio, which is just above Napa Valley in northern California.

LAMB: You tell us all through the book that you at some point are discovered in the midst of all these people as being Jewish.

RONSON: I was kind of out—I was outed as a Jew at a jihad training camp in south London. It wasn't {at the Bohemian Grove}...

LAMB: Jihad training camp?

RONSON: Not—not the best place in the world to be outed as a Jew.

LAMB: Who outed you?

RONSON: Omar Bakhri, Osama bin Laden's man in Great Britain, as he used to call himself until September the 11th.

LAMB: You mean, he did actually pin that on himself before the September 11th...

RONSON: And then on September the 12th, he phoned me up and said, "Why is everybody calling me bin Laden's man in Great Britain?" I said, "Omar." Anyway, I've spent a year with Omar, and it culminated in him inviting me to his jihad training camp. This was in about 1997, I think. And it turned out to be in a place called Crowley, which is a very incongruous location for a jihad training camp. It's kind of near Gatwick Airport. So we were driven there...

LAMB: Near London.

RONSON: Yeah, near London. We were driven there, and it was—it turned out to be a scout hut in a forestry center, with maybe 40 or 50 young jihad trainees beating punch bags, and so on. Still—I mean, no guns, but still not—not the most comfortable place to be. And Omar suddenly hushed the crowd and said, "Look at me with an infidel. Look at me with Jon, who is a Jew." And the whole room went, "Oh!" And they all-...

LAMB: How did—how did he find out? Did you tell him?

RONSON: Well, he—no, I'd never told him. I'd hidden that from him. He said he knew all along. He could see it in my eyes. I don't know when he discovered I was a Jew, but he—it wasn't the best place to reveal it.

LAMB: Now, how old were you then? Was that '97, did you say?

RONSON: Yeah, around '97.

LAMB: How old were you then?

RONSON: I'm 34 now—about 30—29, 30.

LAMB: Is this book, *Them: Adventures With Extremists*—is this your first book?

RONSON: It's my first proper book.

LAMB: It's—it was bought by Simon and Schuster. When did you finish it?

RONSON: I finished it in the—I think probably the winter of 2000, and it got published in England last spring, spring of 2001. And…

LAMB: And what was the reaction in England?

RONSON: Unbelievably good. It became an—it was an instant best seller. It stayed on the best-sellers' charts for about three months and got wonderful reviews. And I kind of figured that—that would be it. I sort of had a profile in England anyway. I've been on TV and I've made TV shows and.

LAMB: Done your own shows?

RONSON: Yeah.

LAMB: What kind of shows?

RONSON: I've done chat shows, and I presented a kind of idiosyncratic chat show, but I've made a lot of documentaries. And in fact, some of the chapters of the book started life as documentaries for British television.

LAMB: Are you worried at all, or have you been worried at all about libel?

RONSON: No, because it's all true.

LAMB: But has anybody questioned what's in here, any of these characters you write about?

RONSON: The anti-Icke brigade, the—the...

LAMB: David Icke?

RONSON: Yeah. I mean, he doesn't like it much. He didn't like what I've done with it.... And I got a little bit of trouble with that. But...

LAMB: Why did these people let you get so close to them? I mean, you traveled with Ian Paisley. You went—spent a lot of time with Tom Robb. You went to—spent a lot of time with Rachel Weaver, the daughter of Randy Weaver.

RONSON: Why did they let me in?

LAMB: How'd you get to them, first of all?

RONSON: Oh, I just phoned them up. I just kind of charmed them.

LAMB: Just called them?

RONSON: Uh-huh. And they all said yes. Everyone said yes.

LAMB: Anybody say no?

RONSON: The Rockefeller Foundation said no. I heard that they were teaching this course on how to make billionaires more philanthropic, and I figured that might make a good chapter for the book, particularly because the name Rockefeller is so synonymous with the grand conspiracy.

LAMB: Did you call the Bohemian Grove and say, "I'd like to come"?

RONSON: No. No, I didn't.

LAMB: Did you call the Bilderbergers and say, "I'd like to come"?

RONSON: No. I—when the Bilderbergers started chasing me through Portugal, I telephoned the British embassy to tell them that this was happening. I got really frightened. I was suddenly being followed by men in dark glasses, who obviously...

LAMB: Really?

RONSON: Yeah. And they obviously presumed I was a crazy extremist, rather than a chronicler of crazy extremists. And I telephoned the British embassy and said, "I'm being followed right now by a dark green Lancia belonging to the Bilderberg group." And the woman said, "Oh!" And she said, "Go on." And I said, "Hang on. I just heard"...

(LAUGHTER)

RONSON: "Stop. Let's rewind. I'm just going to take a breath." And she said, "Did you say the Bilderberg group?" And I said, "Yes." She said, "Do they know you're in Portugal?" And I said, "No." And they said, "Look, you've got to understand. We're just a little embassy. The Bilderberg group is much bigger than we are. We're just an embassy. They're way out of our depth. What are you doing here?"

So I said, "Well, I'm essentially a humorous journalist out of my depth. Maybe you could phone the Bilderberg group and explain that to them." Which is what she did! And called me back to say, "Well, I've spoken to the Bilderberg group and they say that nobody's following you, and how can they call off someone who doesn't exist?"

So I said, you know, "He's behind the tree," and he was. This man in dark glasses was poking up, staring at me from behind a tree. And when I tried to explain to him that I was just a journalist, he—he swatted me away. He didn't want to know who I was. That was kind of frightening.

LAMB: The Bilderberg group stands for what? What's the name from?

RONSON: Oh, from the first hotel where they met in 1954, the Bilderberg Hotel in the Netherlands.

LAMB: Now, when you travel, do you take a recorder with you?

RONSON: Uh-huh. And sometimes a little videocamera.

LAMB: Really?

RONSON: Yeah. In fact, I filmed my Bilderberg car chase. My wife—you see—I tell—you know, I thought I was going to die that day, so I was phoning up everybody to tell them I loved them. I kind of phoned up my wife and said, "I may never see you again."

LAMB: Were you serious?

RONSON: I would—well, I've never been chased by the shadowy henchmen of the secret—I had nothing to compare it to. You see, when I was kind of shouted at by Aryan Nations, I could say, "OK," you know, "I've been to places like this before. I've been to the Klan. It's going to be OK." But I—you know, I couldn't say, "Oh, this is like the time I was chased by the shadowy henchmen of"—you know, "of the secret cabal back in '86." You know, I—so I was completely out of depth. I just—I had nothing to—nothing to root it in…

LAMB: How long have you been married?

RONSON: Seven, eight years.

LAMB: Did your wife ever laugh at you when you called and said it might be over?

RONSON: She did that time. She said, "Oh, you're loving it." And I said—I said, "I'm not loving it." She said, "You're loving it!" And it's only when I got home and showed her what I'd filmed, which was, you know, deserted lanes at twilight with cars with blacked-out windows following me everywhere I went—she thought, "OK, now I can see why you were scared."

LAMB: Now, did—how honest were you with these people when you were with them? And when you found the situation to be humorous, did you laugh at them there, or…

RONSON: Sometimes. Sometimes. And in fact, you know, when I was younger, I thought if I did that, they'd think I was laughing at them and they'd close up. So I tried to hide the laughter. But now I'm—now I'm a little bit older, I realize that it's actually—it's OK to laugh.

LAMB: Did they ever laugh themselves?

RONSON: Yeah, once in a while. Although I kind of liked the people who were—who were so serious and pompous that they don't realize they're being funny. But sometimes they—they do think it's crazy. Although actually, most of the people in this book don't laugh at themselves much at all, when I—when I come to think about it.

LAMB: How close did you get to the Bilderberg meeting?

RONSON: Not very close. But I did get to see the owl-burning ceremony at Bohemian Grove after I was chased away by Bilderberg security.

LAMB: Are there—is there any connection between these two groups, by the way?

RONSON: Not really. There is in the minds of the conspiracy theorists. It's all part of the New World order. But I think in reality, Bohemian Grove is quite right wing and Bilderberg is center-left. Bohemian Grove's Republican. That's why you get Dick Cheney and the Bush family going, and so on. And Bilderberg is much more internationalist, globalist.

LAMB: How often do people go to the Bohemian Grove?

RONSON: That's once a year for three weeks and…

LAMB: Three weeks?

RONSON: Yeah. The owl…

LAMB: People stay there the whole three weeks?

RONSON: Uh-huh. I think quite a lot of the really big names—the Dick Cheneys and the George Bushes—go for the second week. Apparently, the second week's the most popular week. And the second week begins with the—with the "Cremation of Care," the owl ceremony.

LAMB: "Cremation of Care"?

RONSON: Uh-huh. They say that the human effigy they're throwing into the fiery belly of the owl symbolizes all their troubles in the marketplace. And I've got to say, I don't blame the conspiracy theorists for thinking that when—you know, when you put Henry Kissinger together with a berobed, you know, procession, culminating in this, you know, mock human sacrifice, it's kind of no wonder you've got yourself a conspiracy theory.

LAMB: Who owns the Bohemian Grove?

RONSON: The Bohemian Club in San Francisco, which I believe was set up kind of when the railroads came into town. Everyone thought, "There goes the neighborhood."

LAMB: How many go there every year?

RONSON: Oh, a lot. Like, a thousand people.

LAMB: At one time?

RONSON: Yeah. That's why I managed to walk up the drive so easily.

LAMB: And when did you try to get—what year did you try to get in there?

RONSON: This was...

LAMB: Was that the July, 2000?

RONSON: Yeah, that was July 2000.

LAMB: The hundred and twenty-first "Cremation of Care" ceremony?

RONSON: Yeah. Now, I snuck in with Alex Jones, this far-right-wing conspiracy theorist who believed that the "Cremation of Care" proved that the secret rulers of the world practice human sacrifice.

LAMB: Where did you find Alex Jones?

RONSON: He was in Austin, Texas. I'd actually met him at Waco. I was at Waco, the remnants of David Koresh's place, with Randy Weaver. And Alex Jones was rebuilding David Koresh's Branch Davidian church with money donated from his radio listeners. So that's where I met—that's where I met Alex Jones. He did a good job. He rebuilt that church, and I think it's good that that church is rebuilt.

LAMB: Why?

RONSON: Because I think that the Branch Davidians and the Weaver family were—were victims of a—of a government that on both occasions became slightly out of control and messed up and did wrong. And I believe—and I could be wrong, but I believe that neither the Weavers nor the Branch Davidians really were doing anything wrong. I think they were innocent parties.

LAMB: Alex Jones is what kind of a guy, what—how do you explain him?

RONSON: He's—he's 26 years old and looks 10 years older. He's a—he's a hero to the—to the militias. He's a—he's a burgeoning new hero. On one hand, he's kind of like Texe Marrs, you know, a popular underground radio talk show host. But he's also much more than somebody like Texe Marrs. He's an activist. So he rebuilt David Koresh's church. He...

LAMB: Where can you hear him?

RONSON: *Infowars.com* is his Web site. And he broadcasts—and he broadcasts in, like, 40 cities across America. I think it's called the Genesis Radio Network.

LAMB: Did you ever hear him?

RONSON: Yeah. Yeah. I've listened. He's fantastic. I mean, if he wasn't so crazy, he'd be the new Bill Hicks. He's got an amazing way of...

LAMB: Who's Bill Hicks?

RONSON: He was an old comedian who died of cancer in the '90s, and again, was a kind of hero to the Libertarian left, Bill Hicks, because he smoked in the face of cancer and was funny. And—but what happened with me and Alex is that we both witnessed this owl-burning ceremony, and I realized that it was a silly grown-up frat kind of nonsense. And the only thing that shocked me was this is—you know, how the president of the United States wants to spend his summer vacations witnessing this, you know, torchlight procession, which I thought was kind of odd.

But Alex, of course, had his own spin on it, which was that—it was human sacrifice! Maybe that's a real person that—that the—so I went off with my spin, which was, you know, a kind of moderate spin, that it's not that crazy, it's understandable. And Alex went back to his people with his own incredibly crazy spin.

And you know, just a couple of weeks ago, an Alex Jones fan tried to break into Bohemian Grove heavily armed and kill everybody there because he believed Alex Jones's spin of the—of the owl ceremony as being evidence of human sacrifice.

And I remember at the time—because I'm—you know, Alex is an intelligent man, and I remember at the time saying to him, "Alex," you know, "you know that what you're saying about Bohemian Grove isn't true. Now, you're playing with fire here." And Alex said, "Yeah, I'm not going to tell my listeners that." And it's kind of come back to haunt him now.

LAMB: So underlying all this is pretty serious stuff.

RONSON: Oh, yeah, yeah, yeah. I mean, Alex is kind of crazy, funny. And the adventures, you know, that I have in the book are funny. You know, I wanted to write a funny book but always, you know, remembering that these people are chilling people. They may be buffoons, but you know, they resonate.

LAMB: Go back to the Bohemian Grove situation in July of 2000. This event is always held in the summer?

RONSON: Uh-huh.

LAMB: And how far did you get, and how did you get there?

RONSON: Well, I—I agreed to meet Alex Jones in Occidental.

LAMB: California.

RONSON: Yeah, Occidental, California, in a local motel.

LAMB: Where is Occidental?

RONSON: It's kind of above Napa Valley. It's pretty. It's pretty in that kind of, you know, northern Californian hippie way, where if you light a cigarette on the street, somebody a hundred yards down the road will go, "Pooh!" you know, which I always find a little annoying.

And Alex was terrible at being undercover because, you know, he got lost on the way to the motel, in fact. It was dead of night, and he's phoning me from his cell phone saying, you know, "There's fog everywhere! There's people—there's people just standing on the side of the road just staring at me! There's people just staring at me on the side of the road!" And he kind of hung up and phoned back and, you know, said, "Pray for me, Jon! Pray for me!"

And so, you know—and so from the minute Alex arrived in northern California, he'd entered some, you know, paranoid movie in his own mind.

LAMB: Was this his first trip there?

RONSON: Uh-huh. He thought it was—he thought he'd entered Transylvania.

LAMB: OK, so you met at the Occidental.

RONSON: Uh-huh.

LAMB: Or the hotel in Occidental.

RONSON: Yeah, which at night, with the fog and the giant redwoods, plus our mission, you know, to go to Bohemian Grove, was kind of spooky, you know? But then the fog lifted the next morning and, you know, I looked at the breakfast menu, and it's all low-cholesterol egg alternative and breakfast smoothies, and it kind of seemed less—less sinister the next morning!

LAMB: Do you have your camera with you this time?

RONSON: Uh-huh. Yeah, a little camera.

LAMB: And you're shooting this stuff as you go?

RONSON: And Alex was shooting it, too, because he wanted to—he wanted to secretly film the owl ceremony. So he was filming a little documentary about himself trying to—trying to break in because he brought along his girlfriend, Violet, and his producer, Mike. So he came kind of heavily armed with the three guys.

LAMB: So how far'd you get?

RONSON: We got the whole thing. We got in. We witnessed it.

LAMB: You got into the Bohemian Grove?

RONSON: Uh-huh.

LAMB: How?

RONSON: Just walked up the drive, waved, dressed preppily. That was very important. What I found very funny was that Alex is, you know, a far-right-wing Texan, plain-talking kind of guy, but he had to pretend to be preppy. He had to pretend to be kind of Yalie, you know, and—and so he kind of took off his kind of Wild West clothes and put on his chinos and—you know, and his Polo shirt and so on, and was so nervous about coming over as too right-wing and not preppy enough that he rehearsed preppy conversations wandering up and down in his—in his motel room, practicing how to be preppy, which was kind of his version of preppy was, you know, camp, you know, slightly effemi-nate, talking about the dot-com business.

LAMB: Why didn't they check you?

RONSON: I don't know. It's a mystery to me. It's—because we just walked in.

LAMB: All men when you got there?

RONSON: Uh-huh.

LAMB: He didn't take his wife with him.

RONSON: No, she had to stay behind in the motel.

LAMB: All white men.

RONSON: Yeah. Danny Glover's been. He's—and I—out of all the people I researched, Danny Glover's the only black man I know of who's been. It's WASP-y. You know, it's—it's—it's right-wing, white, male, pretty elderly. I think the average age is 65, 70.

LAMB: Did anybody know—or did they ever figure out that you were there?

RONSON: No. And it was—we stood out like such sore thumbs, you know?

LAMB: And did anybody else have cameras going, like you did?

RONSON: No. Well, we—I didn't have the camera, and Alex's camera was—was a secret camera. I think it was on his fake pager, strapped to his belt. He had a secret camera. And the whole—he filmed—he managed to film the ceremony, but in his nervousness, he filmed it upside down and very wide. He never—obviously, he couldn't be zooming in or anything. So all the berobed men are kind of that big.

LAMB: So what'd he do with that film?

RONSON: Put it on the Web, sold it as a video. And it's that film, with his commentary—you know, "Look at the sick stuff they're doing now!"—is what motivated this guy a couple of weeks ago to try and wreak havoc at Bohemian Grove. {*Referring to the "Phantom Patriot" incident.*}

LAMB: So what's your guess, have you tried to get in this year?

RONSON: I don't think we'd get in this year. And you know, maybe it's—I didn't enjoy trespassing. I mean, that's essentially what I did was trespass at Bohemian Grove. I—that wasn't pleasurable to me. I don't get off on the adrenaline or anything like that. But it was where the narrative took me. I was writing a book about how the extremists see our world, and how they see our world is with these cabals in the center of it. And then I was—you know, I had to end the book by going to one of these cabals, so I just had to do it. It was…

LAMB: So what did you conclude, after you saw the Bohemian Grove?

RONSON: I think—well, in terms of Bohemian Grove, I concluded that their worst crime was being dumb.

LAMB: Dumb?

RONSON: I thought so. I thought, you know, these—these are the men that rule the world, yet they're doing these silly ceremonies. And I would see photo boards of—it's a beautiful place, Bohemian Grove. It's a clearing in these giant redwood forests, absolutely wonderful place. And I would picture myself sipping cocktails with, you know, world leaders and discussing the natural beauty. I could completely see why people want to be there.

But then you see the photos of the parties they had the night before on the notice board, and you've got all these men, these CEOs, dressed up in—not only dressed up in drag, which is kind of OK, but...

LAMB: In drag?

RONSON: Yeah. But kind of dressed up with kind of burlesqued, oversized, fake breasts and, you know, ridiculous makeup and—you know, misogynist, I thought. And so what struck me about the place is not clearly that they really are Satanists or, you know, doing all this stuff that the conspiracy theorists say they're doing, but that the leaders of our world seem to be emotionally trapped in their college years.

...LAMB: Of all the things you saw in the writing of this book, what was the—what was the funniest, the lightest?

RONSON: It's kind of—a lot of it's funny, but not much of it's light. I mean, I did love the moment when Alex Jones was practicing how to be preppy, so he could infiltrate the secret place where Henry Kissinger was rumored to—to, you know, attend a berobed owl-burning ceremony. That—that's when he was—was—back in "The Perfect Storm," you know, where all the way—all the weather combines to make this big wave. That was, like, the perfect, absurd moment to me.

LAMB: How has this book, your first book, changed your life, in any way?

RONSON: It's been a success, which I'm so delighted about.

LAMB: How—how many did you sell in England?

RONSON: I think the average sale is what, 2,000, 3,000, 5,000. It's—so far, it's sold about 30,000.

LAMB: In England?

RONSON: Uh-huh. In hardback. It's just come out in paperback in England. Over here, I have no idea, actually, how it's done.

LAMB: How's it changed your life?

RONSON: I'm very—I'm immensely proud of it. I'm really proud that I've managed to write a really good book. And I do think it's—you know, I'm very pleased with the book. It's well written and it's funny, and it's got, you know, interesting things to say about the relationship between our world and their world.

LAMB: Can our—can our viewers that hear about this book watch any of this video? Is it available on any of the Web sites or...

RONSON: You can watch—if you log into my Web site, which is *jonronson.com*—you can see clips. We've got the owl-burning ceremony, we link to. You can see that. The United States has never really wanted to buy any of my documentaries, although I was told the other day that—that they might be able to sell it if they can get Will Smith to re-voice the commentary! So I kind of figured, "OK."

LAMB: Here's the cover of the book. It's about extremists—*Them: Adventures with Extremists*. Those are the words of Jon Ronson. It's a Simon and Schuster book.

Jon Ronson, our guest. Thank you very much.

RONSON: Thank you.

(Interview © 2002, National Cable Satellite Network. Excerpts used with permission.)

Chapter XIV

Senito aliquos togatos contra me conspirare

(I think some people in togas are plotting against me)

ALEX JONES

This interview was conducted live on the "Power of Prophecy" radio show, hosted by Texe Marrs in mid-July, 2000, immediately after Alex and I returned from the Bohemian Grove. I was driving to the TV studio while Alex talked live on the air with Texe on his cell phone, and was present to witness the entire conversation that was heard by thousands of listeners. I wanted to include this interview here because the memory of infiltrating the Grove was still so fresh in our minds. This fact alone makes the interview invaluable as immediate documentation of our experience at the Bohemian Grove, before a single detail could be forgotten.

Texe:…Alex, I understand that you and your cameraman Mike Hanson just got back from the Bohemian Grove, and that you are the first journalists in American history to bring out audio and video of what goes on inside. First, would you just give the listeners an idea of what this place is?

Alex: It's a 121 year-old cult, at the bare minimum—they've actually had the property for 126 years—the Bohemian Club has owned it. And it's known as the "Summer Encampment", or the "Fire Festival" of the Bohemian Club of San Francisco in Northern California. It's about an hour and a half north of San Francisco, 14 miles roughly west of Santa Rosa. It's in a rural area, in the hills and mountains of many uncut, original old-grove Redwood forests. It's a 2,700-acre cult compound; we have confirmed that….And we were able to infiltrate for the kick-off of their two-week summer Fire Festival—the Summer Encampment of the Bohemian Club, as they call it—on July 15th. We were there for two days before, scoping out the area, talking to our inside sources that had worked there in the past, and were concerned about it.

Frankly, Texe, I could hardly believe the rumors I'd heard; that they engaged in human sacrifice before a 45-foot stone Owl: Moloch or Molech of the Bible, 13 times mentioned as the most accursed Demon to worship by God and he'll destroy nations and people that do it.

It takes hours to even tell the story of getting in. It's in the middle of a huge gorge between hills and mountains with some giant Redwoods. We had to go through 3 checkpoints. I mean I have more frustration driving in traffic than I did walking through the checkpoints, being interrogated by Sheriff's deputies, and Secret Service—type individuals. Mike Hanson, my cameraman, and myself were so calm. I'm normally a pretty frantic person to begin with, but I was very calm and God really did comfort us. And I prayed openly on the air, on over 60 radio stations and international short wave and I'm not the type to do that; I'm a private person. I prayed the Lord's Prayer that as we walked through the Valley of the Shadow of Death—it literally is a valley; I didn't know that till I got there—that God protect us if it was his Will. And obviously I really did feel the Spirit of God protecting us, and it was the most religious experience I've ever had. I have come so much closer to God through this and my faith has been redoubled.

...In fact we got in; we tried to stay away from the crowd. They have over a hundred camps. And to call them a camp is really a deception on their part, when you read stories in the mainstream news saying oh, it's just a rich men's get-together with politicians and the heads of business, mainly so-called conservatives. And there are these palatial complexes of log cabins with Jacuzzis and grand pianos built into this gorge, in between these huge hills or small mountains with these Redwoods. And we basically tried to stay away from the crowds, avoid the security that was everywhere. They questioned us—"who are you; what camp are you with?" We didn't even lie; we just said, "oh, we're just guests," didn't even say what camp we were with.

We then went up into the hills, up a very steep incline, up a dirt road. And Mike and myself sat in the woods above them as they had, thousands of them had this huge dinner, dining and chanting. We were just above them looking down from probably 600, 700 feet as they're out there underneath the Redwoods eating. It's a perfect place for a summer-type meeting like this because it doesn't rain there; it's unheard of during the summer in Northern California. So we were looking down on them as they were chanting, and laughing. I actually got some short videos clips of that. Then we came back down as it started getting dark because our sources told us they were going to have the Cremation of Care—the 121st ritual that's been held there.

Think of how bizarre; I mean America is evil today, but 121 years ago doing this—you could easily have gotten hung! Because people didn't put up with this type of activity—at least out in the open back then. And as we came walking—there is a long pond; they call it a lake—it's only probably a hundred yards across, but it's about, I'd say 500 yards, 400 yards long. And at the north front of it you have this 45-, 50-foot Molech stone demon god of Babylon mystery religion and Tyre. And they had an eternal flame burning in front of it, in a large stone lamp that looked like Aladdin's Lamp before it; we actually got some video of it during the day as well. And there are lily pads all around it. And we went around to the east side; security got behind everybody, thousands of men crowded through. They were groaning, saying, "burn him, burn him", pulling out their genitalia in front of each other and urinating in plain view, as some type of weird greeting. And there were thousands of men urinating before the ceremony. It was splattering all over the road, and on my legs. This is true, ladies and gentlemen. They don't just relieve themselves in the Redwoods. I don't understand that ritual; perhaps, Texe, you could shed some light on it.

Texe: I have *no idea* on that one! (Laughter)

Alex: And then the ceremony began; on the other side, on the west side, of the pond—that they call they lake, again—out came a wagon with a flat bed in it with someone bound in black, with two people painted up in skull faces and black cloaks driving the wagon with two large stallions. We got hidden video of this. Before them were about 25 to 30 men in black robes; their faces painted up as Death; about 30 or 40 behind them in brown robes. They then pulled behind, on the other side of the lake, a black cloth that had been unfurled from the trees so you couldn't see. This was some height of the ritual because the old men around me—generally old; some of them were 30, 40 but usually about 70—were groaning with delight, with sexual-sounding relish: "*Mmm, oh yes, do it, do it!*" And I didn't understand that part.

And then across the lake comes a boatman dressed in black with white paint of a skull, and they're playing this sad, sickening music on the sound system and he comes up to the head of these high priests in black and red and the high priest in silver—I'd say about 50 or 60 or 70 of them; quite a large group, I was 175 yards away on the east side of the bank, roughly. And they go into this chant: "*Oh, Great Owl of Babylon, we beseech thee. Give us the Power to destroy Dull Care.*"

Then the boatman brings forward the bound human; and they say "we burn thee in effigy" and it began to beg for its life. We have some actual video clips on InfoWars.com of this.

They bring it forward, the Owl says, *"You must destroy it with my sacred Light"*, so the high priest lights his torch on that. Then he walks over and says, *"Midsummer sets us free."* He kept saying that. Then he lights it and the effigy burns and screams in pain for about 20 seconds. Then there's just…some people say, "oh, this is just some type of fraternal weird behavior"; I could buy that if wasn't for the crowd of about at least 1500 that I was in. It was thousands of people. We were at a higher point above them; that's why in the video you can see their heads when the light illuminates them. They were groaning and saying, *"I can't wait to burn him again! Oh.…!"* Lots of weird curdling laughs. And I would look at the men beside me, the demonic glow in their eyes. Really sick, Texe, and I don't even understand the full import of it. They burned the body, and it was still burning as I left.

We hurriedly walked out, took about 30 minutes to get out. And they didn't bother us as we left security. One man in a black Tahoe was standing there staring at us and began to follow us. We were already out of the main gates. The British media pulled up in their van; they'd been waiting up there. We jumped in and sped away, and of course Violet was waiting at the hotel. She was the one that had actually dropped us off outside the Grove to climb through the woods and up some cliffs, through the first layer of checkpoints to only go through two more after that, where they pull the large…you, once you get into the parking area you get in the back of a old truck, but it's very well upkept with the top cut off with seats in it that says BC on it with an owl, Bohemian Club. Then you go through another checkpoint. When we were first coming in, a truck in front of us was not stopped, but we were stopped; and Sheriff's deputies were around and a woman in a red shirt, black pants, and combat boots, by the way, climbed up in the back; looked like a witch. She stared right at me and I just smiled at her, completely calm. So did Mike. We also have, as we were riding in with some of the acolytes, they were talking about the price of their robes. So we actually caught that on videotape, too. We could spend hours on it, Texe, but the rumors are all true. I don't know that they were actually killing someone. Frankly, it doesn't matter. It's the character of these people; it's the evil that they engage in.

And then you start talking to people like my friend George Humphrey, a former city council member that you know, Texe, here in Austin, Texas; a very successful businessman internationally. He was a liberal. He woke up about 7 years ago right around the same time I did. He actually went there 2 years ago, pulled up to the front gate and he noticed that in Monte Rio—the small town outside of the Grove—that there were mentally ill people everywhere. Men, women. And that he talked to locals and they said that the State Hospital, the mental hospital dumps everyone off there, in this rural, remote area of Northern California. Again, frankly I could barely believe that but I didn't know George Humphrey to be a liar. All we saw—we got it on tape; I don't know if I'll put them on the film, because frankly these mentally ill people don't deserve this; but I may have to, just to document it—we saw dozens, in the 30 minutes we were in town (we were being followed by the Sheriff the day after, before we left we were getting some of the other information); we wanted to get out of there. But all over were autistic men and women walking with their fingers in their faces. And the town is only populated by about a thousand people. We saw homeless women—young; old—looking crazed, all over the streets. This is a place out of Hell.

If Count Dracula—and I don't believe in vampires, but I think the legends have truth in these Satanic cults going back through history: they do drink blood and kill people—if I was Count Dracula, I would pick Sonoma County, I would pick the Bohemian Grove to stay, because at 5 o'clock hours before dark, this dark mist rolls in over the hills. We got video of this. The mentally ill people being dumped off there by the State. All the elitists going there. I *believe*, Texe, now. I believe the stories now. I believe they make snuff films there. I believe they rape children and kill children there. Plus you talk about how Polly Klass' body was found nearby, her throat slit. And by the way, the very weekend we were there—it was in the papers—a camper who was camping in the nearby State park north of there, came up missing and has not been found. Now, that could be coincidence. But this is a nightmarish, hellish place that I would expect Satan to reside in.

Texe: I understand that this is a very exclusive private club, right?

Alex: I'm told for movie stars, even politicians like governors that want to attend, there's a 15 year waiting list, thousands of dollars of yearly dues, also a one-time joining fee. There are different camps of different levels, larger and smaller. I'm told that the Mandalay Camp, in the mainstream articles, is the top camp with Henry Kissinger, and the heads of DuPont, and Dow Chemical and other big international industries. The Bushes are in the second level camp, which is called the Hillbillies. But most of the camp names—and I actually saw as you walked by them—were Demons, Devils, Dragons; or Dragon, Lost Angels...I know there's a vampire movie about that area of California called *Lost Boys*.

It's just really sick to be inside there, and words can't describe; even the video can't describe—I mean it's good video from 175 yards away—but still words can't describe just the evil that was in there. But we were really comforted by God's presence the entire time. Other than the fact that they told us to raise our arms—*"Raise your arms to the Great Owl and beseech it!"*—and I looked over at Mike and we didn't even have to think about it. We just didn't raise our arms. I just couldn't raise my arms to it. And people then really started staring at us, but luckily they looked away. I guess they...but most of the crowd was raising their arms.

We were completely calm the entire time, and that's actually unheard of for me. Mike is very active and a very excitable person. I mean that's the type of people we are. We're concerned about this. But the only time I saw Mike show any emotion was I looked over at him in the lights (because they had some lights up there and fires burning from across the lake; from across the pond really), and Mike had a tear running out of his eye. And I asked him, "Why did you do that?"; he just said, "I never realized how bad we're off, how evil these people are. They want our guns, they want to feed on us," and he just was thinking about his children. It really saddened Mike.

Myself, I was so concerned about getting the video that I wasn't even really focusing too much on the incantations. It was almost like I was there, but I wasn't there. This was like an experience...I've never had an experience like this, Texe. This really changed me. To see and know that it is a purely spiritual battle. Because I've always said I'm a Christian, and I am a Christian, but I've fought it with the nuts and bolts of the secular world that I could prove to people—the high treason, the sell-out, the militarization of our police—these are the issues that I've always covered. But it is purely an Illuminati, Luciferian, Babylon cult; mystery religion being re-visited on us. And *Revelations* is completely true; it is back with us today, more powerful than ever. And I believe we are entering the End Times, Texe.

In fact, several times I thought to myself, "This is ridiculous, this is so stupid," and then I thought, "No, it's deadly serious." Because at 12 years old, my father might have walked into my room and said, "You can't have this shirt with a skull on it. There's nothing cute about death, Son," and at 12 years old in this evil culture I might have been lured to some of this; never getting into it deeply, but it's in the culture, in the video games, in the movies. But now, this is an inward manifestation of what they do in the rest of the world—the phony wars, the death, the vaccines with the toxins in them, the corruption, the evil, the missing children—this is really at the heart of hearts of these people. And to say that it's a mainly conservative meetinghouse…that shows that the phony leaders are misdirecting the Moral Majority, the good people of this country. And it is painful for me. Because I do hate the Democratic Party. I know it is the Beast in this country. But at the same time people keep saying year after year, "Well, why do Republicans fail us? Why do they sell us out? They're so stupid." This is being done <u>on purpose</u>. The leadership of the Republican Party are a bunch of Lucifer worshippers, and I have seen it for myself.

Texe: Alex, do you think that any political party can be the salvation of America?

Alex: I don't think so, Texe. I think we have to be "grassroots" at the cellular level of the body politic. Go into the county commissioners, get *real* Christians elected that know about the New World Order, that know about the secular and the spiritual levels of this. We have to take our local communities back. We have to get the sheriffs elected. Because then there will at least be safe havens where people come into communities, counties that refuse to go along with all these federal programs. I think it's gotten to that point. It's like a doctor diagnosing cancer. I mean if he tells you, or if she tells you, that you've only got, need a Band-Aid when you've really got gangrene and your leg's rotting off, you're gonna die. We have to assess the problem; diagnose it.

This country's already dead. I can't believe that I've actually come to this realization. The evil…all we can do now is try to wake people up, keep our guns, wake up our neighbors, make sure our children are out of the public schools, home school them. Try to get states and counties together against this—like Arizona's doing, getting ready…they just passed a bill to their rules committee now to pull out of the Union if world government is announced or if guns are confiscated.

Plus I've done studies of the massive election fraud in this country. I mean, Texe, I used to be a Republican—going back 8 years ago before I even got involved in radio and television—I was out running around Texas giving speeches for Pat Buchanan and for the Republicans. I was ultra right wing. But I've even realized there...I believe there's election fraud at the Executive level. And we've got a lot of evidence of that. It's so bad. We have...but to fix the problem or even fight it, we have to admit how bad it is first. It's like being an alcoholic—the first step to your recovery is simply admitting that there *is* a problem and having the courage to face it.

...Speaking of the Bohemian Grove, a key point before we run out of time I want to make. My parents live here in town just like you do, Texe, here in Austin, Texas, a great community of decent people here—our little "Moscow on the Colorado"; I guess God's put us here to counter all the corruption here. I got a call from my mother—who has the custom of cooking dinner at about 6 o'clock for my dad who gets home at 7—she kinda always has the TV on back in the background, with CNN on (which always annoys me when I go over because it's pure propaganda, and she knows that) but I can just imagine her sitting there watching this. She called in the morning and said, "Son, I was cooking dinner last night and suddenly I heard something about Bohemian Grove watching your TV show locally after you had aired this footage. I turned around and they were talking about George Bush yesterday—this was the day before—was probably going to announce Dick Cheney as his vice-presidential running mate." And they repeated it on CNN about 6 o'clock (the "Communist News Network") that, "Yes, it's just come out; we already know who it's going to be even though Bush is going to announce it tomorrow; CNN brings you this breaking news." (I interrogated my mother already about what they said; I've now ordered the tape from CNN by the way).

The report said: "Yes, it came out earlier today, from Bohemian Grove: George Bush and Colin Powell were consulting over the telephone with his son, George Bush, Jr., governor of Texas, that they thought Dick Cheney was good and Bush, Jr. agrees—or Governor Bush agrees—that it will be Dick Cheney as his running-mate." So here they were basically saying that George Bush, Jr. got the orders (they said it in kind of a between-the-lines way) from Bohemian Grove. Now I've gone to the University of California Berkley web-site where they've had a few released photos of Presidents and former Presidents and people sitting around a table drinking coffee with a tree behind them, and it's, oh, just a nice little political meeting; no big deal. But they've never just come out on the news to my knowledge and said, "Yeah, we're picking vice-presidential candidates out at Bohemian Grove."

Then I told the story on the radio yesterday and started getting calls that it was reported as well on MSNBC, and we called and confirmed that. So, it's definitely a real news report. I think it's interesting that they're starting to turn up the heat and throw it in our face. What do you think is developing, Texe?

Texe: I think they are trying to sell the American public on the occult, to make it look attractive to us.

Alex: That's why these *Harry Potter* demonic books are being promoted over and over on the front page of the paper internationally. We see it here in Austin. It gets the children acclimated. This is one of the final stages of the Illuminati plan from the information we've had over the years. And now it's all being confirmed to be accurate. It's just horrible. And I never put much stock in Cathy O'Brien's book, *TRANCE-Formation of America*; but Texe, during the break we were talking, you brought up the point...you weren't sure either, this was so shocking. We're told that even worse things happen there. And here she is singling out Dick Cheney as one of the most evil mind-control devil worshippers in this network. And here we're hearing that he's being selected out of Bohemian Grove. But Texe, I had to call you as soon as I got back, because you were really accurate on analyzing the ritual. But, as you repeated on my show—can you repeat it here?—This is just not the Owl of Wisdom. Go into some of the occult details because I'd like to hear it again.

Texe: Well, first of all, Alex, I find it very fascinating when you mentioned that they began to chant and began to worship and to call out for the "Owl of Babylon". That's very significant. Well, I'd like to read, folks, from *the Woman's Dictionary of Symbols and Sacred Objects*. Let's just call this a "witchcraft encyclopedia" of sorts, by Barbara Walker. And on page 404, Alex, she discusses the owl and its meaning in witchcraft and the occult world. Let me just read a part of it.

She says, "...the wise owl appears with witches at Halloween, the Celtic feast of the Dead. It has a past association," she continues, "with many forms of the Chrome Goddess. Also, it is associated with Lilith, Athena, Minerva, and the owl-eyed Goddess, Marie." It says that these goddesses "often were said to take the owl's shape as their own." It goes on to say, "the owl was known as a bird of Death." It says that "to the Babylonians, the owls (the hooting owls) were ghosts of women who died in childbirth, calling for their offspring." It says there's a "time-honored connection" of the midwife goddess with owls. Then, interestingly, it says, "in medieval times the owl was sometimes called the Night Hag, like the daughters of Lilith who were possessed by demonic succubi. Female spirits with owl wings were feared as potential kidnappers of infants." So this a very interesting thing. We're talking about kidnappers of infants; the Night Hag, connected with the great goddess of Babylon. So we have this huge idol of the owl. How did this appear to you? I mean, did they have it draped? Was it menacing? Was there fire about? Tell us a little about that, Alex.

Alex: Well, also just from my reading of history, Texe—going back to the Babylonians and then in Tyre—they kept saying, *"Owl of Babylon, goodly Tyre"*; that they were actually sacrificing their children, throwing it into a hollow owl and burning it. I believe that is biblical. Is that correct, Texe?

Texe: Well, it could be. The bible says that they made their children "pass through the fire". And of course God saw this as a great abomination, we read in the Bible. And that's why he brought great tribulation to Israel. Because they were participating in some of these horrible Pagan child-sacrifice rituals.

Alex: Yeah. Well, basically asking how the Owl looked: we have some photos of it up on *infowars.com*. Someone many years ago smuggled one photo out that was not stopped by security. And I never knew that it was real, but it's obviously a real photo of the priests around it. We've actually got some video of it, and it's this big demonic Owl. And they only lit it—they only had fires and lights that went onto it—when the sacrifice took place as if it was energized by it. The Owl spoke in semi-darkness to them, and told them to do it.

…*"Oh, Great Owl, these holy Halls…"* They also talk about, *"woodland spirits, please bring back the dead of other Bohemian Grove members of the past"*—that's almost their exact words—and, *"let their spirits be with us now"*. So you also have—what's the word for it, necromancy? Conjuring the dead?—I mean you're the occult expert. Do you have any comments on that?

Texe: Well, I would think that would be what it is. They are conjuring up the dead. And here again, *Deuteronomy 18* says this is an abomination to God. And by the way, in this same witchcraft dictionary, on page 180 it says, "The owl is associated with the spirits of the dead". So here again we have the owl in this connection. You remember, Alex, you and I were discussing on your radio program, how a young lady—and I cannot reveal her name because it's in confidence—but her father was the chairman of a Fortune 500 corporation; a multinational, very rich corporation; had been. Now he's retired and lives in a huge mansion, you know, in California. And she stated that he had been a member of the Bohemian Grove, and that he went to their annual meeting. And she said he almost worshipped that meeting. He couldn't wait to go. But he would not tell her, as a little girl, what they did there. But she said all over their house, in every room, they had little figurines of an owl placed about. And that he was frantic to keep that owl in every room. And he made sure that they were tended to by the maid and so forth. And this young lady asked me, she said, "What is the meaning of the owl to the Bohemian Grove? Because my father...it was almost like he worshipped and adored the owl." What do you make of that in light of what you saw going on there?

Alex: One of the Ten Commandments is "don't worship a graven image", and they're sacrificing to this thing. Texe, that's what I got. At a few points I thought, "This is silly", until...then I had a macabre feeling, but I was still calm when I would look at the old men going, *"Yes, oh, oh, yes, burn it again; oh, do it; get him!"*

Texe, do you have any comments about at the start of the ceremony, bringing in this flat-backed wagon with the people dressed up as Death; and when it pulled behind the black curtains, the almost orgasmic relishment that was going on? I don't know what to make of that in the ceremony. Do you have any analysis?

Texe: Well, here again we see the sacrifice going on. I mean, so...back into the witchcraft. I'm sorry I don't have my, let's say my witchcraft calendar with me here. It's not something I keep in my billfold, Alex! (laughs) But in my records we have a Satanic and witchcraft and occult calendar of events. And, let's see...what date were you there?

Alex: They have publicly said that the kickoff of their Summer Encampment of the Bohemian Club is roughly from the 13th through about the 24th.

Texe: OK, well even there we see the 13th, the number 13; in superstition, the number of evil. The 24th—2 plus 4 equals 6—the number of the Beast. The month of July is the month of sacrifice, if I can recall, in the occult world. So everything relates here to what you have discovered at this Bohemian Grove. Now you mentioned also that the priest had a certain symbol, as he attended, let's just say, to this owl figure, this idol. And some of the other priests and associates, they had certain kind of vestments that they wore.

Alex: Yes. There were vastly more priests in black cloaks, some of them with their faces painted up as skeletons, with black circles around the eyes and with teeth. The next most plentiful color of robes was red. And then there were 3 high priests; 2 of which were in silver with stripes of, little flecks of red and green with gold and gold hats on. And then the high priest comes out in pure silver, with little…I saw little bits of green, a little bit of red. And then they stand behind him; 2 acolytes come out in red. And they put this big red, vermilion-red cape on his back, and then he snarls over, and kind of bent over to the side, then his hands out—I was 170 yards away, but he was like bent over with his hands out to the side, curling in his knuckles—and they had some weird symbols around their neck that I couldn't really make out too well. And again that's why I called you, Texe. I'm not an occult expert. I just knew this was some evil stuff. This owl is associated with just ancient human sacrifice. And it was just horrible to witness all this; and Texe, can you go back over the different colors of the high priests, and of course the black and the red robes?

Texe: All of these colors of course have great meaning in the occult world. And I have entire occult witchcraft books talking about the meaning of colors: green symbolizing the Earth, black symbolizing Death, gold representing the great Sun god whom the owl, by the way—even though he's a night creature—represents. So…, at one point you told me that Walter Cronkite had a bit part in all of this?

Alex: Oh, yes. And again it's in the mainstream publications that Walter Cronkite has been a member of the Bohemian Club for over 40 years…But as I would go by the camps, you would see pictures of George Bush, Jr. several times; I only saw one poster hanging on the entrance doors, or on the sides of the wooden fences inside as you would enter, and then go up into the hills where the main buildings were built, which I didn't go into many of. And we also saw pictures of Walter Cronkite; large posters of Walter Cronkite at several of the encampments; and skulls hanging above him—that is, metal skulls; I think they were real skulls. We basically tried to stay out of the camps and stay away from them, because we went into one camp and we were confronted with, "Who are you?" and we just smiled and laughed and left.

Texe: Now Walter Cronkite…was it his voice that was heard over the PA system during this ritual?

Alex: According to these publications, he is the voice of the owl…; the *Economist* and others have written stories about it, and said, "Oh, it's no big deal. They just burn the Club's effigy, Care." And they said they burn an owl; that's not true. And that Walter Cronkite has done the voice of the Owl, yes. And it *did* sound like Walter Cronkite.

Texe: Now how tall is this owl?

Alex: It's on circular steps that are around it, going up to it, and I'd say there's about 20 feet of steps. And then—I was up close to it, about 50 feet away—it's at least 45 to 50 feet tall.

Texe: You know, I recall—talking about Walter Cronkite—he is a globalist. And was it the World Federalists who recently had their big meeting and called for a one-world government?

Alex: And he came out in support of it. And he's huge buddies with Clinton and Gore, and has been photographed out boating at Martha's Vineyard with them on his yacht, so…

Texe: Alex, I'm afraid we've run out of time, but thank you for coming on the show today and sharing your amazing story with us about the Bohemian Grove.

Alex: Thank you, Texe.

(Interview © 2000, Texe Marrs. Reprinted with permission.)

Chapter XV

Manus hoec inimica tyrannis

(This hand is hostile to tyrants)

Alex Jones—Three Years Later

Since the film "Dark Secrets: Inside Bohemian Grove" came out in 2000, many new revelations have come our way. I wanted an updated account from my friend Alex to include in this book, to get his personal recollections of our adventure in his own words. But because we have worked together for so many years, and went into the Grove together, I knew I was too close to the subject to conduct an objective interview with Alex. It was important to me that Alex feel free to say anything about the Grove experience he wanted, without influence from me, and I knew that would not be possible (or journalistically fair) if I interviewed him. So I worked on a list of questions and had a reporter friend of mine conduct the actual interview at a time when I was not present. The result was one of the most candid, relaxed, eloquent (and at times even humorous) interviews I've ever heard Alex give—and in seven years of broadcasting with him, that's saying something.

The date of this interview was February 14, 2003.

Q—How did the idea first come about to try and get into the Bohemian Grove as an uninvited guest?

A—It's funny, you know—I had listeners over the years who would call into my radio show and tell me about the kinds of things that went on at Bohemian Grove, and so I did some research on my own. I went to the mainstream media and found several articles that had been written about this Bohemian Club, that world leaders *do* go to the Grove every summer, that they *do* plan policy in this secret environment, that there was a big owl and some kind of Druid fire ritual that goes on there. I had talked to my friend George Humphrey, a former Austin city councilman and activist, about the Grove, because he had also tried to sneak in there once or twice. The idea was already sort of floating around in my head to try and get in there sometime and find out what it was all about. I even spoke about my desire to do that live on the air to my radio listeners. And then along comes Jon Ronson. He showed up at Waco while we were rebuilding the Branch Davidian church, and said that he wanted to make a film about the Bohemian Grove.

Q—Was that the first time you had met Jon Ronson?

A—He had actually been to Austin a few weeks before, talking to me about his planned visit to Waco on the anniversary, which was April 19th, He asked me if he could come out to the rededication ceremony and bring Randy Weaver with him. That day at Waco, he mentioned Bohemian Grove and asked me what I knew about the place. I told him that I knew about this strange ritual and that they have some 40-foot stone owl God out there. He said, "Well, we're thinking about going out there this summer. Would you like to come along?" I said, sure, it sounded like a good idea, and I thought it was kinda funny, because I had just been discussing that idea on the air recently, so the timing of it seemed exactly right.

I asked Mike Hanson, my cameraman, to come along with me because I knew he had to courage to actually go through with it. I'd seen him display courage in the past, in all kinds of situations. Mike and I have safely gotten into (and out of) some pretty volatile situations before! However, I was the only person under contract with the British producers—Jon Ronson and World of Wonder, the Production Company. We basically had an agreement that they would pay for the trip to California. They flew us out there, they gave us all the maps and stuff we needed to prepare in exchange for us sharing the video we shot with them. We had a verbal contract between us that I would sneak into the Grove, I would shoot the video, and I would take the risk so that he and his company wouldn't have any liability. That way, there wouldn't be any criminal charges brought against them for trespassing. We, on the other hand, had no such protection.

I do distinctly remember in his book, *Them—Adventures With Extremists*, Jon Ronson tried to spin the story a different way. He made it sound like I invited myself along for the trip to Bohemian Grove, and that's not what happened. He enticed us to go, and we were definitely invited, not the other way around.

Q—Did you get to witness any of the Lakeside Chats while you were in the Grove?
A—No, we were just inside for about four-and-a-half hours or so. We walked in about 4 o'clock and left at 9:30 that night. By the time we got inside, which was late afternoon, I think they were done with the Lakeside Chats for the day. Mainly, we were just there to see the Cremation of Care ritual.

Q—These Lakeside chats are perhaps the most important part of the Grove summer camp, because this is the place where policy issues are discussed in the open.
A—Yes, and if you look in the archives at the University of California at Berkeley, you'll actually be able to read the texts of some of the more important Lakeside Talks that have been given through the years. Not all of them are

316

available, but some are. And you can see where future public policy is being shaped privately at the Grove. For example, the "Star Wars" program was hatched there in the 1970s, long before the public was introduced to the space-based initiative and direct energy weapons. And you have the Manhattan Project being hatched there in secret, and the engineering of that. Of course, the profits of warmongering go to the private corporations, which are owned by members of the Bohemian Club. So this is really the place where they set policy and set out the agenda of the New World Order.

Helmut Schmidt, the former German chancellor, wrote in his autobiography *Men and Powers—A Political Retrospective*, that this was a center of globalism for the CFR, the Trilateral Commission, etc....and that they did indeed form policy there at Bohemian Grove. That's on the record by a former German chancellor.

Q—He also said in his book that his visit to Bohemian Grove was the best time he'd ever had in America.
A—It's those Druid rituals. He just loves 'em. (Chuckles)

Q—Ironically, the motto of the Bohemian Grove is, "weaving spiders come not here," quoting from William Shakespeare's *A Midsummer Night's Dream.* They use this motto as a way to remind the campers that this is a place to have fun, no weaving spiders, no business is to be conducted here, but that is a rule that has been discreetly and routinely ignored, hasn't it?
A—Yeah, there's always these double meanings to everything. *Of course* it's about wheeling and dealing. *Of course* it's about business. Alan Greenspan, who had been an opponent of the New World Order's fiat banking system and had written books on it, later went and became a member of the Bohemian Club. Then, like magic, not long after that, Greenspan is announced as the Federal Reserve Chairman. That's just classic double-speak when they say, "weaving spiders come not here." All they do at the Bohemian Grove is weave webs.

Q—And these Lakeside Chats are a case in point—there is serious business being conducted inside Bohemian Grove, and the public is not invited!
A—I've seen photographs of Bush and Bush Jr., the former president and the current president, speaking in front of the owl statue at the Grove. That was in one of the books the Bohemian Club publishes privately, the annals of each decade. I believe that is in the *1986–1996* volume.

Q—So real quick, I'm going to give you the speakers names and topics of a few of these Lakeside chats, and I just want to get your thoughts on them. The year you and Mike were at the Grove, on July 29, 2000, former Secretary of State Henry Kissinger gave a Lakeside Chat titled "Do We Need A Foreign Policy?"

A—Well, we know that Henry Kissinger is a New World Order supergopher, carrying out their activities. I mean, there he is, pushing their whole agenda there at the Grove each year. And Kissinger is a high-level member of the Club. He's practically a God at Mandalay Camp, the most prestigious of all the camps inside.

Q—And how about former Secretary of Defense William Perry, speaking at the Grove in 1998 on "Preventive Defense and American Security in the 21st Century?"

A—And of course, you hear that term a lot now, "preventive." And now we're hearing more and more about "preemptive strikes" and "offensive attacks" against our perceived enemies. So, you can definitely see policy being formed there.

Q—It's fascinating. I mean, this was five, ten, even 20 years ago, these Lakeside Chats at the Grove are laying out exactly what's happening now.

A—Sure. And it's not because these guys are psychic, either. They know what's going to happen well in advance because they are the ones who plan this stuff—and they do a lot of it right there at Bohemian Grove.

Q—Like when former CIA director James Woolsey spoke in 1997 at the Grove, he sure chose an interesting topic: "Rogues, Terrorists, National Security in the Next Century." Or sitting Supreme Court Justice Antonin Scalia speaking on "Church, State and the Constitution?" That might be a speech of interest to the American people, don't you think?

A—Sure. And now you see they have their "Faith-Based Initiative" to take over the churches. Under the 1st Amendment of the Constitution, churches have the right to do what they want. It's the government that's not supposed to be involved. But somehow, they've reversed it all around now so that it's the government that controls the churches. Though the so-called separation of church and state, the church is no longer allowed to have much influence on public policy. But it's what dictators always do when they rise to power—they take control of the churches.

Q—Back in 1991, Elliot Richardson, Secretary of Defense and Attorney General for Nixon, gave a speech titled "Defining a New World Order." Dick Cheney spoke at the Grove that same year on "Major Defense Problems of the 21st Century." Alex, do you think that even then, as early as a decade ago, a plan was already in place to install Dick Cheney as Vice President of the United States in the 21st Century?

A—Well, certainly they had a plan decades ago to put George W. Bush in the White House. His entire cabinet is basically retreads of his father's previous administration, or from Ronald Reagan's administration. They're all a bunch of CIA, intelligence people, and frontmen for global corporations.

Q—I recall listening to your radio show one afternoon, shortly after you and Mike returned from Bohemian Grove in the summer of 2000, and you announced that Cheney was selected to be Bush's running mate from the Grove camp.

A—This was right after we got back from California. My mother called me on the phone and said, "Hey, Alex, they just announced on CNN that they had the exclusive inside track on who Bush was going to be announcing as his Vice Presidential running mate in two or three weeks, and it's going to be Dick Cheney. They said they had this from the summer encampment at Bohemian Grove and the source was Colin Powell." Then, I turned on the TV and actually saw the story for myself, so, yes.

Q—(laughs) So, obviously policy decisions are NOT made at the Bohemian Grove!

A—Well, clearly that one was. A pretty important policy decision.

Q—You are well aware of the fact that human remains have been found on or near the Grove's property, the best-known case is that of Polly Klass. But I wanted to ask you what you make of the story that Paul Bonacci told John DeCamp about the snuff child porn films made there and the actual murder of a boy at the foot of the owl?

A—I've interviewed John DeCamp, and if he says that and hasn't been sued, that's usually a pretty good barometer that it's probably true. He's actually sued people who tried to discredit him over the *Franklin Cover-Up* book and won. I'm certainly not privy to all the information, but John DeCamp does have Paul Bonacci's diary where Paul alleges that he witnessed a murder at the Grove. I know that DeCamp has had those diaries analyzed by experts to determine their authenticity, and that the inks of Paul's handwriting on the page proved genuine and that the inks were of the type being used at the time he made the original diary entries. For those who might be unfamiliar with DeCamp's book, *The Franklin Cover-Up*, he basically uncovered this information about the Bohemian Grove while he was doing research on the Franklin Federal Savings and Loan debacle in Omaha.

Q—It's a pretty twisted web, isn't it? I mean, you've got the Franklin Federal Savings and Loan, run by Larry King, who runs this child pornography business on the side and throws sex parties for important Republican party leaders in order to photograph and blackmail them. And he documents this going on at the highest levels, all the way up to George Bush Sr. and his comrades at the Bohemian Grove.

In this diary, Paul Bonacci claims that he was flown out to the Sacramento Airport in July, 1984 by Larry King in his private jet, they picked up a couple of other young boys on the way, and they were all flown out there for one reason only—to provide sexual favors to these very powerful men. But they were just boys at the time. They were not adults. And they were not paid to do this, like, say a male prostitute would be. I mean, these boys had no idea what was in store for them.

A—In the film, *Dark Secrets—Inside Bohemian Grove*, I didn't even get into that story because it's hard enough for people to believe that there is a place called Bohemian Grove. The general public still has a hard time believing that Bohemian Grove or the Skull and Bones order even exist. And you know, we have their own program cover—the one they gave us that night at the Grove for the Cremation of Care ceremony. And there on the program cover, you can see very clearly the photograph of a skeleton burning underneath the owl. Other program covers I've seen through the years even feature the owl stomping on the body, and you can see the blood running out of the body, which to me implies that this is a *human* body. So there is that common theme of stomping on little people, people that are the size of children. Or burning them in flames. And if you study the ancient Caananite rituals that are described in Leviticus in the Bible, where they talk about sacrificing children to the God Molech, you'll see the famous passage about "give not your children to the fires of Molech." Children were often used in these human sacrifice rituals. The question is—are these customs still being practiced today?

You know, I don't know about snuff films being made at the Grove or children being killed there…I know that information has come out in other publications and books, but I really can't confirm it one way or the other. Certainly, Mike and I witnessed no such thing when we were inside the Grove. Occult experts I've spoken to who have analyzed our film of the Cremation of Care say that this is most likely an outer circle ritual, meaning this is something done more for showmanship than for actually casting any kind of spell. I've been told that a lot of the darker dealings go on in smaller, very private rituals that most of the Bohemians are not privy to and probably aren't even aware go on.

Q—When did you decide to take Mike Hanson along, and what was his reaction when you first asked him to take this risk with you?
A—Mike was there at Waco that day when we both talked to Jon Ronson about the idea, but I think Mike was too busy at that point to pay much attention to the conversation because he had his hands full trying to coordinate the volunteers, get things done…that was his job. Mike was the Volunteer Coordinator on the project to rebuild the church at Mt. Carmel, and his focus was completely on that. So I don't think he took Ronson's proposal seriously at first. But the British kept pushing the idea, and so one day, I asked Mike how he really felt about it, and if he wanted to try and break into Bohemian Grove with me, and he said "sure." Just like that. He didn't say, "let me think about this for awhile…" or anything like that. Mike didn't hesitate. He just said yes.

Besides, I wanted to take my own crew along on this adventure, partly because I didn't entirely trust the British producers from the start. It's hard to explain why I felt that way, but Ronson just struck me as kinda sneaky. So I took Mike and my wife, Violet, along as my own camera crew, and a backup of sorts. I would have brought along more people if I could, but I remember the British would only pay for two of the plane tickets. I had to buy my wife's ticket, but that was fine because I really wanted her to be there, even if she couldn't actually go into the Grove with us. It was so important that we had someone we could trust to drive us to the Grove, drop us off, and wait for us back at the hotel just in case anything went wrong, to have someone we could call if we ended up in jail to come bail us out! I wanted to be as prepared as possible, because I really didn't know what to expect once we got in there.

Q—I wonder if you would tell the readers a brief history of your long friendship and partnership with Mike Hanson. How many years have you known each other?

A—Mike had been down at Austin cable access TV for years, long before I arrived on the scene. He had been producing a show program on local Austin issues. I think the show was called *River City Talk*. About 1995 or so, I started hanging out at access TV and appeared as a guest on a few other shows that were focused on the New World Order, but I hadn't done Mike's show yet. Around 1996, I got my own TV show on cable access, and at that time my cousin was my producer. By this time, Mike and I had become friends, and in '97, I started doing a daily call-in talk show on KJFK-FM, a local radio station. Mike started coming along with me to rallies, protests, and other events as a cameraman, and did a really good job. He also showing up at the studio regularly and volunteered his time to help produce my local TV program, which was called *Exposing Corruption* back then. And our working relationship basically evolved out of our shared belief that these people must be stopped, their activities must be exposed, and both of us felt the same way about things. So, it got to the point where I'd just call him up and say, "Hey Mike, I'm going out to take some footage of this checkpoint on the highway...or, I'm going down to South Texas to catch Delta Force doing combat exercises in a small town...wanna come with me?" So, Mike would always come along and shoot the video and help out in a lot of different ways.

Then, we had the Joe Campana story, which opened up a whole new avenue for us. Joe Campana was a World War II and Korean War veteran who lived here in Austin. Unfortunately, he just died last year after a long illness, but anyway, Mike called me up one day and said, "Alex, I just saw this story on the news that the City of Austin is harassing this poor old man. They're threatening to bulldoze his house because he's been too sick to keep the place up to city code all by himself. That's not right!" So Mike had an idea to get the community together, assemble a group of volunteers to build this man a new house on his property so that the city wouldn't kick him out. This was his property free and clear, by the way—he'd had the house paid off for years.

Mike works in the construction industry, and he knew a lot of builders who donated the lumber and materials, and he really did a great job in coordinating the volunteers. I got on the radio and talked about it, and even *more* folks came out to lend a hand. We got the media interested in following the story, and frankly, we embarrassed the City of Austin by bringing attention to what they were doing to this old guy, Joe Campana, who had already given so much for his country. So, they pushed the permits through in like, 12 days, which is an all time record for the city! (Laughs) All the press coverage of the story we generated turned into a real public relations nightmare for the city, and I think they just wanted to make us go away. So that was probably our first indication that Mike and I were starting to affect some real change, on a local level.

So then, about a year later, Mike and I went out to Waco with a reporter from the nationally-syndicated TV news program *Extra*. They wanted to interview the surviving Branch Davidians, and asked me to help facilitate that meeting. So, we're up there at Mt. Carmel, and there's Clive Doyle (Waco survivor) sitting in his double-wide trailer home, saying, "well, we used to have a church here, but we don't anymore. I sure wish we had a building to worship in again." And Mike spoke up and said, "hey, maybe we could build you a new one." And I agreed that yeah, we could do that. I don't think Clive really believed us. He just kinda smiled and was probably thinking to himself, "well, *that* will never happen."

But Mike and I were serious about this, and we started putting out press releases, talking about the idea to rebuild the church on the radio and TV shows, and sure enough, we quickly assembled a lot of volunteers who turned out to help. Donations started coming in from all over the world. I think we raised about $105,000 for the project. So, we built them a new church in about six months, only working a couple of days a week, because we had to drive all the way from Austin and could only come up to work on the weekends. But we did it anyway.

Y'know, I was just tired of hearing everybody say how bad it was, what the federal government did to the Branch Davidians, but nobody was taking any action. And I wanted to show the Feds that the community didn't appreciate the military and the government going out to this rural church and slaughtering these people. Texans won't stand for that type of massacre in cold blood. We remember the Alamo.

*Alex Jones at Waco, holding a piece of the charred
Branch Davidian church in his hand.*

Q—And as we know, it was the memorial at Waco where you and Mike met
up with Jon Ronson, which, in turn lead you both right to the gates of Bohemian Grove.
A—Precisely.

Q—Once you and Mike managed to successfully get inside the Grove gates,
and you were on your own, free to look around, what kind of internal security
was there? Did you see any microphones or surveillance cameras?

324

A—Yeah. They had little bitty cameras way up in the trees, and we saw a guard shack on the back of the property that had TV monitor screens in it.

Q—The first guard shack you came to was a lucky break, because it just so happened the guard had gone to the restroom, or was out making his rounds—he wasn't there, so you two just kinda breezed right through the first checkpoint. Did you have any other close calls with security where you thought, "well, the jig might be up?"

A—Yeah, more than once. I remember an incident when we got to the second parking lot, and the shuttle truck came along to pick up the Grovers and take them inside. Mike and I were riding along with them, and that's when two of the Bohemians got into a conversation about how much they paid for their robes, and Mike and I started getting a little nervous that we might say the wrong thing to these guys and wind up blowing our cover. We passed another checkpoint while in the shuttle, and one of the guards really stared us down—that was another tense moment.

Then, once we were inside the Grove, walked around to the scenic overlook of the Russian River at the back of the property, and a guy in a sheriff's windbreaker walked up to us and started asking us questions that were worded more like Masonic riddles. I guess we didn't give him exactly the right answers, and probably aroused some suspicion there. He let us go on, but we noticed walking back to camp that we were being followed by two men in dark suits, and…this is actually funny, because Mike turns to me and says, "I think I'm gonna take a run for it, Alex!" And I was trying to tell him to be calm, saying, "no, Mike, we can't do that. Just be cool." Not that I can blame Mike for wanting to run, because these guys were tailing us, walking right behind us for a really long time. Then the men walked up and asked us what we were doing, and we just said, "Oh, nothin'—just enjoying a nice walk," or whatever, and they told us to have a good afternoon and walked on their way. That was a close call, but Mike did a pretty good job of holding his composure under the circumstances, and I think I did, too.

Later, when we were walking down to the "Lake" for the Cremation of Care…well, it's not really a lake. The Bohemians call it a lake, but I call it a large pond. Anyway, the only black man I saw the whole time was working as an usher, handing out programs to the Bohemians as they filed into this amphitheater. This man was very tall, and he said something to us like,

"Trouble yourselves not. Take it easy, here's a program, enjoy yourselves, gentlemen." And I heard some of the old men around me in the darkness, walking under the trees, saying to each other things like, "I can't believe they let those damn niggers in here," and some other pretty offensive stuff. Mike and I just held our tongues and didn't say anything at all. I was incredibly offended by that. It was easy to tell just by eavesdropping on some of their conversations that these were really mean old men—some of them, anyway.

And then while I'm sitting there at the ceremony with this hidden video camera under my arm, in this little shoulder bag, I remember being incredibly nervous. I was so worried because the camera had this little red "record" light on it that was showing through the hole in the bag we had cut, and it was too late to go find some private spot and fix the problem. So Mike and I were just trying to cover up the little red light where the others wouldn't see it and get suspicious. (Chuckles) We must have looked pretty awkward, because people were starting to stare at us, and Mike was trying to step in front of the camera bag to hide the red light, but in doing so, he kept blocking my shot...(laughter)...man, it was really something else!

We almost got found out again later in the ceremony, when they were doing all these pyrotechnics onstage. All of a sudden, there was this great big "BOOM!" and Mike just about jumped out of his skin, the noise scared him to death. And again, all these Bohemians turn around to look at him because they knew that big explosion was coming, it was part of the show, but Mike and I didn't know that. It came as a total surprise, and Mike literally jumped when that thing went off. Then, he covered it pretty well by saying, "Oh! They didn't do that last year!" (Laughs) It's on the video, you can hear Mike saying that—it's totally hilarious.

Q—So once you were both inside, you just tried your best to blend in and had a look around. Can you tell me what you saw—do you remember the camps?
A—Well, they all had demonic-sounding names like "Lost Angels", "Dragons," stuff like that...and some of the camps had some pretty interesting signage out front, too. One of the camps we saw had this big skull hanging on the sign over the camp entrance, strung between the trees, and we got footage of that sign you can see in the film. We saw owl insignias everywhere, all over the place, some of the owls had big glowing red eyes, and that was pretty creepy. They had a big death motif going. And the pirate motif, they were big

on that, too—like the sign with the skull on it was inscribed, *Je Suis Lafitte,* an apparent reference to the French pirate Lafitte.

Just like in the Skull and Bones Order, they are known to have this amazing collection of human skulls. They're absolutely obsessed with the skulls of famous people, like how they have the skull of Geronimo in the Skull and Bones headquarters. In Skull and Bones, they have this initiation rite that goes, "Am I a pirate, am I a king, am I a fool?" They see themselves as modern-day maritime pirates, this organized crime syndicate, and that's why they take the old pirate symbol of the skull and crossed bones as their logo.

To me, Bohemian Grove is sort of the "senior league" of the Skull and Bones, which is more of the "junior league," where they train these men while they are young. The elite doesn't necessarily take their kids and train them in the occult sciences as children. But later, they send the kid off to Yale University, and their children are introduced to the occult through membership in these secret societies. So, going from Yale to a membership in the Bohemian Club seems more like a graduation of sorts, just part of the progression. The Bohemian Club is just a higher level of Skull and Bones, in my opinion.

Q—After the Cremation of Care ritual was over, how did you guys get out of there?
A—When the men started breaking up, the outer initiates who were watching this ritual, we just kinda blended into the crowd as they filed out of the amphitheater. And then we just casually walked the half-mile or so out to the main entrance. We stayed on side paths until we neared the main gate, then we got on the central pathway and just walked right past security. But the Grove members are always walking out and in, going to get things out of their cars and stuff, so it wasn't unusual for us to do that. Let's put it this way—it's a hell of a lot easier to walk out of the Grove than it is to walk in! (Laughs) Once we got outside, the British crew was there waiting for us about a half-mile down the main road, Bohemian Avenue. They were there in their little minivan, ready to pick us up and get out of there as quickly as possible.

Q—And where had the British crew been all that time? Surely they didn't just drive around for four hours waiting for you to come back out of the Grove. That seems a bit risky!
A—Well, one of the cameramen had gone to a local restaurant and drank a lot of red wine, so he was pretty sauced by the time we saw him again. And as for

Jon Ronson, I don't know what he did all that time. He claims in that *C-SPAN* interview (see *Chapter XIII*) that he went into the Grove himself, and I guess I'll take his word for it, although I didn't see him in there. He certainly didn't sneak in with us, although he says that he *was* with Mike and I. I can tell you that part is definitely not true. The tape clearly shows that it was just Mike and I inside the Grove, by ourselves. If he was not being honest, I can't really say as that would surprise me. I mean, after all, what do you expect from the mainstream media?

Q—Obviously, you're aware of the story of Richard McCaslin, the guy who calls himself "The Phantom Patriot," who broke into Bohemian Grove heavily armed about a year or so ago. After he was caught and jailed, he told the media that your film was his inspiration to try this stunt. Your thoughts on that?

A—He was from Austin, or rather, he lived here for a while, and used to watch my TV show pretty regularly, but I never even met the guy. One night, he showed up at the TV studio while I was live on the air. All of a sudden, the studio door swings open, and this guy is standing there holding a stack of the "Phantom Patriot" comic books that he had made. Since I was on the air, he just had to leave them with somebody, but I didn't get a chance to talk to him. That was the only time I ever saw him in person, but we didn't get to speak to each other.

Q—As soon as you returned from the Grove, you did an interview with Texe Marrs on his radio show in which you said that this experience changed your life profoundly, and that it was something you would never forget (see *Chapter XIV*). How do you feel now, almost three years later?

A—Y'know, it was so different from anything I'd ever experienced, its' still like a *Twilight Zone* episode. It's still hard to consciously believe how bizarre this really is, and I think that's a problem a lot of people have. Even I was there saw it with my own eyes, and it's still hard to believe it all really happened. But it *did* change my life, and it served as a reminder to me just what lunatics these world leaders really are, how decadent and crazy they are. But if you look at world history, so many leaders have been involved in stuff like this in the past, that while it might sound crazy to us, to them, it's just normal behavior. That is...let me clarify that...normal behavior for despotic psychopaths!

Q—Alex, how many affiliates now carry your syndicated radio show?

A—About 80 commercial AM and FM radio stations in the United States currently carry the broadcast, and probably over a hundred micro and short wave outlets around the world. And the list is always growing as more and more stations continue to add our show. We're getting the word out there, and as more and more people are waking up to the truth about the New World Order, the show seems to be gaining in popularity.

Q—Alex, thanks for taking the time to talk with us today, and for sharing your Bohemian Grove story with the readers of this book.

A—It's a pleasure to help Mike any way I can. Thank you.

Chapter XVI

cui bono

(for whose advantage?)

Dr. Peter Phillips

Dr. Peter Martin Phillips is an Associate Professor of Sociology at Sonoma State University in Northern California, located fairly near the Bohemian Grove. He is the founder of "Project Censored," a media research organization. (Alex Jones won an award from "Project Censored" for his documentary films in 2003.) Dr. Phillips is also the author of a doctoral dissertation on Bohemian Grove, "A Relative Advantage," which can be read in its' entirety on the Sonoma State University website.

The date of our talk was March 3, 2003.

Q—In researching your Ph.D. dissertation, *A Relative Advantage,* you spent several days at the Grove as a guest. How did you swing an invitation?
A—Al Baxter is the Bohemian Club historian, and I'd been interviewing him on and off for about two years. I'd done a lot of library research, at the Bancroft Library and other archives, and finally he just said, "Well, I think you should come out to Grove and see for yourself."

So I went out to what was called the "Spring Jinks" in 1994, which is a 4-day warm-up in June for the big summer camp in July. The guests for the Spring Jinks are mostly Californians, while the guests that attend the July camp are usually from other places. In fact, you really kind of need special permission to bring somebody in from California during the main summer camp, because they prefer to bring in guests from other parts of the world during that time. But I got a really good feel for what the Grove was like, and I spent a three day weekend there—Friday, Saturday, Sunday—and I took 40 pages of field notes.

Al Baxter is a perfect case in point. He truly believes that there isn't "a relative advantage," that no business is being conducted, which just is not true. I mean, political discussions *do* go on there—he acknowledges that—but he asserts that those discussions inside the Grove don't have any influence on the outside world. He is really quite sincere about that belief, and that's why he invited me.

Yet, when my dissertation was published, Al didn't like it. While he said there was nothing he could find in it that wasn't factual, he didn't like my interpretations. I didn't tell him who my committee was, or that G. William Domhoff was on the committee. Domhoff is a name that is very familiar to the Bohemians, because he wrote a book about the Club in the 1970s that they didn't especially like. So had they known that he was part of my committee, they may have never invited me inside in the first place.

But I was able to dispel a few rumors about the Grove in my dissertation. A lot of the things we hear about the Grove don't check out upon closer inspection. For example, all the homosexual behavior. I saw no evidence of that. And a lot of the prostitute stuff. You know, if 1 percent of the guys there "jump the river"—that's what they call it—I would be surprised. But it's sure joked about a lot there.

Q—What about the "no girls" policy at the Grove? Did you see any women inside?
A—I did observe women there, at the bar, in groups. And I did observe club members coming and sitting down with them. And they've brought busloads of women there in the past. So, I mean, if you put 3,000 rich guys together in one place, of course there are going to be some of them who "jump the river".

(Author's Note: Apparently, none of the Bohemians bothered to clue Dr. Phillips in on the fact that the "girls" he saw hanging out at the Grove bar were strippers and prostitutes. He seemed to be unaware of this. Stands to reason that the Bohemians would not tell him the truth, as he was an invited guest writing a critical piece about the Club, and naturally, the Grovers wanted the most favorable coverage possible.)

Q—What do you think the biggest myth is about the Bohemian Grove?
A—Probably the biggest myth is the Cremation of Care ceremony. It has been characterized as Druid-like, with the burning of bodies and stuff, and there have been a lot of spooky tales that float around the Grove, even murder mysteries written about the Club.

Then, there's the guy in Texas, the talk jock *(Alex Jones)*, who did a big expose' on the club a few years ago and claimed they might be doing human sacrifice there. He went in the same day the British filmmaker *(Jon Ronson)* did—in fact, I know the people who helped them get in—but Alex didn't want to go in with the British as planned, he ended up going off and doing his own thing. He marched through the poison oak out by the parking lot and somehow got in with his camera.

Then, last year, a guy who had watched Alex's film broke into Bohemian Grove *(Richard McCaslin, the so-called "Phantom Patriot.")*, heavily armed, because he said he wanted to stop the murder of innocent children. He got caught, was arrested, and is now serving time in jail. He honestly believed he was going to go in there and save children from human sacrifice.

Q—I have to disagree with you there, because I work with Alex Jones, and I was the cameraman who went in the Grove and helped him film the ceremony. We were both completely shocked by what we saw. We understand that they were probably not sacrificing a human being up on the altar, but Alex did raise the question in his film: "how do we know for sure that Dull Care is only an effigy?" Then, the mainstream media picked up on that comment and took it out of context, it became a rumor.
A—Well, it's the crazy rumors like these that get started by people like Alex Jones. I mean, if you look at the film Jones made, he actually *says* he observed sacrifice that *could have been* a human being. While he may not come right out and say that they *are* burning a human body, he strongly implies it, saying that it is a "human-like body." And he says things to the effect of, you know, "if they catch me, will they burn me alive?" that sort of thing.

Q—But isn't the Cremation of Care a strange thing for our world leaders to do?
A—Admittedly, the Cremation of Care ceremony is a little bizarre. I have witnessed it myself. Basically, you've got 15 or 20 guys dressed in long, colorful robes with bishop-like hats on, and they come up on stage and shout to the Creator, "banish our cares from the world!" And to them, the whole thing is symbolic of coming there in companionship, leaving the cares of the world behind.

They bring an effigy of Care across the lake in a canoe. There are a lot of guys standing around in robes carrying these big torches. I've heard these robes described as Ku Klux Klan type outfits, but...I don't know. A robe is a robe. Whether it's a Druid robe or a Klan robe or a Bishop's robe from the Catholic Church..., but the visual of the ceremony, with the men wearing these robes, it does *look*...semi-religious. I'm told it has nothing to do with worship. It is not a religious ceremony. It's not intended to be. In the minds of the men at the "Cremation of Care" ceremony, it has nothing to do with worshipping the owl, or anything to do with any religious connotations whatsoever. It's more like a silly fraternity tradition.

Q—That's not what it looked like to me! (Laughs)
A—Certainly, for an outside observer to look at it, seeing this ceremony for the first time, anybody would say, "Oh, this is bizarre." And it is, you know? I

mean, if you just saw only the "Cremation of Care" ceremony, and you didn't know all about the Bohemian Club and its' traditions, and what they were doing there, it would look...it would look very bizarre.

So, once they've brought the effigy of Care to the stage, they try to light him on fire, and the funeral pyre doesn't light. Care mocks them: "Ha, ha, ha—you can't kill me!" And there is a whole funeral procession with horses and a horse-drawn carriage and guys playing bagpipes, and it's all part of this ceremony. And finally the flame, the true flame of the Spirit of Bohemia is emitted from the giant owl, and that in turn is finally able to ignite Care.

Care is burned up, and then there's fireworks and everything at the end. They actually damn near set the place on fire one year when I was there! (Laughs) I don't know how they manage to set fireworks off in the woods like that and the fire department lets them get away with it. But the Bohemians actually have their own fire department on premises, and they came out and hosed down the tree that had caught on fire.

Q—What do you know about the giant owl they have above the altar there?
A—The 45-foot stone owl is symbolic of the club, it represents wisdom to them. It's been part of their club's tradition for over 100 years. Now, the giant owl statue at Bohemian Grove is actually made of concrete, and it's been there for more than 70 years now. I think they covered it with some moss to make it look real, like a big old rock that had been there for thousands of years.

Q—When Alex and I were in Northern California to make our documentary film, we interviewed a lot of local residents, and we were surprised to find that so few of them knew about the Grove. When we told them about the "Cremation of Care" ritual, these folks didn't believe us. They thought we were crazy. In fact, several of them didn't even believe that there was a Bohemian Grove. Why is this place such a secret, after being in existence all these years?
A—It's not a secret. (Chuckles) There have been books written about it and many newspaper and magazine articles through the years as well. But over the decades, the Club has become much more defensive, especially since Mary Moore's group started protesting there. But I think it's safe to say a lot of locals know it's there.

Public access to the Grove has been closed off since the 1880s. Back then, the residents of the little town of Guerneville used to go have family picnics out there. So, when the Bohemians bought all that land, the people of Guerneville were very upset because they lost access to this beautiful old redwood area. I mean, it really is pretty. There are huge trees all around you, it's gorgeous.

Up until the 1930s, the local papers carried regular announcements of the events there and who was in attendance each year, so in those days, the Grove was very well known to the people of San Francisco. The ceremonies, the "Creation of Care" ceremony in particular, has been rewritten several times over the years. I have copies of many past year's ceremonies in my files. It's meant to be a symbolic dismissal of the cares of the world, as the men who are coming there are coming in friendship, to have a good time, a party, and entertain each other with plays and music. Supposedly, they just gather there to celebrate the arts.

Q—A lot of famous people have gone to the Grove, and not just politicians and dignitaries. What can you tell me about some of the important artists, writers, musicians and Hollywood stars who have been Grovers?
A—The Bohemians have always maintained a close association to the arts, literature, theater. That's how the club was originally conceived, by a bunch of local newspaper writers who wanted to do some self-entertaining. Jack London was one of the early Bohemians. Samuel Clements (Mark Twain) was a guest. I'm not sure if Bret Harte was a member or not. Ambrose Bierce was, too—until he went off and fought the Mexican war.

A lot of famous people went there and still does to this day. As far as the Hollywood connection goes, there is a history book written by the Los Angeles camp, which is probably the camp where most of the Hollywood people would stay. Although not necessarily. The Lost Angels camp is the name of the camp, and it's on what they call "snob hill," because there are several very rich camps up there. I did not go into the Lost Angels camp myself, but did visit some of the other camps nearby on snob hill, and let me tell you, these are some very wealthy people. But the Lost Angels club is the LA contingent, and they published a book. A lot of the camps have written history books.

There is that "Teddy Bears' Picnic" movie out about the Club, which is actually very good. Harry Shearer, who made the film, had been inside the Grove before as a guest, and therefore knew all the little inside jokes and was able to make a convincing film about it, even if it was a comedy.

Q—How far away from the Grove is Sonoma State University, where you teach?
A—About 40 minutes away.

Q—So you obviously know the area around the Grove very well from personal experience.
A—Yes, I live up there. In the area.

Q—You went to the Grove as an invited guest in 1994. Have you been back since?
A—No.

Q—Could you tell the readers a little bit about the topics you covered in your dissertation, *A Relative Advantage*? What was the main point you tried to make?
A—What I'm saying is that powerful men get together at the Grove and build consensus; they help each other out. Like being in a club—well, it *is* a club. And these men use the connections made at the Bohemian Grove in other aspects of their day-to-day lives, including, most importantly to me, their business dealings. So that gives them an advantage in the world. So, if anything, that's what its' about.

I also write about how they do all kinds of skits, theatrical performances, orchestra concerts, banjo groups...its entertainment. It's fun. But some of it is deadly serious. They have off-the-record talks there, given by high level political people—and about one out of five people there is somebody very important in the world. People can actually read my dissertation about Bohemian Grove on the web. It's public information, and is available on the Sonoma State University website. You're welcome to quote from it in your book.

Q—Thank you, Dr. Phillips. I appreciate your time, and next time you're in Austin, look us up. Alex and I would be pleased to meet you.
A—I'll actually be in Texas next month to speak at Southwest Texas University.

Q—Great. Hope to see you then.

Chapter XVII

quaere verum

(seek the truth)

Mary Moore

Mary Moore is the founder of the Bohemian Grove Action Network, and for more than 20 years has organized protests outside the Grove during each midsummer encampment. She also publishes a great deal of insider information in the BGAN's newsletter and website, available at sonomacountyfreepress.org.

This interview was conducted via phone from her home in Sonoma County, California on February 13, 2003. A verbatim transcript of our conversation follows.

Q—Can you begin by just telling the readers a little bit about yourself, and how you started the Bohemian Grove Action Network?
A—I'm a 67 year-old woman who has spent the past 40 years working basically as an activist. I got started in 1962 working in the civil rights movement, then later the women's movement, also environmental and anti-nuclear work. I guess you would call me a "card-carrying lefty" (chuckles). I certainly see the world we're living in now as very corporate-controlled, what with all the corporate influence on our government. But I *do* believe there is a point where the left and the right do come together, such as protesting Bohemian Grove. We can all agree on that.

I moved to Sonoma County in northern California in 1974, and was totally unaware of Bohemian Grove, until I read a book by G. William Domhoff *(The Bohemian Grove and Other Retreats)*. He's a professor at Santa Cruz who has done a lot of study on the ruling class. After reading his book, I then realized I was living about 5 miles away from one of the places he wrote about, which was the Bohemian Grove. So I, of course, grew much more interested after that, and had become a little more, uh...*sophisticated* in my political views than when I had started out in 1962. And so I was part of a group at that time that was bringing issues before the public such as the dangers of nuclear energy, nuclear power, and nuclear weapons. This was back in the late 1970s, early 1980s.

In 1980, we decided to start researching the Bohemian Grove to see who up there was connected to the nuclear industry. We started doing the organized protests outside the Grove in 1980. We were pretty much a single-issue organization at that time. I've always believed in building coalitions with like-minded people, and by 1982, we had a coalition with more than 70 other groups because it became apparent that these men at the Grove were very prominent also in the nuclear power industry. And you know, no matter what your particular issue is, I think you can always find several of your prime suspects there at the Bohemian Grove.

Q—When you first started doing this back in 1980, did the Bohemian Club allow African Americans or women as members?
A—Oh, no. There were a few black members of the club who were musicians back then. Because you've got your political elites here, but they all agree that their main reason for coming to the Grove is the arts. They do theater and have concerts up there and need the best talent they can get. But they have many members who are very well known in the arts, popular cultural figures—not necessarily political figures. It took them forever to finally admit black men to join the club, and still to this day, there are only a handful of them within the ranks, a token few.

Of course, this is an exclusively all-male club, so definitely no women are allowed as members. Women are only allowed at the Grove as employees. But before 1980, they didn't even allow women there to work, which of course, is totally against the law in California. You can't discriminate on the basis of sex for employment here, so they (the Bohos) called up the State of California and said they needed some additional parking lot attendants or something, and they specified "men only," and the State of California told them, "well, you can't do that, it's against the law." And the Club's response was, "but we are the Bohemian Grove, we do what we want." So we had to take them to court for a fight that lasted maybe three or four years…first, it won in our favor, then they appealed and it went in their favor, then we finally got it settled in the California Supreme court.

Q—When Alex Jones and I went in, we did not see any women once we got past the parking lot. Is that the only place women are allowed to work at the Grove?
A—Well, they either have them working in the dining room or the parking lot. Women are certainly not allowed to…in fact, most of the help is really not allowed to wander around. They are confined to their assigned areas. Some of the camps have workers—stewards, valets—and of course, there are more than 200 individual camps at the Grove. And they have people who work just for this camp or that camp. The main place of employment for women at the

Grove has been the dining room. They are taken to and from work on shuttle buses. They don't see much else.

Q—So, as far as you know, you haven't heard of any women actually going up into the hills and into the camps?
A—Well, you know, I'm sure there have been some "working women" up there (laughs). Prostitution is, of course, one of the main things we could talk about that goes on up there, but technically, most of the prostitutes do rent rooms along the Russian River, near the Grove. They rent homes nearby and these men allegedly leave the camp and go to these rented places to do whatever. I'm sure, although I have no way to prove that women have managed to get inside the various camps.

Q—Is this a rather exclusive residential area we're talking about? What's the average home price for a home near the Grove?
A—On the contrary, this is a rather economically depressed area. It's traditionally been very poor people, but of course, that is changing. Sonoma County has been gentrified...you gotta understand the timeline here. The Grove has been there for over 100 years. When they first came up there, the area was very rural, you know, sparsely populated. It was really being used more for summer homes for people in the Bay Area who would come up here to vacation. There were always natives who lived around here, but back in those times, most of the people were visitors. Bohemian Grove was allowed to function with a lot of anonymity for decades, because the area was so perfectly secluded. Nobody had really called any attention to them until William Domhoff's book and later when we started our protests outside the Grove in 1980. Things have changed a lot since then. People live around here full-time a lot more these days, and the home prices are going up.

But one of the things I objected to in Alex Jones' description of this area was that he basically was insulting the people who live around here. I know he tends toward exaggeration, perhaps, but it was kind of insulting the way he described people who live here. There are lots of old hippies here, who left the city and moved up here to the country; it's actually pretty diverse. We have a lot of veterans living here, too. People who have become rather disillusioned with the system, maybe kinda wanting to "drop out." This was a place where basically a lot of the '60s counterculture came to "drop out." Now, you've got your average families moving up here, because it's one of the few places left in

Sonoma county that's still affordable. Where the Bohemian Grove is situated is in the little town of Monte Rio, which is about 10 miles west of Guerneville, and Monte Rio has always been very economically depressed.

Q—I think where Alex got that impression, as I remember, was that two reliable sources told him that the State of California were basically releasing a lot of patients from a nearby mental hospital into that town. Is that not true?
A—No. I have lived here now for 30 years. I just have to say that is not true. I know a lot of people who've heard him say that, and of course, the locals were pretty insulted by that. I think his statement was something to the effect of, "they're using the people around Monte Rio to do experiments, mind control experiments and things like that on." It was very insulting to the people of our community.

Q—Well, you set the record straight on that one. We will correct it in the book.
A—Thank you.

Q—From the time you started protesting the Grove in 1980 to the year 2000, which issues about the Grove have become the most important to you personally?
A—Well, certainly the Lakeside Talks, and I'd have to say the Cremation of Care. The Lakeside Talks is really what I, after 22 years, have really focused on. What the Lakeside Talks are is that, at Bohemian Grove which is totally private and where there is no public scrutiny, they have daily talks. Most of them are held twice a day, by very influential people from the corporate world, the military, and the financial and political elite circles. And these are *mind-numbing* when you put them all together. It would take me hundreds of pages to tell you about every single one they've done up there. But what we've managed to do is to get most of the schedules out over the years. That's how we get a lot of our information—we have helpers inside the Grove, and the first thing I ask them for every year is to get me the Lakeside Talks schedule. Because that is the most revealing information about what really goes on inside the Bohemian Grove.

Q—Is that on your website? (*sonomacountyfreepress.com*)
A—Yes. In fact, you may reprint the list of Lakeside Chat topics in your book. You can learn so much about the policy issues being discussed there just by looking at the topics of the Lakeside Chats and the speakers. For example, the

issue of what the government may be hiding about UFO's has been a hot topic in recent years. Well, here's a Lakeside Chat given on July 17, 2001 by Richard Mueller, who is Professor of Physics at U.C. Berkeley. His topic was "Military Secrets of the Ocean, Atmosphere, and UFO's." Now, that's just one example. Clearly, they're talking about some very important stuff inside the Bohemian Grove, and I think it behooves the American public to start taking this seriously.

Q—Now, we're up to the year 2000, when Alex and I got in with our video cameras. I want to get your perspective on what happened that summer, when you met with Jon Ronson and the British filmmakers. How did they first approach you?
A—(laughs) Well that's a very interesting story because when Jon Ronson approached me, I believe that he had never met Alex Jones.

Q—I'm not sure when that took place, but both Alex and I had met Jon Ronson before when we were rebuilding the Branch Davidian Church in Waco, Texas. He visited the site and brought Randy Weaver (of the now-infamous Ruby Ridge incident) with him to meet us. That would have been in April 2000.
A—Well, the story Jon Ronson told me, which may or may not be true, and if not, this would be a good place to clear it up, is that it was just himself and his British crew that would be attempting to get into Bohemian Grove. He called me a few months before coming here in July, and just asked me if he could come up and look at my files on Bohemian Grove. You see, his whole thesis, which we now know but were not told at the time we provided our cooperation, was that he was going to basically "hang out with extremists." That means you and me, Mike—even if we don't share the same politics. He's defining *us* as the extremists (laughs), which gets my dander up a little bit! When he did arrive here in July of 2000, he had Alex and Violet and yourself in tow. He did call me up and ask me to come meet you three, but my daughter was very ill and I had to tell him that regrettably, it was just not a good time for me to get away for a meeting. I did want to meet you guys then, but it didn't happen.

Q—So I understand that you were the one who put us in touch with Rick the lawyer, who is seen in our film, *Dark Secrets—Inside Bohemian Grove*. Since he is still a practicing attorney in the area, we withheld his last name to protect his identity, so we just call him "Rick the Lawyer." When we interviewed him, he advised us not to try to sneak in through the woods like we actually did. The original plan, given to us by him, was to try to get in by boat, coming across the river that way.

A—We've gotten people in there before. Even before the 2000 Grove camp, we had successfully gotten reporters in there before. Now I know that Rick and Dr. Peter Phillips and some others actually had gotten in before the same way you actually ended up doing it.

Q—Tell me about how you helped to get reporters from *Mother Jones* and *People* magazine into the Grove before.

A—The reporter for *People* was Dirk Matheson, he was the Bureau Chief in San Francisco and was interested in doing a story about it. We had previously helped another reporter from *Time* magazine get in, but their story had been killed by the editorial powers on high. I was a little leery of the idea at first, and told him so. I explained how I had gone to great lengths to help people get in there before, only to have the story get squashed and never see the light of day. He assured me that wouldn't happen, that he was the one with the power to make that decision. So I said okay, and I made arrangements with one of my contacts who got Dirk in there. He got his story, but *People* censored it. The whole thing ended up with Dirk getting fired from the magazine.

Q—You know, after Alex and I returned from the Grove, Alex went on his radio show and told the world what we had done. So the next thing you know, we're getting calls from all these newspapers expressing interest in the video we shot. They were all promising, "oh, this is going to be BIG, top story!" They would write their story, an editor above their heads would kill it, and they never got published.

A—Yes, it's always the same old story. The reporters who try and write exposés on the Grove have the best of intentions. But obviously they are not the ones who make the final decisions. In both the cases of *Time* magazine and *People* magazine, both of them were squelched by people who were members of the Club or hung out with the Bohemians. Both stories got killed in the upper echelons of the editorial hierarchy.

Q—The way Alex and I finally got into the Grove was we just sort of befriended two older men who were club members, and we just walked right in with them! I guess the guards just looked at us and thought we were all together. They actually seemed to think we were their "dates." (Laughter) Is that something that is not considered out of the ordinary there, to see old men hanging out with much younger men like that?

A—It would depend on the demeanor and the dress of the men. Of course, I understand you guys went shopping for "the right clothes" to wear before you went to the Grove. Now, obviously, whatever you and Alex did worked, because you waltzed right in. The way we had done it in the past, like the first reporter we got inside the Grove was the *Mother Jones* reporter, in 1980. We got them in there through a man who was a union steward who had come out and introduced himself to us. He told us that if we could just find the right person who looks the part, that he could get him into the Grove as a waiter. So, of course, we looked around at our little scruffy group and there was nobody that qualified and literally, two hours later, the *Mother Jones* reporter came by to see what we were doing up there with the protests. It just so happened he was on vacation in the area with his family and stopped to talk to us. Well, he was perfect, he fit the part, you know, very clean cut, we thought he could easily blend in with the Grovers. When we told him about the idea, he didn't want to do it at first, because he was on vacation. Then, he called the magazine to see what they thought, and they talked him into doing it. We got him in through the front door as a legitimate waiter. The other people we got in were literally through the back door. People who hiked in through the back woods, took their costume in a bag, and changed into their nice clothes before they entered the Grove itself.

Q—What kind of security do they have there? I've heard all kinds of stories about surveillance cameras and microphones in the trees...

A—You know, I don't believe it. We have enough people who have gotten in there over the years who have been on our side, and they all agree that is just not true. Either all of them are very unobservant or...in fact, I think security there is much more lax than what is perceived.

Q—Do you think that they have increased security at the Grove since they've had more break-ins in recent years, and in the aftermath of 9/11?

A—I would think so. I'll give you an example of how Philip Weiss, the *Spy* magazine reporter came to me, I helped him to get in. Now that article actually did get published, by some miracle—I guess the establishment figured nobody really takes *Spy* magazine seriously, anyway, so they let that article go forward. Philip actually got in and out of there seven times before he got his story. He didn't want to stay there too late at night, obviously, because he didn't have a camp to go to and sleep. When he went in 1989, that was the same year that CBS News flew a helicopter over the Grove and filmed some of the "Cremation of Care" from the air. It was so funny because Philip and I were sitting there watching the CBS News report where they were saying, you know, "Security is so tight at the Bohemian Grove, nobody can get past it, etcetera, etcetera…" and we were just laughing our heads off, you know, because he had just come from there! And it was so easy, really. So, I think a lot of the effectiveness of their security is the perception that the place is a lot better guarded than it actually is. And of course, they don't want to insult their members by enforcing this heavy police presence over them—after all, this is a place where they are supposed to feel free to let their hair down.

As far as recent changes in security, I do know that the Club is clamping down on employees a lot more than they used to. The other thing that they have changed is, in the early days, even up until about 1983 or so, guest lists—which are full of information—were just floating all around the camps. Membership lists and schedules of events were much easier to come by. When the Bohemians realized that we were using the guest list in our research, they really put a lid on that. Now the guest list is displayed under glass at the Grove, so if anybody wants to go have a look at it to see who-is-bringing-who this year, they have to make a special point to go see it. Lists aren't photocopied and freely distributed in the camps anymore.

Q—Let's move into the "Cremation of Care."
A—Ah, yes—the big ink blot! (Laughs)

Q—Has your research given you any indication as to why they do this? Why do they bring a bound effigy of a human body on a wagon to be cremated onstage in front of this 45-foot stone owl statue?
A—Their big ritual. It's just the most elaborate, ridiculous, I mean it goes anywhere from the extremely silly to the extremely gross and unbelievable. That's the spectrum of beliefs around the "Cremation of Care." I can see why people might read some pretty sinister things into it. I've seen the footage you and Alex took of the ceremony, but Alex did not prove, at least in my mind, that the body they were cremating was that of a baby. I don't believe it because I have had people on the inside for 20 years, and I trust them.

Q—But do you think the bound body symbolizes a human being in effigy?
A—It symbolizes…now that is where you get into the real big ink blot…what exactly is it symbolizing? Is it just a silly little Druid ceremony? The fact that they use hooded robes, I mean…you show a picture of the "Cremation of Care" ceremony to a black person, and you know what their first thought is going to be. It would probably look like a KKK rally to them. I think that most black people I know would be highly offended by that image.

It's so…open to interpretation. When people try to pin me down and ask me "what is the meaning of the Cremation of Care?" I can say only that it covers everything in that spectrum.

Q—Well, let me ask you this: I live down here in Texas where the FBI and ATF raided David Koresh's church at Waco, they characterized the Branch Davidians as "cult members." That makes me think, when I go into the Bohemian Grove and see what our world leaders are doing in rituals like the Cremation of Care, what kind of "cult" are these people involved in, and why don't we refer to them as a cult? I mean, I never saw the Branch Davidians dress up in Ku Klux Klan robes and dance around in pagan rituals, offering sacrifices to an owl God.
A—(Laughs) Yes, exactly. *Exactly*. They're doing the same thing right now, diverting the public's attention to the supposed "weapons of mass destruction" that Iraq has, to keep us from asking—"well, what about the ones we have?" I mean, it's so hypocritical, if you look at it from that point of view.

Q—There are also many different interpretations of this 45-foot owl at the Grove. What do you think about it?
A—Well, we pretty much know that it's a stone owl, made out of stone.

Q—Yes, I walked right up to it, and rapped on it. It felt like real stone. That thing must weigh a ton…do you have any idea how they got that thing in there?
A—They probably carved it there.

Q—Our research shows that long before the owl statue was placed at Bohemian Grove, they used to have a large Buddha statue there, made of Plaster of Paris. This would have been from about 1892 to approximately 1928, when they replaced it with the stone owl statue. Did you know anything about that?
A—Really? No, I didn't know anything about the Buddha. That's fascinating!

346

Q—What struck me as odd is that when Alex and I went around Monte Rio, asking the locals if they knew anything about this giant owl at Bohemian Grove, most people had never heard of it, and they didn't believe that it is really there.
A—Maybe you just happened to ask the wrong people that day, but a lot of people up here know about it. The Bohemian Grove Action network has been getting the information out for over 22 years now—about the Cremation of Care at the bottom of a 45-foot stone owl. To assume that nobody up here knows about the Cremation of Care is just a wrong conclusion.

Q—Paul Bonacci, one of the key witnesses in former Nebraska State Senator's book, *The Franklin Cover-Up*, alleges in his diary that he personally witnessed, and was forced to take part in, a child porn snuff film made at the Bohemian Grove. He claims that he saw the ritual murder of a young boy take place at the bottom of the owl altar. In your many years of experience researching the Grove, have you ever heard of such activities taking place?
A—I've heard stories like that floating around before, but I've never found any of them to be credible. I mean, first of all, show me the proof. *(Author's note: I will refer both Mary and the skeptical reader to the next chapter, where the story is told in the victim's own words.)* The reason that I object to this kind of speculation is that—the men who do business inside the Grove cause more deaths globally with the wars they wage—and those deaths are not inside the Grove. This kind of thing to me is kind of counter-productive talk. It takes away from the main message we're trying to get across here, which is strictly about these powerful men making decisions inside the Bohemian Grove that affect the outside world.

Q—We've heard that the Sonoma County Sheriff's department works very closely with the Bohemian Grove, almost like the Grovers' own personal police force. Is there any truth to that?
A—It's true, yes, but to the extent...let's face it...I don't know if you and I will agree politically on this or not, but my personal belief is that law enforcement exists for the purpose of keeping the status quo. And so, if these men at Bohemian Grove are the absolute pillars of the status quo, law enforcement certainly exists there primarily to keep them safe. I have had good cooperation in the past from the Sheriff's office when we protest at the Grove, and on the other hand, I've also been betrayed by them before, too. For example, on a couple of years, we were protesting—and we have the legal right to pro-

test—up to that property line. Well, Mike, you know; you've been there, that sign at the end of the road that says, "go no further?" And a couple of times, including last year, we were "pushed back" by the riot police to 100 yards down the road from there. We had 1000 people out there protesting in July, 2001—and the police always do this when they expect we're going to have a larger turnout in certain years. And I think it's really all about what they "perceive" to be the size of the demonstration.

Q—We actually sent Ed Hohmann, an *infowars.com* reporter out to do a follow-up story on the Grove in July, 2001, and I believe he met with you and filmed the protest. We have footage of that and broadcast a report on our weekly television show. But what I saw in that video was not just Sonoma County Sheriff's, but also CHP (California Highway Patrol), and…looked like some other divisions as well.
A—Yeah, the highway patrol, and they had buses there just waiting to take us away. Which they didn't use, but they were there.

Q—How did the Bohemian club members get into the Grove with all the protesters blocking the roadway?
A—Well (laughs), technically, we stood to the side of the road. And to answer your question honestly…they got in *very slowly*.

Q—And did the media cover that event like it should have been covered?
A—No.

Q—Well, when a thousand people show up anywhere to protest something, *that's news*. No doubt about it.
A—Well, we garnered quite a bit of news coverage over the years. There was an incident in 1984 where 50 of us were arrested for actually sitting down and blocking the street completely.

*Mary Moore being arrested for engaging in civil disobedience at the Grove, 1984.
(Photo courtesy of Mary Moore, the Bohemian Grove Action Network)*

Q—Tell me more about that.

A—That was a year we had done a teach-in ahead of time, about a week before, and we fully expected to be arrested, of course. We knew they weren't just going to pat us on the head! (Laughs) And you know, Mike, because you've been to the Grove, you know how narrow that little road going in is. It's a very easy road to block. And that was the year we had a bunch of women from the San Francisco area who had made these hundreds and hundreds of yards of spider webbing, done with regular yarn—because they have that motto at the Grove about "weaving spiders come not here," you know? And they actually managed to "net" the police cars, the buses they were going to use to take us away in, the policemen got all entwined...I mean, everybody got mixed up in that stuff! We have photos of that. It was actually very funny. But the point that we actually did get across in the media that year about our protest was that we were not blocking them out, but *rather blockading them in* so that their greed wouldn't spread. And we were successful in getting that message out, the media kinda liked that and latched onto it.

Q—Why do you think it has been nearly 30 years since a book has been published about Bohemian Grove, exclusively?
A—(sighs) Boy, is *that* ever a good question. Let me just answer the question with a question: Why does it take the American people so long to make the connection between the quality of their life and the ruling class? I mean, why is it that some people are so slow to understand that, you know...? (Laughs)

Q—There have been chapters included in other books about the Grove, such as Domhoff's 1974 book, *The Bohemian Grove and Other Retreats*, and more recently, Jon Ronson's *Them—Adventures with Extremists*. What did you think of their portrayals of what's happening inside Bohemian Grove. Were they accurate?
A—Well, William Domhoff's book is still the best that's been done about the Grove to this date. At least, in my mind. And of course, I was unhappy with Alex Jones' portrayal of it and Jon Ronson...even worse. He made Alex and I both look bad in his book! I mean, Alex and I may disagree, but I think we *both* got screwed by Jon Ronson. It's a shame to me, really, because it trivializes the whole thing.

Q—What is the ethnic spread of the Bohemian Club's membership?
A—Well, of course, it's always been almost totally WASP-ish, you know White Anglo-Saxon Protestant. Henry Kissinger is one of the few Jews who are members. African Americans, Asians, and Hispanics are a pretty rare sight at the Grove.

Q—I want to ask you about one of the Grove's strangest customs. Now, as you know, they have plenty of public restroom facilities there, but for some weird reason, nobody uses them. Everybody pees on the trees! (Laughter) What is *that* about?
A—Well, of course, Northern California has always historically been full of very earth-friendly, very environmentally-conscious people. And the symbolism behind peeing on these great grand, incredible redwoods trees...I mean, you gotta admit, these are some *amazing* trees...it's almost like a nature-hating act. This is just how I see it, understand—I have no perception of what is inside the minds of these men, but—to me, it's symbolic of man's dominion over nature. Just that arrogance of "I can pee on this great, beautiful living

thing." It's almost a parable of how they behave out there in the real world, too. It symbolizes their attitude of "hey, I run the world—I can pee on any damn thing I please." And I just find it so disgusting.

Q—And these men REALLY DO rule the world!
A—Yes, I believe so. There certainly are individuals who go to the Grove who are not powerful, although nearly all of them are rich. It's not those men that we are targeting necessarily. The point that we are making is that when they gather up there, these men are the elite of the corporate, financial, military and governmental circles. And they meet there without public scrutiny; they listen to future policy ideas floated up there without any input from the people they rule.

Q—To me, the whole concept of that is un-American.
A—And even if they didn't have the Lakeside Talks, there's still that "ruling class bonding" that makes things happen at the highest levels. You know, if you meet say, Joe Smith up there at the Grove, and you become friends, then later, when you have a big business contract to give, you're going to remember Joe Smith and...well, you see where I'm going with this. They're creating partnerships in there that carry over to the business they conduct in the outside world.

Q—The men who attend Bohemian Grove, are most of them Freemasons?
A—Well, certainly the ideas of the rituals they do are quite similar. Um, the Freemasons, to my knowledge, just like the Kiwanis and Rotary clubs in every small town, has that same sort of "good-old-boy network" of prominent men in the community getting to know each other through a social club. But when you get to the level of the Bohemian Grove, it's a very global network. And much more powerful.

It's the exclusivity of this bonding we see among high-level elites at Bohemian Grove that makes us wonder. You know, they might say, "hey, we're just having a little summer vacation here. We're putting on some plays, listening to music..." Well, yes they *are* doing that. But they are also talking about some very serious subjects, and that's where I draw the line. If they were just up there harmlessly dancing around to banjo music, well, who would care?

Q—Have Secret Service or federal agents ever approached you when you were demonstrating outside Bohemian Grove?

A—Not to my knowledge. But that's not to say I haven't been "looked at" by them. But no one identifying themselves as Secret Service or FBI has ever walked up and questioned me about it. And they do realize that I've been doing this for many years now, I do get a lot of media attention of this issue, and I've built up a lot of credibility in this community. And as you know, I just can't say it too many times, our bottom line issue is that we are concerned with the actions of these men inside the Grove and how they affect us in the outside world. Now, if I knew for a fact or even slightly believed that they were killing babies in there, I would be ABSOLUTELY OUTRAGED. I mean, I'm a grandma! I have three children and four grandchildren. But by having the focus on things we cannot prove, I think it takes the focus off of things we can already prove as fact.

Q—The whole time that Alex and I were inside the Grove, I have to confess I was afraid. I didn't know what was going to happen to us if we got caught. You know, I was thinking, "am I going to end up in jail, or in court for three years, or what?" So, what do they usually do with people who sneak into the Grove and get caught?
A—I'd say that you guys were pretty lucky (laughs), because you certainly could have been arrested, at the very least. That was a definite possibility. For instance, one of the informants we had inside one year, posing as a worker, was caught with a tape recorder. I believe he was trying to tape one of the Lakeside Talks. He was simply fired and they never pressed any charges against him. Mainly because, one of the things they don't want is publicity. And that's one of the things we've been able to do...is to get media attention on them.

Q—You know, another odd thing we observed when we were inside was we only saw one pay phone in the whole place, and that was down by the little gift shop where they sell postcards and souvenirs. And I just remember thinking to myself, "these are some of the most powerful businessmen in the world, and they're unable to conduct business by phone?" And I've heard jokes about these power elites, you know, standing in this long line just to use one telephone. But I guess these days they probably all conduct their business on their personal cell phones, right?
A—Actually, no, not at the Grove. Up until very recently, cell phones didn't work up here. This is a very remote area and we had no cell towers for a long

time. I think they've actually passed a new rule in recent years that no cell phones are supposed to be allowed in the Grove, anyway.

Q—Why? Because cell phones today can be used as cameras, and that would violate the "no cameras" rule at the Grove?
A—I might guess that's the reason, probably.

Q—Alex and I had a chance to walk into a few of the camps while the Bohemians were all off at dinner, and what really surprised me was the splendor that these men are living in. Some of these camps were very richly furnished, some with grand pianos, you know…these guys aren't exactly roughing it!
A—Oh, yes, exactly. I actually wrote a story, sort of tongue-in-cheek about 15 few years ago about that, and proposed the idea that we open up Bohemian Grove to the homeless! (Laughs) There's plenty of land and tents that people could live in year-round in these very plush surroundings. You know, 2000 people could live up there! We'd solve the homeless problem! And besides, what do the Bohemians really need it for the other 11 months of the year, anyway? (Laughs)

There is a definite pecking order within the camp system at the Grove, with Mandalay Camp probably being the most exclusive of all. It's the one with probably the most influence, a lot of old money families like the DuPonts—and that's the camp Kissinger belongs to. The only ex-President who is in that camp is Gerald Ford, who never even won an election. Interestingly, Nixon was a Caveman. He belonged to the Caveman camp.

Q—Well, Mary, I want to thank you for this interview. It's been fascinating. And it's also good to see people from the left and the right banding together on an issue and finding out we actually have a lot more in common than people might think we do. I think that's pretty refreshing.
A—You know, we actually *do* agree more than we disagree on a lot of issues. I'm actually with you on the 2nd Amendment issues as well. I mean, I worry when the police are armed and the citizens aren't. To tell you the truth, I'm a little more afraid of the police than I am the criminals these days. Sometimes, they're interchangeable.

Q—When the people fear their government, that's tyranny. When the government fears the people, *that* is liberty.
A—Absolutely.

For more information on BGAN, write to:

The Bohemian Grove Action Network
PO Box 296
Occidental, California, 95465

Or visit *sonomacountyfreepress.com*

Chapter XVIII

Parea non serving

(I obey but not as a slave)

John DeCamp

Former Nebraska State Senator John DeCamp, Esquire, investigator and author of *The Franklin Cover-Up*, spoke with Alex Jones live on the radio in 2001, and gave some startling new information that had not been previously published in his book. Since this updated information specifically concerns Bohemian Grove and includes testimony from an eyewitness to what may have been a real human sacrifice there, I wanted to include it in this chapter.

John DeCamp's book, *The Franklin Cover-Up*, includes Paul Bonacci's personal diary entries about a snuff film being made on July 26, 1984 in an exclusive Northern California campground in "an area that had big trees." After his book was published, DeCamp told a group in Santa Rosa, California (near the Grove) that he had edited out Bonacci's diary references to an enormous, moss-covered owl and men in hooded red and black robes. Why? Because at the time Mr. DeCamp did not know about the Bohemian Grove and thought it "too far fetched for people to believe."

What follows is a transcript of the radio interview Alex conducted with John De Camp on his nationally syndicated GCN Radio Network broadcast. This chapter comes with a strong warning that the content is very graphic, often of a sexual and violent nature. **IT IS NOT SUITABLE FOR MINORS OR THE FAINT OF HEART!** Parts of it are absolutely *disgusting*, and so deeply disturbing that I find it hard to fathom, let alone read. I include it here for your consideration, with that important disclaimer. You, the reader, must decide for yourself if you believe or disbelieve Paul Bonacci's testimony about the disturbing goings-on at Bohemian Grove.

(Interview Transcript)

Alex Jones (AJ): Senator DeCamp, tell us a little bit about your work. Tell us how you got into this. You didn't get into this Franklin Federal Credit Union investigation to find all these horrors involving children. I understand your committee was initially formed only to investigate some money that went missing. You were basically there to disprove it for the [state] Senate, right?

John DeCamp (JD): I was. Let me give the story real quick. In North Omaha, Nebraska, there was a credit union, a federal credit union, and a man named Larry King ran that. Not the Larry King on *CNN*, this is a different Larry King altogether. He was often written about in the *New York Times* as you mentioned, and a number of other state and national publications. He was officially listed as the, quote, "Fastest-rising black star in the Republican party". Some of you listening out there may have attended the 1984 or 1988 Republican conventions and you heard him sing. One was in Texas, I remember I was there for the one in New Orleans, then…

AJ: You're a Republican. Now let's get that out there.

JD: I guess.

AJ: I'm the same way.

JD: Anyway, Larry opened both those national conventions as some of you may remember. Larry opened both of them by singing the National Anthem. He's a great singer. A great whatever you call it. Baritone or alto or whatever those strange things are, but anyway…

AJ: a vocalist.

JD: I knew it was one of those, (laughs) but anyway, Larry is the man singing there at the opening convention and on the election day for George Bush, Sr. in 1988.

The story begins when the Feds raided this little credit union in North Omaha. It was supposed to be serving the minority community, specifically the black community, and they shut it down. They said there was a lot of missing money. Stories started floating out as always happens when some incident like that occurs, and some of those stories were really strange. They were coming from kids all over. Young kids; 16, 14, 13 year-old kids telling about how they had been on Larry's private jet to this party or that party. Or that they had been at the Republican National Convention here or they had been at this political event in Washington, and the stories had to with that they were there and were used as drug couriers. 13 or 14 year-old kids back then going through the airport could get through security easily without anyone asking twice about anything. They'd pack them full of cocaine or whatever, little backpacks they'd carry on their bodies, or in the girls' handbags. I mean, young boys, young girls—and these kids were telling much stranger tales that seemed bizarre at the time.

They'd say that they had had sex with this or that famous politician or businessman and I was the one who stood up and said, "this has got to be the most hilarious, ridiculous story I've ever heard!" First of all, I knew Larry King. What the heck! I was head of banking at the time he was when he was doing his banking stuff, the senate banking committee here in

Nebraska. It's *absurd*. All the stories started (prompting) more and more and I said, "look, if I believe even *one* of these crazy stories I'd be one of the first one's to stand up and demand that something be done." Then, I got a letter from a kid named Paul Bonacci.

AJ: Now later, you took his diary that went back like 5 years and ink experts and forensics experts looked at it and he had all this stuff written down.

JD: That was the strange thing about this kid. I wish I had been able to do that throughout life but apparently when he was a little boy, he was about 18 when I had met him in jail, 17 or 18. And as a young kid his uncle or grandfather or somebody had taught him religiously to keep a diary where you mark everything down, every day. Well, he did it in detail. So when I went and visited with him and he told me these strange tales and then you had to hear the psychiatric medical institutions in the state university say "Hey, This kid he ain't crazy. He's a multiple personality. He's probably telling the truth because multiples don't need to lie. They just switch personality."

Anyway, to make a long, long bizarre story short, I found out that he was in jail because he had been in one of those intimately involved in all this, and he had to be shut up real quick. Now, at the time I didn't realize that but, they locked him up and charged him with touching another boy on the outside of his pants, his cousin or something.

AJ: Senator, talk right into your telephone please.

JD: Anyway, they have him there, and I finally agreed to represent him and that led to a long, long tale that's got me deeply involved in researching and investigating the collapse of the credit union and the personalities involved. Ultimately, on the advice of my best friend, closest friend, godfather, whatever...I wrote this book because he told me that this would be the best way to protect myself, and that person was a man named Bill Colby. Bill, as you know, was once the head of the CIA and ended up floating dead in a pond somewhere. But I won't get into that right now. Anyway, I wrote the book, and as I started working on it, one of the things I did do was obtain the diary of this young boy to see just what he *did* say and then I had them checked.

AJ: And it wasn't just that. I mean they've got...

JD: Forensic experts and the forensics were because somebody said he could have just made this all up later. He could have made this up later, and I wanted to make sure that this wasn't done. So we had forensic examiners check it out, and they said that this ink was done at a certain time and this could have only been done at that time, and on and on. Anyway, to get to the heart of the discussion...

AJ: One more point, Senator DeCamp, because I've actually seen the *Discovery Channel* documentary that never aired and we actually played it here locally on TV in Austin. I'll send you a copy of it. They found hundreds of videotapes in King's office when they raided it. The police saw those tapes and freaked out, hid it away somewhere and have never released it. But some actually got convicted of this stuff.

JD: Oh, yeah.

AJ: I want people to understand—this all *really* happened, folks.

JD: This isn't a fantasy. I ended up winning a million dollars judgment against awful, awful, *awful* overwhelming odds, including the *Omaha World-Herald* newspaper that attacked me so viciously because one of the key individuals I got locked up in prison was one of their top editors! There's another individual but anyway...

AJ: But the point is...People *are* going to prison for this...

JD: He just got released from prison here about 8 or 10 months ago.

AJ: Hold on. You were actually just out of senate and you were hired to go whitewash the operation because, you know, this sounds ridiculous.

JD: That's what I was hired for.

AJ: Yeah.

JD: But I did the opposite.

AJ: Well, I call you an *impeccable* witness. Go ahead.

JD: Anyway, so I won the million-dollar judgment in federal court...finally...and it wasn't easy. I want to talk about that a little, because some of the stuff coming out about pedophilia in the churches now...well, these same types of stories were written in my book way back then. But anyway to get to the heart of the matter that you called about, as I understand it...I simply took the diaries of Paul Bonacci and I printed a good portion of them in my book, and one of the areas described a trip to Northern California in 1984. I could even read part of it here. He was taken to an area around Sacramento where they had the great big tall trees in this grove and then they went in where there is some owl. Some big huge carved owl or something....

AJ: When we get back from break I want to read that on the air.

JD: O.K.

AJ: Well please continue. Go ahead.

JD: Anyway, so there was what he claimed. I wasn't there, so I don't know. That's the closest I've been to Bohemian Grove. He took me out and showed me where it was, and indeed there is such a place there. And I didn't know there was a place called Bohemian Grove. I didn't write about Bohemian Grove in my book because I didn't know what it was back then. I'd never heard of it until after the fact. I just took his diary. Anyway, it clearly is where he was taken and he was taken out there for a ceremony in which they committed some pretty horrible things on another boy. Three boys—and they filmed it—and I just took his testimony and the names he wrote there. They're right there in the book.

And by the way just to answer your next question...Yes, I put names in the book, dates and everything that I could just as they were. Why? For example, a number of threatening calls came after the first edition came out. People said, "This is the most libelous, slanderous thing we've ever heard!" I said, "fine. I think I've done enough to prove it, and I'm satisfied". I mean, if somebody said these things about me, I'd sue them for libel or slander.

AJ: Here you are 10 years later, and you're *winning* lawsuits.

JD: Well, there was one libel suit as a result of the book. But, that was one I filed against some group called Great Atlantic Telecast Company. They're some TV network on the east coast when they had one of the characters of the book, who also happened to be running for president at the time, going around saying, "Oh, don't believe this, and don't believe that. The book is a lie." The TV network reported those statements, and I sued. Well they ended up paying me off, backing down and reaching a settlement.

AJ: Stay right there Senator. This is powerful info. It's all coming up after this...

[station break]

AJ: Continuing...you actually have passages in your book out of the diary...

JD: Well, I have…I have right here the diary itself. Do you want me to read a little? Understand that I didn't know that this place he describes was Bohemian Grove back then, nor did the kid when he was writing it. All he knew was he was taken to this place. Let me just read it. It'll take three minutes. Is that O.K.?

AJ: Go ahead.

JD: "I went in January", now this is Bonacci, this is Paul Bonacci writing this. This is directly word for word from his diary.

> "I went in January of '84 on every trip. I was paid by men (Larry) King knew for sex. The summer of '84 sometime I went to Dallas, Texas, and had sex with several men King knew in a hotel. I flew private charters, YNR Airlines and Kam Airlines normally for King. I never had much personally to do with King; I only went where he told me to go.
>
> In or on July 26th, I went to Sacramento, California. King flew me out in a private plane from Eppley Airfield [in Omaha] to Denver where we picked up Nicholas, a boy who was about 12 or 13. Then we flew to Las Vegas to a desert strip and drove in to Las Vegas and to some ranch and got something. Then flew on to Sacramento.
>
> We were picked up by a white limo and taken to a hotel. I don't remember the name of it. "We," meaning Nicholas and I, were driven to an area that had big, big trees, it took about an hour to get there. There was a cage with a boy in it who was not wearing anything. Nicholas and I were given these Tarzan things to put around us and stuff like that.
>
> They told me to, I won't use the word, "blank" the boy and stuff. In other words have sex with. At first I said no and they held a gun to my genitals (again, I won't use the wording Paul used since we're on the radio) and said, 'do it or else lose them' or something like that. I began doing it to the boy and stuff. And Nicholas had anal sex with him and stuff. We were told to "blank" him and beat on him. I didn't try to hurt him. We were told to put our "blanks" (private parts) in his mouth and stuff and sit on the boy's penis and they filmed it. We did this stuff to the boy for about 30 minutes or an hour when a man came in and kicked us in the genitals and picked us up and threw us. He grabbed the boy and started "blanking" him and stuff. The man was about; I'm not sure how to say this, but the man was about ten inches long and the boy screamed and stuff. The man was forcing his "blank" into the boy all the way. The boy was bleeding from his rectum and

the men tossed me and him and stuff and put the boy right next to me and grabbed a gun and blew the boy's head off.

The boy's blood was all over me and I started yelling and crying and the men grabbed Nicholas and I, and forced us to lie down. They put the boy on top of Nicholas who was crying and they were putting Nicholas's hands on the boy's backside. They put the boy on top of me and did the same thing. They then forced me to "blank" the dead boy and also Nicholas..."

JD: Alex, I'm sorry—I'm reading directly from the diary here, and—it's pretty crude. I just want to apologize for that to your listeners, because it's about to get even worse. Paul continues in his diary:

"They put a gun to our heads to make us do it. His blood was all over us. They made us kiss the boys lips and a few other things. Then they made me do something I don't even want to write, so I won't.

After that the men grabbed Nicholas and dragged him off screaming. They put me up against a tree and put a gun to my head but fired into the air. I heard another shot from somewhere and then saw the man who killed the boy drag him like a toy. Everything including when the men put the boy in the trunk was filmed. The men took me with them and we went up in a plane. I saw the bag the boy was in. We went over a very thick brush area with a clearing in it. Over the clearing they dropped the boy. One said "the men with the hoods" would take care of the body for them.

I didn't see Nicholas until that night at the hotel. He and I hugged and held each other for a long while. About two hours later, Larry King came in and told us to go take a shower since we'd had only been hosed off at some guy's house. We took a shower together and were told to put on the Tarzan things. After we were cleaned up and dressed in these things we were told to put on shorts, socks, a shirt and shoes and were driven to a house where the men were at with some others. They had the film and they played it. As the men watched it, they passed Nicholas and I around as if we were toys and sexually abused us.

They made Nicholas and I "blank" each other and one of the men put the dead boy's "blank" in mine and Nicholas' mouth. I didn't want to write this because the man forced me to bite the boys' penis and testicles off. It was gross, and I saw the film where it happened and started freaking out, remembering what they made us do afterwards to the boy. They showed us doing everything to the boy. I was there for about 5 days attending parties but only recall cutting my wrist, which

Mike Hanson

is why I stayed two days in a hospital under a name I can't recall. Some guy paid for me."

AJ: Stay right there, Senator DeCamp. We'll be right back. This is what the New World Order wants to do to your kids.

[station break]

AJ: I want to go back into the investigation. That's one of the clearest pieces of evidence. Tell us how they tried to stop it. How one of the investigators was obviously killed. Do you think this is a good place to continue?

JD: That's when I brought Colby in. Bill Colby was, like I say, a very close friend with this investigation. Gary Caradori, the one the senate had hired to do the investigation, called me from Chicago one day. He had gone there on a trip to pick up a bunch of material. His plane crashed, and he was killed in the "accident."

It was a remarkable coincidental thing that one of the central characters of the book, Robert Wadman, had been the police chief of Omaha at the time of these events. I'm not suggesting anything; I'm just saying it's one of the most remarkable coincidences in the world, and since that time I've learned more from the sheriff's office that was first on the scene. They told me how FBI or other federal officials moved into the crime scene and took stuff out of there quick. They seized pictures and things that they found laying around, and told the sheriff's deputy who was there: "You've not been here. You've not seen anything. If you talk, you're in trouble. Compromising a federal investigation is a crime…," etc.

Anyway, Gary Caradori and his friend were both killed in that accident, and of course, he didn't get to testify. But the evidence just kept coming in. Some little strange thing would happen, which would lead me to the next bit of evidence I needed. It keeps proving once again when they say, "this didn't happen," or "this couldn't have happened," or whatever, some new little piece of information comes forward that proves it. And in this case it was a call from a policeman, the detective who was head of the patrol.

He claimed he was head of the State Patrol in Oregon and he told me that they had just arrested someone and seized a bunch of material. They found a copy of my book, *The Franklin Cover-Up*, which we're talking about right now, and this person had my book in his possession, with certain pages underlined. I said,

"What's the person's name?" He told me, "It is Russell Nelson."

Eventually…to make a long, long story short, I got him out of prison and got him up here to testify and bring pictures and tried to see other pictures to confirm the story in the courts. He was a key witness then that ended up in a million-dollar judgment. He was Larry King's private photographer who had been going to the various things and taking pictures of "Comprised Politician A" or whatever with a kid or with this or that.

AJ: Yeah, the report produced by the *BBC* people that never aired on *the Discovery Channel* actually showed the police admitting all this. I mean, they grabbed all these videos and photos. It's just like "The Finders" organization in DC.

JD: I know it extremely well. I went there.

AJ: Yeah.

JD: That was another story!

AJ: I can't even mention what was in that warehouse. It's all too profane. This is something just like from the pit of hell.

JD: See, I know people listening right now will think, "this is la-la land, this is make believe, these people are fruitcakes talking about that stuff, this couldn't happen." Particularly, with prominent people. "They wouldn't be fiddling with little kids, would they?"

Unfortunately, I also believe that. I guess I *want* to believe that. But I'll guarantee you that bad things have happened out there. They *do* happen. One of the coincidences that I think is going to rock the people very shortly is one of the centerpieces of this thing was using a lot of kids out of a place called Boys Town.

Boys Town of course, is one of the most respected institutions in this country, as it should be. It's done more for young boys throughout the last 75 or 100 years probably than just about any other institution you want to mention. At the same time, corruption can occur anywhere. Even the best apples can get rotten by it. In this case, as I identified very clearly in my book, Larry King was operating and getting kids out of there and using them. Well, of course the *Discovery Channel* that sent a team in from Britain spent about half million dollars doing things and I think that was one of the centerpieces of their documentary film. You've seen that one, right?

AJ: Oh yeah. We actually put it on TV here in Austin. My friend Mike Hanson and I do a local television show, and we aired that for our viewers several times.

JD: Anyway, the head of Boys Town is now an 87-year-old man, a monsignor. Guess who his newest attorney is? He's hired me because he's getting old and is worried about wanting to get some things told and get some truth out before it's too late. His newest attorney is a young; well he's not young anymore is he? (laughs) A man named John DeCamp who wrote a book *called The Franklin Cover-Up*, and if anybody would have a reason to want to attack me it was him. Instead he is doing the opposite.

AJ: Now repeat that again.

JD: He hired me within the last week or ten days as his private attorney because of some of things you've been reading in the national press regarding pedophile priests and so on.

AJ: And who is he again?

JD: He was the head of Boys Town.

AJ: Oh. O.K. Monsignor…

JD: He also was the only catholic priest ever appointed as a delegate to the United Nations. He was a special delegate appointed by I think, two different presidents as a representative to the United Nations on behalf of children.

AJ: And he's going to blow the whistle?

JD: He's going to provide some information that I think will rock some people and they will immediately denounce him, of course, and try to shut him up.

AJ: That's incredible. I tell 'ya, you're a very busy man these days. You're all over the place. You were also helping some of the victims' families with lawsuits involving the Columbine High School shooting case, right?

JD: I was hired by the family of one of the teachers who was killed at Columbine to represent them. We have filed a federal lawsuit because these kids (Erik Harris and Dylan Klebold) that killed all these people were absolute unlimited addicts of a couple of video games that are just training kids to be cold-blooded killers.

AJ: *Doom* is a military game, they now admit. The military developed it.

JD: That's correct. That's correct.

AJ: Because they've found in soldiers, in Vietnam especially most people will not fire up close on somebody and through the video games it trains them to disconnect and do it. And this will be our S.W.A.T. teams of the future. So, getting back into the *Franklin Cover-Up*.

JD: Bill Colby looked into the death of our investigator, Gary Caradori. He basically told me, "you're never going to know the answer." Anyway, so I was sitting with him and his wife at his place one night. I said, "I don't know what to do next. I see prosecutors who are afraid to prosecute. I see politicians who shouldn't be there. I see institutions of government who have surrendered because they've been comprised or corrupted or threatened or whatever," I said, "I just don't know what to do!"

He said, "I'm going to tell you what to do." I said, "Thank goodness!" He told me, "Get as far away from this thing as you can! Forget you ever saw us or know it, heard about it or anything else." I said, "Wait a minute! You're telling me this, as the former head of the CIA?" I said, "You're telling me that I should just walk away from this and pretend it didn't happen?"

He said, "John, I love you. I love your kids. I love your family. This is just a little more serious than you think. Let me tell you a story". So then he begins: "Last night I returned from Moscow". I said, "What the blazes is the former head of the CIA doing in Moscow?" He says, "Believe it or not, we were there to, along with some others who's names you'd recognize, try to make sure that nobody pushes a button and does the wrong thing, because things are unstable." Now this occurred exactly, this conversation, exactly three weeks before the famous revolution and the fall of communism, you know what I'm talking about where they held Gorbachev hostage for awhile. Remember?

AJ: Yeah.

JD: What's his name? Yeltsin, that's it. Exactly three weeks before that happened, he says things are "unstable". Then he says, "You know, the night before I was to leave, I couldn't sleep. I was thinking about the momentous event that I was participating in". He says, "I couldn't sleep and instead just wanted to go for a walk. Of course, I knew that was forbidden. Everybody knew who I was and thought the guards wouldn't let me out. They just ignored me as I walked past them, and out into Red Square. I walked up to the door of the Kremlin at two o'clock in the morning; guards were watching me, but nobody paid any attention, nobody cared. And then it struck me". I said, "What struck you?"

He said, "It's over! The cold war is over! We won!" Remember, this is three weeks before all this broke loose and the whole thing collapsed and then I said, "Ah-ha". And then he said something else struck him and I asked, "Gosh, what was that?" He says, "Here I was, the former head of the CIA, who had fought the Russians for forty years, walking alone in Red Square in the middle of the night, and nobody even cared. I realized that this was going to be the only victory parade all the Cold War warriors and I would ever have. We wouldn't have tickertape parade down Madison Avenue like the soldiers in WWII. There wouldn't be any victory parade."

I said to him, "Well, Bill—that's a real interesting story but, for heaven's sake, what's my great lesson I'm to learn here?" He answered, "Well, I guess what I'm trying to tell you is, John, sometimes there are forces too big and too evil. Even though we know they are there and we know it *absolutely*, for us to deal with it the way we would want or should is out of our league. Therefore, you have to turn and walk away. If you want to live to fight another day. These forces are too big and too evil and too powerful. You're going to get killed if you keep playing around! I don't want that!" I said, "You mean there's nothing I can do?" Colby said, "Well, you have to do something. The safest thing, the best thing you can do for your own safety is write your story. Tell it all. You'll get ridiculed, and you may not be believed, but at least if you tell it there's no reason for them to do you in. They'll just try to ridicule you."

AJ: Yeah, because that'll make them even more powerful. They don't want to make you a martyr.

JD: Yep.

AJ: There are so many facets to this. How many children were you able to confirm were involved in this there in Nebraska?

JD: I can't confirm a total number. I dealt with I think probably 25 or 30 that were really intimately involved.

AJ: These children didn't even know each other. Yet, they're all telling exactly the same stories involving the same people, right up to the Bush family. The usual suspects.

JD: Well yes, absolutely. In other words, it wasn't that one kid said this, or that he and all his friends made up this terrible hoax. But I've heard that accusation before. People have said, "it's all a hoax perpetrated by these absolutely penniless poverty children who all got together somehow and told this tale." Get real!

AJ: There were criminal convictions in these cases. You wrote the book and nobody sued you because...probably because it's all true. I mean, how could a kid who has never even been to California before know how long it takes to drive from Sacramento to the Bohemian Grove? Every detail Paul Bonacci described in his diary about the Grove is correct. And I can only say this because I've been inside the Bohemian Grove and seen it for myself. I've been there for the Grovers' big summer fire festival and the Cremation of Care, which Mike and I captured on a hidden video camera. And just in case you haven't seen it, John, they bring an effigy of a human body up to the stage, and they burn it. The body screams in pain and that's just the stuff they do there. They engage in mock human sacrifice.

This year, another journalist managed somehow to get hidden camera video footage out of an initiation ceremony at Yale University's Skull and Bones society, and what they captured was every bit as strange and maca-bre. I mean, they even showed this tape on *Fox News*, of a woman lying in a coffin while a man slits her throat, and you can see the fake (at least, we hope it's fake) blood squirting out. Why isn't there a police investigation? John, if my neighbors saw me slitting women's throats and burning bound human bodies in my backyard, even if only in effigy, wouldn't they call the cops on me? Wouldn't the cops have probable cause for the search of my house?

JD: I sure think so.

AJ: I would expect to see the police ripping out my walls. If I saw my neighbor doing this and I reported it to the police, I would expect a warrant and a search.

JD: Yeah, I know. As I say, the problem is that gap between something outrageous and what the average human being is capable of believing based on their own human experiences.

AJ: Is that what the New World Order does, on purpose, I wonder? Do they do everything in plain sight so overtly, so arrogantly? Doing things that are so insane that the average person just can't even process it men-tally?

JD: Well, I'm not sure what the plan is or isn't. I guess I'm not smart enough to know. I do know that what I wrote about and what occurred here, I absolutely know and believe this occurred, and it's pretty horrible that if this is a part of some larger program or plot, then I'm really worried! I'm scared for us all, so to speak.

AJ: So some of these people you convicted in Nebraska are now getting out of prison?

JD: Larry King got out, the *Omaha World-Herald* editor got out. A couple of the others got charged and paid a fine and then got felonies dropped to misdemeanors. For all practical purposes, anybody who was in prison has been redeemed and is somehow holy now.

AJ: Thank you for taking the time to talk with us today, Mr. DeCamp.

JD: It's been my pleasure, Alex. Thank you.

Chapter XIX

Ne timeo nec sperno

(I neither fear nor despise)

David Icke

David Icke may well be the most controversial writer, researcher and nemesis of the New World Order in the patriot movement today. He has appeared on numerous media outlets worldwide, given thousands of public speeches, and authored more than a dozen books on the subject. He has an encyclopedic knowledge of history, ancient occult rituals, secret societies, and trauma-based mind control. He shared much of his expertise on the Bohemian Grove (among many other things) in a phone interview with me from his London home on February 12, 2003.

Q—First of all, David, could you just tell the readers a little bit about yourself and how you became involved with spreading the word about the New World Order?

A—What happened to me is that I was a professional soccer player in Britain. My sports career was ended by arthritis at age 21. I then became a journalist, doing newspaper and radio work from the early 1970s onwards. Through the 1980s, I was a television reporter and anchor for the BBC, working on things like *BBC News* and those sorts of programs. Then towards the late '80s, I became a national spokesman for the British Green Party, which was very important to me because it allowed me to see politics from the inside. And I learned that while people from the Green Party claim to be a "different version" of politics, it's really just the same old blueprint under another guise. I learned that politics was not part of the solution at all—it was massively part of the problem. And I also realized that people that I saw hurling abuse at each other on the television and at public debates were doing anything but that behind the scenes, and it started me thinking, "hey, there is something more to know about all this."

So I left the Green Party, left politics altogether because it just sickened me. Then I went through what you might call a transformation of my perception of reality. And it was a very painful time because everything I thought the world was just collapsed in my mind…and I came out of it seeing the world in an entirely different way. I could see things that I couldn't see before. It was a painful time in my life because all of the bridges to the past were gone. So, I left the BBC and had no job, anything…and just started writing a book about what had happened to me. When the book came out, I got fantastic ridicule in Britain, because I was already a public figure due to my work on TV. But I knew this was a road I had to walk, no matter what people said about it, or said about me, and I gradually began to lose my concerns about what other people thought.

In a nutshell, I learned that there were other explanations to life that were not taught in the schools or broadcast through the media. And I started...just intuitively...investigating what was *really* going on. And from the early '90s, the information I had was just a trickle. But now, I've been walking this path for several years, traveling to other countries researching this stuff. And an amazing world has opened; in which I've realized that for people to understand the nature of what's happening in the world, they just need to forget everything they ever learned and start all over again with a blank sheet of paper. We live in *Alice in Wonderland*—what is, *isn't*—and what isn't, *is*. We are living in a movie. It's a movie that's projected to us minute-by-minute by *CNN* and *FOX News*, but it's not what's going on in the world at all; it's what those authorities *want us to believe* is going on in the world. And what I've learned to do is to look behind the movie screen and see what's really going on, and see what that movie is basically designed to obscure. It's a cesspit, and the world is not just a little bit like we thought it was; the world is *nothing* like what we thought it was.

Q—When did you first find out about the Bohemian Grove?
A—Well, I first started coming across this name shortly after I started researching all this, and I guess it was in 1996 I was traveling around America doing speaking engagements on a three-month trek. The main benefit of it was to meet many, many people—whistleblowers—people on the inside of the system who had experience, women who had been abused in these rituals by the elite and sexually abused by some of the most famous names in America. This name Bohemian Grove became a bit of a mantra with the people I was talking to, because the thing that staggers you when you first start looking into this is how these world-famous people who we see on the news day after day—these people who are "fated" to be great statesmen—are actually involved in some of the most appalling child abuse, satanic ritual, and that this stuff has been going on for thousands of years.

Throughout history, the elite classes have engaged in these sorts of activities—we all read about it and know it to be true. But we naively thought that these things only went on in the ancient world, and that these bizarre customs had not survived. But that's simply not true. It still goes on now, all the time. So it was mind-blowing to me to realize not so much that this was still going on, I could sort of get my mind around that, but…the scale of it staggered me. And the Bohemian Grove is one of the more…in fact, because of researchers and journalists who've helped expose it, has actually become *the* best known of all the secret places these men gather. But it is just the tip of a very enormous iceberg of ritual abuse that these people are involved in.

The names that come up most around the Bohemian Grove in recent years have been The Bush family, Dick Cheney, Henry Kissinger…those are the same names that also keep coming up in the conversations I've had with victims of mind control who name these men as the key perpetrators of that abuse. Some have said that they were actually abused at Bohemian Grove, among many other places where these sorts of rituals were done. So yes, from the mid-1990s on, Bohemian Grove became a consistent theme that kept showing up in my research.

Q—Have you studied John DeCamp's book, *The Franklin Cover-Up?*
A—Yeah, I've read that, and everything the book says about George Bush, Sr. is massively consistent with the common themes that I've picked up through the years. Father George Bush is one of the most infamous pedophiles and child abusers and child killers in the world, in terms of the rich and famous. So the things that are talked about in that book are indeed absolutely dead-on accurate, as far as fitting together with what I've heard from other sources as well.

Q—A victim named in that book, Paul Bonacci, claims that he witnessed another child being murdered in a snuff porn film made on the altar at the base of the giant stone owl statue at the Grove. Had you heard about that?
A—Not that specific story, no—but it fits absolutely with what I've found about the general themes of this Illuminati elite. It gets more and more bizarre. If you go back to historical accounts, and you talk about making human sacrifices to the Gods…well, what are these Gods, and why the human sacrifice? And you realize when you do the research with an opened mind, and not edit things you don't like out because of your belief system, you find that…and this is kind of mainstream science: when you look through your eyes, you're not seeing everything there is to be seen. You're looking within a certain frequency range that your five senses can access, the eyes in this case.

Now, when you're in a room with a cat, for example, and the cat is jumping around, acting very animated, play fighting with something that appears to be empty space, the cat is not reacting to empty space, it is reacting to something it can actually see. The visual frequency range of a cat is much greater than the human range, so what appears to be thin air to the human is not empty space to the cat, you see? Beyond the five-sense reality is infinity, and just beyond the five-sense realities are entities that are vibrating that at a resonance that is beyond the human five-sense ability to tap into. We can't perceive it, which is the origin of so many of these folklores and ancient stories in cultures all over the world about these Gods. Because people of a psychic nature who can expand their capability beyond that of the normal human range…can see these things. And also, these entities can briefly come into this five-sense reality, and some people can see them then because the entity has entered their frequency range.

Now, where I'm going with this is…it's very clear from my research in over 40 countries that these entities, hidden just beyond the frequency range of human sight actually feed off the human energy field, particularly fear. And so when these people who are controlled by these entities, these so-called "Illuminati elite," one of the reasons they are into human sacrifice ritual is that they're literally making a sacrifice to their "Gods," as the ancients talked about. In those cultures, there is an old belief that when you ritually kill someone, as the ritual builds up, the victim knows that they are going to be sacrificed. All this ritual creates enormous terror in the victim. And when the ritual comes to that point where it kills the body, all that energy, the energy of the person is released and absorbed by these entities that are in that same energy field while this ritual is going on. If you go back thousands of years, and you look at the stories of this ancient phenomenon—and no historian seems to have a problem with acknowledging that these things *did indeed go on* in the ancient world—you will see clearly that precisely the same thing still goes on today.

The author with David Icke on a visit to Texas, 2003.

Q—What is your understanding of this 45-foot stone owl that they appear to be worshipping in the "Cremation of Care" ceremony?

A—Another key theme that I've picked up over these years that these Illuminati types are massively, *tremendously* obsessed with symbolism. Everything is symbolism: names are symbolism, corporate logos contain strong symbolism, and places that they choose to do things are also full of symbolism. They surround themselves with symbols in the spot where they plan to do ritual work because it gives the whole thing power. If you look at basic psychology, you'll see that the mind deals not in words, but primarily in images. And so they have created this in society as well, always carefully placing images in our subconscious minds. Symbols do affect the subconscious mind, and those subliminal thoughts and images eventually filter through to the conscious mind. By that time, we think we're having our own thoughts. What we might think is pure inspiration may actually be a subliminal suggestion that was made to us previously through our subconscious mind.

So we've established that use of symbols in ritual work has been common throughout the ages, with different symbols meaning different things. What I've read about the meaning of the owl, is that in the ancient world there was a goddess called Lilith, who is still kind of a satanic Illuminati goddess, and that she was traditionally represented by the owl. But there are other interpretations as to what the owl represents—some believe the owl at Bohemian Grove is meant to represent Molech, or Moloch, the God that families sacrificed their children to in the Old Testament. But what is for sure is that the owl is a major symbol for these guys. Of course, traditionally, the owl is the bird that can see in the dark, and symbolically, the Illuminati operates in the dark, in the shadows.

Another fascinating thing about the owl: if you look at the street map of the roads within the complex of the Congress building in Washington, you will see that it depicts very clearly an owl. And you will see that the Congress building is located right in the belly of this owl on the street plan. Just look at a basic map of Washington DC—any old map will do—and you should have no trouble seeing it. And not only that, the way the streets come down from the Congress building on the map, you will see further that this owl is sitting atop a pyramid. So the owl is definitely a major part of their symbolism, one of their Gods to which they sacrifice humans.

Sacrificing humans also takes many forms. It's not just that they put one man or woman on an altar and sacrificed them, as in the ancient cultures. In more recent times, they have escalated this to mass sacrifices. All the soldiers who died in World Wars I and II, and every other war of the 20th Century are an example. Another example would be the slaughter of hundreds of thousands of people in Iraq and Afghanistan. Those 3,000 people who died in September 11th were sacrificed. This is the Illuminati's sick idea of modern day human sacrifice.

Q—What about Waco, where they literally sacrificed 76 men, women and children in a raging bonfire?
A—Oh, absolutely, Waco. Even the date of April 19th in the satanic calendar relates to fire. This is the day that Hitler sent the flame-throwers into the Jewish ghettos. April 19th is when they bombed the Murrah Federal Building in Oklahoma City. And of course, that's when they did Waco. And the sacrifice of all those children in fire was a *ritual killing*. And it didn't happen by coincidence. To Satanists, every detail of a ritual work is planned out well in advance

for optimum power, including the date on which it is performed. I mean, does anyone really think that September 11, 9-1-1, the number you call for help in an emergency in America, was just a coincidence? Of course it wasn't! It was planned on that day because the "numbers" were right.

Waco is a classic example of how an apparently random event was *a coldly calculated sacrifice* on a day of sacrifice, using the means of ancient human sacrifice—fire. That's what Waco was really about. I mean, these people are deeply sick and imbalanced, and once you start to understand that because they are so ritualistic, because they are obsessed with these things, they become ridiculously predictable. Because they follow such ritualistic cycles in their behavior.

Q—As you know, Alex Jones and I got into the Grove with a hidden camera during the summer 2000 camp and captured the ritual on tape. You probably saw the footage in England as part of Jon Ronson's documentary film, *The Secret Rulers of the World*, produced by Channel 4. And I know that you also took part in the making of that film and you were interviewed by Jon Ronson for his book *Them*. What are your thoughts on how Bohemian Grove was portrayed there in Britain?

A—Yes, they actually did include an interview with me in his film—that was the year you had gone into Bohemian Grove. What I've been told by several women who were ritually abused there, is that first there is the opening ritual, the "Cremation of Care," which you saw live in person. And you know, even if you don't believe that is a human body that is being burned, even if this is being done only in effigy, it's still *amazing* that the people running the world are involved in that stuff. But what these woman tell me is that the actual ritual sacrifice that goes on inside Bohemian Grove actually take place elsewhere in the camp, in smaller groups containing the really elite people. It would be pretty easy to hide…I mean, it's a 2,700-acre campsite—they think that they can do anything in there they bloody well like. So I'm told the really horrible stuff goes on during the week and doesn't involve the mass majority of people there. Also, from what people have told me, there are some underground rooms at Bohemian Grove where these things go on, places that the other low-level club members would be totally unaware of.

Anyway, so Ronson interviewed me as part of this five or six-part series for British television, *Secret Rulers of the World*. One of those episodes was about me, and about the efforts people have made to stop me from having a public platform, and then I was also in the other episode he made about you and Alex Jones going into Bohemian Grove. But as I wrote in my latest book, the film that you and Alex produced yourselves (*Dark Secrets—Inside Bohemian Grove*) was actually far better than the Ronson documentary because Ronson's film sort of pours water on all the so-called "conspiracy theories" and tries to make fun of some very serious issues. His film was seeking to discredit all the work done by researchers who had gone before.

You see, I have experiences with Jon Ronson dating back to about the mid-1990s when I wrote a book called *The Truth Shall Set You Free.* I mentioned Ronson in that book—in passing—because he had written an article in a British magazine. And he was speaking from a Jewish point-of-view, because he is Jewish, and he was basically saying to the Jewish hierarchy, "hey, you've got to change your attitudes. People are leaving the Jewish faith in droves because it's not relevant anymore to them in this modern world." And I just mentioned this article in my book, in a chapter where I write about how religions of the world are imposing their will on people. And he called me just after the book came out in 1995 and said that he'd like to interview me for a major British newspaper called *The Guardian.* So he came around and interviewed me, then the article appeared the following weekend. And it was...*staggering.* I mean, there were people here who witnessed the interview being done, people who are knowledgeable of how journalists work, and even they were absolutely staggered by the quotes used in the article versus what was actually said in the interview.

You know, I've had so much shit written and said about me over the past 13 years that it's become like water rolling off a duck's back to me. But this piece that Ronson wrote was so appallingly misrepresented that I actually wrote to the editor of *The Guardian* and said, "hey, you need to know that what appeared in your newspaper was nothing like what was said to your journalist." And I got the usual excuse letter back from the editor, telling me that he stood behind the story because he had looked at Jon Ronson's notes. And I thought, "well, that's interesting, because he didn't take any notes at the interview." Well, needless to say, Ronson and I had no further contact with one another for a few more years after that.

Then, in 1999, I got this very sheepish communication from Jon Ronson saying he was making this series of documentaries about the New World Order, and said that he wanted to do one of the episodes about me...just following me around with a camera, that sort of stuff. So I sat down and thought about it long and hard, because I had my reservations about this guy already based on past experience. And one of the key elements in this man's article that really upset me was that he implied that I was somehow anti-Semitic! Which staggered my Jewish friends. So when he came back in 1999, he was quick to apologize for that and say, "yeah, yeah, I know you're not anti-Semitic, and I've talked to members of the British board of Jewish Deputies, and they do not believe you are anti-Semitic, either." But even after offering that apology, I was still hesitant to take part—mainly because I wouldn't trust Jon Ronson to tell me the time of day. But what made me eventually agree was that I figured what's really important is getting the information across to as many people as possible. Regardless of whatever spin Ronson chooses to put on it, people with a brain who watch this program will be able to see though the spin. And you know people who don't see through the spin are probably not ready to understand this information, anyway. And that is exactly how it worked out. The program he did on me had a tremendous impact on my work here in Britain, and brought a lot of new people my way who were interested in what I was doing and how they could learn more about the New World Order.

But the main problem I encountered with Ronson is that he was just desperately uninformed about the subject. And therefore, when it came to him interviewing the European chief executive of the Bilderburg Group or whatever, he just simply didn't have enough information to be able to expose him in the interview. So, while his film had some positive aspects, at least as far as waking people up somewhat, the film is sadly tainted by his own lack of knowledge. And also his tendency to try and editorialize and say, "these people are all silly" towards the end of each film. Especially in the one he did about Bohemian Grove, where at the very end of the film, he goes out of his way to make Alex Jones look like some kind of nut. But let me tell you, I've seen the hidden camera footage you guys brought out of there, and it's very clear to me what's going on with the "Cremation of Care." And by the way, the audio is excellent, so I could really hear the words of the ritual as they were being spoken. I mean, just the fact that this is the first video footage that has *ever* gotten out of the Grove in itself makes this a major story. And people should be asking some major questions about what's going on in there. And there should have been major media coverage of what you guys did—but of course, there wasn't.

Q—Did you see the interview Ronson did on C-SPAN (*Booknotes*) where he said he also went into Bohemian Grove that year?

A—You mean...in 2000, the same year you guys did? So, he is now saying that *he* went into Bohemian Grove?

Q—Yes. That's what he said in the C-SPAN interview.
A—Well, that's very interesting to me, because in the film he did on Bohemian Grove, he makes it very clear that he didn't go inside at all. It was clear to me he didn't.

Q—He personally told me that the reason he used Alex and I to infiltrate in the first place is so that the Bohemian Club wouldn't sue him. We served as a shield, going in so that he didn't have to, and therefore, no liability for him or *Channel Four*. Now, let me ask you—is *Channel Four* a major network in the UK, like *ABC* or *NBC* in the U.S.? Can you give our American readers some sense of how big this network is?
A—Yeah, basically in Britain, we have four major television channels. The main ones are *BBC1* and *ITV1*, then *BBC2* and *Channel Four*. But *Channel Four* is the major independent network in England, so the programs Ronson produced would have probably reached an audience of several million people.

Q—Do you ever worry about your own safety when you're out there spreading this information to the public? Or do you feel safer because you're in the spotlight?
A—Well, first of all, let me say in my case that they have tried...and failed. Not to kill me, but to assassinate my character. It got the point where they were trying to keep me from speaking in public, tried to get my books taken off the shelves...and they failed miserably.

My feeling is that you create your own reality. I would pass this on to other journalists, researchers, and other people out there trying to communicate this message: when I first came to America in 1996 to speak about these issues, I met many whistleblowers, and the one common theme ran through every story I heard. That central theme is that the whistleblowers that were operating in fear of the consequences got the consequences they feared. We attract to us what we most fear, and our experiences usually reflect our belief. Belief is so powerful in creating our reality. If we believe that we are powerless, then we will live powerless lives. Either we give our power away by acknowledging and accepting the possibility that these silly, brainless people will try to stop us...or, we will not allow that possible reality to enter our minds. We need to move forward with the absolute belief that nothing or no one can ever stop us.

If I will not allow the thought of being stopped enter my reality, then I *cannot be stopped*. I simply do not accept that it is possible for anybody to stop me. I refuse to even let that thought enter my mind.

When people have bodyguards, it's kind of funny to me in an *Alice in Wonderland* sort of way. I mean, what is a bodyguard? A person having a bodyguard in the first place is sending out the message of: "By having a bodyguard, I accept the possibility that something bad is going to happen to me." You're actually *projecting* that fear out into the universe when you walk around with a bodyguard, yet you think you feel safe. Fear is just not in my reality. And my reality is much more powerful than that of these sick, twisted, imbalanced people, these world leaders who only feel "powerful" because the people keep giving their power away to them every single day. They have no power in their own right. They only have the power that people have *given to them*.

For example, if President Bush came out one day and said, "We've decided that the people are going to do such-and-such..." well, remember that he only has power if the people say, "Okay, Mr. President, we'll do it." But if the people were to say instead, "Oh, go stuff yourself—we're not doing that!" then where is the power? Answer: there is none. The people manipulating us only have the power to do so if we give it to them. I refuse to give my power away. Especially not to them!

Q—Do you feel a sort of "mass awakening" going on out there in your travels around the world? Are you seeing more and more people who are "getting it"? A—Without question, yes. I've traveled to over 40 countries now, and so I guess I'm a pretty good barometer, and yes, many more people are getting the bigger picture, especially since September 11. There has been a very demonstrable awakening that I see. People are realizing that there definitely is an agenda going on here. And what's interesting is that even now, until very recently when they deployed these 450 troops to Heathrow Airport with their bloody tanks and stuff...Uh, the question was actually being asked in the media: "now hold on a minute. This is a bit too convenient, isn't it? You're trying to sway public opinion to invade Iraq, and now suddenly this happens? Are you kidding me?" And then when this hilarious Bin Laden tape appeared out of nowhere a few days ago where he supposedly aligns himself with Iraq, just at a time when they are desperately trying to prove some connection between Al Queda and Iraq to justify invading a sovereign country, even the media are getting skeptical of what's going on here. And so these questions are now being asked, and people are becoming a lot more cynical. I mean, you'd have to travel a long ways now in Britain to find one person who feels they can trust a word Tony Blair says anymore. Because he's been caught in so many lies publicly.

When you are in fear, when you are panicking, when you are desperate and stressed, you stop thinking straight. And these leaders are getting more and more nervous by the day, because they realize that there *is* an awakening going on, and their agenda is in trouble. One of the things I think they've absolutely been shocked by is the lack of longevity of the public's reaction to 9/11. They thought they were going to get far more mileage out of that, over a longer period of time than they are actually getting. So they are now panicking to keep the agenda going. And in doing so, they are making some *massive* mistakes. Which only helps our cause because it puts the idea in people's minds that there is more to this story than they're being told. This is a great time for us to be living in. It's a challenging time, yes, because on a global scale, the human mind is awakening to the reality of its' plight. And once enough people wake up, it's just a matter of time before this movement becomes completely unstoppable. We can change anything, move any mountain, even though this New World Order thinks they are immovable, they are not. Not at all. There is only going to be one winner in this tussle. We will be living in a completely different world ten years from now—and I'll tell you, it ain't gonna be the kind of world the Illuminati *think* it's going to be.

I always say, "don't think it, *know* it." Because if you try to get your head around some of these different concepts of what's going on in the world, it's hard to do, as we've all been programmed by society, by the schools, by the churches…into a false belief system that is not reality. The reality *they* want us to have is the reality that suits the agenda. We're programmed daily from cradle to grave. But if you *feel* it, if you feel the truth of this information intuitively in your gut rather than just *think* it, you'll probably be very surprised to see how bizarre and extreme some of it really is. Like famous people in politics sacrificing children. And yet, something deep within you is saying, "yes, yes, this *is* actually true."

There are a number of people who've written to me through the years after maybe having read one of my books, saying, "I shouldn't believe in any of this stuff you're writing about because it's so bizarre, but…it just rings true, and I can't tell you why." That's going beyond the conscious mind that's pro-grammed to believe the manipulated reality into other levels of consciousness which know far more, and that's through *intuition* and *feeling* and *knowing* rather than *thinking*.

Q—Before we close, could you please tell people a little bit about your books, and where people can go to find out more about David Icke? And also please clarify how to properly pronounce your name, because everybody gets that wrong!
A—Yeah, For the record, my last name is pronounced "Ike." And the best source for information would be my website, which is *www.davidicke.com*. The website consists of more than 5,000 pages of information, plus it's con-stantly updated every day. My latest book is *Alice in Wonderland and the World Trade Center Disaster: Why the Official Story of 9/11 is a Monumental Lie*, which is 500 pages long, looking not just at the events of 9/11, but putting it in con-text of the bigger picture; how the world is being manipulated by men who create problems so that they may be the ones to offer the solutions, controlling society as a result. It's a process I often refer to as "problem, reaction, solu-tion," which is actually classic Hegelian dialectic.

What happened on September 11, 2001 is the most blatant example I've ever seen of creating a problem (the terrorist attacks), blaming it on someone else (Osama Bin Laden, Al Queda), and getting the public outraged to where they literally beg their government to "do something about it!" Then, of course, the New World Order rubs their hands together with glee because they can then offer the solution: increased surveillance and police powers, destroying your personal privacy.

Even as we speak, Mike, Britain has 450 troops with *tanks* at Heathrow Air-port here, all as part of this "war on terrorism," which has all been a result of the 9/11 aftermath. And just to throw the Bohemian Grove angle in here—people have an understandable problem getting their heads around the fact that these powerful people actually sit around some big table somewhere and orchestrate the deaths of 3,000 people in the World Trade Center, The Pentagon and on the hijacked planes. But when you consider that the people doing it are the same people who sacrifice human beings in rituals at places like the Bohemian Grove and elsewhere. People who would take part in human sacrifice and blood-drinking rituals obviously would have no qualms whatsoever about killing 3,000 innocent people in a single day.

One of the things I always say to people is: if you pre-judge what these people will do, you're never going to understand the plot here. Because the people we're talking about here do not have the same mental mechanisms that most normal people have. The thought of killing 3,000 people on September 11th and another 5,000 Afghan civilians in retaliation for a horrible act that they themselves had done—we would find it impossible to do a thing like that because naturally, we would have natural human empathy for the innocent people who were going to be the victims of our actions. But these Illuminati types do not have that same human empathy. They are like empty shells, they are emotionless people, and therefore they do not have the same fail-safe mechanism that stops normal people from engaging in outrageous, grotesque behavior. Like I've said, the same mentality that could sacrifice a child, or worse—sexually abuse a child and then sacrifice it—because that's what these people do, is not gonna have any problem with killing 3,000 people on 9/11. They're not human in the sense that we understand "human." They do not have the same human emotional or mental responses that the vast majority of people have. Without that emotional fail-safe mechanism, anything goes. Because the people doing it feel no emotional consequences for doing it. I mean, the term "cold blooded" was made for these people.

Q—How many people do you think make up this New World Order global elite?
A—Well, I think it works like a pyramid. Basically, they've created our society to be a compartmentalized pyramid so that the Illuminati can more easily control it. And when you get to the top of the pyramid, I think you're dealing with basically a handful of people who really run the world. That's the center of the web, the peak of the capstone. When you come down from the pyramid, or out from the center of the web, and you start seeing hundreds who are in awareness of the ultimate agenda, and below that, thousands more with a fairly high awareness. The further down you go from that, you're dealing with people who don't know the big picture, but are willing to play their part in a particular part of the operation. For example, the CIA, who will work for the Illuminati, but the majority of them are not in full awareness of what they're involved in and what the real game is. And the real game is to create a new global version of Nazi Germany. A global fascist state with a world govern-

ment dictatorship, a world army, a world bank, world currency, and a micro-chipped population.

A microchipped population is the jewel in their crown, because...and I've talked to CIA scientists about this, people who are desperate to get out but can't because of the way they're caught in this web, but...the microchip is the biggest thing this Illuminati wants, more than anything else. The reason is because once they get that thing inside of us, they will have the ability to manipulate our mental and emotional processes from one central command center, if you will. They will be able to easily isolate an individual and target them, including killing them with the microchip by stopping the person's heart, or causing cancer, or any of a variety of ways they can do this. It also enables them to target people *en masse*, and what one of the CIA scientists told me is, once the microchip is inside us, which is actually far more sophisti-cated technology than the public has been led to believe, that there can be mass aggression or mass docility and submission, the emotional states of a large group of people can be manipulated from afar. And again, things like the war on terrorism, or this recent string of highly publicized child kidnappings, child murders...are used in propaganda to convince parents to put a microchip in their children "for their safety." That's absolute crap. I mean, I don't think that having a microchip in their bodies would have been any help at all to the people who were inside the World Trade Center that morning, except to help identify their remains, which is horrible.

This is the main point I'm trying to get across in my books—all these things we're talking about are connected! It may sound strange at first, but Bohemian Grove, deadly toxins in the vaccinations, the banking scams, the Bush family, Rupert Murdoch and the media...these should not be viewed as separate events or entities, because these people all work together on every aspect of controlling society. They connect under the banner of an agenda, which is to turn human beings into cattle controlled by a fascist, centralized global dicta-torship. And the Bohemian Grove is one of the playgrounds of the people who are working to achieve that.

For more information about David Icke, visit *www.DavidIcke.com*

EPILOGUE

acte est fibula

(The play is finished)

9/11

"Every nation in every region now has a decision to make:
Either you are with us or you are with the terrorists."

—*President George W. Bush*
addressing the U.S. Congress,
September 20, 2001.

"You must choose, and right now, whether you want to be with us, or against us."

—**Nazi scientist Hans Hoerbiger,**
published declaration, 1925.

Now that you've reached the end of the book, I'd like to leave you with a few thoughts on the events of September 11, 2001 and how the cold and unemotional eye of history may eventually view those events. I have chosen to make my final point with numbers. Only two simple numbers: nine and eleven, but they say it all.

DO THE MATH

- The date of the attack: 9/11 (9 + 1 + 1 = **11**)
- Each building had **110** stories.
- The first plane to hit the towers was Flight **11**.
- After September 11th there are **111** days left to the end of the year.
- September **11**th is the 254th day of the year: (2 + 5 + 4 = **11**)
- **119** is the area code for Iraq/Iran. (1 + 1 + 9 = **11**, 911-119 are opposites)
- The Twin Towers, standing side by side, looked like the number **11**.
- The WTC towers collapsed to a height of **11** stories.
- The State of New York was the **11**th State added to the Union.
- "New York City" has **11** letters.
- "Afghanistan"—**11** letters.
- "The Pentagon"—**11** letters.
- "Ramzi Yousef"—**11** letters (convicted of orchestrating the attack on the World Trade Center in 1993).
- Flight 11—92 on board (9 + 2 = **11**) The Flight 11 call letters were AA11.
- Flight 11 had **11** crewmembers onboard.
- Flight 77—65 on board (6 + 5 = **11**)
- Flight 77 was 155 feet long. (1+5+5 = **11**)

Napoleon Bonaparte once said: "What is history but a fable agreed upon?" Former U.S. President Franklin D. Roosevelt echoed those sentiments when he remarked that "nothing in the course of history is coincidental." So, what exactly am I getting at here?

Certain members of the U.S. Government, Military and Intelligence community knew the 9/11 tragedy was going to happen *because they are the ones who planned it, funded and trained the terrorists, and allowed the event to take place.*

Don't believe the whitewash that is being sold to us as "fact" in those 9/11 Commission hearings on Capitol Hill—it's nothing more than the new millennium's version of The Warren Commission, and every bit as believable. The FBI, CIA, and Pentagon did not make "mistakes" when they missed the numerous warnings about an impending attack on America. They didn't "miss" the warnings. Individuals at the highest levels ignored the warnings ON PURPOSE, up to and yes, *including* the President of the United States. These people worked together with Osama bin Laden (a known CIA asset, whose family has had a long history of business dealings with the Bush family) to bring this horrific event to pass. That's my story, and I'm sticking to it.

There are now numerous books, newspaper and magazine articles, websites, and documentary films made since September 11, 2001 that ask the hard questions and bring forward troubling evidence that points to the true perpetrators of the darkest day in American history. This information is available to you from a variety of credible sources. Even Michael Moore got most of the facts right in his controversial film *Fahrenheit 9/11*, give or take a few mistakes, errors in editorial judgment, or whatever personal agenda he was pushing. Therefore, I will not spend too much time here focusing on the semantics of what actually happened that horrible day. Rather, I want to bring your attention to the overwhelming occult and numerological "clues" surrounding the event that simply do not add up to coincidence.

The entire September 11 attack was underlined with the number 11. Practiced high-level occultists worldwide knew exactly what had happened and who had done the deed, based on the terrorists' distinctive numeric signature. Once you know what to look for, and simply "do the math," the picture becomes much easier to see clearly.

For example, did you know that it was on **September 11**, 1609, when the explorer Henry Hudson sailed into New York harbor and discovered Manhattan Island and the Hudson River, near the very location on which the Twin

Towers were constructed? Or that construction on the Pentagon officially began on **September 11, 1941?** Isn't it rather strange that the Pentagon was attacked 60 years later *to the day?* Remember the big American flag that was so proudly hoisted over the Pentagon during the recovery effort? It's interesting to note that Old Glory flew for the very first time on **September 11, 1777,** at the Battle of Brandywine. (Incidentally, the Redcoats won that time, if you're keeping score.)

The world was "introduced" to terrorism on **September 11, 1972,** at the Munich Olympic Games. There were 121 participating countries **(11X11=121),** and **11** Israeli athletes were killed. Exactly 29 (2+9=11) years to the day later came the largest terrorist attack ever on American soil. Why would Arab terrorists choose this particular date? Perhaps it could have something to do with the landmark British mandate that was put into effect in the Palestine on **September 11, 1922.**

This mandate imposed British rule over Palestine, and Arabs protested it robustly, calling this bold move an outright occupation of their lands. Every since that time in our history, the Holy Land has never been the same, torn by warring factions who are still fighting over a piece of ground each side believes is rightfully theirs. And Allied hands helped to create this entire unfortunate, bloody mess.

The British government wanted to establish a permanent home for Jews in Palestine. After discussions within the cabinet and consultations with Jewish leaders, the decision was made public in a letter from Lord Arthur James Balfour to Lord Rothschild, written in the 11th month of 1917. The contents of this letter became known as the Balfour Declaration, dated November 2 (11+2=13), it was incorporated into Article **22** of the Covenant of the League of Nations, which became the mandate of **September 11, 1922.**

The United States Congress and President Warren G. Harding gave the Balfour Declaration their full support without question. This essentially put Palestine under British control until 1948 (1+9+4+8=**22**), when the State of Israel was officially created by the United Nations. The UN established a Special Commission on Palestine (UNSCOP) to devise a solution.

Delegates from **11** nations decided the fate of Palestine, concluding the only workable solution was to divide the Jews and Arabs by partitioning off their lands. The majority recommendation for partition was subsequently adopted 33-13 on November 29, a date that also has the numerological value of **13**.

Fascinating "coincidence," isn't it?

11—The Master Number

I have zeroed in on the number 11 here, because this number is scrawled across the pages of history like a clue, inviting us to figure out who the real culprits of the 9/11 tragedy are. It may or may not surprise you to learn that President George W. Bush's name has the numerological value of 11. An experienced occultist would arrive at this calculation by utilizing the ancient Chaldean and/or Pythagorean Tables. Here's how it works:

The Pythagorean Table is numbered 1 to 9, each number having certain letters of the alphabet associated with it. The Chaldean Table works in a similar way except it is numbered 1 to 8 and the letters associated with each number are differ as well. Numerologists use these two methods for calculation with the Chaldean table being the oldest and most accurate. For example, using the Chaldean method "September" adds up to another 11.

These two charts are used by most serious skilled occultists, and certainly by the Illuminati. The Chaldean was probably the method used in the days of the Tower of Babel by Babylonian priests, and we will also use it to determine the number value for each letter in President Bush's name. Then, we simply take all the letters in "George W. Bush" and add them up:

G + **E** + **O** + **R** + **G** + **E** (3 + 5 + 7 + 2 + 3 + 5) =	25
W (6)	6
B + **U** + **S** + **H** (2 + 6 + 3 + 5) =	16
Sum-->	47 (4 + 7 = **11**)

July 6, 1946 is George W. Bush's birthday. It can be reduced to the power number **33**, sacred to all Freemasons (The 33rd Degree is the highest grade in freemasonry):

$$7/6/1946 = 7 + 6 = 13, 1946 = 1 + 9 + 4 + 6 = 20.$$
$$20 + 13 = 33$$

George W. Bush's birthday equals the master number **33** and it was Bush (whose name equals the master number **11**) who ordered all flags be flown at half-mast until September **22**! September 22 was **11** days after the event. It completed the sacred Masonic triangle of **11, 22, 33**, which I will explain in more detail below.

As before mentioned, the number 11 has special significance. In Numerology it is not reduced to a single digit. It is a power number as is 22, 33 etc. According to Freemasons, the number 11 represents a vision. The number 22 combines vision with action. The number 33 offers this "vision" to the world. The master numbers 11, 22, and 33 represent a triangle. A triangle of enlightenment or illumination, sacred to all Freemasons.

33

11   22

Why is the number 11 important to the occultist? As 19th Century occultist W. Wynn Wescott explained, "*...so 11 is the essence of all that is sinful, harmful, and imperfect.*"

Eleven is the general number of magic or sorcery and magicians. It is the number of war and the battle with the demonic element. It's an unlucky number to Hebrews, yet is sacred to Muslims. To them, it is the number of the knowledge of God, which can only be bestowed after the individual has gone through 11 steps, or "tests." Eleven is also the symbol of martyrdom to Arabs. It's interesting to note that the blue cord of the Mason masters is 11 cm. long. In the Hermetic Order of the Golden Dawn there are also 11 steps, or degrees of initiation. Aleister Crowley once said that the whole object of magick was the 5 (yin) with 6 (yang) =**11**!

In ancient Egypt, King Tutankhamen's tomb had combinations of 11 in the jewelry he wore, and he had 11 oars placed on the floor surrounding his tomb. In Tolkein's The Lord of the Rings, the number 11is described as a curious number, and reaching your 111th birthday is an event. The USA skipped sequence numbers on the Apollo moon missions to ensure it was Apollo 11 that landed on the moon.

I'm going to share with you just a few examples of other seminal events in American history that were also underscored with the master number 11. In a later section, we will delve into the power and significance of the number 9. I will include here not only events that took place on the 9th or 11th of a month, but further show you events whose numerological values add up to 9 or 11 (or some multiple of 11, such as 22 and 33). It's a quick crash course in what I call "history by numbers."

HISTORY BY NUMBERS

The first American president to publicly call for a "New World Order" was Woodrow Wilson during the First World War. In a January 1917 address to Congress, Wilson laid out his plan for a League of Nations, describing his vision of a New World Order to the Senate. Former President George H.W. Bush would later echo that statement in an address to Congress on **September 11**, 1990, announcing his decision to invade sovereign Iraq. **11** years to t*he day* before 9/11, the President's father had sent out the call for WWIII. And if he couldn't be in office to start it himself, his son would.

World War I officially ended on Monday, **November 11**, 1918 at **11** a.m., the 11th hour of the 11th day of the **11**th month. Think *that's* a coincidence? To further define the occult signature upon this event, we need only to do a bit more simple math. The date November 11 adds up to 22 **(11+11=22)**, and when you add up the "three elevens" that represent the **11**th hour, **11**th day, and **11**th month of the Armistice, you get the master number 33. **(11+11+11=33)** November 11 became known as "Armistice Day," and is still celebrated as a national holiday in many former Allied nations, although America only observed this holiday through 1953, abandoning it for the more generalized "Veterans Day" to include veterans of all American wars.

Never was the number **11** so firmly stamped on such an important moment, at least not until the events of September 11, 2001, 83 years later. As a footnote, probably not coincidentally, 83 has the numerological value of **11**. (8+3=11)

When the Illuminati assassinated President John F. Kennedy, he was killed according to the occult number signature of eleven and within the sacred Masonic pyramid of **11, 22, and 33**. His murder took place in the **11th** month, on the **22nd** day, and on the **33rd** parallel in Dealey Plaza, a public structure

394

built by Dallas Freemasons. President Kennedy had arrived in Dallas just after **11** a.m. that morning.

For most Americans living today, this is probably the worst national tragedy they can recall prior to September 11, 2001. The Kennedy Assassination pre-dated the 9/11 attacks by 38 years, which also has the numerological value of 11. (3+8=**11**)

REVOLUTION No. 9

The number 9 is also sacred to the Illuminati. Just one important example of this would be May 1, 1776, the official date when the Illuminati Order of Freemasonry was founded.

$$5/1/1776 = 5 + 1 + 1 + 7 + 7 + 6 = 27.\ 2 + 7 = 9$$

So, why did the Illuminati choose this specific date for the official founding of their secret order? A look back into history provides us the answer. The origin of May Day as a day for celebration dates back to well before the birth of Christ. And like many ancient festivals, it too has its' origin in the old Pagan religion.

For the Druids of the British Isles, May 1 was the second most important holiday of the year. This was when the festival of Beltane took place. It was thought that the day divides the year into half. The other half was to be ended with the Samhain on November 1. In those days, the May Day custom was the setting of new fire, meant to purify and regenerate the earth. It was also a time for observing the ancient fertility rites traditionally associated with the coming of spring, thus kicking off "the lusty month of May." Young ladies dancing in a circle around the obviously phallic Maypole was one of these Olde English fertility customs.

The Maypole tradition survived religious persecution, and later resurfaced in France. Merely changing its name, the Maypole became the "Tree of Liberty" and was the symbol of the French Revolution. Back across the pond, Colonial Puritans frowned on May Day festivities because it was not a Christian holiday. As a result, May Day has never been celebrated with as much enthusiasm in the United States as in the more secular European nations.

One of the Illuminists' primary goals was to use magick, combined with science, philosophy, and politics to create war and unrest in the world. To experienced occultists, this is a well-known practice known as "chaos magick." Then, being in positions of high power, these same men would then be perfectly poised to offer a solution—they would bring "order" (A New World Order) out of the chaos *they themselves had created*. It's the classic Hegelian dialectic of "problem—reaction—solution." First you create the problem, wait for the public's inevitable reaction that "something must be done about it!"—then, you conveniently offer the desired solution. Let's take an example based upon the birth of the Illuminati:

Exactly 110 years later after the founding of this secret Order in Bavaria, May 1, 1886 became an important date in American history, when a series of organized and violent labor strikes were all coordinated to take place on that date in different cities. For late 19th century Victorian Americans, this was their September 11. An immaculately timed and carefully-conceived series of simultaneous attacks that could conveniently be blamed on "terrorists" (Back then, we called them "anarchists" and "agitators.") Probably not coincidentally, May 1, 1886 adds up to the master number **11**. (May 1—5+1=6. 1+8+8+6=23. Reduce 23 to a single digit by adding 2+3=5. Then, add the date and year values together. 6+5=**11**.)

The events of May 1, 1886 set off a worldwide firestorm on the question of labor. In 1889, an association of French Socialists called the Second International, declared that May Day should be a holiday devoted to labor and its problem. They renamed it "Labor Day" and it became the occasion for important political demonstrations. In France, the Maypole was already regarded as the symbol of the French Revolution. Perhaps the French union was partly motivated by that spirit behind the day. Then again, the original Illuminati had played a seminal role in agitating the French Revolution, so is it inconceivable that this event would also bear their signature?

"MAYDAY, MAYDAY!"

Every war since the French Revolution has been promoted by the Illuminati operating under various names and guises. Immediately after the Napoleonic Wars, the Illuminati assumed that all the nations would be so desperate and so weary of wars that they would be glad for any solution. So, the stooges of the

Illuminati set up what they called The Congress of Vienna. At this meeting they tried to create the first League of Nations, their first attempted one world government. They held the theory that all the crowned heads of Europe were so deeply in debt to them that they would willingly or unwillingly serve whatever agenda was proposed. But the Czar of Russia caught on to the plot, and completely sabotaged it.

The enraged Illuminati then vowed that some day they would destroy the Czar and his entire family. And this very threat was later accomplished in 1917, first with the abdication of Czar Nicholas II, then with the brutal execution of the entire royal family on July 16, 1918 (7+1+6=14. 1+9+1+8=19. 19+14=the master number 33). Three centuries of Romanov rule were quickly replaced by a new system of government in Russia—communism—sold to the citizenry as a "people's revolution," an overthrow of the Old World Order.

In 1848, Karl Marx wrote the *Communist Manifesto*, under the direction of one group of Illuminists, while Professor Karl Ritter of Frankfurt University wrote the anti-thesis, under the direction of another group of Illuminists. The First World War was to be fought so as to enable the Illuminati to destroy Czarism in Russia, as vowed by the International Bankers after the Czar had torpedoed their scheme at the congress held in Vienna, and to transform Russia into a stronghold of atheistic Communism. After the war ended, Communism developed a firm stronghold in Russia, exactly according to plan. Henceforth, May 1 became known as the celebration of the Russian Communists. It was in the 1920s that they inaugurated the annual May Day parades. Even in today's Russia, the holiday is still observed with parades and a rather bizarre display of the most modern weapons and seemingly endless troops of soldiers in Moscow.

While on the subject of weapons, soldiers, and war, no examination of the significance of the Illuminati's most sacred date, May 1st, would be complete without a mention of the event that drew the United States into the First World War. On May 1st, 1915 (which adds up to the master number 22: 5+1=6. 1+9+1+5=16. 16+6=22), the British liner *Lusitania* set sail from New York, bound for Liverpool, with more than 100 Americans on board. Of course, we all know of her unfortunate fate. The first clear indication of peril to *Lusitania* was the extraordinary notice placed in American newspapers by the German Embassy on May 1, 1915, the very day the Cunarder sailed. The notice strongly warned all vessels traveling into the war zone that any and all ships flying the British flag could be legitimate targets for attack.

Despite this "take heed" notice from the Germans, the *Lusitania* charged straight into dangerous waters off the southern coast of Ireland, where three British merchant ships had just been sunk by the Germans. Then on May 7, *Lusitania* Captain William Turner not only forged ahead on this doomed course, but actually slowed the great ship *down*, as if to allow the Germans an easy shot at her! Once the German U-boat had successfully delivered its torpedo, it was only a matter of 18 (1+8=9) minutes before the *Lusitania* sank, killing 1,195 of her 1,959 passengers and crew. 132 of the dead were Americans, and the outrage felt in the USA made our entrance into the First World War a certainty. Up until that time, we had remained officially neutral and isolationist, with the majority of Americans wanting no part in what they considered Europe's war. The *Lusitania* tragedy changed all that.

Some avid *Lusitania* historians claim that the British Admiralty, and in particular First Lord Winston Churchill conspired to put the ship in harm's way ON PURPOSE, planning to spark an incident that might pull the U.S. into the war. Many now believe the ship was secretly loaded with munitions, that *Lusitania* was illegally disguised as a passenger ship in international waters when in fact, it was an operational battleship. This may explain why the Germans felt justified in firing at what they considered an "enemy" vessel, and all those explosives stored down below certainly helped to make a big explosion even more spectacular for the news photographers.

Oh yes, the Americans would be very upset about this, just as they were about the *Maine* in 1898, later at Pearl Harbor on December 7, 1941, and in the 1964 Gulf of Tonkin incident that led us to Vietnam. It's the oldest trick in the book: stage an attack with tragic loss of life (problem), find a "bully" to blame it on, and wait for the angry masses to demand revenge (reaction). Then, use the event and it's unfortunate victims to facilitate a war or invasion of some foreign land (solution). Starting to sound familiar? It should, for the September 11 attack on America followed this old blueprint to the letter, only exchanging outdated ships from the maritime era of warfare with a more modern alternative, airplanes. But that's about the only difference.

The sinking of *RMS Titanic* is generally regarded as the biggest and most mysterious maritime disaster of the 20th century. This great "unsinkable" ship went to the bottom of the Atlantic Ocean on her maiden voyage from Liverpool to New York on April 14, 1912. (April 14= 4+1+4=**9**. 1+9+1+2=**13**. 13+9= the master number **22**.) *Titanic* struck the iceberg that would sink her in the 11th hour, exactly at 11:40 p.m. Her speed at the time of the collision was an unthinkable **22 ½** knots. *Carpathia's* speed while passing through that same treacherous icefield a few hours earlier had been only **9** knots. There were originally **33** lifeboats planned for *Titanic*, but the White Star Line's designers thought the decks would look too cluttered. The number of lifeboats was reduced by **13**, a decision that as we now know, would directly cause the deaths of 1,503 (1+5+0+3=**9**) passengers who could not escape the ship as it went down.

Of the many conspiracy theories about what really happened to the *Titanic*, perhaps the most widely-believed is that the White Star Line secretly switched *Titanic* with her sister ship *Olympic*, which had been badly damaged after several collisions, running aground, and a scrape with *HMS Hawke*. Knowing *Olympic* was going to cost a fortune to repair, White Star planned to deliberately sink her and recover a fortune in insurance money on the more valuable *Titanic*. Of course, they didn't plan on anybody actually being killed—plenty of other ships were supposed to be in the vicinity to rescue all persons aboard, but somehow their scheme had gone horribly wrong. The White Star Line now had a problem. They could claim money on the *Titanic* sinking but they would have to pay a lot of it out to the bereaved. In the end, the White Star Line did make money out of the disaster, and many people believe that the real *Titanic* (sailing under the name of the *Olympic*) served the company faithfully for another quarter-century without incident.

THE IDES OF APRIL

Just as Caesar was warned to "beware the Idea of March" in Rome, perhaps America should pay more attention to the "Ides of April." Is it a coincidence that April 15 just happens to be the dreaded deadline date for all Americans to pay their taxes? Was this day simply chosen at random? Doubtful. Yet, even before there was a Federal Income Tax in this country, the Ides of April were always unlucky for us. Just as *RMS Titanic* sunk off the eastern coast of America on April 14, 1912, that same date already had two other national tragedies stamped upon it. The Civil War had begun at Ft. Sumter on April 14, 1861.

Four years later to the day, actor John Wilkes Booth assassinated President Abraham Lincoln at Ford's Theatre in Washington.

The date of Lincoln's assassination was of deep religious and patriotic significance to the country. Besides being the anniversary of Ft. Sumter, it was also Good Friday. Yet, to the "illuminated," April 14, 1865 would carry a more sinister significance:

April 14, 1865—4+14=9. 1+8+6+5=20. 20+9=29.
2+9=11.

On that evening, all Washington was aglow with festivities. The long weary war had just ended, and many commemorative events were also planned to observe the four-year anniversary of the fall of Sumter. One of these was a special Good Friday performance of the play *Our American Cousin*, originally planned for Grover's Theatre instead of Ford's. As a matter of fact, on April 13, the manager of Grover's, C.D. Hess, had penned an invitation to the first couple. In a bizarre twist, Hess would later remember that he was reminded to do so by none other than John Wilkes Booth. The exact contents of their chat are very telling indeed, as if spoken in code:

> "He seated himself in a chair," Hess remembered, "and entered into a conversation on the general illumination of the city that night…He asked me if I intended to illuminate. I said yes, I should, to a certain extent; but that the next night (April 14) would be my great night of the illumination, that being the celebration of the fall of Sumter."
>
> "Do you intend to invite the President?" Booth asked casually.
>
> "Yes," Hess answered, and then added, "that reminds me; I must send that invitation."
>
> (*Wilkes Booth Came to Washington.* By Larry Starkey. Random House, 1976. P. 89)

It may also interest you to know that the date of President Lincoln's public funeral in Washington was April 19, 1865.

APRIL 19

Although the fighting had officially begun at Fort Sumter, the first bloodshed of the Civil War came on April 19, 1861. Tensions had escalated in Maryland between secessionists and Union troops in what became known as the "Baltimore Riot." This critical event led to the occupation of the city by Federal troops, and declaration of martial law. These imposed mandates would last throughout the entire war. But April 19 was already a significant date in American warfare long before the Civil War.

85 years previously (8+5=**13**), the **13** American Colonies rebelled against the British and the American Revolution begun on April 19, 1776. Perhaps not coincidentally, this is also the first day of the 13-day Satanic celebration, "The Bloody Sacrifice of the Beast." **13** days later, the Order of the Illuminati was founded on May 1, 1776 in Bavaria. This is NOT a coincidence, folks. Is it any wonder that the "Ides of April" have always brought dark days for our nation?

In 1993 (selected because it is a "power year" to occultists: 1+9+9+3=the master number **22**), a new kind of war started in America. The "war on terrorism" was officially launched with the first bombing of the World Trade Center towers on February 26. The Clinton administration used this event to push Congress for more funding and police powers to guard against such future attacks by foreign terrorists. Back then, the public at large just weren't all that interested in the idea, and the proposed anti-terror legislation didn't pass. The new tactic was to simply shift the focus from foreign to domestic terrorists, the ones who could be living in Anytown, USA. They could be like the people next door, you know, nice clean-cut All-American folks. Good people. Simple God-loving Christians. A conservative little Texas town like Waco would do just fine for what was next on the agenda.

Just two days after the 1993 World Trade Center bombing, on February 28, the U.S. Bureau of Alcohol, Tobacco and Firearms (BATF) conducted a military assault upon the Branch Davidian Church outside Waco. **6** people died that first day, both Davidians and federal agents. After a 51-day (5+1=**6**) siege, the Davidians' home was burned to the ground by the federal government, killing more than eighty men, women and children on April 19, 1993.

Just as with the case of Ft. Sumter 128 (1+2+8=11) years before, the Federal government may have lost the first battle with the Confederates, but they were determined to come back and finish the job. From 1863 to 1865, the Confederates at Fort Sumter withstood a 22-month siege by Union forces. During that time, the fort was reduced to brick rubble. When the ATF botched the first raid at Waco, they weren't going to take that kind of defeat lying down. They wanted revenge for the deaths of their fellow agents, and for being publicly humiliated over their inept handling of the situation. David Koresh and his entire flock could have been peacefully arrested, and the whole tragedy avoided. Reducing the "compound" to ashes and sending all the Davidians inside to a fiery death was no simple solution to the problem. It was *revenge.* But there was also a much bigger agenda at work here.

When you "do the math," the numbers connect the dots between Waco and what happened exactly two years later to the day in Oklahoma City on April 19, 1995:

> **April 19, 1993** = 4+1+9=14. 1+9+9+3=22. 22+14=36. 3+6=**9**.
> **April 19, 1995** = 4+1+9=14. 1+9+9+5=24. 24+14=38. 8+3=**11**.

Do you see the common thread here? The numerological value of the event at Waco adds up to **9**, the numerological value of the Oklahoma City "domestic terrorist" bombing is **11**. Both of these seminal events lead us directly to the **9/11** attacks on America and the now-global "war on terror." If you've ever wondered if all these strange "coincidences" are connected, now you know for sure. Rather than simply "connecting the dots," you can "do the math" of numerology instead.

Exactly **911** days after September 11, 2001, terrorists attacked a commuter train in Madrid, Spain, killing 191 (1+9+1=**11**) passengers and injuring more than 1400. The date was March 11, 2004; just three days before Spain's national elections were to take place. At the time of this obviously staged attack, President Bush *just happened to be in New York City to speak at the groundbreaking ceremony for the 9/11 Memorial. Gee, what a coincidence, eh?* If that isn't rubbing our noses in it, I don't know what is! However, should you require any further evidence that the Madrid bombing was an act of "Illuminati terrorism," just take a closer look at the numbers.

A total of **13** bombs were placed on the train, coordinated to go off almost simultaneously. 10 bombs exploded within three minutes, beginning at 7:40 a.m. (7+4+0=**11**). 3 other bombs, possibly timed to kill rescue workers, were thankfully found and defused. The pre-selected date for this horrible attack was **3/11**, exactly two years and six months after **9/11**. When you "do the math," you may be astonished to learn that exactly **911** days elapsed between these two events:

730 days (365 x 2) + 182 days (6 months) = 912.

Subtract one day to allow for a leap year, and you have **911**!

But there's more—There are 6 letters in Madrid, 5 letters in Spain. Add them together and you have **11** letters. Also, the date of the attack adds up to **11**: (3+1+1=5. 2+0+0+4=6. 5+6=**11**).

As the final flourish in this unfolding tragedy, Hamas spiritual leader and founder Sheik Ahmed Yassin was killed in an Israeli airstrike on March **22**, 2004, exactly **11** days after the train bombing in Madrid. This entire event was cleverly underscored with *Three Elevens* (the time, date, and place of the attack all have the numerological value of **11**)—remember that about **3/11**.

Six months after the September 11 attacks, on March 11, 2002, New York City was "illuminated" by 88 (8 x 11 = 88) powerful light bulbs (*"a thousand points of light?"*) that lit up the night sky from the former World Trade Center site. The next morning, on March 12, 2002, the bodies of **11** FDNY firemen were recovered from Ground Zero.

By using numerology to get a closer look at the thread which has connected most of the truly important dates in our history, I wanted to make the point that what we call prophecy is nothing more then a collection of future events which are agreed upon by men. If you *still* don't believe this, read on and see what happened one year after 9/11.

On the morning of the first anniversary, September 11, 2002 the names of 2,801 victims were read at a Ground Zero Ceremony from a recently "revised" official death toll list compiled by the New York City Medical Examiners' office. (2+8+0+1 = **11**).

Later that evening, the evening numbers drawn in the New York Lottery were **9-1-1!**

Oh—*that's* a coincidence, for sure. Luck of the draw, they explained.

"The numbers were picked in the standard random fashion using all the same protocols," lottery spokeswoman Carolyn Hapeman told the Associated Press. "It's just the way the numbers came up." *(Wink, wink, nudge, nudge…)*

In an even more amazing twist of "fate," the September Standard & Poor's 500 futures contract closed at **911**.00 on the same date—the one-year anniversary of 9/11.

There was some buzz on the Chicago Mercantile Exchange stock index futures trading floor about why that happened. Could it be collusion? Price-fixing? "It was bizarre, it was strange, but it wasn't manufactured," said Richard Canlione, vice president of institutional financial futures at Salomon Smith Barney in an AP story. "It was just the rules of coincidence…That's just where the market was." Some thought that perhaps suspicious activity could have taken place, but most brushed it off as a "patriotic rally" and didn't see the harm in it.

Now, the question is…do YOU see any harm in it?

BACK TO BABYLON

If you've read this entire book and don't yet believe that our "elected" leaders are indeed utilizing numerology and the occult to influence world events, I urge you to read this last chapter again. You don't have to be an alchemist to figure this stuff out. Just do the math.

There hasn't been a war or revolution since Oliver Cromwell that didn't employ secret societies and the occult, to prepare not only the target country, but also the invading country for the onslaught that was to follow. Astrology, divination and numerology have been used throughout the ages to plan and guide the course of conquest.

I made the decision to close this book with the breakdown of the occult symbolism of 9/11 because the events of that day have now plunged this nation into an endless, disastrous war with Iraq. I believe we are now fighting WWIII, the last war. Some may call it Armageddon. And isn't it a coincidence that we're seemingly coming to the end in the land where it all began?

Modern day Iraq is located upon the former site of Babylon. It is also on the 33rd parallel, located at 33 degrees N, 44 degrees E. Both President Bushes waged war on Iraq. The Bushes (along with their buddies at Bohemian Grove) are obsessed with ancient Babylon; not just strictly for its' natural treasures that can be exploited for profit, but for its' spiritual and historical treasures as well.

The second Gulf War began on March 19, 2003. 3 + 19 = **22**. The master number 22 is part of the triangle, representing vision combined with action to produce the desired result. By this formula, the occultist would look at the events by numbers to reconstruct the "sacred pyramid" of the Illuminati, thus giving us the roadmap outlining the entire future plan. Here it is: the number **11** represents the beginning (September 11 Terrorist Attacks). The number **22** represents the action (the war), and the number **33**, the top of the pyramid, signifies the end result (complete global domination by a Luciferian, tyrannical, militarized one world government). But don't take it from me. Better to let you read it in the Illuminati's own words:

> *"No one will enter the New World Order unless he or she will make a pledge to worship Lucifer. No one will enter the New Age unless he will take a Luciferian Initiation."*

—David Spangler, Director of Planetary Initiative,
United Nations

...AND NOW, THE *REAL* KICKER!

Now that I've covered hundreds of years to make my point, that 9/11 was an event carefully orchestrated by adepts at high levels of initiation and knowledge, I'll take you back thousands of years for a little GOOD NEWS. And I'm sure by now you've *got* to be ready for some, so here goes:

Historian Dr. Ernest L. Martin first began to publish his findings about the birthday of Jesus in 1976, and again as *The Birth of Christ Recalculated*. In 1991, the book was re-released as *The Star that Astonished the World*. Dr. Martin revealed in his book that the signs in the sky on the night of Jesus' birth occurred on only one day in 3 BC, and they occurred exactly on **September 11,** 3 BC between what would now be 6:15 PM and 7:49 PM eastern standard time. Is September 11th the birthday of Jesus Christ?

Now let's travel back to September 11, 4000 BC. According to some Hebrew historians, September 11, 1999 was the 6,000th anniversary of Adam's creation, and year 1 on the Hebrew calendar. These new revelations on human history may help us to better cope in a nation still mourning the events of September 11, 2001, and hopefully bring us to a much deeper understanding of the problems facing mankind here and now.

As this epilogue hopefully illustrates, many significant events occurred on September 11 throughout history, but perhaps none could be as significant as the last two I've shared with you here. Could it be that God has chosen to use September 11 so many times in history to dramatically intervene in world affairs?

As for the events of September 11, 2001, I feel that this was no disaster made by the hand of God. Quite the opposite, my friends. I believe that the Illuminati, possessed of this powerful and ancient knowledge, are trying to strike at God through using September 11 and the number "11" so many times to mark some of the worst tragedies in world history. The Bible assigns "11" to Antichrist in *Daniel 7:7-8*, thus the Illuminati absolutely *adores* the number **11**, and would be committed to use this number to "give power" to staged events on important dates. This formula would be considered critical to the Godless Global Brotherhood working to speed the arrival of the coming Antichrist.

Who else would use the horror of September 11 to facilitate a war in the Garden of Eden (near modern-day Fallujah, Iraq)? If the collapsing World Trade Center Towers symbolically represented the fall of The Tower Of Babel, what are the odds that event would lead us to bomb Baghdad, site of ancient Babylon?

And is it any wonder that the masterminds of WWIII (the war to end all wars) would be George Bush and his Bohemian Grove cronies? After reading this book from cover to cover, you can hardly find that information surprising.

In these final pages, I've given you a lot to think about. We have examined so many important events in history engineered by occult numerological formulas and methods that your head may be swimming from all these numbers! We have revealed so many examples of the numbers 9 and 11 underscoring important dates, their significance, and key events on past September 11ths, that the chances of all these occurrences being accidental is absolutely zero!

I think there is a much bigger reason for this endless global "War on Terror" than the people are being told, for as they say—*NUMBERS DON'T LIE.*

Politicians do.

APPENDIX A

sine cura

(without a care)

List of Camps at Bohemian Grove, A-Z

NOTE: The individual camps at Bohemian Grove have changed quite a bit through the years. Some camp names have changed (such as the politically incorrect *Swastika* Camp, which quietly disappeared after WWII). Other camps were disbanded when members passed away, as several Grove camp names were the proper name of the families who owned that particular private camp (a good example would be the Taft-Henry Camp, reserved for the former president's family and friends). To illustrate the changes over a 52-year period, I have included both a 1992 camp list and a 1930 list of camps for comparison.

While much has changed, some camps remain ever constant, such as Bromley Camp, which has traditionally served as a catchall for members or guests who are not housed in private camps. The Grove's musicians and performers occupy Aviary, Jinks Band, Orchestra, and Tunerville Camps. Campsites at Bohemian Grove usually contain no more than 20 members; some consist of only one individual or family, while others (such as San Francisco Bank Camp) reflect a corporate identity.

In 1992, Bohemian Grove had 116 campsites; in 1930 there were 162. Over the past 50 years, the Grove has grown in square miles as the club continued to purchase surrounding lands for expansion. The Bohemian Club's membership rolls have grown substantially, too—but in more recent years, camps have been consolidated, with more men assigned to each camp—before that, most campsites at the Grove were very small, often consisting of only one family or group of friends. This old tradition has for the most part been done away with, as the 1992 camp list suggests. The ever-changing list of camp names at the Grove are a useful cross-reference against membership lists, and are also a useful indicator of how this tightly-knit community has slowly evolved over the club's 130 year history.

1992 Camp List

ABBEY	BALD EAGLE
AORANGI/SWAGATAM	BAND
AVIARY	BELLA UNION

BETTER 'OLE
BROMLEY
CAMELS
CARELESS
CAVE MEN
CLIFF DWELLERS
COOL-NAZDAR
CROSSROADS
CROW'S NEST
COOKOO'S NEST
DERELICTS
DOG HOUSE
DRAGONS
DRUIDS
EDGEHILL
EL TORO II
ESPLANDIAN
FARAWAY
FIVE EASY PIECES
FORE PEAK
FRIENDS OF THE FOREST
GREEN MASK
HALCYON
HAVEN
HERMITS
HIDEAWAY
HIGHLANDERS
HILLBILLIES
HILLSIDE
HUALPAI
IDLEWILD
INTERLUDE
IRON RING
ISLE OF AVES
JINKS BAND
JUNGLE
LADERA
LAND OF HAPPINESS

LANDS END
LAST CHANCE
LOST ANGELS
MADRONE
MANDALAY
MATHIEU
MEDICINE LODGE
MEYERLING
MONKEY BLOCK
MOONSHINERS
MORO
NECATAMA
OUTPOST
OWLERS
OWL'S NEST
OZ
PARSONAGE
PELICANS
PIEDMONT
PIG 'N WHISTLE
PINK ONION
POISON OAK
POKER FLAT
POW WOW
PUMA
RATTLERS
RED FIRE
RENDEVOUS
RIVER LAIR
ROARING
ROMANY
ROUGH 'N READY
SAHARA
SANTA BARBARA
SEMPERVIRENS
SEQOUYAH
SEVEN TREES
SHELDRAKE LODGE

SHOESTRING
SILVERADO SQUATTERS
SKIDDOO
SKYHI (SKY-HIGH)
SLEEPY HOLLOW
SNUG HARBOR
SONS OF REST
SONS OF TOIL
SPOT
STAR AND GARTER
STOWAWAY
SUNDODGERS
SUNSHINERS
TARRYTOWN
THALIA
THREE THREES (333)
THE BINDERS
TIMBUKTU

T-N-T
TOTEM IN
TOYLAND
TURNERVILLE
UPLIFTERS
UTUKULU
VALHALLA
VALLEY OF THE MOON
WAYSIDE LOG
WEB
WHISKEY FLAT
WHOO CARES
WILD OATS
WOHWOHNO
WOOF
YE MERRIE YOWLS
ZACA

1930 Camp List

ABBEY
ACACIA
AFTERGLOW
AMES
ANCHOR WATCH
AORANGI
ARTISTS
AVIARY
BALD EAGLE
BAND
BATES-FORD
BEACH
BEACON
BETTER 'OLE
BLUE HERON
BOTTS-ZIMMERMAN

BROMLEY
CAMELS
CARLTON
CASITA LINDA
CAVE MAN'S
CHETOLAH
CHICAGO
CHORUS
CLARK-MAGEE-OLNEY
CLIFF DWELLERS
COPPERHEAD
CRIPPLES
CROCKER-STILLMAN
CROSS ROADS
CROWS NEST
CUCKOO'S NEST

DARK ROOM
DERELICTS
DRAGONS
DUNNE, A.B.
DUNNE, F.H.
EL CAPITAN
EL TORO
ELWORTHY
ESPLANDIAN
EXILES
EXPRESS
FES-DEN
FORE PEAK
'49 CAMP
GREEN MASK
GREGORY-SCHINDLER
HALCYON
HALL
HALL-HAMLIN
HATFIELD
HAVEN, THE
HERMITS
HICKS
HILL BILLIES
HILLSIDE
HOWELLERS
HUALAPAI
ICONOCRABS
INTERLUDE
ISLE OF AVES
JAVA
KATY DID
KEBYAM
KELLOGG-WHITE
KIAWALLA
KLINK-RUNYON
KONTENT
KROGNESS

KURAN
LADERA
LAND OF HAPPINESS
LAST CHANCE
LOBINGIER
LOG
LOOP
LOST ANGELS
MACE
MADRONE
MANDALAY
MARYLAND
McLAREN
MEDICINE LODGE
MEESE
MIDWAY
MITCHELL
MONASTERY
MOONSHINERS
MORO
NAZDAR
NEC NATAMA
ORCHESTRA
OUTPOST
OWLS NEST
PAINT POT
PARSONAGE
PEBBLE BEACH
PELICANS
PIEDMONT
PIG AND WHISTLE
POISON OAK
POMEROY
POW WOW
PUMA
RAINBOW
RATTLERS
REDFIRE

RIXFORD-SYMMES
ROARING
ROBERTSON
ROBINSON, WALTER H.
ROGERS
ROMANY
RUSSELL
SAN FRANCISCO BANK
SANS GENE
SANTA BARBARA
SCHNEIDER
SELDOM INN
SEMPER VIRENS
SEQUOIA
SEVEN TREES
SHIELS
SINE NOMIE
SKIDDOO
SLOSS-DIAMOND
SNUG HARBOR
SONS OF REST
SONS OF TOIL
SPOT
STAR AND GARTER
STEINMETZ
STERLING
STEWART

STOWAWAYS
STROLLERS
STYX
SUNDODGERS
SUNSHINERS
SWALLOW
SWAGATAM
SWASTIKA
TAFT-HENRY
TANTALUS
TARANTULAS
TARRYTOWN
THALIA
TIE BINDERS
T-N-T
TOIYAK-OAYAK
TOTEM INN
TOYLAND
TUNERVILLE
UPLIFTERS
WANDERER
WAYSIDE INN
WELAKAHAU
WOOF
YE COUNTY GAOL
YE MERRIE YOWLS
YOUNG

APPENDIX B

Non illigitamus carborundum

(Don't let the bastards get you down)

Bohemian Grove Member List, 2010

NOTE: This is the most recent membership list the publisher could obtain. Members are listed alphabetically by last name, first name, and middle initial. Their camp affiliation appears next to the member's name.

In addition to the names on this list, there are a number of participants who attended as guests or as speakers at annual enclaves whose names are not listed because they are not officially members of Bohemian Grove.

This is taken from an actual copy of the club's official membership list, obtained from Norcaltruth.org.

MEMBER	CAMP
A	
Abbey Douglas D.	Sundodgers
Abbott Frank W. Jr.	Moonshiners
Abernathy G. D. Jr.	Whoo Cares
Abernethy David Beaven	Sempervirens
Abnee A. Victor	Five Easy Pieces
Acquistapace James S.	Dragon
Adams Clifford S.	Valley of the Moon
Adams David Bruce	Tunerville
Adams Edward E.	Aviary
Adams Griffith H.	Totem In
Adams James T.	Meyerling
Adams Michael C.	Meyerling
Adams Peter S.	Skiddoo
Adams William H.	Meyerling
Agius Tancred E. A.	Valhalla
Aigner Dennis John	Jungle
Akers John F.	Mandalay
Aldinger William F.	Uplifters
Alexander Matthew D.	Pink Onion
Allen Francis Frederick	Wild Oats
Allen Peter Thatcher	Three Threes
Allen Rex	Totem In
Allen Robert H.	Wild Oats
Allen Wheatley	Wayside Log
Allison Ben M.	Puma
Alpert Bernard S.	Hill Billies
Alvarez Walter	Pelican
Ames Lawrence C. Jr.	Sons of Rest
Anderson Brenton W.	Sempervirens
Anderson Bruce Garrett	Web
Anderson David L.	Owls Nest
Anderson F. Allan	Totem In
Anderson Gunnar D.	MonkeyBlock
Anderson James G.	Aviary
Anderson Mark S.	Aviary
Anderson Martin	Sempervirens
Anderson Martin Carl	Cave Man
Anderson Ross S.	Silverado Squatters
Andrew Paul B.	Meyerling
Angeli Primo	Madrone
Aoun Joseph E.	Spot
Arguelles Romeo A.	Pelican
Argyros George L.	Lost Angels
Armacost Michael H.	Mandalay
Armacost Samuel H.	Mandalay
Armstrong David A.	Wayside Log
Armstrong Paul A.W.	Tunerville/Crossroads
Arnelle H. Jesse	Tarry Town
Arnold Carl D. III	Pig 'N Whistle
Arnold Robert M.	Hill Billies
Arnott Peter R.	Shoestring
Arscott David Gifford	Aviary
Ash Glenn J.	Dog House
Ashby Peter R.	Idlewild
Ashenfelter Orley Clark	CaveMan
Ashley Wm. Whitley	Sundodgers
Ashton Harris J.	Mandalay
Ashton William S.	Tunerville
Aspevig Clyde R.	Seven Trees
Atcheson David M.	Rendezvous
Ateljevich Sava	Band
Atkins Victor K. Jr.	Stowaway
Atkins William T.	Wild Oats
Atkinson Earle	Band
Atkinson Franklyn R.	Shoestring
Atkinson James B.	Sec. Natoma
Atkinson Richard C.	WildOats
Atwater H. B. Jr.	Mandalay
Augustine Norman R.	Pelican
Austrian Robert "Boz"	Aviary
Avery Bruce	Pink Onion
Ayres Bruce	Tie Binders
B	
Baanstad Paul H.	Dutch
Bacon Milton Edward	Green Mask
Bacon Thomas Edgertoo	Snug Harbor
Bade John E. Jr.	Cool-Nandar
Baggott Kenneth B.	Owl's Nest
Bailard Thomas E.	Santa Barbara
Bailey Arthur E.	Halcyon
Bajpai K. Shankar	Totem In
Bakaly Charles G. Jr.	Lost Angels
Baker Cameron	Thalia
Baker G. Leonard Jr.	Spot
Baker James A. III	Woof
Baker William Leonard Jr.	Romany
Ballachey John Maturin	Sundodgers
Ballard Robert D.	Mandalay
Baltimore David	Silverado Squatters
Bancroft James R.	Owlers
Bancroft Paul III	Hill Billies
Bancroft Paul Marshall	Owlers
Banker William H. Jr.	Crow's Nest
Bannan C. Forrest	Lost Angels
Barbour Haley	Bascom
Bark Dennis Laistner	Sahara
Barker Dwight L.	Lard's Em
Barker Peter K.	Stowawa
Barlow Edward L.	Lard's Em
Barnard Bailey Stone	Valley of the Moon
Barnard David H.	Jinks Band
Barnard Timothy Henry	Wet
Barnard William M.	Aviar
Barnes William B.	Tunerville
Barnett Thomas W.	Tunerville
Baron Barry C.	Five Easy Piece
Bartlett Philip C.	Skiddoo
Barton Philip E.	Aviary
Barton Thomas Lewis	Spot/Aviar
Bass James E.	Isle of Ive
Bass Lee M.	Zaca
Bass Richard D.	Midway
Bates Charles W.	Pink Onion
Bates Nicholas L.	Pink Onion
Baum Marc Hampton	Band
Baumgartner J. Peter	Silverado Squatters
Baxter Charles Baker	Tie Binder
Baxter Thomas W.	Tie Binder
Beach Robert S.	Medicine Lodge
Beall Donald R.	Mandalay
Beardsley R. Duncan	Bella Union
Bechtel Gary H.	Care Less
Bechtel Riley P.	Mandalay
Bechtel S. D. Jr.	Mandalay
Beck Joseph Charles	Tunerville
Beck Bill	Fore Peak
Beckett John R.	Sempervirens
Bedford Peter B.	Sahara
Beebe Bruce Elliott	Medicine Lodge
Beebe Morton Pritchet	Land of Happiness
Behrendt Richard John	Woo
Beim Robert B.	Hermits
Bell Martin T.	Aviary
Bell Robert F. Rich	Aviary
Bellis G. Gordon	Piedmont
Belushi James A.	Woof
Bennington James L.	Totem In
Bennington William J.	Totem In
Benson John E.	Tyland
Benson Mark	Jinks Band
Bentley Clay	Valley of the Moon
Bentley Donald C.	Thalia
Bentley William	Moonshiners
Benway Randall Mark	Aviary
Berens Thomas P.	Pig 'N Whistle
Berg Shelton	Owl's Nest
Berggruen John	Uplifters
Berglund William R.	Tie Binders
Bergman John	Band
Berolzheimer Charles P. II	Land of Happiness
Berry Jeffrey G.	Piedmont
Berry Kenneth G.	Skiddoo
Bertero Richard J.	Skyhi
Bertges Jack R.	Ye Merrie Yowls
Besser Kenneth Holt	Outpost
Bethards Jack M.	Dog House
Bettis Harry	Last Chance
Bice Richard Edwin	Jinks Band
Bickel John H.	Medicine Lodge
Biggs Anthony Harcourt	Tie Binders
Biggs Michael H.	Tunerville
Bigham Michael F.	Midway
Billington James H.	Hill Billies
Bingham Robert C.	Totem In
Bingham Wheelock Richard Jr.	Tunerville
Bjorkluod David	Sequoyah
Black Charles A. Jr.	Care Less
Blackman Richard B.	Crow's Nest
Blake Anthony F.	Tunerville
Bliss William W.	Piedmont
Blumenkranz Mark	Abbey
Board Charles L. Jr.	Thalia
Boardman Eric Charle	Shoestring
Boardman William K. Jr.	Aviary
Bobrow Morris David	Poler Flat
Bodine Murray G.	Cuckoo's Nest
Bodman Richard S.	Midway
Boeck Lawrence G.	Aviary
Boesch Robert J.	Band
Bogardus Andrew L.	Totem In
Bogardus Peter B.	Totem In
Bohannon David D. II	Tie Binders
Bohannon Scott E.	Tie Binders
Bohn John A. Jr.	Sempervirens
Bolton George	Skyhi
Bonaparte Robert Edward Lee	Ants
Bond Charles	Pelican
Bonney J. Dennis	Cave Man
Borda Richard J.	Sempervirens
Borgwardt John	Star & Garter
Borgwardt Kurt	Star & Garter
Boring Dix	Pig 'N Whistle
Boring Douglas	Pig 'N Whistle
Borwick Jamie	Moro
Bosch Mark Alan	Mathieu
Bosche John Volkman	Whisky Flat
Bosche Lawrence M.	Seven Trees
Boskin Michael J.	Hill Billies
Bost Frederic W.	Whisky Flat
Bostan Andrei S.	Tunerville
Boswell G. Michael	Dog House
Boswell James W.	Moonshiners
Bowes William K. Jr.	Hill Billies
Bowman Michael L.	Outpost
Bradley Michael P.	Cliff Dwellers
Bradley Richard J.	Cliff Dwellers
Bradley Steven G.	Highlanders
Bradner James R.	Meyerling
Brady David W.	Sempervirens
Brady Nicholas F.	Mandalay
Brady Patrick H. (Ret)	Idlewild
Brady William J.	Totem In
Brandenburger Don	Tarry Town
Brandin Mark S.	Druids
Breck Peter Beaudoux	Stowaway
Breed George G.	Hideaway
Brennan Craig D.	Aviary
Brennan James E.	Band
Bresler Michael Jay	Band
Bressie Elbert Paul	Wild Oats
Breyer Charles R.	Shoestring
Briggs Donald T. Jr.	Sunbinders
Bright Lee	Band
Brill John Marty Jr.	Hermits
Briner Robert Lee	Brakula
Brink Benjamin M.	Aviary
Brink Robert R.	Fore Peak
Brinton William W.	Pig 'N Whistle
Briscoe Lawrence W.	Spot
Bronson William H.	Owlers
Brooks Peter Kendall	Poler Flat
Brooks T. Anthony	Derelicts
Brose William George	Hideaway
Brown Douglas Minge	Sempervirens
Brown Ned	Santa Barbara
Brown F. Frederick	Lard's End
Brown Keith Lapham	Woof
Brown Philip F. Jr.	Faraway
Browne Christopher P	Medicine Lodge
Browne Merrick Jr.	Rough 'r Ready
Browne Timothy Otis	Medicine Lodge
Brownson Howard E.	Aviary
Brucher Peter V.	Lani's End
Brummel Jon	Tunerville
Brush Gerald F. Jr.	Cool-baxdar
Brush Spencer M.	Crows Nest
Bryan Hamilton V. II	Piedmont
Bryan J. Stewart I	Owlers
Bryan John M.	Hill Billies
Bryan Parker S.	Tie Binders
Bryant Ernest A. III	Lost Angels
Buck Richard P.	Silverado Squatters
Buckley Christopher	HillBillies
Buffett Jimmy	Wayside Log
Bulkley Edward L.	Druids
Bull Donald	Meyerling
Bullard Edward Dickinson	Fiends of the Forest
Bullas Will	MonkeyBlock
Bulley Allan E. Jr.	Crows Nest
Bulotti Richard C.	Woof
Bundschu James T.	Band
Burdick Harold Hunt	Tarry Town
Burkett William C.	Timbuktu
Burnham Clark James	El Toro II
Burnham DeWitt K. Jr.	Wayside Log
Burress Richard T.	Wayside Log
Burrow Gerard Noel	Spot
Burrows F. Robert	Land of Happiness
Burrows William D.	Land of Happiness
Bush George H. W.	Hill Billies
Bush Michael J.	Ye Merrie Yowls
Busterud James P.	Faraway
Butler Dean Moore	Aviary
Byers Brook H.	Hill Billies
Byrnes Bryant H.	Snug Harbor
C	
Cagley James R.	Totem In
Cahill Edward Lyons	Friends of the Forest
Cahill J. Peter	Hualapai
Cahill John E. Jr.	Hill Billies
Cahill Richard F.	Hualapai
Cahill William R.	Pink Onion
Cakebread John E.	Tarry Town
Caldwell James E. Jr.	Dragon
Calhoun Alexander D.	Last Chance
Calkins John Thiers	Romany
Callan John C. Jr.	Sleepy Hollow
Callander Bruce Hardaway	Piedmont
Callander Charles L.	Faraway
Callander Clark N.	Midway
Callander John Kendrick	Cliff Dwellers
Callander John N.	Faraway
Callander Peter W.	Uplifters
Callaway Howard H.	Pelican
Callender William C.	Monastery
Camargo Carlos A.	Pelican
Cameron Anthony E.	Puma
Campbell Donald B.	Hualapai
Campbell Duncan H.	River Lair
Campbell Thomas Gordon	Band
Capobianco John	LOH/Jinks Band
Carey Michael R.	Owlers
Carlson Dane D.	Tunerville
Carlson Donald W.	Interlude
Carlson Mark D.	Skyhi
Carmassi Herman L.	Hideaway
Carmona Richard H.	Moro
Carroll Duane C.	Band
Carroll Fred L.	Stowaway
Carroll Philip J.	Wild Oats
Cartan Jim	Web

MEMBER	CAMP
Carter Brian Frank	Monkey Block
Carter George H	Edgehill
Carter James A.	Land of Happiness
Carter Timothy James	Aviary
Carter Todd	Aviary
Carter William	Owl's Nest
Casey Lyman H.	Uplifters
Cashin Skip	Camels
Casper Donald Andrew	Fore Peak
Cassiday Paul Richard	Sundodgers
Castellini Robert H.	Santa Barbara
Castle Donald George	Camels
Caufield Frank J.	Poison Oak
Caulkins William	Song Harbor
Cay John Eugene III	Valley of the Moon
Cella Peter Michael	Skiddoo
Cerny Keith J.	Aviary
Cerruti George	Zaca
Chalberg Thomas Walter Jr.	Aviary
Chamberlain David M.	Hill Billies
Chamberlain John W.	Cool-Nazdar
Chapman Duncan A.	Hill Billies
Chapman Philip D.	Whoo Cares
Char Devron H.	Ye Merrie Yowls
Charles Glen G.	Roaring
Charles Stanley Peter III	Tunerville
Chase Andy	Hualapai
Cheng Gregory	Aviary
Chick Warren Hyde	Ladera
Chiles Earle M.	Pow Wow
Chiles John G.	Rendezvous
Chinn Warren D.	Spot
Choper Jesse Herbert	Isle of Aves
Christie Dick	Woof
Cinelli Steven A.	Toyland
Clack David A.	Fore Peak
Clahan Eugene E.	Woof
Clair Pierson E. III	Owlers
Clapp John D.	Monkey Block
Clark James W.	Land of Happiness
Clark Michael C.	Aviary
Clark Richard J. III	Five Easy Pieces
Clark Richard W.	Aviary
Clarke Frederick	Unkulu
Classen James S.	Rough 'n Ready
Classen Willard J. Jr.	Rough 'n Ready
Cleary Joseph S.	Monkey Block
Cleary Mark W.	Cliff Dwellers
Cliff Lee H.	Tarry Town
Clopp Larry	Hideaway
Cloyd Marshall Preston	T-N-T
Cobb Charles E. Jr.	Owl's Nest
Coblentz William K.	Hill Billies
Coghlan John Philip	Care Less
Cohn Robert	Mandalay
Colbert Lester L. Jr.	Cuckoo's Nest
Colburn Greg	Tunerville
Colebourn Donald G.	Faraway
Coleman Lewis W.	Isle of Aves
Coleman William R.	Dog House
Collier Russell	Fore Peak
Collins Charles M.	Iron Ring
Collins Craig Bennett	Aviary
Collins George Robb	Green Mask
Colman Robert S.	Valley of the Moon
Colmery Harry W. Jr.	Piedmont
Colyer Wayne Allen	Jinks Band
Comann Tyler K.	Spot
Comartin Robert A.	Skyhi
Commanday Robert Paul	Aviary
Congdon Jeffrey H.	Timbuktu
Conger Harry M.	Isle of Aves
Conley Patrick	Moro
Conley Scott	Medicine Lodge
Connelly James D.	Sundodgers
Connick Robert E.	Aorangi/Swagatam
Connolly Will	Aviary
Conover C. Todd	Madrone
Conquest Edwin Parker Jr.	Shoestring
Conrad Barnaby III	Hill Billies
Considine Terry	Cave Man
Conte David	Aviary
Cook Robert E.	Land's End
Cook Sam B.	Last Chance
Cooke Lowell Thomas	Aviary
Cookson David E.	Jungle
Cookson James H.	Jungle
Cookson Michael David	Faraway
Cookson Richard	Jungle
Cookson Robert C.	Faraway
Cooley A. Crawford	Friends of the Forest
Cooley Floyd Owen	Band
Cooley Robert A.	Friends of the Forest
Coonan Kevin	Web
Cooper Allen B.	Camels
Cooper Barry	Sons of Toil
Cooper John L.	Thalia
Coppola John Michael	Jinks Band
Corbett Mike B.	Owl's Nest
Coriston James Michael	Edgehill
Cormia Neil	Band
Corneliuson William D.	Madrone
Cornish Hugh De Golia	Hualapai
Costello James Funsten	Outpost
Costello Joseph V. III	Moonshiners
Costello Joseph V. Jr.	Skyhi
Costigan Carlton G.	Seven Trees
Costle Douglas M.	Five Easy Pieces
Coulter Jamie B.	Dragon
Covington Christopher	Cool-Nazdar
Cowing Eric C.	Camels
Craft Cecil I.	River Lair
Craig Mitchell	Band
Craig Peter C.	Meyerling
Craig Robert W.	Five Easy Pieces
Crandall L. Dale	T-N-T
Crane Philip A. Jr.	Green Mask
Craves Evan	Tunerville
Crawford Bradley Cort	Aviary
Crawford J. Brooks M.D.	Abbey
Crocker Charles	Stowaway
Crocker William H.	Zaca
Cronan Daniel P.	Sleepy Hollow
Cronan Michael Patrick	Poker Flat
Cross James Allin	Tie Binders
Crossley John Parshley III	Nec Natama
Crow Harlan	Dog House/Midwas
Crumley Roger L.	Crossroads
Cullum James A. Jr.	Owl's Nest
Cummins Donal Casey	Wayside Log
Cunningham David E.	Care Less
Cureton Stewart Jr.	Valley of the Moon
Curlett John N. Jr.	Totem In
Curry James T. Jr.	Mandalay
Cushing Francis C. Jr.	Wayside Log
Cuthbert David L.	Mathieu
Cutter Curtis Brooks	Isle of Aves
D	
Dachs Alan M.	Hill Billies
Dagley William F.	Sunshiners
Dailey Peter H.	Pelican
Dailey William F.	Highlanders
Daley Scott	Tunerville
Dalrymple Brian	Band
Dalrymple James M.	Band
Daly Leo A. III	Stowaway
D'Amico Steven Joseph	Tunerville
Damner Bert	Whisky Flat
Danielsen Paul	Monastery
Danielson Lee	Santa Barbara
Dannemiller Thomas E.	Last Chance
Dapper Samuel M.	Sempervirens
Dart Stephen	Lost Angels
Davalos Gerald C.	Jungle
Davanzo Loris P.	Tunerville
Davenport David	Cave Man
Davey Craig S.	Pink Onion
Davidow William H.	Bella Union
Davies Paul L. Jr.	Piedmont
Davies Paul Lewis III	Piedmont
Davis Charles G. Jr.	Pelican
Davis Donald W.	Iron Ring
Davis James Edward	Jinks Band
Davis William L.	Sahara
Dawkins M. Vance Jr.	Bella Union
Dawson William J.	Monastery
Day Douglas W.	Totem In
Day Robert A.	Whoo Cares
Day T. J.	Tie Binders
Deane Andrew D.	Ye Merrie Yowls
Deane William	Dog House
deBenedetti John F.	Meyerling
Decker Frederick S.	Skiddoo
Decker Richard W. Jr.	Parsonage
Dedo Herbert H.	Land's End
DeFeo Neil P.	Land of Happiness
Dehmel Richard C.	Aviary
Delagnes R. Michael	Crossroads
DeLanoy Drake	Interlude
De Luchi Stephen F.	Five Easy Pieces
DeMaria Phillip A.	Five Easy Pieces
Demmon Roy Earl	Hualapai
Dennis Harry L. E.	Wayside Log
Dennis Reid W.	Midway
De Rosa Donald V.	Tarry Town
Derr K. T.	Mandalay
Desautels Marc Pierre	Faraway
De Silva Lytton	Tunerville
Desjardin Dennis Edmund	Lost Angels
DeSorrento James	Bella Union
Devening R. Randolph	Hermits
Devine Timothy A.	Lost Angels
De Voto Terence Alan	Moonshiners
Dewey Richard R. Jr.	Monastery
Dickason Bradford S.	Tie Binders
Dickenson Charles H.	Halcyon
Dickey Jonathan C.	Nec Natama
Dickey Mark M.	Sleepy Hollow
Dickover Stanley Jr.	Sheldrake Lodge
Dickson John D.	Woof
Diffenderfer G. Edward	Jinks Band / Monkey Block
Dingman Michael D.	Whoo Cares
Dingwell Scott	Madrone
Dini Robert Louis	Aviary
Dinnean Lawrence	Aviary
Ditz William Wallace	Moonshiners
Dixon Donald R.	Owl's Nest
Dobelle Evan S.	Land of Happiness
Dobies Joshua	Aviary
Docker W. F.	Sempervirens
Dockson Robert R.	Cuckoo's Nest
Docter Kenneth G.	Idlewild
Dodd Bill	Halcyon
Dohrmann Bruce P.	Seven Trees
Dohrmann Eric B.	Seven Trees
Dolan Arthur J. III	Crow's Nest
Doll Dixon Raymond	Midway
Domann William A. Jr.	Friends of the Forest
Donahoe Daniel J. III	Spot
Donner Alexander B.	Poison Oak
Donner Joseph W.	Poison Oak
Dorman David Wyatt	Stowaway
Dorsey Michael C.	Faraway
Dorward Donald F.	Wild Oats
Dostart Steven P.	Aviary
Doumani Peter J.	Wild Oats
D'Ovidio Gene J.	Idlewild
Down Gerald C.	Interlude
Downey Paul A.	Five Easy Pieces
Doyle Patrick F.	Medicine Lodge
Doyle Richard P. Jr.	Faraway
Drake Peter M.	Medicine Lodge
Draper Jerome C. Jr.	Sundodgers
Draper Timothy C.	Hualapai
Draper William H. III	Hill Billies
Dressel Chris J.	Sundodgers
Drewes Doug	Cool-Nazdar
Drewes John Frederick	Moonshiners
Drewes Robert C.	Cool-Nazdar
Drysdale George M.	Thalia
Duboc Robert M. Jr.	Wayside Log
Du Bois Grant P. III	Sheldrake Lodge
Duckhorn Daniel James	Cool-Nazdar
Ducommun Robert C.	Pink Onion
Duff Michael Patrick	Mathieu
Dunham Keith	Lost Angels
Dunlap William R.	Lost Angels
Dunne Robert M.	Tarry Town
Durney Michael K.	Five Easy Pieces
Duryea Leslie N. II	Lost Angels
Dwight Herbert M. Jr.	Sempervirens
Dyke James Trester	Pelican
E	
Eagan Thomas E.	Tunerville
Eastwood Clint	Roaring
Eberhard Andrew J.	Crossroads/Jinks Band
Eberhardt Douglass M. II	Roaring
Eberhardt Douglass M.	Roaring
Eberwein William W.	Aviary
Eckard George R.	Moonshiners
Eden Theodore A.	Sons of Toil
Edwards Cree A.	Hualapai
Edwards Paul C.	Hualapai
Edwards William L.	Hualapai
Edwards William C.	Hill Billies
Egan Gerald E.	Skyhi
Egan Mark	Monastery
Elachi Charles	Spot
Elder John W.	Hualapai
Elicker Paul Hamilton	Owlers
Elliott George	Crossroads
Ellis Stephen A.	Hill Billies
Ely George W. Jr.	Abbey
Ely Leonard W.	Sempervirens
Engel Albert O.	Ladera
Englert Joseph S. Jr.	Snug Harbor
Englert Stephen L.	Snug Harbor
Epstein Charles J.	Tunerville
Erskine R. Andrew	Sheldrake Lodge
Ervin Howard Guy III	Highlanders
Escher Caspar H. Jr.	Whisky Flat
Escher Thomas C.	Derelicts
Eshima Shinji Takane	Tunerville
Esrey William T.	Mandalay
Essert William	Tunerville
Evans Andrew W.	Camels
Evans Julian	Isle of Aves
Evans Richard B.	Pelican
Evans Robert Beverley Jr.	Tie Binders
Everdell Coburn D.	Shoestring
Evers Albert John II	Whisky Flat
Evers Henry K.	Hill Billies
Evers William D	Hill Billies
Evers William Dohrmann Jr.	Faraway
Evers Williamson M.	Hualapai
F	
Faggioli Justin M.	Silverado Squatters
Farley William E.	Timbuktu
Farwell G. Nicholas	Interlude
Faulhaber Charles	Isle of Aves
Fay Michael George	Pow Wow
Fay Paul B. III	Stowaway
Federal William Aubrey Jr.	Moonshiners
Felchlin J. Christopher	Owlers
Feichlin James A.	Wayside Log
Feld Alan D.	Valley of the Moon
Felder Louis E. Jr.	Last Chance
Felton Paul Jacques	Cliff Dwellers
Ferdon Jonathan	Fore Peak
Ferguson Robert K.	T-N-T

MEMBER	CAMP
Fernbach Stephen A.	Band
Fessler Daniel W.	Ladera
Fesus George J.	Totem In
Feulner Edwin J. Jr.	Cave Man
Field Gregg	Owl's Nest
Field James L.	Moonshiners
Field Robert W. Jr.	Moonshiners
Fields Robert A.	Band
Filter W. Jeffrey	Idlewild
Fimrite Ronald D.	Meyerling
Finger Jerry Elliott	Wild Oats
Finger John William	Monkey Block
Finn Howard J.	Roaring
Fisher Kenneth L.	Owlers
Fisher Robert	Owl's Nest
Fitzmyers Thomas J.	Edgehill
Fitzpatrick Michael J. Sr.	Uplifters
Flanigan Peter M.	Mandalay
Flax Robert J	Aviary
Fleischer L. Walter	Oz
Fleming Tod N.	Band
Fletcher James Jay	Monastery
Flood James C.	Stowaway
Flynn Gregory Grant	Cliff Dwellers
Fogelberg Earl V.	Monastery
Fogelsong Norman A.	Moro
Foley Dennis	Sequoyah
Foley S. Robert Jr.	Hillside
Folger Lee Merritt	Zaca
Folger Roy A. Jr.	Pig 'N Whistle
Follett Alan Lee	Medicine Lodge
Ford Bernerd J.	T-N-T
Forrester Eugene P.	Toyland
Forster Nicholas S.	Rattlers
Forward Robert H. Jr.	Totem In
Foscue Charles T.	Woof
Foster T. Jack III	Aviary
Foster Paul S. III	Sunshiners
Foster T. Jack Jr.	Owl's Nest
Fotre Terry Vincent	Sundodgers
Fournier Dudley J.	Pink Onion
Fournier Dudley J. Jr.	Rough 'n Ready
Fox Fred	Tunerville
Franich Steven	Rough 'n Ready
Frank Anthony M.	Bald Eagle
Frank Joseph P.	Hillside
Frank Randall Palmer	Bald Eagle
Fraser Michael Edward	Wild Oats
Fraughton Edward J.	Wayside Log
Frazier Peter B.	Medicine Lodge
Fredrich Daniel S.	Tunerville
Freeberg Don	Wayside Log
Freeman Bradford M.	Lost Angels
Freeman Robert A.	Bella Union
Freemon Richard D.	Last Chance
French John Stephenson	Moonshiners
Freund James C.	Midway
Fridell Squire	Ukukulu
Friedman Gary D.	Band
Friedman Jerry	Woof
Friedman Tully M.	Midway
Friedman Michael A. M.D.	Lost Angels
Friedrichs Edward C. III	Bella Union
Friedrichs Jay H.	Bella Union
Fritz Lynn C.	Monastery
Frye Lawrence J.	Sundodgers
Fuery Charles P.	Aviary
Fuller Charles A.	Sons of Toil
Fuller Charles E.	Highlanders
Fuller Richard L.	Highlanders
Fulstone Richard N.	Green Mask
Fung Kenneth Hing Cheung	Owlers
Funsten James Johnston III	Crow's Nest
Furlotti Alexander	Woof
Furman Will	Aviary

G

MEMBER	CAMP
Gaither H. Rowan III	Friends of the Forest
Gaither James C.	Friends of the Forest
Galante Edward Elio	Cuckoo's Nest
Galvin Eugene G. M.D.	Hideaway
Galvin Sean	Zaca
Gamble George Thomas	Timbuktu
Gamble James A.	Land of Happiness
Gamble Launce E.	Piedmont
Gammill Lee M. Jr.	Land's End
Ganz Michael A.	Valhalla
Gardiner John J. III	Skyhi
Gardner Robert K.	Woof
Gardner Trent Rigel	Jinks Band
Garlinghouse Richard E. Jr.	Shoestring
Garrett Michael L.	Sons of Toil
Gasser Nolan Ira	Five Easy Pieces
Gates Milo S.	Derelicts
Gavin John A. G.	Lost Angels
Gazzaniga Michael S.	Dragon
Gee Sonny B.	Aviary
Gellert Fred Jr.	Silverado Squatters
Gelles George	Tunerville
Gensler David	Monastery
Gensler M. Arthur Jr.	Land of Happiness
Gentschel Richard Paul	Red Fire
Gergen David	Owl's Nest
Gerstner Louis V. Jr.	Midway
Giovannoni James P.	Bella Union
Giddings Dan	Mathieu
Giddings Daniel Arthur Jr.	Mathieu
Gidwitz Ronald J.	Midway
Gilbert Robert J.	Isle of Aves
Gilleran James E.	Sundodgers
Gilley R. Stevens	Pow Wow
Gilligan Patrick	Valley of the Moon
Gilmer Wendell Jerome	Romany
Ginn Samuel L.	Mandalay
Girard Stephen A.	Meyerling
Glenn Roger	Bella Union/Jinks Band
Gloger Robert Michael	Camels
Goddard C. Convers	Fore Peak
Goity Jean M.	Faraway
Goldman Kenneth S.	Tunerville
Goldsmith Robert H.	Cliff Dwellers
Good David E.	Medicine Lodge
Goodan Roger	Shoestring
Goode John G.	Green Mask
Goodrich Herbert A.	Aviary
Goodwin Kenneth James	Aviary
Goonewardene Nihal W.	Tie Binders
Gordon Dan	Ladera
Gordon Lindsay H.	Wild Oats
Gordon Robert Cochran III	Tie Binders
Gordon Stuart M.	Cliff Dwellers
Gore Gordon C.	Band
Gorman Timothy	Web
Goss Thomas A.	Sunshiners
Gotcher Peter C.	Haalapai
Gould Charles L. Jr.	Bromley
Grady Mark F.	Ukukulu
Grady Tyler V.	Owlers
Graffis Richard Dunn	Dog House
Graham Lawrence	Tie Binders
Grant Jack P.	Skiddoo
Gray Howard K.	Highlanders
Grayson Ellison Capers Jr.	Hillside
Grayson William Ellison	Seven Trees
Green Edward	Tunerville
Green J. Jeffrey	Wayside Log
Green Russell H. Jr.	Dog House
Green William Carbine	Hideaway
Green William George	Madrone
Green William L.	Whisky Flat
Greenberg Maurice R.	Cave Man
Greene Frank Perry	Camels
Greene J. J.	Aviary
Greene James H. Jr.	Uplifters
Greenlee Gordon W.	Idlewild
Greenwood Robert Hilliard	Jungle
Gregory David	Puma
Gregory Quintard	Moonshiners
Grether John M.	Friends of the Forest
Griesedieck Joseph E. Jr.	Totem In
Griffin Andrew	Skiddoo
Griffin Anthony	Shoestring
Griffin Cyrus Richard	Shoestring
Griffin Noah Webster	Sons of Toil/Aviary
Griffinger Theodore A. Jr.	Derelicts
Groen Eugene G.	Aviary
Grogan Thomas J. Jr.	Web
Grout Jack Miller	Rough 'n Ready
Gruber Frederick Wm.	Monastery
Grupe Greenlaw "Fritz" Jr.	Pelican
Gualco Ross	Jinks Band
Guggenheim David J.	Star & Garter
Guggenhime Richard J.	Midway
Guibara Albert	Land of Happiness
Guittard Gary	Owl's Nest
Gullett John M.D.	Bella Union
Gundunas Lewis Peter	Hillside
Gunther Erik C.	Pow Wow
Guppy George W.	Outpost

H

MEMBER	CAMP
Haas Robert Douglas	Isle of Aves
Hachman Timothy J.	T-N-T
Hackbarth Alfred E. Jr.	Land of Happiness
Haff John P.	Skiddoo
Hagerman David H.	Aviary
Halbe Stephen A.	Tunerville
Hale James C. III	Pink Onion
Hale Prentis C. III	Zaca
Hale Robert V.	Monastery
Hall Dwight La Rue	Band
Hall George G.	Cool-Nazdar
Hall Lee	Aviary
Hall Roderick C. M.	Haven
Hall Ted W.	Medicine Lodge
Hall William A.	Wild Oats
Halloran Michael J.	Sundodgers
Halverson Philip	Monastery
Hambrecht Wm. R.	Midway
Hamilton William R.	Mathieu
Hamlin Oliver D. III	Cool-Nazdar
Hammer Joseph F.	Woof
Hammersmith William C. III	Red Fire
Hammond Chaunce W. III	Dragon
Hammonds William E.	Woof
Hampson Dirk	Sons of Rest
Hampton Gregory J.	Poison Oak
Hancock John W. III	Dog House
Hanes R. Philip Jr.	Lost Angels
Hanna John Paul	Sempervirens
Haansel Henry	Monastery
Hansel Stephen E.	Land's End
Haansen John C.	Five Easy Pieces
Hansen Robert C.	Medicine Lodge
Hanson John E.	Cool-Nazdar
Hanson Paul Jr.	Aviary
Hanson Victor Davis	Pelican
Hardie John I.	Lost Angels
Hardwick Richard J.	Dog House
Hardwick Robert D.	Haven
Hardy Richard E.	Sundodgers
Hargrave Alexander W.	Aviary
Harley Alan D.	Care Less
Harp Vernon C. Jr.	Band
Harper Stephen S.	Star & Garter
Harries D. Griffith III	Totem In
Harris Jerrold B.	Totem In
Harris Lawrence W. III	Zaca
Harris Robert C. Jr.	Cliff Dwellers
Harrison Michael A.	Sempervirens
Harrison Walter F. III	Valley of the Moon
Hart Bruce W.	Pig 'N Whistle
Hart Douglas E.	Pig 'N Whistle
Hart George D. Jr.	Pig 'N Whistle
Hart Mickey	Hill Billies
Hart Thomas A.	Jinks Band
Harvey D. Peter	Derelicts
Harvey Robert A.	Sunshiners
Harvey Thomas E.	Hideaway
Harwood Edward S.	Rendezvous
Haskell Jeffrey R.	Tunerville
Hasler William A.	Spot
Hauer John R.	Mathieu
Hauser Kurt	Roaring
Hawley Philip M.	Mandalay
Hawley Stephen H.	Tie Binders
Haynes David A.	Sundodgers
Haynes Gilman B.	Jungle
Hazard Geoffrey C.	Druids
Hazard James Lockwood	Puma
Hazen Paul	Uplifters
Hazlehurst Thomas B.	Stowaway
Hazlett William S.	Camels
Hearney Richard D. USMC (Ret)	Outpost
Hearst William R. III	Owl's Nest
Hebert Victor A.	Midway
Hecht Kenneth G. Jr.	Wild Oats
Hedrick William Scott	Valley of the Moon
Heidrich A. Grant	Highlanders
Heidt John M.	Monastery
Heil Ross F.	Poker Flat
Heimbucher Robert A.	Sheldrake Lodge
Heinmiller Dale R.	Band
Heintz Frank T.	Tunerville
Hemphill Charles L.	Poison Oak
Henderson Brian E.	Fore Peak
Henderson James A.	Seven Trees
Henderson Wellington S. Jr.	Uplifters
Hendrix Clifford R. Jr.	Idlewild
Henninger Daniel P.	Five Easy Pieces
Henriksen Thomas H.	Cave Man
Herbeck Robert William	Whoo Cares
Herrick Jerome Neal	Puma
Herrick Stephen Brooks	Piedmont
Herrington John S.	Parsonage
Hewett Arthur E.	Valley of the Moon
Hewlett Walter B.	Tunerville
Hewlett William A.	Highlanders
Heydorn William H.	Hideaway
Heywood Robert G.	Aviary
High Kenneth G. Jr.	Crow's Nest
Higson John W. Jr.	Meyerling
Hildreth Robert	Sempervirens
Hilger Leslie Guy M.D.	Sequoyah
Hill Brian A.	Hideaway
Hill Frank de Milt	Sundodgers
Hill George C. III	Land of Happiness
Hill Kent Walthall	Hermits
Hill Scott Clayton	Hermits
Hill William W.	Medicine Lodge
Hillis J. Stanley	Whisky Flat
Hills Austin E.	Last Chance
Hilton John R.	Wild Oats
Hinckley Robert C.	Dragon
Hoar Joseph P. USMC (Ret)	Wayside Log
Hobin Patrick S.	Dragon
Hockenberry Tim	Wild Oats
Hoffman Robert Butler	Midway
Hofmann John Richard Jr.	Thalia
Hogan William H. III	Jinks Band
Hogan R. Stephen	Lost Angels
Hogan V. Michael	Pelican
Hoganson John A.	Toyland
Hogland William D.	Piedmont
Holt Benjamin D.	Outpost
Holt Benjamin D. III	Outpost
Holt Douglas G.	Outpost
Holt Nicholas	Outpost
Holt Nicholas V	Outpost
Holt Peter M.	Wayside Log
Holt W. Stanley	Wayside Log
Honeyman David E. Jr.	Pink Onion
Honour Roger W.	Band
Hood Michael M.	Web
Hooker Anthony S.	Timbuktu
Hooper Ralph Wilson	Meyerling
Hoopes L. Scott	Cliff Dwellers

MEMBER	CAMP
Lundquist Weyman J.	River Lair
Lurie Robert A.	Shoestring
Luther Homer L. Jr.	Woof
Lynn Douglas G.	Snug Harbor
Lyons Irving F. III	Moonshiners

M

MacAllister John	Aviary
MacBride Thomas J. Jr.	Bella Union
MacColl William B. Jr.	Midway
MacCorkle Emmett W.	Bella Union
MacDonald Graeme L.	Highlanders
MacDonald Kirkpatrick	Silverado Squatters
Macdonald Peter S.	Highlanders
MacDonald William John	Crossroads
MacDonnell Robert I.	Uplifters
MacGeorge James A.	Bella Union
Machette Michael H.	Cool-Nazdar
Mackenzie Roger D.	Medicine Lodge
Mackinlay Ian	Wayside Log
MacLean Angus L. Jr.	Hill Billies
MacNaughton Malcolm Jr.	Camels
Macurdy John	Sundodgers
Madden James S.	Dragon
Madden Richard B.	Midway
Madding Bruce W.	Thalia
Magnuson Richard A.	Midway
Mahany Brian Douglas	Monkey Block
Maher John F.	Lost Angels
Maier Robert W.	Wayside Log
Main Stephen T.	Tunerville
Mallari R. Peter	Aviary
Maloney Graham	Timbuktu
Maloney Michael J.	Owlers
Malott James S.	Mathieu
Malott Robert H.	Silverado Squatters
Maltbie Roger I.	Whoo Cares
Mancini Brooks T.	Bella Union
Mancini Jay C.	Wayside Log
Mancini Philip Woodson	Skiddoo
Mandigo Clark R. II	Five Easy Pieces
Mandle Roger	Dragon
Manning Edward M. III	Web
Manseau Robert B.	Aviary
Marcelli Victor Ottavio	Monkey Block
Marchesi Silvano B.	Tunerville
Mardikian Haig G.	Cave Man
Margaretten William	Abbey
Margolin Edwin Alan	Jinks Band
Markison Robert E.	Tarry Town
Marks Robert Thomas	Puma
Maroney John F.	Piedmont
Marquardt David F.	Zaca
Marshall Donald Ian	Tarry Town
Marston Jeffrey L.	El Toro II
Marston Michael	Wayside Log
Marszal Edward R.	Wohwohno
Martin Christopher J.	Zaca
Martin David Orem	Tunerville
Martin Francis A. III	Uplifters
Martin Fredric Wayne	Aviary
Martin George F. Jr.	Hideaway
Martin Jay R.	Land's End
Martin John F.	Sheldrake Lodge
Martin Richard Wilson	Aviary
Martz C. Thomas	Monastery
Maryatt David E.	Owlers
Marymor Rodman J.	Band
Maslin Philip Star II	Aviary
Mason Arthur D.	Bella Union
Mateo Segundo	Piedmont
Matheson James	Tunerville
Matthews Christopher J.	Dragon
Mathews Scott	Hill Billies
Matthews William C. Jr.	Silverado Squatters
Maus Donald M.	Web
Mayne Stephen S.	Isle of Aves
Maze George S.	Snug Harbor
McAfee Ward M.	Dragon
McAuliffe Richard Charles Jr.	Monastery
McAuliffe Stephen B.	Cool-Nazdar
McBaine J. Patterson	Five Easy Pieces
McCabe Charles K.	Puma
McCabe Eugene A.	Iron Ring
McCall Ernest H.	Tarry Town
McCann Edward Francis II	Outpost
McCann William D.	Valhalla
McCarthy John J. Jr.	Band
McCarthy Steven Brian	Parsonage
McCaulou Kenneth H.	Tunerville
McCaw Bruce R.	Wohwohno
McClatchy J. J.	Highlanders
McClatchy William Briggs	Better 'Ole
McCloud Kimball P.	Poison Oak
McComish John H.	Pig 'N Whistle
McCorkle Chester O.	Jungle
McCown George E.	Land of Happiness
McCoy Bowen H.	Owl's Nest
McCrea Peter	Medicine Lodge
McCrea Thomas P. III	Tie Binders
McCrea Frederick H. II	Medicine Lodge
McCrohan James J.	Tunerville
McCubbrey J. Bruce	Aviary
McCullough Goodall W. Jr.	Skiddoo
McCune Allan A.	Interlude
McCune, USN (Ret.) J.	Denver Hideaway
McCune James D.	Ladera
McDonald Ian Bruce	Band
McDonald Paul Joseph	Better 'Ole
McDonald T. J.	Cool-Nazdar
McDowell W. Patrick	Bella Union
McElnea Jeffrey K.	Tie Binders
McElnea William H. Jr.	Tie Binders
McEsdy John D.	Shoestring
McEvoy Nion T.	Poison Oak
McGarry Christopher T.	Tunerville
McGettigan Charles C.	Zaca
McGinley Michael	Aviary
McGovern Francis E.	Owl's Nest
McGowan Matthew B.	Parsonage
McGowan Michael B.	Parsonage
McGuinness Joseph Patrick	Ladera
McGuire Michael T.	Utukulu
McHugh Robert Anthony III	Skyhi
McIlhenny Paul C. P.	Sahara
McKannay Richard H. Jr.	Owlers
McKay Brendan Patrick	Tie Binders
McKee W. Stuart	Roaring
McKelvy Alfred D. 'Tod' Jr.	Aviary
McKenna Edward A.	Aviary
McKennon Keith R.	Sunshiners
McKissick Carson R.	Tie Binders
McKnight Paul C.	Tie Binders
McLaughlin Andrew C. III	Pig 'N Whistle
McLaughlin Peter Bennet	Sleepy Hollow
McLaughlin Thomas O.	Esplanadian
McLellan Bruce B.	Seven Trees
McManigal Roderick A.	Moro
McMicking Henry C.	Haven
McMurtry Burton J.	Woof
McNab James III	Skiddoo
McNabb Mark Hopkins	Aviary
McNamara Daniel Forbes	Pig 'N Whistle
McNaughton Raymond J.	Utukulu
McNay John Wesley	Valhalla
McNear Denman K.	Uplifters
McNeil Dennis A.	Owl's Nest
McNeill H. Russell	Medicine Lodge
McNellis John E.	Interlude
McNiff Kevin L.	Aviary
McNulty Michael Thomas	Web
McPherson Michael C.	Sleepy Hollow
McQuade Donald A.	Hideaway
McQuarrie Robert Bruce Jr.	Poker Flat
McReynolds Thomas P.	Sunshiners
McWilliams Keith B.	Thalia
Mead Harold B.	Crossroads
Meakin James W.	Jungle
Meakin Thomas E.	Jungle
Meblin Matthew B.	Jinks Band
Mechan William E. III	Sempervirens
Meese Edwin III	Cave Man
Megeath Samuel A. III	Cuckoo's Nest
Megert Van	Utukulu
Mehran Alexander R.	Stowaway
Meister E. H. "Ned"	Monastery
Mel Howard Charles	Silverado Squatters
Mellor Robert E.	Whisky Flat
Melvoin Jeffrey D.	Aviary
Mendelson Alan C.	Cliff Dwellers
Merchant Michael A.	Zaca
Merrill Steven L.	Woof
Merriman Dwight L. III	Santa Barbara
Merriman Dwight L. Jr.	Santa Barbara
Merten David F.	Abbey
Messmer Harold M. Jr.	Mandalay
Metheny Alan E.	Meyerling
Metheny Johnny	Hermits
Mettier Stacy R. Jr.	Totem In
Metz Thomas F.	Lost Angels
Meunier Louis M.	Aviary
Meyer Donald R.	Last Chance
Meyer Nation	Fore Peak
Meyersieck Kenneth W.	Tie Binders
Michael Jay Dee	Land's End
Michael Peter Z.	Spot
Michelson Michael W.	Uplifters
Mielke Frederick W. Jr.	Toyland
Milam Kenneth E.	Cliff Dwellers
Miles Chipman	Crow's Nest
Millar Richard W. Jr.	Idlewild
Millar Roger J.	Highlanders
Miller Anthony T.	Totem In
Miller Arjay	Sempervirens
Miller David Earl	Valhalla
Miller Edward D.	Star & Garter
Miller Henry S.	Meyerling
Miller J. Sanford	Highlanders
Miller O'Malley M.	Lost Angels
Miller Peter B.	Mathieu
Miller Richard S.	Green Mask
Miller Robert Gordon	Medicine Lodge
Miller Ronald Dean	Star & Garter
Miller Stephen R.	Cool-Nazdar
Miller Stephen T. B.	Bella Union
Miller Steven H.	Poison Oak
Miller Terry	Wild Oats
Milligan Marshall C.	Friends of the Forest
Milne Robert	Land of Happiness
Minor David R.	Owlers
Miottel W. John Jr.	Wayside Log
Mitroff George B.	Sheldrake Lodge
Molnar David M.	Nec Natama
Mondavi Michael	Midway
Monfredini James Joseph	Skiddoo
Monson Dwight Lindsay	Red Fire
Montgomery George G. Jr.	Santa Barbara
Montgomery H. DuBose	Sundodgers
Montgomery Matthew	Tunerville
Montgomery Thomas	Dog House
Moore Douglas G.	Pig 'N Whistle
Moore George B.	Haven
Moore James Rolph Jr.	Pig 'N Whistle
Moore James Thaddeus III	Pink Onion
Moore Joseph Gartland	Pink Onion
Moore Peter Martin	Pink Onion
Moore Robert B. Jr.	Sleepy Hollow
Moore Stephen A.	Tunerville
Moore Thomas E.	Land's End
Moore Thomas W. Jr.	Cuckoo's Nest
Moores William York	Tunerville
Morey Charles L.	Whisky Flat
Morgan Charles F.	Stowaway
Morgeas Edwin H.	Mandalay
Morley H. Barclay	Sunshiner
Morris Charles Kendrick	Spot
Morris Thaine R.	Mathieu
Morris William C.	Lost Angels
Morrish Tom	Wayside Log
Morrish William B.	Puma
Morrison R. Scott Jr.	Whisky Flat
Morrison Richard H. Jr.	Hideaway
Morrow Robert P. III	Derelicts
Morse Bryan F.	Aviary
Morse James R.	Tarry Town
Mortarotti John L.	Tunerville
Mortensen Earl L. Jr.	Tunerville
Motlow John Geoffrey	Derelicts
Moulin Thomas M.	Edgehill
Mourier Pierre-Francois	Three Threes
Moxley Michael	Aviary
Muhs E. H. Ted	Druids
Muhs Peter L.	Druids
Mule Deer Gary C.	Whoo Cares
Mulford David A.	Star & Garter
Mulford David Campbell	Mandalay
Mullane John J. Jr.	Idlewild
Muller Martin	Three Threes
Muller Richard A.	Moro
Muller Timothy Matthew	Green Mask
Mullin Peter W.	Skyhi
Mullins Brian Thayer	Spot
Mumford H. G. (Toby)	Faraway
Munks Greg	Hualapai
Murakami Michael T.	Hillside
Murdoch Colin	Pig 'N Whistle
Murdock Deroy	Medicine Lodge
Murphy Leo J	Skiddoo
Murray Daniel Buntin	Cliff Dwellers
Murray Dwight H. Jr.	Hermits
Murray John Creighton	Pelican
Murray John Robert	Poker Flat
Murray Thomas J. Jr.	Monkey Block
Musto Peter Johnson	Medicine Lodge
Myatt J. Michael	Wayside Log
Myers Jack E.	Aviary
Myers Michael E.	Roaring
Myers Richard B. USAF Ret.	Midway

N

Nachtrieb Harold C.	Shoestring
Nagel Kenneth C.	Rendezvous
Nally Patrick Louis	Cliff Dwellers
Nash Jeffrey P.	Skiddoo
Nauman Peter B.	Outpost
Nawrocki W. A.	Jinks Band
Neblett G. Rives	Wayside Log
Nees John Morgan	Valhalla
Neff Thomas J	Haven
Nelson Bruce R.	Aviary
Nelson Fredric C.	Cool-Nazdar
Nelson Kipp MacQueen	Crossroads
Nelson S. Victor	Skyhi
Nelson Ward T.	Sunshiners
Nevolo Gary J.	Snug Harbor
Newbigging David K.	Cave Man
Newman Paul	Fore Peak
Nichol Harold	Wild Oats
Nichols Alan Hammond	Silverado Squatters
Nicholson William H.	Sons of Rest
Nicholson W. John	Highlanders
Niello David F.	Pow Wow
Niello Richard L.	Hillside
Niello Rick	Faraway
Niello Roger W.	Pow Wow
Niggeman L. Peter	Pow Wow
Nim Kenneth	Shoestring
Nishkian Levon H.	Toyland
Nixon Thomas Arthur	Bella Union
Noelke Carl B.	Aviary
Norris William F.	Wohwohno
North D. Warner	Silverado Squatters/Aviary
Nott Robert H.	Whisky Flat
Nouri Edmond J.	Zaca
Nouri Michael	Zaca
Nova Brian Kauakea	Poison Oak
Nowlin Wade T.	Tarry Town

MEMBER	CAMP

O

Oakley John B.	Sons of Rest
Oberndorf William Edward	Hill Billies
O'Brian Dillon	Midway
O'Brien George D. Jr.	Wayside Log
O'Connell Kevin A.	Dragon
O'Connor Jay H.	Wayside Log
O'Connor Scott H.	Faraway
O'Donnell James J.	Sons of Toil
Ogburn Matthew M.	Skiddoo
Ogburn Raymond R.	Tie Binders
Ohleyer Michael L.	River Lair
O'Keefe Sean	Wayside Log
Olcott Cornelius IV	Piedmont
Olds William Jr.	Abbey
Olds William Lee III	Abbey
O'Leary Paul A.	Medicine Lodge
Oliphant Patrick	Lost Angels
Olmsted Jonathan	Derelicts
Olsen George H. Jr.	Land of Happiness
Olson John F.	Haven
Olson Perry V.	Piedmont
O'Malley Peter	Cuckoo's Nest
O'Neill George D. Jr.	Romany
O'Neill Jeffrey Bryan	Skyhi
O'Neill Joseph I. III	Web
Ong John D.	Hill Billies
O'Reilly David J.	Mandalay
O'Reilly Terry	Bella Union
Osborn James R.	Tarry Town
Osborne Brent W.	Totem In
Osborne David H. III	Land's End
Osterling Ralph S.	Bella Union
Osthimer Charles E. III	Zaca
Otellini Paul S.	Monastery
Otter Richard C.	Medicine Lodge
Otto J. Gregory	Valhalla
Owens Bill USN (Ret.)	Silverado Squatters
Owsley John Q. Jr.	Land's End

P

Padian Kevin	Hideaway
Palm Charles G.	Cave Man
Palmer Barnaby	Tunerville
Pannill William G.	Pelican
Papadopoulos Panos	Sons of Toil
Parfit Matthew	Band
Parish Jeffrey J.	Aviary
Parker Harry S. III	Thalia
Parker Jack S.	Pelican
Parker Joseph L. Jr.	Valley of the Moon
Parker Robert Ted	Tunerville
Parkhurst Paul	Pig 'N Whistle
Parma Leon W.	Spot
Parry Dana G.	Wild Oats
Parsons Gerald E.	Faraway
Pattee Gordon Burleigh	Stowaway
Patterson Robert E.	Sempervirens
Patton Paul Lyon	Pig 'N Whistle
Paul Hartley	Whoo Cares
Paul James Cameron	Whoo Cares
Paulson Christopher L.	Pink Onion
Peck Rodney R. Esq.	Thalia
Pedley Dean A.	Druids
Pedley Eric A.	Druids
Pedley Rick	Care Less
Pelkan John R.	Ye Merrie Yowls
Pelosi Paul F.	Stowaway
Pendergast Gene E. Jr.	T-N-T
Perez Vincent	Monkey Block
Perry James Warren	Poker Flat
Perry Mark W.	Cliff Dwellers
Person Evert B.	Aviary
Petersen Neal L.	Band
Peterson Edward H.	Roaring
Peterson John H.	Isle of Aves
Peterson Kirk L.	Hideaway
Peterson Stephen F.	Isle of Aves
Petkevich J. Misha	Interlude
Pettit Tom	Wild Oats
Pettus David Wingfield	Dragon
Pfau George H. Jr.	Hill Billies
Pfeifer William L.	Nec Natama
Phelan Michael Aloysius	Midway/Fore Peak
Phelps J. Barton	Sempervirens
Phillips Dave	Lost Angels
Phillips William W.	Piedmont
Phipps Allen M.	Puma
Phleger Peter M.	Derelicts
Pickering Frederick B. Jr.	Derelicts
Pickford Stephen T.	Woof
Pierson Peter O'Malley	Madrone
Pigott Charles M.	Uplifters
Pigott Mark	Mandalay
Pillsbury Thomas E.	Rendezvous
Pinger Edward B. Jr.	Friends of the Forest
Pitts Thomas H.	Puma
Placzek F. Anthony	Timbuktu
Pliska Gregory L.	Five Easy Pieces
Podesta Robert Anthony	Five Easy Pieces
Poe David A.	Better 'Ole
Poe Robert C.	Better 'Ole
Poett Henry Williams III	Derelicts
Pogue Richard W.	Pelican
Pohli Richard R.	Tie Binders
Poland Bill R.	Hermits
Policy Carmen A.	Midway
Pollock James M.	Totem In
Pond Robert M. Jr.	Rough 'n Ready
Poole Bruce Christopher	Sleepy Hollow
Poole Christopher K.	Sleepy Hollow
Poole David W.	Owlers
Poole Edward G.	Owlers
Poole George A. Jr.	Crow's Nest
Pope Wayne E.	Shoestring
Popoff Frank P.	Sunshiners
Porter James W.	Tie Binders
Porter Mark Edward	Outpost
Porter Timothy C.	Rendezvous
Potochny James	Tunerville
Powell Colin L. USA (Ret.)	Mandalay
Powers Gilbert C.	Outpost
Prater Doy	Tunerville
Pratt James C.	Iron Ring
Prezant William A.	Hill Billies
Price P. Anthony	Thalia
Price P. Buford	Isle of Aves
Price William Stanley III	Hill Billies
Prindiville G. David	Meyerling
Pringle Mark L.	Sleepy Hollow
Priske Joseph L.	Utukula
Prusiner Stanley B.	Silverado Squatters
Prussia Leland S.	Sempervirens
Puckett Allen	Whoo Cares
Pulling Thomas L.	Edgehill
Pursell William Whitney	Totem In
Pynchon William E.	Tunerville

Q

Quarre Wilson Charles	Abbey
Quigg Thomas M.	Dragon
Quinn John	Wild Oats
Quist Robert L.	Sleepy Hollow
Qvale Bruce H.	Moonshiners
Qvale Jeffrey	Whoo Cares

R

Radke Edward Frederick III	Wohwohno
Rafferty Joseph V.	Hideaway
Raggio Nicholas O.	Sleepy Hollow
Raisbeck Clifford C. Jr.	Rattlers
Ralston Joseph W. USAF	Stowaway
Ramsey Brian E.	Aviary
Rasmuson Edward B.	Druids
Rawlings Kenneth Blair	Roaring
Rawson David R.	Monastery
Rawson Ronald Craig	Highlanders
Rayner Arno A.	Idlewild
Read J. Peter	Land of Happiness
Read Steven M.	Five Easy Pieces
Redlich C. R. Jr.	Zaca
Reed Thomas C.	Land of Happiness
Reeder Milton K.	Tie Binders
Rees W. Mason	Fore Peak
Reichardt Carl E.	Mandalay
Reilly James R. (Reg)	Cool-Nazdar
Reilly William K.	Sempervirens
Reinhart Floyd	Tunerville
Reininga John	Sempervirens
Reis Thomas S.	Dragon
Reiter Charles P.	Mathieu
Reiter James F.	Tunerville
Rendell Kenneth W.	Bella Union
Rennick Mark Eugene	Romany
Reppas George S.	Hillside
Reppas Robert G.	Hillside
Resh Vincent H.	Isle of Aves
Revill Clive Selsby	Shoestring
Reyes Carlos A.	Ladera
Reyes Julio	Ladera
Reynolds Jon Q.	Wild Oats
Reynolds Jonathan R.	Tie Binders
Reynolds Robert Joseph	Wayside Log
Reynolds Thomas B.	Crossroads
Reynoso Raul	Sunshiners
Rhodes John W. Jr.	Hideaway
Rice Henry F.	Whisky Flat
Rich Donald L.	Poker Flat
Rickards Peter C. M.D.	Toyland
Richardson Charles M. Jr.	Seven Trees
Richardson H. Leonard	Aviary
Richardson Harold L.	Edgehill
Richardson W. H.	Aviary
Richardson William C.	Monastery
Richart Ralph M.	Five Easy Pieces
Riehl Donald R.	Better 'Ole
Riley Benjamin K.	Sundodgers
Riley Patrick G.	Dragon
Riley William Thomas	Dragon
Ring Stewart Andrew	Oz
Ripsteen Jack B.	Ladera
Rissel Richard Carl	T-N-T
Ritchie C. Stewart III	Land of Happiness
Rivasplata Alfred A.	Tunerville
Robarts Drew Leland	Pig 'N Whistle
Robbins Lindsey Chaloner	Esplandian
Roberts George R.	Uplifters
Robertson Channing Rex	Highlanders
Robertson David G.	Monkey Block
Robertson Mark Owen	Monastery
Robinson Billy E.	Band
Robinson John F.	Uplifters
Rocha Antonio L.	Aviary
Rockefeller David	Stowaway
Rockefeller David Jr.	Stowaway
Rodenbaugh F. Hase	Sons of Rest
Rodriguez Carlos A.	Hermits
Rogers David N. USN (Ret.)	Sunshiners
Rogers Jack	Aviary
Rogers Roy G.	Dragon
Rogers Stephen John	Highlanders
Rogers T. Gary	Pelican
Rogich Sigmund	Midway
Rohn R. Jeffrey	Skiddoo
Rohr James E.	Land of Happiness
Rohr Thos	Roaring
Rojas Vincent R.	Dog House
Rollandi Victor Lawrence Sr.	Pink Onion
Romig Clifton S.	Aviary
Roosevelt Michael A.	Totem In
Rosati Mario M.	Isle of Aves
Rosch Thomas L.	Tie Binders
Rose Anthony Frederick	Shoestring
Rosekrans Adolph S.	River Lair
Rosekrans John S.	River Lair
Rosekrans Peter R.	River Lair
Rosenblatt Toby	Hill Billies
Rossi Robert D.	Totem In
Roth Douglas H.	Hualapai
Rowan Thomas Patrick	Woof
Rowe Peter Hamlin	Cool-Nazdar
Rowell Robert W.	Monastery
Rumsfeld Donald H.	Hill Billies
Runnels Charles B.	Cuckoo's Nest
Ruprecht David Martin	Woof
Rush R. Stockton III	Woof
Russell James N.	Fore Peak
Russell Thomas R.	Abbey
Rutherford George W.	Rendezvous
Ryan Donald Vincent	Edgehill
Ryan Gregory Paul	Thalia
Ryan Joseph	Lost Angels
Ryan Michael D.	Tunerville
Ryan Stephen J.	Cave Man
Ryan T. J. III	Tie Binders
Ryan Timothy P.	Sons of Toil

S

Saavedra Kevin C.	Band
Saffir Richard A.	Mathieu
Sakakeeny Gabriel	Tunerville
Salazar Phillip	Rattlers
Salestrom James Kevin	Five Easy Pieces
Salewski Anthony J.	Aviary
Salt Haddon N.	Wohwohno
Saltzer David L.	Aviary
Saltzer Rudolph B.	Wild Oats/Aviary
Sample Steven B.	Mandalay
Sample Wilton Wade	Faraway
Sandman John "Bert"	Parsonage
Saul B. Francis	Pelican
Saveri Guido	Esplandian
Saveri Richard Alexander	Esplandian
Sawyer Frederic A.	Sheldrake Lodge
Saxton Andrew E.	Land of Happiness
Scafidi Joseph A.	Shoestring
Scales Jeffrey M.	Sunshiners
Scarborough Phillip	Aviary
Schadlich Scott F.	Puma
Schadlich Stephen H.	Puma
Schafer H. James	Druids
Schatz Joseph L.	Tie Binders
Schellerup Mark Baxter	Tie Binders
Schemel J. David	Pelican
Schenkkan Gerard	Aviary
Schiff Albert J.	Five Easy Pieces
Schilling Alexander H. Jr.	Owlers
Schley Kenneth C.	Camels
Schmidt Chauncey E.	Tie Binders
Schmidt Eric Clausen	Hillside
Schmidt Jon Eugene	Aviary
Schmoke Kurt L.	Hill Billies
Schnitzer Jordan D.	Moro
Schreck Albert R.	Iron Ring
Schreck Thomas A.	Iron Ring
Schroder Donn	Tunerville
Schroder John S.	Tunerville
Schulte Bernard H. Jr.	Cool-Nazdar
Schumacher Robert J.	Hualapai
Schwartz Edwin J.	Abbey
Scollin Bruce	Valley of the Moon
Scott Conley Jay II	Aviary
Scott Edward B. II	Wild Oats
Scott Norman M. Jr.	Hideaway
Scott Thomas Wright	Wayside Log
Scully John H.	Sunshiners
Sears John H.	Cool-Nazdar
Sechrest Dennis G.	Idlewild
Seeligson Arthur A. III	Zaca
Seidel Bruce	Medicine Lodge
Sellers Eldon	Tunerville
Semple Lloyd A.	Santa Barbara
Sepos Charles	Tunerville

422

Mike Hanson

MEMBER	CAMP
Setrakian Scott H.	Silverado Squatters
Settlemier Brock Reid	Land of Happiness
Seward George C.	Seven Trees
Sfarzo Ronald A.	Bela Union/Jinks Band
Shanley Kevin	Medicine Lodge
Shapiro A. Horton	Thalia
Sharon William F.	Sons of Rest
Sharp Neil	Tunerville
Shattuck Paul C.	Pig 'N Whistle
Shattuck William M.	Sleepy Hollow
Shattuck William N.	Sleepy Hollow
Shea Peter Owen	Land's End
Shearer Frederic George	Fore Peak
Shearing George A.	Tunerville
Sheldon George O.	Land of Happiness
Shenk John C.	Sundodgers
Shepard Roderick W.	Piedmont
Sherman James Edward	Totem In
Sherman Robert S. III	Seven Trees
Shields Robert M. Jr.	Crossroads
Shine Raymond E.	Nec Natama
Shirley David Arthur	Wayside Log
Shoemaker Alvin V.	Mandalay
Shoptaugh Philip	Band
Shulgin Alexander T.	Tunerville
Shultz George P.	Mandalay
Siart William E. B.	Midway
Sibley Peter E.	Isle of Aves
Sibley Scott	Ladera
Sickel Edward T. III	Umkulu
Simens Mark F.	Last Chance
Simon Donald Stewart	Whisky Flat
Simons Carlton Barrett	Shoestring
Simpson Alan K.	Pelican
Singer Sam	Interlude
Singleton Dennis E.	Cool-Nazdar
Sitzmana Gary Russell	Land's End
Skinner Jeffrey A.	Whisky Flat
Skinner Paul W.	Woof
Skye Robert Brighten	Jinks Band
Slattery Dennis D.	Whisky Flat
Sloan David B.	Aviary
Slusser James W.	Bella Union
Smiell Joseph E.	Tunerville
Smit Steve P.	Timbuktu
Smith Brannan T.	Ladera
Smith Bruce C.	Sundodgers
Smith Budge H.	Ladera
Smith Christopher J.	Interlude
Smith E. Del	Dog House
Smith F. Allen	Jinks Band
Smith H. William III	Wayside Log
Smith Hawley Dwight	Shoestring
Smith Jeffrey C.	Outpost
Smith Lloyd Herbert	Sons of Toil
Smith Richard W.	Parsonage
Smith Sydney C.	Band
Smith William McFate	Owlers
Smyth John E.	Owl's Nest
Snavely Christian M.	Whisky Flat
Snavely Stephen V.	Ye Merrie Yowls
Sochor Jim L.	Sons of Toil
Soher Thomas J.	Oz
Solari Jerome P.	Dragon
Solinsky Frank IV	Whisky Flat
Soracco Peter A.	Mathieu
Sorenson Eric	Tunerville
Spalding Philip Foster	Skiddoo
Spalding Richard C.	Zaca
Spane Robert J.	Midway
Spellman Zachariah	Band
Spence G. Stuart Jr.	Green Mask
Spence Robert L.	Bella Union
Spencer John	Woof
Spencer M. Hunter	Parsonage
Spencer Norman A.	Cliff Dwellers
Spiegel Andrew E.	Three Threes
Spicker R. Tod	Sleepy Hollow
Spicker Warren "Ned" E. Jr.	Valley of the Moon
Spight Richard D.	Hideaway
Spilhaus Athelstan F. Jr.	Sons of Toil
Sprague Norman F. III	Druids
Sprole Frank A.	Hill Billies
Squires Kendall B. Mooers	Madrone
Stafford Robert M.	Spot
Stanford Alan G.	Sundodgers
Stansbury Herbert E. Jr.	Highlanders
Staples John N. III	Camels
Starke Rodman D.	Monastery
Starr Kenneth W.	Cave Man
Starr Kevin	Sons of Toil
Steele Bob J.	Jinks Band
Steele James A.	Better 'Ole
Steele Robert Gantt	Monkey Block/Aviary
Stegmiller Kenneth Lawrence	Aviary
Steil Peter	Dragon
Stein Jeffery D.	Cliff Dwellers
Stenovec P. Andrew	Puma
Stephan Christopher Q.	Five Easy Pieces
Stephens Craig Arthur	Midway
Stephens Donald R.	Uplifters
Stephens Paul H.	Hill Billies
Stephens Robert L.	Woof
Sterling Clark	Dog House
Sterling Peter	Skyhi
Stern Hans L.	Meyerling
Stevens Richard W.	Tunerville
Stewart William Paul	El Toro-II
Stiffler Terry C.	Timbuktu
Stimson Michael R.	Poison Oak
St. John Eugene M. Jr.	Santa Barbara
Stock John Van Maren	Tie Binders
Stolz Peter A.	Mathieu
Stone Prescott W.	Faraway
Stone William A.	Aviary
Stoney Carl J. Jr.	Isle of Aves
Stough Brooks	Rendezvous
Strader Brett	Aviary
Stratmann Erich Wolf	Aviary
Street Reginald W.	Skyhi
Strickland J. Robert Jr.	Jinks Band
Stricklin John	Idlewild
Stringer James Quinton Jr.	Nec Natama
Stromberg Arthur H.	Dragon
Stuart Charles R.	Wayside Log
Stuart Robert D. Jr.	Stowaway
Sugg John William Jr.	Web
Sullivan Brian J.	Aviary
Sullivan John L. Jr.	Cool-Nazdar
Sullivan Walter H. III	Stowaway
Sulpizio Robert E.	Jinks Band
Sultan Edward D. Jr.	Wild Oats
Summa Terry L.	Tunerville
Sumner William O.	Land of Happiness
Supple Frederic E. Jr.	Dog House
Sutcliffe Robert J.	Sahara
Suter William K. USA (Ret.)	Star & Garter
Sutherland William D.	Highlanders
Sutter Mark Louis	Sequoyah
Sutton Garrett Zook	Rendezvous
Sutton James Hepburn	Dragon
Swain Robert J.	Cave Man
Swan John	Star & Garter
Swanson W. Clarke	Haven
Swartz Eric C.	Land of Happiness
Swartz Thomas B.	Land of Happiness
Swig Steven L.	Abbey
Swindells William R.	Toyland
Swinden James Irvine	Pelican
Swinerton James B.	Dragon
Sylia John R.	Sheldrake Lodge
Symington James W.	Hill Billies
Symonds J. Taft	Seven Trees

T

| Taggart Robert W. | Poker Flat |
| Tappan James C. | Monastery |

Taranik James V.	Wayside Log
Taube Seth B.	Uplifters/Tunerville
Tayler Christopher John	Poker Flat
Taylor Charles E. Jr.	Lost Angels
Taylor James Emmanuel	Abbey
Taylor John Brian	Cave Man
Taylor Kenneth John	Aorangi/Swagatam
Taylor Matthew J.	Rendezvous
Taylor Robert M.	Cool-Nazdar
Taylor Vernon Jr.	Owl's Nest
Taylor Vernon III	Owl's Nest
Teich Steve Emery	Tunerville
Tellez Stephen C.	Lost Angels
Tevis Michael L.	Sundodgers
Thacher David J.	River Lair
Thacher John Pomeroy	River Lair
Thacher William	River Lair
Thayer Edward C.	Sheldrake Lodge
Thayer Rufus G. Jr.	Idlewild
Theurer Richard	Band
Thiele Ted	Jinks Band
Thieriot Peter E.	Zaca
Thirkell Edward D.	Bella Union
Thomas Arthur Norman	Owl's Nest
Thomas E. J. Ned II	Faraway
Thomasson Dan King	Cave Man
Thompson John	Tunerville
Thompson Morley P.	Cave Man
Thompson Peter Henry	Tunerville
Thomson David Gwynn	Aviary
Thomson Keith	Isle of Aves
Thomson Peter A.	Land of Happiness
Thornton C. B. Jr.	Lost Angels
Thornton William Laney	Midway
Thurlow Stephen C.	Hermits
Thurlow William L.	Tunerville
Thurston Michael Kent	Jinks Band
Tiernan Liam	Cliff Dwellers
Tierney Thomas J.	Hill Billies
Tight Dexter C.	Faraway
Tight Tim	Faraway
Tilden Calvin B.	Sundodgers
Tobin Joseph O. II	Poison Oak
Todd Joseph Z. III	Wild Oats
Toguazzini Roland E.	Whisky Flat
Tolles R. P. Dee	Skyhi
Tombrello Thomas A. Jr.	Sons of Toil
Tomsic Ronald P.	Hermits
Toole James F.	Land of Happiness
Tooley William L.	Owl's Nest
Topham Ned	River Lair
Tornga Thomas H.	Pig 'N Whistle
Torrance Anthony L.	Halcyon
Toth Bryant A.	Hill Billies
Touw Paul C. M.	Midway
Townes Charles H.	Isle of Aves
Townsend Lawrence G.	Hideaway
Traitel David T.	Crossroads
Trent Darrell M.	Parsonage
Tresan David I.	Band
Tribble Todd	Band
Trione Victor S.	Dog House
Tripaldi David R.	Cool-Nazdar
Tripp Marv	Aviary
Trotter Tracy L. M.D.	Crow's Nest
Tudor W. Pendleton	Land of Happiness
Tuller Robert M.	Roaring
Tully Herbert B.	Piedmont
Tunney Peter W.	Land's End
Tupin Joe P.	Sons of Toil
Turner Bruce Gordon	Aviary
Turner David	Band
Turner Marshall C. Jr.	Shoestring
Turner Thomas A.	Wild Oats
Tyler Carl D.	Pig 'N Whistle

U

| Unobskey Sidney R. | Cuckoo's Nest |

| Urstadt Charles J. | Midway |
| Usher Kirk Jr. | Faraway |

V

Valentine Peter B.	Dragon
Vanderhoof Larry N.	Sons of Toil
Van Dine Robert G.	Skyhi
Van Genderen Warren	Care Less
Van Horn William G.	Idlewild
Van Praag H. John	Woof
Vaughan James S.	Medicine Lodge
Vaughan Richard Haylett	Tunerville
Veach Jay	Sunshiners
Veit Robert J.	Aviary
Verzhbinsky Alyosha G.	Wayside Log
Vestal Peter L.	Medicine Lodge
Vickers Robert M.	Poison Oak
Viel Jean-Pierre L.	Puma
Vinson Donald E.	Sahara
Violich Paul A.	Thalia
Violich Peter Christopher	Tunerville
Vitalie John R.	Aviary
Vogelheim Paul C.	Tarry Town
Volk David R.	Cuckoo's Nest
Volk Richard R.	Crow's Nest
Volkmann William	Sleepy Hollow
von der Lieth Robt. H.	Meyerling
von Galen Ferdinand	Whoo Cares
von Platen Henrik	Owlers
Vosti Laurence	Skyhi
Vukasin George J.	Sahara

W

Wade David M.	Aviary
Wagner H. A.	Tarry Town
Wagner Henry W. III	Aviary
Wait Bradford M.	Aviary
Waligore Robert S.	Aviary
Walker Brooks III	Stowaway
Walker Brooks Jr.	Pink Onion
Walker James Leslie IV	Pink Onion
Walker Vaughn	Owl's Nest
Wallis Edward James	Whisky Flat
Walsh David P.	Aviary
Walsh Richard	Totem In
Walsh-Wilson Alexander	Tunerville
Walters Frank L. Jr.	Zaca
Walters James Douglas	Totem In
Walton Gary M.	Sons of Toil
Wangeman Conrad	Tie Binders
Ware Leonard	Tarry Town
Warren Benjamin S. III	Tie Binders
Warren David	Band
Warren James D.	Hillside
Warren James D. Jr.	Lost Angels
Warren Jeffrey Earl	Isle of Aves
Washington Gene A.	Hillside
Waste James M.	Monastery
Waste William Harrison II	Esplandian
Watkins Richardson L.	Faraway
Watson Edward J.	Totem In
Watson Franklin H. III	Wayside Log
Watterworth Scott	Monastery
Wattis Paul L. Jr.	Crow's Nest
Watts H. David	Tunerville
Watts Jack Loy II	Sempervirens
Wayne Patrick John	Skyhi
Weber Barrett H.	Sundodgers
Webster Robert L.	Tie Binders
Webster William H.	Wayside Log
Weeks David	Totem In/Jinks Band
Weidkamp Noel D.	Band
Weinberg Peter M.	Tunerville
Weir Robert	Rattlers
Welborne John Howard	Pig 'N Whistle
Welk Robert E.	Ladera
Welker Richard Philip	Band

423

Selected Bibliography

Ex Libris

(From the library of)

AUTHOR'S NOTE: This list by no means in meant to give a complete list of all the stacks of books, newspaper and magazine articles, documents, photographs, web sites, videotapes, and other materials that I accumulated while writing this book. Such a list would be far too lengthy to include in these pages. Any source materials not listed here are cited within the text of the previous chapters. My goal in providing this selected bibliography is to give the reader suggestions for further reading and research on the Grove and related topics covered in this book.

BOHEMIAN CLUB OFFICIAL SOURCES

Most of the Bohemian Club primary source documents cited here are available at the University of California Bancroft Library Manuscript Division, California Historical Society and California State Library.

Bohemian Club Midsummer Encampment Guest Lists—1968, 1970, 1976, 1978, 1979, 1980, 1981, 1993.

Bohemian Club Membership Lists—1887, 1914, 1941, 1945, 1951, 1964, 1966, 1968, 1970, 1972, 1988, 1990, 1997, 2000.

Bohemian Grove Members Camp Lists—1930, 1938, 1941, 1952, 1956, 1968, 1969, 1971, 1981, 1987, 1992, 1993, 1997.

Bohemian Grove Midsummer Encampment programs—1940, 1951, 1971, 1975, 1979, 1980, 1981, 1982, 1983, 1986, 1989, 1991, 1992, 1993, 2000.

Bohemian Club, By-Laws-Officers, 1969, Published by The Club, San Francisco, 1969.

Bohemian Club, By Laws and Rules, Published by the Club, San Francisco, 1931.

Annals of Bohemia, Volume VI, 1973–1987. Published by: The Bohemian Club, San Francisco, 1987.

The Annals of the Bohemian Club, 1907–1972, Alexander T. Case, Editor, Volume II, 1972.

Annual Report of the Chairman, 1940–1941, The Hoover Library on War, Revolution and Peace, Stanford University Press, CA, 1941.

United Nations and the War Years in Bohemia. By William C. Bacon. The Annals of the Bohemian Club, Volume V, 1972.

The Great Organ of the Grove, Bethards, Jack M. Annals V, 1907–1972, pp. 413–414.

The Lost Angels Camp History—Bohemia 1908–1958. By Preston Hotchkiss. Ward Ritchie Press, July 1958.

Semper Virens: the Bohemian Club Grove Play, 1923. George G. Clark. MSS 0054, located at the Mandeville Special Collections Library, Geisel Library, University of California, San Diego.

Saul, A Grove Play. Purrington, Benjamin Allen. Music by Charles Hart. San Francisco: The Bohemian Club, 1940. Printed by The Grabhorn Press.

The Centennial Grove Play—Celebrating the 100th Anniversary of the Bohemian Club. By Robert B. England. Music Director Charles Dant. A compendium of highlights from Grove Plays over the Years. 8volumes published by the Bohemian Grove 1972.

July 17, 1920 Cremation of Care Ceremony. Bohemian Club Publication.

The Visual Arts in Bohemia. By Dr. Kevin Starr. *The Annals of the Bohemian Club.*

From Time to Time: A History of the Wayside Log Camp, The Bohemian Grove, 1893–2000. By Dr. Kevin Starr. Privately published by the Bohemian Club, 2000

BOOKS

The Bohemian Grove and Other Retreats—A Study in Ruling-Class Cohesiveness. G. William Domhoff, Harper & Row, New York, 1974.

Who Rules America. By G. William Domhoff. Prentice-Hall, Inc., Englewood Cliffs, N.J., 1967.

Higher Circles. By G. William Domhoff. Vintage Books, NY, 1970.

America's Secret Aristocracy. By Stephen Birmingham. Little, Brown and Company, Boston, Toronto, 1987.

The Greatest Men's Party on Earth by John van der Zee, Harcourt Brace Jovanovich, Inc., New York, 1974.

Them: Adventures with Extremists. By Jon Ronson. Simon & Schuster, New York, 2001.

Friends in High Places: The Bechtel Story. The Most Secret Corporation and How it Engineered The World. By Layton McCartney. Simon and Schuster, New York, 1988.

The Memoirs of Chief Justice Earl Warren. By Earl Warren. Doubleday and Company, Inc., Garden City, NY, 1977.

"Father, Son & Co.—My Life at IBM And Beyond" by Thomas J. Watson, Jr. and Peter Petre. Bantam Books, New York, 1990.

Men and Powers: A Political Retrospective. By Helmut Schmidt. Random House, New York, NY, 1989.

Big Green Circus, Inside the Environmental Movement. By Charles Galvin Murphy, Jr. Paw Mark Publishing, Gulf Breeze, FL, 1994.

Sex Work: Writings by Women in the Sex Industry edited by Frédérique Delacoste and Priscilla Alexander, Cleis Press, San Francisco, 1987.

The Occult—A History. By Colin Wilson. Vintage Books/Random House, New York, 1974.

The Occult Underground. By James Webb. Open Court Publishing, La Salle, Illinois, 1974.

Perdurabo: The Life of Aleister Crowley. By Richard Kaczynski. New Falcon Publications, 2002.

Trance Formation of America—The True Life Story of a CIA Mind Control Slave by Cathy O'Brien with Mark Phillips. Reality Marketing Incorporated, 1995.

Thanks for the Memories—The Truth Has Set Me Free! By Brice Taylor. Published by the Brice Taylor Trust, 1999.

Common Sense—An Introduction to the New World Order. By George Humphrey. Common Sense Press, Austin, TX 2000.

Uncommon Sense—Your Choice: The Blue Pill or the Red Pill? By George Humphrey. Common Sense Press, Austin, TX 2001.

9/11—The Grand Illusion. By George Humphrey. Common Sense Press, Austin, TX 2002.

9-11: Descent into Tyranny. By Alex Jones. AEJ Publishing, Austin, TX, 2002.

The Franklin Cover-Up: Child Abuse, Satanism, and Murder in Nebraska. By John W. DeCamp. AWT Inc., Lincoln, NE, 1996. Second Edition.

Fossilized Customs—The Pagan Sources of Popular Customs. Strawberry Islands Publishers, Louisville, KY, Special Edition 3rd printing.

The Waco Whitewash—The Mt. Carmel Episode Told by an Eyewitness to the Trial. By Jack DeVault, Major USAF (Ret.). Rescue Press, San Antonio, 1994.

Ancient Mystery Cults. By Walter Burkert. Harvard University Press, Cambridge, MA, 1987.

The Nazis and the Occult. By Dusty Sklar. Dorset Press, New York, 1977.

Who Is Witter Bynner? A biography by James Kraft. University of New Mexico Press, Albuquerque, 1995.

The Biggest Secret. By David Icke. Bridge of Love Publications, Scottsdale, AZ, 1999.

Children of the Matrix. By David Icke. Bridge of Love Publications, 2001.

Alice in Wonderland and the World Trade Center Disaster. By David Icke. Bridge of Love Publications, 2003.

The Eye in the Pyramid. Robert Shea and Robert Anton Wilson.

The Great Republic—A History of the American People, Vol. 2, Third Edition. D.C. Heath and Company, 1985. (See *A New World Order on* page 666! Imagine that!)

A Literary History of the American West, Texas Christian University Press, Ft. Worth.

Sketches of the Sixties by Bret Harte and Mark Twain. John B. Howell, ed., San Francisco, 1927. second edition.

Mark Twain and Bret Harte. By Margaret Duckett. University of Oklahoma Press Norman, OK, 1964.

Americans and the California Dream, 1850–1915. By Kevin Starr. Oxford University Press, New York, 1976.

The Valley of the Moon. By Jack London. New York: Macmillan, 1913.

The Acorn-Planter: A California Forest Play. By Jack London. New York: Macmillan, 1916.

Shakespeare—Creator of Freemasonry. By Alfred Dodd, Editor of the Alfred Dodd Edition of Shakespeare's Sonnets. Rider & Co., London, Paternoster House.

The Norton Shakespeare. Edited by Stephen Greenblatt. New York: W.W. Norton & Co. Inc., 1997.

Shakespeare on Fairies and Magic. **By** Benjamin Darling. Prentice Hall Press, 2001.

Mozart: The Golden Years 1781–1791. By Howard Chandler Robbins Landon. Thames and Hudson, London, 1989.

Mozart and the Masons: New Light on the Lodge "Crowned Hope." By Howard Chandler Robbins Landon. Thames and Hudson, London, 1982.

Wagner's Ring and Its Symbols: The Music and the Myth. By Robert Donnington. 3rd ed. London: Faber and Faber, 1984.

Music: Its Secret Influence throughout the Ages. By Cyril Scott. Rider, London, 1933.

Beethoven Essays. By Maynard Solomon. Harvard University Press, Cambridge, MA, 1988.

Beethoven and the Voice of God. By Wilfred Mellers. Faber and Faber; New York: Oxford University Press, 1983.

Fatal Links: the Curious Deaths of Beethoven and the Two Napoleons. By Gail S. Altman. Anubian Press.

Beethoven's Hair by Russell Martin. Broadway Books, 2000.

OTHER PUBLICATIONS/PERIODICALS

A Relative Advantage: Sociology of the San Francisco Bohemian Club. Dissertation by Peter Martin Phillips, for Doctor of Philosophy degree in Sociology, Office Of Graduate Studies of the University Of California, Davis, 1994.

Bohemian Grove Action Network Newsletters. 1983–2002. Mary Moore, Bohemian Grove Action Network.

Mary Moore—The Woman Behind the Protest. The Paper, July 9–15, 1982.

Justice Scalia Plans Speech to Bohemians. By Eileen Clegg. *Santa Rosa Press Democrat*, July 24, 1997.

From the *San Francisco Chronicle*:

November 13, 1910 *New Home of the Bohemian Club is Dedicated.*

August 17, 1908 *Money to Build Bohemia's Nest*

May 19, 1919 *Mermaids Invade Sacred Precincts of Olympic Club*

July 20, 1922 *Bohemian Club's Midsummer Jinks Now in Progress*

July 28, 1922 *Bohemian Wives Entertain While Clubmen at Camp.*

May 13, 1932 *Clubs Building Plans Approved*

May 30, 1933 *Bohemia Bids Ladies from Exile*

January 19, 1934 *Steady Progression New Bohemian Clubs*

November 7, 1949 *Bohemian Club is Notoriously Publicity Shy.*

July 16, 1982 *Bohemians Taking to the Grove-Protesters will be there too.*

July 17, 1983 *Bohemians Are Back and So Are the Protesters.*

September 11, 1987 *Bohemian Club's Illegal Construction.*

October 13, 1987 *Bohemians Love Women.*

Inside Bohemian Grove. Masters of the Universe Go to Camp. By Philip Weiss. Spy magazine, November 1989.

Power Playground by John van der Zee, Business Month magazine, July/August 1988.

Is Trouble Brewing for the Paradise of the Rich? By Jack Anderson. Parade Magazine, February 22, 1981.

Among The Giants, By Allan Fotheringham, Maclean's, 8/5/2002, Vol. 115, Issue 31

Move Over, Bohemian Grove, By Toddi Gutner, Business Week, 02/19/2001

Power Camps, Time Magazine, 07/20/98, Vol. 152, Issue 3

Newt Draws Fire, By William F. Buckley Jr., National Review, 9/11/95, Vol. 47, Issue 17.

Gingrich Joins The Jet Set, Common Cause Magazine, Fall '95, Vol. 21, Issue 3

Gergen Quits Bohemian Club and 17 Other Organizations. By Frank J. Murray. The Washington Times, June 11, 1993.

Bohemian Blues, By Lucy Howard, Joel Stein, Newsweek, 8/10/92, Vol. 120, Issue 6

Pouvoir: le club le plus fermé du monde. By Jean Sébastien Stehli, Le Point magazine, August 27, 1994.

Beer and Loathing at Bohemian Grove. By Greg King. West Sonoma County Paper, July 17–July 23, 1986.

Power at Play: The Boho Boys Club. By W. Hampton Sides, Regardie's magazine, January 1991.

The Male Manager's Last Refuge by Walter McQuade, Fortune magazine, August 5, 1985.

Inside Bohemian Grove: The Story People Magazine Won't Let You Read. Extra! Magazine November/December 1991.

Capital Reporter, Public Hearing Transcripts, Franchise Tax Board Hearings on Regulations 17201 and 24343, Sacramento, CA, June 16, 1987.

What Happened when People Magazine dropped in on the Bohemian Club. By Jeff Cohen. Press Democratic, December 2, 1991, p. B-5.

Why Bush Walked Out of the Grove, By Robert Novak. San Francisco Chronicle, August 9, 1993, p. 21.

Hijinks at the Bohemian Grove. By Bill Soberanes. The Argus Courier, July 18, 2001.

Bohemian Grove & Global Elite. Movers, shakers from politics, business go Bohemian: Annual Sonoma fete draws Bushes, Kissinger, Powell, Gingrich. By Suzanne Bohan. Sacramento Bee, August 2, 1999.

A Lodge Gone Black. By R.V. Scheide. Sacramento News and Review, July 25, 2002.

Ruling Upheld—Women can Work at Boho Grove. By Lisa Amand. The West Sonoma County Paper, March 5–11, 1987.

The West's Hidden Summit at Bohemian Grove. By Geoffrey Godsell. The Christian Science Monitor, July 23, 1982.

Disharmonious Convergence Returns to Bohemian Grove. By Gaye LeBaron. Santa Rosa Press Democrat, July 1, 2001.

Weaving Spiders, Come Not Here—Bohemian Grove: Inside the Secret Retreat of the Power Elite. By Rick Clogher. Mother Jones, August 1981.

Bohemian Grove: Power Camps Out. By Lori Berger. "M" Magazine, October 1983.

Burying the Branch Davidians. By Judith Vinson. Published on LewRockwell.com, July 20, 2000.

Finishing Off the Branch Davidians. By Judith Vinson. Lewrockwell.com, March 3, 2000.

Skipping Scotty and the Exit. By Judith Vinson. LewRockwell.com. March 6, 1999.

Art Linkletter Says the Greatest Things. An Interview with Art Linkletter. The New Sun Newspaper, Issue#14, 2001.

Beethoven, The Illuminati and the Recycled Themes. By Derek Strahan. Sydney Music Diary, February 1989. Also published (slightly abridged) in The Sydney Morning Herald, Tuesday, October 19, 1982.

Fantasy and Occult Themes in Classical Music. A talk given by Alan R. Pendragon in two parts. Part I on the 1st of June 2001, Part II on the 7th of September 2001 at Outlanders Club Seminar, Leicester, England.

Concerto for Magic and Mysticism: Esotericism and Western Music. By Gary Lachman. Theosophical Society of America's *Quest* Magazine, Jul/Aug. 2002 issue.

Thelemic Numbers and Words. By David Cherubim (Frater Aurora Aureae). The Order of the Thelemic Golden Dawn, 1991.

The Impact of Freemasonry on Elizabethan Literature. By Ron Heisler. Article originally published in The Hermetic Journal, 1990.

VIDEO

Dark Secrets—Inside Bohemian Grove.   Alex Jones Productions, Austin, TX. This is the original film that Alex Jones and Mike Hanson shot inside the Bohemian Grove. Available from *powerofprophecy.com*

For additional information about the Bohemian Grove, please visit Texe Marrs' website: *powerofprophecy.com*. Texe offers not only the video, *Dark Secrets—Inside Bohemian Grove*, but also numerous CDs and audiotapes on this and other interesting topics.

Index

About the Author

veni, vidi, vici

(I came, I saw, I conquered)

Mike Hanson

Mike Hanson is a TV producer, small business owner, philanthropist, author, political candidate and civil rights activist. Hanson is a native of Austin, TX. After graduating from Travis High School in 1982, he attended college at the United States Army Signal Center in Fort Gordon, GA, and went on to the 249th Signal Battalion as a radio operator. During his military career in the Army and National Guard, Mike won several awards including the Army Achievement Medal, Outstanding Service Award, Distinguished Achievement Award, and the Adjutant General's Individual Award.

Mike has earned a strong reputation for volunteerism, donating his money, time, and materials to building homes for disadvantaged and low-income families. As an award-winning TV producer, his work with longtime comrade-at-arms Alex Jones has been seen on British Television Channel Four, ABC-TV's 20/20 and Good Morning America, CNN, Court TV, and Hard Copy. In 2000, Alex and Mike produced a film about the events portrayed in this book: Dark Secrets—Inside Bohemian Grove.

Mike Hanson comes from a family dedicated to public service; his brother, Billy Hanson, is an Austin Police officer, and his father, Otto Hanson, Jr., became known as an American hero when he saved many lives as an Emergency Medical Technician during the UT Tower shootings of 1966. In 1984, Mike married his high-school sweetheart, Melissa. They have two children, Justin and Krystal.

RECOMMENDED PRODUCTS ON THIS AND SIMILAR TOPICS:

BOOKS:

Conspiracy of the Six-Pointed Star—Eye-Opening Revelations and Forbidden Knowledge About Israel, the Jews, Zionism, and the Rothschilds, by Texe Marrs (432 pages) $30.00

Circle of Intrigue—The Hidden Inner Circle of the Global Illuminati Conspiracy, by Texe Marrs (304 pages) $25.00

Codex Magica—Secret Signs, Mysterious Symbols, and Hidden Codes of the Illuminati, by Texe Marrs (624 pages) $40.00

Conspiracy World—A Truthteller's Compendium of Eye-Opening Revelations and Forbidden Knowledge, by Texe Marrs (432 pages) $30.00

Dark Majesty—The Secret Brotherhood and the Magic of a Thousand Points of Light, by Texe Marrs (304 pages) $23.00

Mysterious Monuments—Encyclopedia of Secret Illuminati Designs, Masonic Architecture, and Occult Places, by Texe Marrs (624 pages) $40.00

Bloodlines of the Illuminati, by Fritz Springmeier (624 pages) $50.00

The Gods of the Lodge, by Reginald Haupt (208 pages) $23.00

The Illuminati—Facts and Fiction, by Mark Dice (415 pages) $23.00

VIDEOS:

Die, America, Die!—The Illuminati Plan to Murder America, Confiscate Its Wealth, and Make Red China Leader of the New World Order, by Texe Marrs (80 min. DVD) $30.00

Dark Secrets: Inside Bohemian Grove/Order of Death (by Alex Jones, DVD) $30.00

Architectural Colossus—Mysterious Monuments of the Illuminati Enshroud the World With Magic and Seduction, by Texe Marrs (60 min. DVD) $30.00

Baal's Shaft and Cleopatra's Needle—Phallic Architecture and Sex Monuments of the Illuminati, by Texe Marrs (60 min. DVD) $30.00

Face to Face With the Devil—Close Encounters With Unexpected Evil, by Texe Marrs (60 min. DVD) $30.00

Secret Societies and the Illuminati, by Texe Marrs (60 min. DVD) $25.00

The Sun at Midnight—Pyramids of Mystery, Temples of Blood, by Texe Marrs (60 min. DVD) $30.00

Thunder Over Zion—Illuminati Bloodlines and the Secret Plan for A Jewish Utopia and a New World Messiah, by Texe Marrs (60 min. DVD) $30.00

Where the Rich and Famous Dwell—Architectural Secrets of the Rothschilds, the Vanderbilts, the Rockefellers, the Astors, and Other Storied Bloodlines and Dynasties, by Texe Marrs (60 min. DVD) $30.00

AUDIOS:

Blood Sacrifice and Debauchery at the Bohemian Grove—Shocking New Revelations, by Texe Marrs (60 min., CD or Tape) $13.00

Exposé of the Bohemian Grove, Texe Marrs interviews Alex Jones (60 min., CD or Tape) $13.00

Illuminati Architecture as Global Battleground, by Texe Marrs (60 min., CD or Tape) $13.00

Sex Cults of the Illuminati, by Texe Marrs (60 min., CD or Tape) $13.00

Two on a Saddle—Unmasking the Sexual Perversions of the Illuminati, by Texe Marrs (60 min., CD or Tape) $13.00

Unmasking the Order of Skull and Bones, by Texe Marrs (3 hours, CD or Tape) $23.00

The Wicked Men of the Bohemian Grove (by Texe Marrs, 60 min., CD or Tape) $15.00

ALL PRICES INCLUDE SHIPPING AND HANDLING
Visa/Mastercard/Discover Accepted

To order, see website below, or phone 1-800-234-9673,
or send check or money order to:

Power of Prophecy
1708 Patterson Road, Austin, Texas 78733

Check Out These Web Sites for these and more invaluable books, videos,
audios, and for breaking news and informative articles:

www.powerofprophecy.com
www.conspiracyworld.com